CAMBRIDGE

Brighter Thinking

A/AS Level Computer Science for WJEC/Eduqas
Student Book

Mark Thomas with Alistair Surrall and Adam Hamflett

CAMBRIDGE
UNIVERSITY PRESS

University Printing House, Cambridge CB2 8BS, United Kingdom

One Liberty Plaza, 20th Floor, New York, NY 10006, USA

477 Williamstown Road, Port Melbourne, VIC 3207, Australia

4843/24, 2nd Floor, Ansari Road, Daryaganj, Delhi - 110002, India

79 Anson Road, #06 -04/06, Singapore 079906

Cambridge University Press is part of the University of Cambridge.

It furthers the University's mission by disseminating knowledge in the pursuit of education, learning and research at the highest international levels of excellence.

www.cambridge.org
Information on this title: www.cambridge.org/9781108412728 (Paperback)

First published 2017

20 19 18 17 16 15 14 13 12 11 10 9 8 7 6 5 4 3

Printed in Great Britain by CPI Group (UK) Ltd, Croydon CR0 4YY

A catalogue record for this publication is available from the British Library

ISBN 978-1-108-41272-8 Paperback
ISBN 978-1-108-41276-6 Paperback with Elevate enhanced edition

Cambridge University Press has no responsibility for the persistence or accuracy of URLs for external or third-party internet websites referred to in this publication, and does not guarantee that any content on such websites is, or will remain, accurate or appropriate. Information regarding prices, travel timetables, and other factual information given in this work is correct at the time of first printing but Cambridge University Press does not guarantee the accuracy of such information thereafter.

All exam-style questions and sample answers have been written by the authors.

....

Contents

Introduction

This full-colour, illustrated textbook has been written by experienced authors specifically for the Eduqas AS and A Level Computer Science syllabus.

Computer Science is more than just the study of how to write code and this book will help you to understand how and why computer systems behave in the way that they do.

Almost every aspect of our lives is recorded, processed and supported by computer systems of one sort or another. Computers provide us with methods of communication, automated manufacturing, improved design methods and managing vast quantities of data. A greater understanding of how computer systems work, from the low level processing right through to the seamless integration of technology that many people take for granted, will allow you to develop new solutions to problems and to better appreciate the decisions made by developers of both hardware and software.

The presentation of the chapters in this book reflects the content of the syllabus:

- The book covers the theory content for the syllabus. Some programming examples are provided in a range of languages where the content overlaps with practical programming content (e.g. data structures)
- Each chapter defines a set of learning objectives which closely match the learning objectives set out in the syllabus.
- Each chapter ends with a series of questions that will help you to gauge your understanding of the content as well as links for further research or suggested key phrases to search online.

How to use these resources

The Cambridge A/AS Level Computing for WJEC/Eduqas suite of resources covers the full AS and A Level specifications for the Eduqas (England) and WJEC (Wales) qualifications. This outline explains how to use these resources to teach the different pathways.

A/AS Level Computer Science for WJEC/Eduqas

Component 1

This section is designed to prepare students for written examinations. It covers Component 1 of the Eduqas A Level specification (England) and Unit 3 of the WJEC A Level specification (Wales). It also covers Components 1 and 2 of the Eduqas AS Level and Units 1 and 2 of the WJEC AS/A Level specifications.

Component 2

This section is designed to prepare students for written examinations. It covers Component 2 of the Eduqas A Level specification (England) and Unit 4 of the WJEC A Level specification (Wales). It also covers Components 1 and 2 of the Eduqas AS Level and Units 1 and 2 of the WJEC AS/A Level specifications.

It is available as an eBook publication on our Cambridge Elevate platform.

AS Level

The AS Level specifications for England and Wales are identical. However, the content in these products is presented in the order in which it is studied at A Level in England

and A2 in Wales, so you will need to approach it in a slightly different order to teach AS Level.

Here's how we suggest you approach the AS Level content:

1 **Hardware and communication:** Component 2 Chapter 10
2 **Logical operations:** Component 1 Chapter 2
3 **Data transmission:** Component 2 Chapter 11
4 **Data representation and data types:** Component 2 Chapter 12
5 **Data structures:** Component 1 Chapter 1
6 **Organisation and structure of data:** Component 2 Chapter 13
7 **Databases and distributed systems:** Component 2 Chapter 14
8 **The operating system:** Component 2 Chapter 15
9 **Algorithms and programs:** Component 1 Chapter 3
10 **Principles of programming:** Component 1 Chapter 4
11 **Systems analysis:** Component 1 Chapter 5
12 **Software engineering:** Component 1 Chapter 7
13 **Program construction:** Component 1 Chapter 8
14 **The need for different types of software system and their attributes:** Component 2 Chapter 17
15 **Practical programming:** Component 3
16 **Data security and integrity processes:** Component 2 Chapter 17
17 **Economic, moral, legal, ethical and cultural issues relating to computer science:** Component 1 Chapter 9

If you're co-teaching AS and A Level in England, we'd suggest that you approach the content in this way for the first year of teaching, and then review it when you teach the added A Level content in the second year.

How to use this book

Throughout this book you will notice particular features that are designed to aid your learning. This section provides a brief overview of these features.

Learning Objectives

A short summary of the content that you will learn in each chapter.

Learning objectives

- Draw truth tables for Boolean expressions consisting of AND, OR, NOT and XOR logical operations.
- Extend this to include NAND and NOR logical operations.
- Apply logical operations to combinations of conditions in programming, including clearing registers and masking.
- Extend this to include encryption.
- Simplify Boolean expressions using Boolean identities and rules.
- Simplify Boolean expressions using de Morgan's laws.

Tip

Useful guidance about particular types of code or software, as well as common errors to avoid and tips to help you prepare for exams.

 Tip

There are different symbols used for Boolean algebra and it is important to be familiar with all of them.

Symbol	Alternatives
$\wedge$	.
$\vee$	+
$\neg A$	$\bar{A}$
$\leftrightarrow$	$\equiv$

Computing in Context

Provides examples of how the concepts you are learning fit within real-life scenarios.

 Computing in context: high profile failure of the Waterfall approach

In 2010, the American President Barack Obama set out to reform healthcare in the USA. He aimed to provide health insurance to US citizens who couldn't afford the expensive premiums charged by private healthcare companies and were therefore very vulnerable if they fell ill.

Chapter Summary

A short summary to recap on the key concepts and topics and that you have learnt in that chapter.

📎 **Chapter summary**

- A stakeholder is anyone who has a vested interest in the development of a system. Common stakeholders include:
  - user
  - programmer
  - project manager
  - system analyst.

End-of-Chapter Questions

Questions designed to test your learning of the material in the chapter you have just studied.

End-of-chapter questions

1   Explain the purpose of a virtual machine (VM) when using a programming language which is both compiled and then interpreted by a virtual machine.   [6]

Further Reading

A list of additional sources where you can find further information on a particular topic.

Further reading

Lexical analysis in detail	
Building a compiler – Lexical and syntax analysis	
Introduction to instruction sets	

A Level only icon

This icon indicates where material is specific to the A Level only. The green line extending from the icon shows you clearly where the A Level only content starts and finishes.

Introduction

Translation programs

We use the term 'translators' to cover all the types of software that convert code from one form to another. Compilers, interpreters and assemblers are all types of translators.

Activities

Questions and exercises designed to help you practice what you have learnt throughout the resource.

Activity 9.1

Join Twitter and follow technology correspondents from major news outlets. Re-tweet anything you are sent that involves technology and the law.

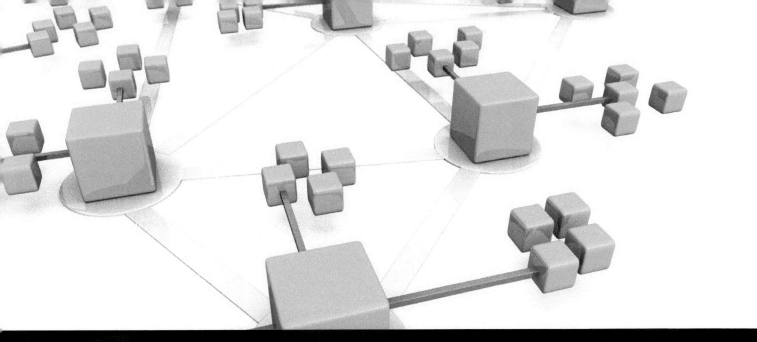

Chapter 1
Data structures

Learning objectives

- Describe, interpret and manipulate data structures including one-dimensional arrays, two-dimensional arrays, three-dimensional arrays, stacks, queues, trees, linked lists, hash tables and records.
- Represent the operation of stacks and queues using pointers and arrays.
- Represent the operation of linked lists and trees using pointers and arrays.
- Select, identify and justify appropriate data structures for given situations.

Introduction

A data structure is a collection of related data items held in a computer's memory. There are hundreds of different data structures available to programmers but at this level you need only understand a few of the most common ones:

- one-dimensional arrays
- two-dimensional arrays
- three-dimensional arrays
- records
- stacks
- queues
- binary trees
- linked lists
- hash tables.

Data structures usually fall into one of two categories: static and dynamic. In static data structures, the size of the data structure is set at the beginning of the program and cannot be changed. This is very limiting (and inefficient) because it means that you have to know in advance how large your data structure needs to be. However, static data structures are easy to program and you always know how much space they will take up. In contrast, dynamic data structures do not have a limited size and can expand or shrink as needed. They also tend to be more complex to implement.

It is also very common for more complex data structures to be made of simpler ones. For example, it is normal practice to implement binary trees by using a linked list, or to create a stack by using an array. It is important to remember, however, that data structures can be implemented in different ways. The idea behind a data structure (the abstract data type) is the important aspect to learn. How the data structure is implemented is up to the person coding the implementation. There are many ways of implementing the same data structure.

You will need to perform various operations on your data, such as inserting, sorting or searching data. The efficiency of such operations varies depending on the data structure in use. Generally speaking, you want to use the most efficient data structure possible. This is particularly important when you have large data sets. Your choice of data structure can have a big impact on the run time of your program. You can find out about the efficiency ratings (using Big O notation) of the data structures you need in the 'Further reading' section at the end of this chapter.

So why do we use data structures?

Data structures are a convenient way of organising data relating to a real problem.

One-dimensional arrays

Arrays are the simplest of all data structures. An array is a collection of variables of the same data type grouped under a single identifier. Each variable in the array is called an element and is accessed using its position in the array as an index.

This code shows how to declare an array (holding five names) using Python:

```
Names = ['Sam', 'Lucy', 'James', 'Jack', 'Jane']
```

Figure 1.1 shows how this is held in the computer's memory.

Tip

NB: These examples use Python, which doesn't support arrays but uses lists instead. The examples here demonstrate the same properties as arrays.

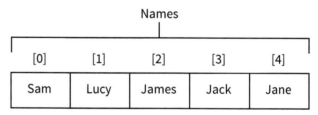

Figure 1.1: A one-dimensional array.

Changing or accessing the data in an array is simple. You simply refer to the element number (index) of the piece of data you want. For example, `print(Names[1])` would print the word 'Lucy'. `Names[3]='Sarah'` would change the value of element 3 from Jack to Sarah.

It is important to recognise that the element numbers (indices) of arrays usually start at 0.

Arrays are normally static data structures, so once they have been declared they can't grow beyond their initial size. As a result, the array in our example can never contain more than five items. If you were to write `Names[6]='David'` you would get an error message.

Two-dimensional and three-dimensional arrays

You can also create arrays with more than a single dimension. In theory, you can have arrays with a large number of dimensions, but this becomes very hard to visualise and at A-Level you only need to go up to three (at AS-Level you only need to go up to two).

This code shows how to declare a two-dimensional (2D) array using Python:

```
Names = [['Sam', 'Lucy', 'James', 'Jack', 'Jane'], ['Peter',
'Sarah', 'Adam', 'Karen', 'Verity'], ['Emily', 'Edward',
'Dominic', 'Justin', 'Jake']]
```

The implementation of multidimensional arrays differs from language to language. In Python, you simple create an array and then place another array inside each element of it.

Names

	[0]	[1]	[2]	[3]	[4]
[0]	Sam	Lucy	James	Jack	Jane
[1]	Peter	Sarah	Adam	Karen	Verity
[2]	Emily	Edward	Dominic	Justyn	Jake

Figure 1.2: How a 2D array is held in the computer's memory.

Changing or accessing the data in a 2D array is the same as in a 1D array. You simply refer to the element number (index) of the piece of data you want. For example, referring to Figure 1.2, print (Names[2][1]) would print the word 'Edward'. Names[0][3]='Alistair' would change the value of element (0, 3) from Jack to Alistair.

Notice that the element index operates in the same way as the coordinates on a map or graph.

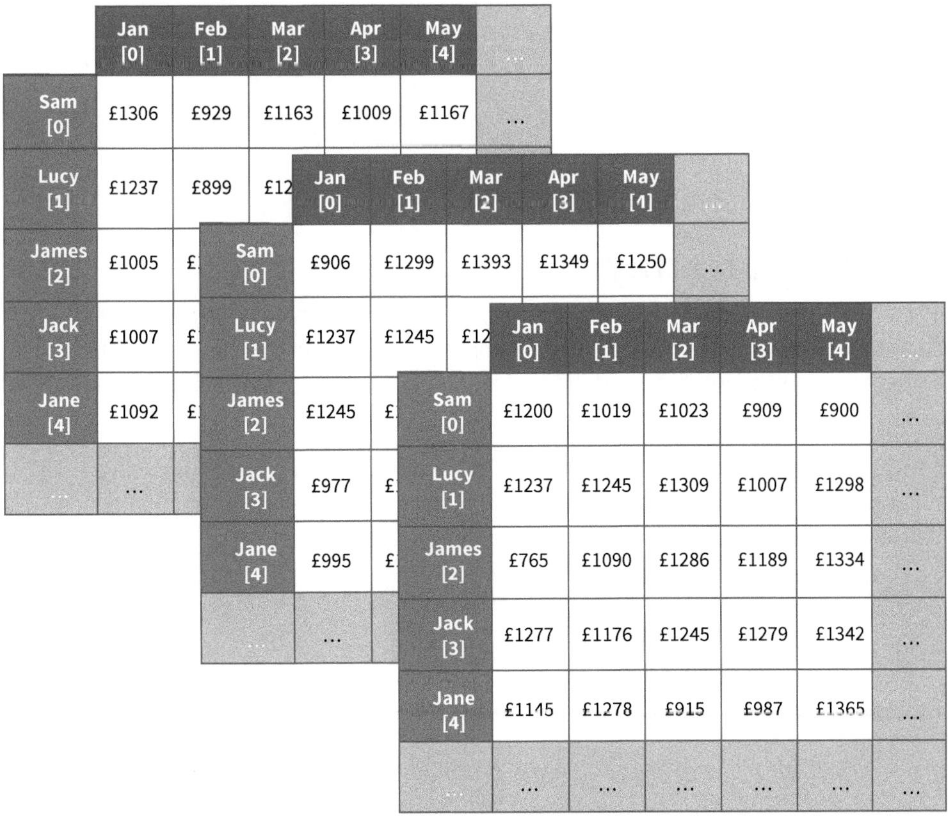

Figure 1.3: The sales figures for different salespeople in the first five months of the year over a number of years. These data can be stored in a 3D array.

The disadvantage of using 3D arrays is that they are more complex to program.

3D arrays can be thought of as an array of 2D arrays (see Figure 1.3). They can be defined in a similar manner as 2D. Consider a set of computing classes, as shown in the tables below.

Name	Tutor group
Sally	7TU
Bert	7AB

Name	Tutor group
Martin	7AB
Susan	7PB

A single row in each table can be represented by a 1D array, for example `['Sally', '7TU']`. The entire table can be represented by a 2D array. As we have two classes worth of data we can move to the third dimen.sion by expressing the final array as being the set of classes.

```
computingClasses = [[['Sally', '7TU'], ['Bert', '7AB']],
[['Martin', '7AB'], ['Susan', '7PB']]]
```

The first class will have an index of 0 while the second class will have an index of 1. To access Susan's tutor group we could use the notation `computingClasses[1][1][1]`.

To display the contents of both classes, a nested loop will be needed. The code example below uses three loops, one for each dimension.

```
for classes in computingClasses:
  for student in classes:
    print ('name tutor group')
    for data in student:
      print (data)
    print('')
```

Searching an array

Arrays are normally immutable, so you can't increase their size once they've been created. However, you can search through to find any empty spaces and put your new data in there. This has the added bonus that you don't waste memory reserving space for empty array elements.

This Python function takes a piece of data and searches through the array until an empty spot is found. If an empty element is found, the data is inserted and the function returns true. If there are no empty elements left, the function returns false.

```
def add_data (data):
  for x in range (0,len(array)):
    if array[x] == "":
      array[x] = data
      return True

  return False
```

As you might expect, it is also impossible to remove elements from an array once it has been created. You can, however, set elements to 'empty' or 'NULL' to signify that they are available to store data in:

Names[1] = ""

Computing in context: Big O notation

An algorithm's efficiency is usually described using Big O notation. Big O notation gives an idea of how well an algorithm scales. For example, how long it will take to search an array of 10 items compared to an array of 10 000 items. Big O notation generally gives the worst case scenario, that is, the maximum possible number of steps required to complete the algorithm.

If an algorithm always takes the same time to complete, regardless of the size of the data set (n), it is said to be **O(1)**. For example, reading the first element of an array will be **O(1)** because it makes no difference if the array is 10 items long or 100 000 items long. The algorithm will take the same number of steps to complete.

If the length of time taken to complete an algorithm is directly proportional to the size of the data set (n), it is said to be **O(n)**. For example, carrying out a linear search on an array is **O(n)** because the number of checks carried out is directly proportional to the number of items in the array.

If the time to complete an algorithm is proportional to the square of the amount of data (n), it is said to be **O(n^2)**. This is very common in algorithms that have nested loops, such as the bubble sort algorithm.

All common algorithms and data structures will have a generally accepted Big O notation efficiency rating. It is up to the programmer to make sure that they choose the most efficient data structure for the job.

See Chapter 3 for more details on Big O notation.

Activity 1.1

Make a list of some common searching and sorting algorithms. Use Big O notation to find out which is the most efficient.

Records

A record is a set of data items all related to a single entity. Unlike an array, a record may contain data items of more than one data type. The following data structure may be used to store the details of an organisation's members:

Field Name	Data Type
Member ID	Integer
First name	String
Surname	String
Gender	Character
DOB	Date

Stacks

Stacks are Last-In, First-Out (LIFO) data structures. This means that the most recent piece of data to be placed onto the stack is the first piece to be taken off it (Figure 1.4).

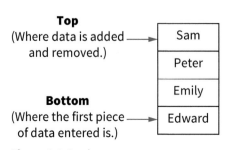

Top
(Where data is added and removed.)

Bottom
(Where the first piece of data entered is.)

Figure 1.4: Stack.

Think of a stack like a pile of pancakes. The pancake on the top is the last one to be added to the pile and will be the first one to be taken off.

Adding data to the stack is called pushing and taking data off the stack is called popping.

Stacks are easily implemented using an array or a linked list to hold the data, and a variable to point to the top of the stack.

The code below shows how Python could be used to implement a simple stack using an array. Calling the pop function will remove a piece of data from the stack; calling the push function will add some data to the top of the stack.

```python
myStack = ['Edward', 'Emily', 'Peter', 'Sam', 'Empty', 'Empty']


def pop(pointerTop): #LIFO, so removes the value from the top
of the stack and returns it
  value = myStack[pointerTop]
  myStack[pointerTop] = 'Empty'
  pointerTop = pointerTop - 1
  return value, pointerTop


def push (data, pointerTop): #add a new piece of data to the
top of the stack
  pointerTop = pointerTop + 1
  myStack[pointerTop] = data
  return pointerTop
  print (myStack)


pointerTop = 3 # points to the last valid element- the top of
the stack
  value, pointerTop = pop(pointerTop)
  print("Removed " + value)
  print (myStack)
  pointerTop = push ('Alex', pointerTop)
  print (myStack)
```

Queues

Queues are First-In, First-Out (FIFO) data structures. This means that the most recent piece of data to be placed in the queue is the last piece taken out.

Think of queues like the ones you find at supermarket checkouts. The first person in a queue is the first person to leave it (Figure 1.5).

Queues are easily implemented using the simple Python code shown here. It contains an array and two variables; one variable points to the first item in the queue, the other points to the next free space:

```python
myQueue = ['Sam', 'Peter', 'Emily', 'Edward', 'Empty', 'Empty']
def pop(pointerFront): # FIFO, so removes the value from the
front of the queue and returns it
```

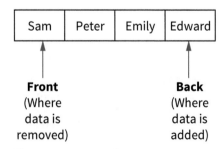

| Sam | Peter | Emily | Edward |

Front
(Where data is removed)

Back
(Where data is added)

Figure 1.5. A queue data structure.

```
    value = myQueue[pointerFront]
    myQueue[pointerFront] = 'Empty'
    pointerFront = pointerFront + 1
    return value, pointerFront

def push(data, pointerBack): #add a new piece of data to the
end of the queue
    myQueue[pointerBack] = data
    pointerBack = pointerBack + 1
    return pointerBack

pointerFront = 0 # points to the front of the queue
pointerBack = 4 # points to the back of the queue
    print (myQueue)
    value, pointerFront = pop(pointerFront)
    print (myQueue)
    pointerBack = push ('Alex', pointerBack)
    print (myQueue)
```

Binary trees and binary search trees

Binary tree data structures are composed of nodes (sometimes called leaves) and links
between them (sometimes called branches). Each node has up to two others coming off it,
which creates a structure like the one shown in Figure 1.6.

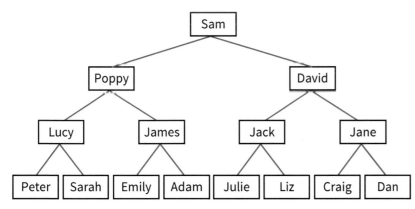

Figure 1.6: A binary tree.

Binary trees are used to implement another data structure called a binary search tree.
These are identical to binary trees but have the additional constraint that the data on
the left branch of a node must be less than the data in the node. Likewise, the data on
the right branch of the node must be greater than the data in the node. All the following
binary trees are also binary search trees.

Unlike stacks and queues, there are a range of different ways to traverse binary tree data
structures. Each method will return a different set of results, so it is important that you use
the correct one.

We'll use the binary search tree shown in Figure 1.7 to demonstrate the different methods
of traversal.

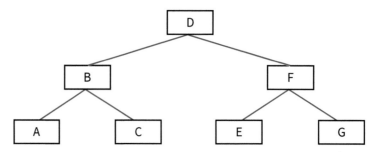

Figure 1.7: A binary tree.

- *Pre-order traversal (depth first search)*: Start at the root node, traverse the left sub-tree, then traverse the right sub-tree. This would give: *D B A C F E G*.
- *In-order traversal*: Traverse the left sub-tree, then visit the root node, and finally traverse the right sub-tree. This would give: *A B C D E F G*.
- *Post-order traversal*: Traverse the left sub-tree, then traverse the right sub-tree, and finally visit the root node. This would give: *A C B E G F D*.

Implementing a binary tree

Just like stacks and queues, it is possible to implement a binary tree using an array or a linked list. It is more useful to use a linked list as this allows the binary tree to be dynamic and grow to any size.

Using a linked list, the nodes of a tree are made up of a piece of data as well as pointers to the addresses of the nodes on the left and right. It is also sensible to include a pointer to a node's parent (the node above it) to aid in navigation. The C++ code below shows how this can be achieved:

```cpp
class Node
{
public:
Node(string dataInput, Node* left=NULL, Node* right=NULL,
Node* parent=NULL);

  void setData(string dataValue);
  void setLeft(Node* leftNode);
  void setRight(Node* rightNode);
  void setParent(Node* parentNode);

private:
  string data;
  Node* left;
  Node* right;
  Node* parent;
};
const string& getData() const;
const Node* getLeft() const;
const Node* getRight() const;
const Node* getParent() const;
```

However, binary trees can also be created using an array. The first element would contain the root, at index 0. From that point on you would find the index which contains the left and right nodes using the formula:

Left index $= 2n + 1$

Right index $= 2n + 2$

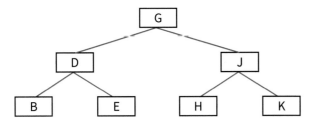

Figure 1.8: A binary tree.

Figure 1.8 would be encoded in the array below. To find the index for H, we start at 0. In order to go right we do the calculation $2n + 2$ or $2 \times 0 + 2$ which is 2. From index 2 we go left using the calculation $2n + 1$ or $2 \times 2 + 1$ which is 5. 'H' is at position 5.

```
myTree = ['G', 'D', 'J', 'B', 'E', 'H', 'K']
```

Adding data to a binary search tree

You can add data to a binary tree by following these simple steps, starting at the root of the tree:

1 Compare the data you want to add to the current node.
2 If the new data is less than the node, follow the left pointer, otherwise follow the right pointer.
3 Repeat this until you reach the end of the tree.
4 Update the pointers of the last node to point to the new one.

The Python code below gives you an idea of how this can be done.

```python
class node:
  def __init__(self, data, parent):
    self.left = None
    self.data = data
    self.parent = parent
    self.right = None


def addToTree(self, currentNode, data, parent):
  if currentNode == None:
    newNode = node(data, parent)
  else:
    if data <= currentNode.data:
      addToTree(currentNode.left, data, currentNode)
    else:
      addToTree(currentNode.right, data, currentNode)
```

Removing data from a binary tree

Removing data from a binary search tree is more complicated. The method required differs depending on the number of branches coming off the node to be removed.

Case 1: a leaf with no branches

If the node to be removed is a leaf with no branches coming off it, removal is simple. You can delete the node and set the original pointer which is referencing the node to be null. In this example (Figure 1.9), node A is simply removed along with the pointer from node B.

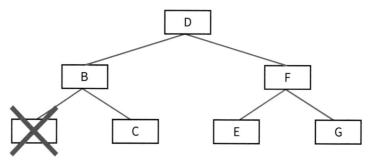

Figure 1.9: A binary tree.

Case 2: a leaf with a single branch

If the node has a single branch, you must update the pointer of the parent to point to the address of the child of the node to be deleted. Then you can delete the node without losing any information. In this example (Figure 1.10), the left pointer of node D is updated to point to node C before node B is deleted.

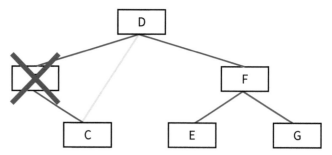

Figure 1.10: An element is removed from a binary tree and the necessary branches are updated.

Case 3: a leaf with two branches

If the node to be deleted has two branches, things are slightly more complicated. First you must use in-order traversal to find the smallest node beneath the one to be deleted, which is known as the successor node. The successor node has its left, right and parent pointers updated so that they are the same as the node to be deleted. Only then can the target node be removed from the tree. Although this may seem complicated, it is vital if the structure of the binary search tree (with small values on the left and large values on the right) is to be preserved.

Linked lists

Linked lists are probably the most common type of dynamic data structure. Being dynamic means that, unlike arrays, they can grow to whatever size is required and their size isn't set when they are declared at the beginning of the program.

Linked lists are made up of nodes, with each node linked to the next node in the list. They are really flexible, powerful data structures and can be used to implement almost every other type of data structure you need to know about.

Nodes in a linked list consist of two things: data and a pointer to the next piece of data in the list (Figure 1.11).

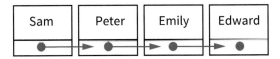

Figure 1.11: A linked list.

The best way to implement a linked list is using an object-oriented language such as C++; this allows the list to be completely dynamic:

```
class Node
{
public:
  Node(const Node* next=NULL);

  void setData(const string& dataValue);
  void setNext(constNode* nextNode);
  string getNext();
private:
  string data;
  Node* next;
};
```

Each node is made up of a piece of data and a pointer to the memory address of the next node in the list. This information is stored in the private section of the Node class. A node is created by calling the public Node constructor and passing it the data value of the node and a pointer to the next node.

Adding data to a linked list

Adding new data to the end of a linked list is easy. The first step is to create a new node (Figure 1.12):

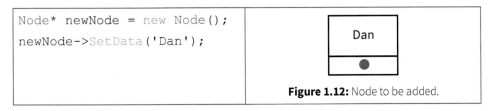

```
Node* newNode = new Node();
newNode->SetData('Dan');
```

Figure 1.12: Node to be added.

The second step is to update the last item in the current list so that it points to the new item (Figure 1.13):

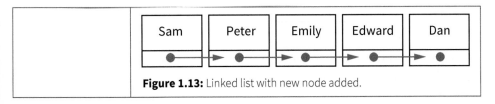

Figure 1.13: Linked list with new node added.

Of course, there is no reason why you have to put your new item at the end of the list. Imagine you want to create a linked list that is sorted in a particular order. You can easily insert a new node in the correct place by working out where you want it, adjusting the node that is currently there to point to the new node and then telling your new node to point to the next node in the list (Figures 1.14 and 1.15).

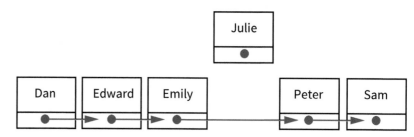

Figure 1.14: Linked list with node to be inserted.

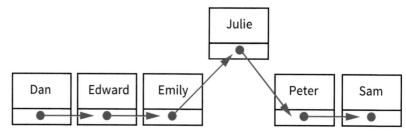

Figure 1.15: Inserting data into a linked list.

Removing data from a list

It is also very simple to remove an item from a list. We simply need to adjust the item before it to point to the item after it. Doing this removes the node from the list and preserves the order of items.

Hash tables

A hash table has two components, a table where the actual data is stored and a mapping function (called a hash function or hash algorithm). The hash function uses the data that is going to be entered in the table to generate the location in the table where the data should be stored.

In this example, we want to use a hash table to hold some names. The initial table shown below is the easy part; it looks like any other table:

Index	Name
0	
1	
2	
3	
4	

Next, we need to decide on our hash algorithm; let's say that we will take the length of the name entered and divide it by the size of the table (using the modulo (MOD) operation); the remainder gives the name's index number.

Let's say we want to enter the name 'Sarah' in the table. The length of the string is 5 and the length of the table is also 5:

5 MOD 5 = 0

So we'll store the name in index 0 as shown in the table below:

Index	Data
0	Sarah
1	
2	
3	
4	

To insert a new, name such as Adam, we carry out the same operation (4 MOD 5) and get 4, so the name Adam goes in index 4:

Index	Data
0	Sarah
1	
2	
3	
4	Adam

It's not hard to see that with our simple hash algorithm we'll soon have problems. If I want to add Jane to the table, her name is the same length as Adam's so the algorithm will try to overwrite Adam to insert Jane. Not ideal! There are many solutions to this problem, the most useful of which is called separate chaining.

Separate chaining uses the original table to store a dynamic data structure (like a linked list). When a new item creates the same hash result as an existing piece of data, a new node on the linked list in that location is created to hold the new data. While good at avoiding collision, this technique will slow down finding the data again, as once the hash location has been computed the linked list will need to be searched as well. It is important to pick a hash function which spreads data evenly over the table to minimise collisions and the potential slow down caused as a result.

Chapter summary

- Data structures are organised stores of data in a computer's memory. Each data structure has its own strengths and weaknesses that make it suitable for a given situation.
- Arrays hold data of a single type in rows and columns; they have one or more dimensions.
- The different sections in an array are called 'elements' and are accessed using an index (which usually starts from 0).
- A record is a data structure that allows items of data of different types to be stored together in a single file.
- Data is removed from linked lists by deleting the node and pointing the item behind it to the item in front of it.
- Stacks are Last-In, First-Out data structures that hold data in the order in which it was entered.

- Data is removed or added at the top of the stack.
- Queues are First-In, First-Out data structures in which the last piece of data entered is the last piece of data retrieved.
- Tree data structures consist of nodes (leaves) and branches. Nodes contain data and the branches link nodes together.
- Linked lists represent each piece of data as a node which holds the data and a link to the next piece of data in the list.
- Hash tables use mapping functions to calculate where in the table a new piece of data should be stored.

End-of-chapter questions

1   What notation is used to describe the efficiency of a data structure or algorithm?   [1]

2   What is an array?   [2]

3   What do the nodes in a linked list contain?   [2]

4   Give the name of a First-In, First-Out data structure (FIFO).   [1]

Further reading

Efficiency of data structures	bigocheatsheet.com
Big O notation	Search for an article on Big O notation on www.khanacademy.org
Linked lists	Search for an article on Linked List Basics on Stanford's Computer Science library
Binary trees	Search for an article on Binary Trees on Carnegie Mellon's Computer Science website
Stacks and queues	Search for a lesson on Data Structures on Virginia Tech's Computer Science department website.

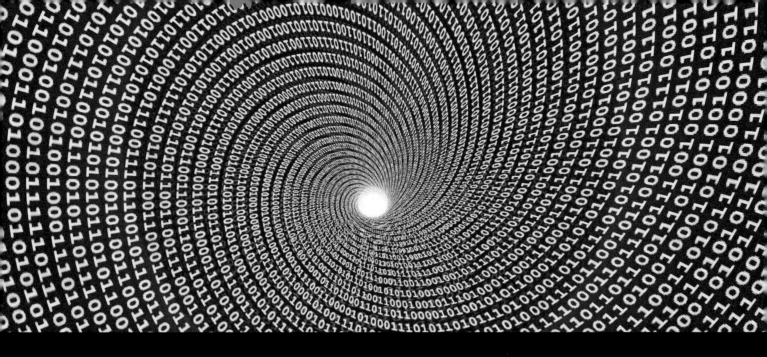

Chapter 2
Logical operations

Learning objectives

- Draw truth tables for Boolean expressions consisting of AND, OR, NOT and XOR logical operations.
- Extend this to include NAND and NOR logical operations.
- Apply logical operations to combinations of conditions in programming, including clearing registers and masking.
- Extend this to include encryption.
- Simplify Boolean expressions using Boolean identities and rules.
- Simplify Boolean expressions using de Morgan's laws.

Introduction

Computers are binary devices that use 1 and 0 to represent all data. Boolean algebra is about looking at statements that, when evaluated, will result in true or false. Propositional logic, which is where a statement or proposition is defined in terms of true and false, follows mathematical rules that allow manipulation of the propositions. This, in turn, allows logical statements to be simplified or derived. In this chapter you will learn about propositional logic and some of the tools that can define real-world problems as propositional statements. You will also learn some of the key tools that can be used to derive and simplify these logical statements.

Propositional logic

Let *P* be 'it is raining'

Let *Q* be 'I have an umbrella'

Let *T* be 'I will get wet'

Logical propositions such as 'it is raining' can have either a true or a false value. Statements such as 'what is the weather', which can produce multiple answers, cannot be considered to be logical propositions. A proposition is an atomic value or place holder and is represented algebraically by assigning letters to each proposition. In the statements above, we used *P* to represent the proposition that 'it is raining'. We have also used *Q* and *T* to represent two different propositions. Most of the rules used to simplify logic do not rely on the meaning of the propositions, but rather focus on how a logical statement is structured. It is useful, when defining problems, to give meaning to our propositions to give them more context. It is also possible to allow our propositions to have more of a programming focus by assigning them conditional expressions. For example, we could write 'Let *P* be N < 5' or 'Let *Q* be N >= J'. These would be acceptable logical propositions as each one can evaluate to true or false only.

Propositional logic makes use of a number of symbols to represent logical connectives. A summary of these connectives can be seen in the table below. A propositional statement, therefore, will be a combination of propositions connected by logical connectives. To aid understanding, colloquial (informal) terms have been given to each symbol as well as their formal names, as shown in the table below. It is important that you use formal names when discussing propositional logic; their colloquial versions are only included to help your learning.

Symbol	Formal term	Informal term
∧	Conjunction	AND
∨	Disjunction	OR
¬	Negation	NOT
⊕	Exclusive disjunction	XOR
↑	Alternative denial	NAND
↓	Joint denial	NOR
→	Implication	IF
↔	Biconditional equivalence	Equality

 Tip

There are different symbols used for Boolean algebra and it is important to be familiar with all of them.

Symbol	Alternatives
∧	.
∨	+
¬*A*	*Ā*
↔	≡

Conjunction (AND)

Consider the conjoined proposition: 'it is raining outside *and* I have an umbrella'. The keyword in this statement is the word 'and'. For this statement to be true, both of the propositions represented by *P* and *Q* must be true. If one is false, the whole statement becomes false. Conjunction can be represented in the simple truth table below:

P	Q	P AND Q
T	T	T
T	F	F
F	T	F
F	F	F

Figure 2.1: Diagrammatic representation of an AND gate.

When we join two propositions together using conjunction, it is represented by the full stop symbol. If P represents 'it is raining' and Q represents 'I have an umbrella', we can represent the conjunction of these two propositions as the statement $P \, . \, Q$.

Disjunction (OR)

Sometimes we want to see if one thing or another is true. The truth table of two propositions connected using disjunction is shown in the following truth table:

P	Q	P OR Q
T	T	T
T	F	T
F	T	T
F	F	F

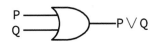

Figure 2.2: Diagrammatic representation of an OR gate.

Disjunction is represented by the + symbol and to represent the disjunction of two propositions we would simply write $P + Q$.

Negation (NOT)

When the negation of a proposition is needed, for example 'it is *not* raining', we can make use of the negation ¬ operator, colloquially known as NOT. Negation is a unary operator and will apply to the proposition immediately following it. So if P represents 'it is raining', we can represent the negative by a bar above the statement, $\bar{P}$.

P	NOT P
T	F
F	T

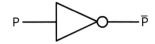

Figure 2.3: Diagrammatic representation of a NOT gate.

Exclusive disjunction (XOR)

Sometimes we want to see if **only** one thing or the other is true (but not both). The truth table of two propositions connected using exclusive disjunction is shown in the following truth table:

P	Q	P XOR Q
T	T	F
T	F	T
F	T	T
F	F	F

Exclusive disjunction is represented by the ⊕ symbol and to represent the disjunction of two propositions we would simply write $P \oplus Q$. For a practical example of the XOR logical operator in use, please refer to encryption at the end of the chapter.

Additional Boolean operators

In the AL specification, you will also need to be familiar with two other logical operators. These are the alternative denial (NAND) and the joint denial (NOR).

The logical NAND is an operation where the values of two propositions produce a value of false if both propositions are true. In other words, it produces a value of true if at least one of the propositions is false. The truth table for the logical NAND of two propositions is shown below:

P	Q	P NAND Q
T	T	F
T	F	T
F	T	T
F	F	T

We can represent the logical NAND of these two propositions as the statement $P \uparrow Q$.

The logical NOR is an operation on two propositions that produces a value of true if both of its propositions are false. It produces a value of false if at least one of its operands is true. The truth table for the logical NOR of two propositions is shown below:

P	Q	P NOR Q
T	T	F
T	F	F
F	T	F
F	F	T

We can represent the logical NOR of these two propositions as the statement $P \downarrow Q$.

Implication (IF)

P = 'it is raining'

Q = 'I have an umbrella'

T = 'I will get wet'

When certain propositions are true, we can infer or imply other elements of truth. Consider the proposition $P \wedge Q$. If it is raining and you have an umbrella, we can infer that you will not get wet, or $\neg T$. Implication is represented using the symbol →, so our keeping-dry proposition could be fully written as $P \wedge Q \rightarrow \neg T$. This would be read as 'if P and Q then not T' or 'if it is raining and I have an umbrella, I will not get wet'.

P	Q	P∧Q
T	T	T
T	F	F
F	T	T
F	F	T

Tautologies

A propositional logic formula is a tautology if, regardless of what truth values each proposition has, the entire statement will always remain true. Below are some examples of tautologies:

$$X + \overline{X}$$
$$\overline{\overline{X}} \rightarrow X$$
$$\overline{\overline{X.\overline{X}}}$$

If you substitute truth values for any of the above formulae, they will always evaluate to true. Consider the truth table for $\overline{\overline{X}} \rightarrow X$:

$\overline{\overline{X}}$	X	$\overline{\overline{X}} \rightarrow X$
T	T	T
F	F	T

Replacing a simple proposition, X, with another formula will always result in a tautology. Consider the formula $P + Q$. If this formula replaces X for the tautology $\overline{\overline{X}} \rightarrow X$, we get the formula $\overline{\overline{P+Q}} \rightarrow (P+Q)$. When the truth table is calculated for this, regardless of the truth value of P or Q, the full statement will still evaluate to true. No matter how complicated you make the substitution, the final result will always be the same. Tautologies always evaluate to true and this logical deduction is useful when deriving further formulae.

P	Q	$P + Q$	$\overline{\overline{P+Q}}$	$\overline{\overline{P+Q}} \rightarrow (P+Q)$
T	T	T	T	T
T	F	T	T	T
F	T	T	T	T
F	F	F	F	T

Biconditional equivalence (Equality)

Biconditional equivalence joins two propositions together using the $\leftrightarrow$ symbol, and means that the truth on both sides is equivalent. For example, 'if and only if it is raining will I get wet' can be represented as $P \leftrightarrow T$. It is equivalent because if both sides are true, the whole statement is true, while if they are different, the statement is false. The statement will also be true if both are false as, if it is not raining, I will not get wet, which maintains logical integrity. For biconditional equivalence to be true, both sides must evaluate to the same truth value.

P	Q	$P \leftrightarrow Q$
T	T	T
T	F	F
F	T	F
F	F	T

Boolean identities

Biconditional equivalence showed that if both sides of the formula are equivalent, the overall formula is true. We can use this property to show the equivalence of formulae and prove that they are tautologies. Boolean algebra has certain laws that can be used to help with further derivations. This section covers commutation, association, distribution and double negation. It is important to remember that each of these equivalencies is a tautology, that is, it is true regardless of what we replace the propositions with.

Commutation

$$P.Q \leftrightarrow Q.P$$

$$P+Q \leftrightarrow Q+P$$

P	Q	P.Q	Q.P	P.Q↔Q.P
T	T	T	T	T
T	F	F	F	T
F	T	F	F	T
F	F	F	F	T

The laws of commutation for both conjunction and disjunction are shown above. Commutation essentially refers to the idea that the order of propositions for both conjunction and disjunction do not matter and they can be interchanged. The truth tables for both $P.Q$ and $Q.P$ are exactly the same. This means they are biconditional.

Association

$$T.(P.Q) \leftrightarrow (T.Q).P$$

$$T+(P+Q) \leftrightarrow (T+Q)+P$$

The order in which we combine multiple conjunctions or disjunctions does not matter. There is a biconditional equivalence regardless of the order, as long as they all use conjunction or disjunction, not a combination. As in standard algebra, statements in brackets are always evaluated first. In the statement, $T.(P.Q)$ the conjunction in brackets is evaluated first and the result is conjoined with T. Likewise in the second statement, $(T.Q).P$, the conjunction in brackets is evaluated first and then conjoined with P. The resultant truth tables below show that the two statements are equivalent and that they are tautologous:

P	Q	T	(P.Q)	(T.Q)	T.(P.Q)	(T.Q).P	T.(P.Q)↔(T.Q).P
T	T	T	T	T	T	T	T
T	F	T	F	F	F	F	T
F	T	T	F	T	F	F	T
F	F	T	F	F	F	F	T
T	T	F	T	F	F	F	T
T	F	F	F	F	F	F	T
F	T	F	F	F	F	F	T
F	F	F	F	F	F	F	T

Distribution

$$T.(P+Q) \leftrightarrow (T.P)+(T.Q)$$

$$T+(P.Q) \leftrightarrow (T+P).(T+Q)$$

This law is a bit more complicated than the others, but distribution for Boolean algebra works in the same way as in standard algebra. Consider the statement $x(y+z)$; this can have x distributed over $y+z$ resulting in $xy+xz$. All we have done is multiplied everything inside the brackets by x. If you consider multiplication to be conjunction and addition to be disjunction, we can see a bit more clearly how the distribution really works.

$$T.(P+Q)$$

$$\equiv T.P+T.Q$$

$$\equiv (T.P)+(T.Q)$$

Brackets are needed to ensure that the resultant equivalency is a tautology and that it is clear in which order the conjunctions or disjunctions must be evaluated. Distribution is not associative, that is, the order of the brackets matters; however, the contents of the brackets are commutative. A simplified truth table proves that the law of distribution is a tautology:

P	Q	T	$T.(P+Q)$	$(T.P)+(T.Q)$	$T.(P+Q) \leftrightarrow (T.P)+(T.Q)$
T	T	T	T	T	T
T	F	T	T	T	T
F	T	T	T	T	T
F	F	T	F	F	T
T	T	F	F	F	T
T	F	F	F	F	T
F	T	F	F	F	T
F	F	F	F	F	T

Double negation

$$\overline{\overline{P}} \leftrightarrow P$$

You may already be aware that a double negative results in addition. For example, $2--2$ is the same as $2+2$. In logic, a double negative always results in the original truth value. So any proposition that is negated twice is the same as simply writing the proposition with no negatives. This equivalency, like all of the others, is a tautology and can be seen in the truth table below. In fact, double negative was one of the statements we saw to explain the concept of tautologies.

$\overline{\overline{P}}$	P	$\overline{\overline{P}} \leftrightarrow P$
T	T	T
F	F	T

de Morgan's laws

$$\overline{P+Q} \leftrightarrow \overline{P}.\overline{Q}$$

$$\overline{P.Q} \leftrightarrow \overline{P}+\overline{Q}$$

de Morgan's laws are named after Augustus de Morgan, who died in 1871; he introduced laws into propositional logic. He proposed that the negation of disjunctions is the conjunction of the negations and that the negation of conjunction is the disjunction of the negations. Putting this into plain English, consider an example. If we consider the case that $\overline{P+Q}$ is true, this could only come about if both P and Q are false. This is because disjunction, as we know, is true if either proposition is true. This leads to the truth table below, which clearly shows that there is only one case where the statement can be true:

P	Q	$P+Q$	$\overline{P+Q}$
T	T	T	F
T	F	T	F
F	T	T	F
F	F	F	T

Following through with this logic, we can infer that both P and Q must be false if the entire statement is true. As such, we can say that P must not be true, $\overline{P}$, and Q must not be true, $\overline{Q}$. Notice that the word 'and' has been used, which we already know as conjunction. Therefore, once we pull the logic together, we are left with $\overline{P}+\overline{Q}$.

A simple way to remember this is that you can always split a long bar, so long as you replace an AND with an OR, or you replace an OR with an AND. Similarly, you can join two individual bars, so long as you replace an AND with an OR, or an OR with an AND.

Defining problems using propositional logic

So far in this chapter, you have seen the different notations and laws relating to propositional logic, but mostly in the theoretical sense rather than the practical. What propositional logic enables us to do is to define problems as statements containing propositions and logical connectives. Consider the statement 'If I own an old car which fails the MOT then I can either repair it or buy a new car'. This simple problem can be expressed in propositional logic by first splitting the sentence into propositions. Next, we can analyse the sentence to see what logical connectives we can use. Implication and disjunction are easy to spot: look for the key words 'if' and 'or'. However, the conjunction in this sentence is slightly more cryptic. The way the sentence is phrased, using the word 'which', suggests that both of these things must be true for the implication to be true. As we know, if we need two things to be true, we can use conjunction. Sometimes you have to consider the statement in a bit more detail rather than blindly looking for command words. In the following example, Figure 2.4 helps us to see the correct logical symbols to use.

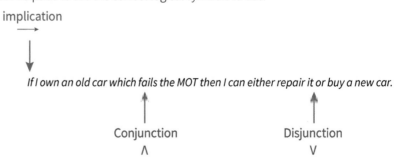

Figure 2.4: Identifying command words and logical symbols.

W = 'own an old car'

X = 'fails MOT'

Y = 'repair car'

Z = 'buy new car'

$$W.X \rightarrow Y + Z$$

Consider the statement 'All old cars always fail the MOT and need to be repaired'. It is trivial to spot the conjunction by looking at the keyword 'and', which gives us $X.Y$. However, linking old cars to this statement is a bit more complicated. We are essentially saying that old cars are synonymous with failing the MOT, and we could say 'Cars which fail the MOT and need to be repaired must be old'. We have two implications here, as shown by the propositional statements below:

$$W \rightarrow X.Y$$

$$X.Y \rightarrow W$$

When you get a situation where you can reverse the implication and still have a true statement, we have a bidirectional condition. As such, the correct form of this propositional logic is:

$$W \leftrightarrow X.Y$$

It is also possible to bring programming constructs into play. Consider a simple ball, not governed by gravity, bouncing around the screen. When the ball nears the edge of the screen, it needs to reverse direction. We can model this, using five propositions, one for each edge and one to reverse direction:

Let A be 'Ball is near far left edge, $x <= 0$'

Let B be 'Ball is near far right edge, $x >=$ width'

Let C be 'Ball is near the top edge, $y <= 0$'

Let D be 'Ball is near the bottom edge, $y >=$ height'

Let R be 'Reverse direction'

$$A \rightarrow R$$

$$B \rightarrow R$$

$$C \rightarrow R$$

$$D \rightarrow R$$

$$A + B + C + D \rightarrow R$$

We can combine the initial implications to form a compound disjunction of all four of the initial propositions. Based on the laws of association and commutation, it does not matter in which order we put the propositions, as $A + B + C + D \rightarrow R \equiv D + C + B + A \rightarrow R$.

Using propositional laws to derive and simplify statements

$$\overline{X.Y} \equiv \overline{X} + \overline{Y}$$

Truth tables are a great way of testing the equivalency of two propositional statements. The $\equiv$ symbol means identity and is used when we want to say that two statements are identical, regardless of the truth values assigned to the propositions. $\overline{X} + \overline{Y}$ is a simplified version of $\overline{X.Y}$, which can be derived using the propositional laws already encountered:

X	Y	$X.\bar{Y}$	$\overline{X.Y}$	$\bar{X}+Y$
T	T	F	T	T
T	F	T	F	F
F	T	F	T	T
F	F	F	T	T

Consider the statement $\overline{X.\bar{Y}}$; it has a negation outside the brackets and looks very similar to de Morgan's law $\overline{P.Q} \leftrightarrow \bar{P}+\bar{Q}$. We can use this law on our original statement, which leaves us with $\bar{X}+\bar{\bar{Y}}$. As we know, a double negative is the same as having no negatives at all (the double negation law), so we can remove them, leaving $\bar{X}+Y$. When applying both laws you must set out the simplification as shown below, always stating which law is applied at any given stage:

$$\overline{X.\bar{Y}} \equiv \bar{X}+\bar{\bar{Y}} \text{ de Morgan's law}$$

$$\overline{X.\bar{Y}} \equiv \bar{X}+Y \text{ Double negation law}$$

In the above example, we derived one logical statement from another using propositional laws. It is also possible to make use of the laws to simplify logical statements. In the example below, you can simplify a statement by using the commutation and distribution laws:

$$(X.Z)+(Y.Z) \equiv (Z.X)+(Z.Y) \text{ Commutation law}$$

$$(Z.X)+(Z.Y) \equiv Z+(X.Y) \text{ Distribution law}$$

$$\overline{\overline{X.\bar{Y}}.\overline{\bar{X}.Z}} \equiv X+(Y.Z)$$

Sometimes, when a statement needs to be simplified, you must break things down into a number of steps. It is not always possible to jump from the statement on the left-hand side to the right in one step. When tackling problems like this, it is important that you know and understand the laws so that you can recognise when they must be used. $\overline{X.\bar{Y}}$ has a negation outside the brackets, which matches de Morgan's law in the same way that $\overline{\bar{X}.Z}$ does. $\bar{Z}$ is a double negation and de Morgan's law has left us with four double negations. As such, the second step will be to remove them. Finally, we are left with X distributed over two bracketed statements. The distribution law allows us to remove this from the each pair of brackets as long as the conjunctions and disjunctions are correct and match the law. The full derivation is shown below:

$$\overline{\overline{X.\bar{Y}}.\overline{\bar{X}.Z}} \equiv (\bar{\bar{X}}+\bar{\bar{Y}}).(\bar{\bar{X}}+\bar{Z}) \text{ de Morgan's law (twice)}$$

$$(\bar{\bar{X}}+\bar{\bar{Y}}).(\bar{\bar{X}}+\bar{Z}) \equiv (X+Y)(X+Z) \text{ Double negation law (four times)}$$

$$(X+Y).(X+Z) \equiv X+(Y.Z) \text{ Distribution law}$$

Activity 2.1

Open up the propositional logic calculator at http://www.inf.unibz.it/~franconi/teaching/propcalc/

Enter the formulae found in this chapter to see the truth tables and the expressions' various properties. Use it to test all of the tautologies, which will light up the green 'taut' icon.

X	Y	Z	$\overline{\overline{X.\bar{Y}}.\overline{\bar{X}.Z}}$	$X+(Y.Z)$
T	T	T	T	T
T	F	T	T	T
F	T	T	T	T
F	F	T	F	F
T	T	F	T	T
T	F	F	F	F
F	T	F	F	F
F	F	F	F	F

The above truth table shows that the two statements have the same truth values, which is not immediately obvious just by looking at them.

Applying logical operations

Masking

Sometimes, it is necessary to discover the value of a bit stored in memory. The following example shows data stored in an 8-bit reigster, where the value of the **third** most significant bit needs to be determined.

10111011_2

The masking process can perform this task by applying the AND logical operator to the data with a mask 00100000_2.

Original Data	10111011_2	
Mask	00100000_2	AND
Result	00100000_2	

In this example, the value of the third most significant bit is 1_2. Had the value been 0_2, then the AND logical operation would have returned 0_2.

Clearing registers

When data stored in registers needs to be cleared, the AND logical operator may be applied. In the following example, data is stored in an 8-bit register:

$$10011001_2$$

By applying the AND logical operator on the data above with a clear mask, the register will be cleared.

Original Data	10011001_2	
Mask	00000000_2	AND
Cleared register	00000000_2	

Another method of clearing the register is to apply XOR to itself, which does not require an additional register which is already cleared.

Original Data	10011001_2	
Mask	10011001_2	XOR
Cleared register	00000000_2	

Encryption

Encryption is used to convert data into cipher text that cannot be easily understood by people without the decryption key. Data can be encrypted using the XOR logical operator. When encrypting data, the XOR logical operator is performed on the original data and a *key*. The key is a secure binary number, known only to the sender and recipient.

In this example, we will encrypt the data 10101010_2, using the key 11010001_2.

Original Data	10101010_2	
Key	11010001_2	XOR
Cypher text	01111011_2	

The original data, 10101010_2, is now encrypted and can be transmitted as 01111011_2.

To recover the original data, the recipient will XOR the cypher text with the key.

Cyphertext	01111011_2	
Key	11010001_2	XOR
Original Data	10101010_2	

Chapter summary

- Conjunction: both sides of the proposition must be true.
- Disjunction: either side of the proposition can be true.
- Negation: reverses the truth of a proposition.
- Implication: if something is true then we can infer that something else is also true.
- Commutation: the order does not matter when using conjunction or disjunction.
- Association: the order does not matter when we link multiple conjunctions or multiple disjunctions; this does not hold true if we start mixing conjunctions and disjunctions.
- Double negation: two negations cancel each other out.
- de Morgan's law: the negation of disjunctions is the conjunction of the negations.

commutation law for conjunction	$P.Q \leftrightarrow Q.P$
commutation law for disjunction	$P+Q \leftrightarrow Q+P$
association laws for conjunction	$T.(P.Q) \leftrightarrow (T.Q).P$
association laws for disjunction	$T+(P+Q) \leftrightarrow (T+Q)+P$
distribution law 1	$T.(P+Q) \leftrightarrow (T.P)+(T.Q)$
distribution law 2	$T+(P.Q) \leftrightarrow (T+P).(T+Q)$
de Morgan's law for disjunction	$\overline{P+Q} \leftrightarrow \overline{P}.\overline{Q}$
de Morgan's law for conjunction	$\overline{P.Q} \leftrightarrow \overline{P}+\overline{Q}$
double negative law	$\overline{\overline{P}} \leftrightarrow P$

Table 2.1: List of rules

Tip

Make sure you can recreate truth tables for any given Boolean expression. It is worth practising by writing out a logical statement and then creating a truth table for it.

You need to learn the different laws and when they should be applied. Remember that most of them come in multiple formats depending on whether disjunction or conjunction was used.

End-of-chapter questions

1   $\neg(P \wedge Q) \leftrightarrow \neg P \vee \neg Q$ is an example of de Morgan's laws. Explain what this
    law means using examples.   [4]

2   Explain, using the correct symbols, what the following terms mean:

    a   Conjunction   [2]

    b   Disjunction   [2]

    c   Implication   [2]

    d   Negation   [2]

3   Using the laws of deduction, show that the following statement
    is correct.   [3]

$$\neg(A \vee \neg B) \leftrightarrow B \wedge \neg A$$
$$\overline{A + \overline{B}} \leftrightarrow B.A$$

4   An elevator, when it is allowing people on and off, can be described using the
    following propositions:

    P = 'doors are open'

    Q = 'Lift has arrived'

    T = 'You can enter'

    R = 'Lift is full'

    For each of the following statements create a way of representing it using
    Boolean algebra.

    a   You cannot enter if the doors are not open.   [2]

    b   You can only enter if the doors are open and the lift has arrived.   [2]

    c   If the lift has arrived and the doors are open, but the lift is full,
        you cannot enter.   [3]

5   Using truth tables, show the difference between implication
    and biconditional equivalence.   [4]

Further reading

Introduction to propositional logic	Go to mathpath.org and search for Propositional Logic
Natural deduction	Search for Natural Deduction on Cornell's Computer Science website
Propositional logic (video)	Search for propositional logic on the Universidad de Navarra's Youtube card

Chapter 3
Algorithms and programs

Learning objectives

- Explain the term algorithm and describe common methods of defining algorithms, including Pseudocode and flowcharts.

- Identify and explain the use of constants and variables in algorithms and programs.

- Describe why self-documenting identifiers, annotation and program layout are important in programs.

- Give examples of self-documenting identifiers, annotation and appropriate program layout.

- Describe the scope and lifetime of variables in algorithms and programs.

- Explain the purpose and effect of procedure calling, parameter passing and return, call by reference and call by value.

- Explain the use of recursion in algorithms and programs and consider the potential elegance of this approach.

- Identify, explain and use mathematical operations in algorithms, including DIV and MOD.

- Identify, explain and apply appropriate techniques of validation and verification in algorithms and programs.

- Explain the need for a variety of sorting algorithms both recursive and non-recursive.

- Describe the characteristics of sorting algorithms: bubble sort, insertion sort, quicksort.

- Explain the effect on the efficiency of a sorting algorithm of storage space requirements, number of comparisons of data items, number of exchanges needed and number of passes through the data.

  Use Big O notation to determine the efficiency of different sorting algorithms in terms of their time and space requirements and to compare the efficiency of different sorting algorithms.

- Explain and apply a linear search algorithm.

- Explain and apply the binary search algorithm.

- Explain and apply a shortest-path algorithm.

- Describe appropriate circumstances for the use of each searching technique.

- Use Big O notation to determine the efficiency of linear and binary searches in terms of execution time and space requirements and to compare the efficiency of different searching algorithms.

- Follow search and sort algorithms and programs and make alterations to such algorithms.

- Write search and sort algorithms and programs.

- Identify, explain and use sequence, selection and repetition in algorithms and programs.

- Identify, explain and use counts and rogue values in algorithms and programs.

- Follow and make alterations to algorithms and programs involving sequence, selection, and repetition.

- Write algorithms and programs involving sequence, selection, and repetition to solve non-standard problems.

- Identify and explain the nature, use and possible benefits of standard functions, standard modules and user defined subprograms.

- Identify, use and explain the logical operators AND, OR, NOT, XOR, NAND and NOR in algorithms and programs.

- Write and interpret algorithms used in the traversal of data structures.

- Explain data compression and how data compression algorithms are used.

- Compare and explain the efficiency of data compression algorithms in terms of compression ratio, compression time, decompression time and saving percentage.

- Select appropriate test data.

- Dry-run a program or algorithm in order to identify possible errors, including logical errors.

- Explain the purpose of a given algorithm by showing the effects of test data.

- Use Big O notation to determine the complexity and efficiency of given algorithms in terms of their execution time, their memory requirements and between algorithms that perform the same task.

Algorithms

An algorithm is a set of mechanical and sequential steps that are followed in order to take some form of input and process it to form an output. Algorithms are a mathematical concept rather than just being something we use in computer science. In order to create an algorithm we must first know what it is to accomplish, what input it will be provided with and what form the output will take, as shown in Figure 3.1.

Figure 3.1: Diagrammatic representation of an algorithm.

Identify inputs and outputs of an algorithm

Figure 3.2: Input and output of a problem.

Before an algorithm can be properly written, the inputs and outputs must be carefully defined. This is not as simple as just stating the data type. We must consider what are the permissible values allowed, what structure the data will take, how many arguments the input will form and what the preconditions are. In order to help exemplify this we can look at the game noughts and crosses. Because this contains numerous algorithms, we will break the problem down first and only consider one part, as shown in Figure 3.3. For each part, the identification of the inputs and outputs will be the first stage in developing a solution.

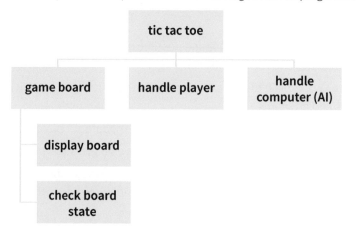

Figure 3.3: Top-down design of a noughts and crosses game.

When deciding on the inputs and outputs, there are a number of important considerations to make, which are summarised in the table below.

Consideration	Explanation
Data type	To ensure only the correct data is passed to the module enabling the developer to abstract away from any concerns over incompatible data.
Structure of the data	Will it be a primitive data type or a data structure? For example, will it accept a string or a list of strings?

Consideration	Explanation
Validation	Will the input be restricted in any way? For example, only numbers from 1 to 10 or a maximum list of 100 elements.
Number of arguments	Does it require multiple items of information? For example, withdrawing money from a bank account will require the amount and the account details.
Where will the input come from or where will the output go?	Will it be passed to/from a function or saved into a file? Will a database be involved? Is it going to be interactive?
Are there any preconditions?	Does anything need to have occurred first before the problem can be solved? For example, we would need a digitised map in order to do route finding.

As an example, consider the 'Handle player' module. The purpose of this module would be to allow the user to decide where they want to take their turn. The input to this module will be the square the player wants to pick. If this were a text based game then the input could be a number corresponding to the square the user has chosen. The output will simply update the current game board with the player's selection.

Consideration	Handle player
Data type	Integer
Structure of the data	The game board will be stored as a one dimensional array. Each element within the array will be 0 (square is available), 1 for player and 2 for the computer.
Validation	The number must be a valid square starting from square 1. If that square does not currently contain 0 then the player must select again.
Arguments	The game board array and the user's selection.
Where will the input come from or where will the output go?	The game board will be passed to the module as a one dimensional array. The user's selection will come from the console.
Are there any preconditions?	The game board array should be pre-initialised. The player and computer should be taking their turns in order. This module will assume it is the player's go when called.

When dealing with input, validation is going to be in place as this will help restrict the problem domain and ultimately make the solution simpler. This is best done before development occurs as many bugs occur due to incorrectly implemented validation rules. Input to a system is also the door for security threats, which makes validation a crucial consideration when defining input. If invalid data is allowed into a module then bugs may occur which could crash the module or allow hackers to bypass security mechanisms. For example, SQL injection allows hackers to run SQL commands by carefully submitting data through web forms that have poor validation. This is doubly important if modules are daisy chained together (e.g. the output of module A provides the input to module B) because a rogue input could be propagated throughout the system.

Representing an algorithm

Once an algorithm has been defined and developed we must represent it in a way that shows how it works and can lead to a developer implementing it as part of a larger program. Pseudocode is a common method used to represent algorithms while flowcharts can be used to represent simpler algorithms. Both methods will be shown in this section.

Pseudocode

Pseudocode is a generic programming language that is not meant to be run directly or compiled, but rather used to represent algorithmic ideas. There are many subtly different ways to represent Pseudocode but they all have one thing in common: they must be interpretable by a programmer and show exactly the process that they represent. Below is a list of programming ideas and how they are represented in Pseudocode.

Programming statement	Pseudocode
Variable	```z= 5``` ```name="bob"```
Global variable	```global userid = 432```

Casting	```int("64") casts to 64```
	```str(32) casts to "32"```
	```float("7.8") casts to 7.8```
	```Note - strings are shown in quotation marks.```

Output	```print "hi"```
	```print "my age is" + age```
	```output "goodbye"```

Text input	```hobby = input ("what is your hobby? ")```

For loop	```for i =1 to 10```
	``` print i```
	```next i```

While loop	```i = 1```
	```while i<=10```
	``` print i```
	``` i = i + 1```
	```end while```

Modulus and integer division	```print 17 MOD 10 -> will print 7``` ```print 17 DIV 10 -> will print 1```

Selection	```if a == 1 then```
	``` print "hello"```
	```else if a == 2 then```
	``` print "hi"```
	```else```
	``` print "bye"```
	```end if```

Programming statement	Pseudocode

Functions	```function areaOfCircle(r)```
	 ``` return 3.14 * r * r```
	 ```end function```

Array	```array names[3]```
	 ```name[0] = "bert"```
	 ```name[1] = "sally"```
	 ```name[2] - "fred"```
	
	 ```print "I like" + name[2]```

2D and 3D array	```array grid[[3,3], [5,6]]```
	 ```grid[0][1] = "x"```
	
	 ```array grid[[3,3][6,7]],[5,6[8,9]]```
	 ```threeD = grid[5,5,5]```
	 ```print grid[2,1,1]```

Comments	```// this is a comment!```

Below is an example of an algorithm written in Pseudocode.

```
word = INPUT "Enter a word"
start = 0
end = LEN(word) - 1
WHILE (word[start] == word[end] AND start < FLOOR(LEN(word) / 2))
  start = start + 1
  end = end - 1
END WHILE
IF start >= LEN(word)/2 THEN RETURN TRUE
ELSE RETURN FALSE
```

It is not important if the keywords are written in uppercase or lower case. In the above example, they are uppercase to make them stand out more. Also, notice two functions, which have not been defined, FLOOR and LEN. In Pseudocode, you can make use of functions, which are not defined, as long as their intention is clear. Floor is a common function in most languages and will round a floating-point number down. Len is another common function used to return the length of strings or arrays. When using these extra functions it is important to decide if they are commonly available in most languages (not just one specific one) and that their purpose and usage is unambiguous.

Flowcharts

Flowcharts are less commonly used for representing algorithms but can be used to represent the same structures as Pseudocode. They are more commonly used to represent smaller algorithms. Figure 3.4 is an example flowchart representing a serial search algorithm.

The flowchart mixes parts of Pseudocode together with some English statements. As long as the meaning of each part of the flowchart is clear then you can use whichever terms you deem expressive enough. When creating flowcharts it is important not to over generalise, for example the flowchart in Figure 3.5 would not be considered expressive enough.

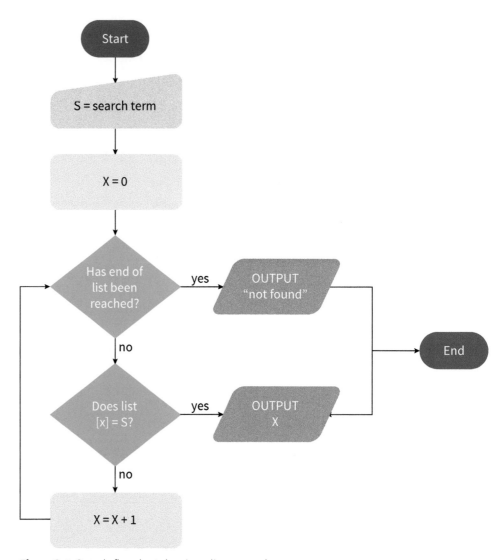

Figure 3.4: Sample flowchart showing a linear search.

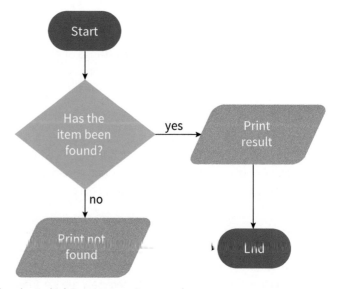

Figure 3.5: Flowchart which is not expressive enough.

The shapes of a flowchart are as follows:

Shape	What it represents
⬭	The start or end of a flowchart.
◆	A decision or selection. It will always have two lines coming off it.
▱	Manual input which is used to gather information from the user (equivalent to INPUT in Pseudocode).
▭	Process. A process is something which happens internally in the flowchart and does not directly produce input or output.
▱	This is commonly used to show output.

Constants and variables

Variables

A variable is a named location in the computer's memory that a programmer can use to store data whilst the program is running.

All computer systems have some form of storage or memory. You will probably be familiar with RAM (Random Access Memory) as shown in the image in Figure 3.6.

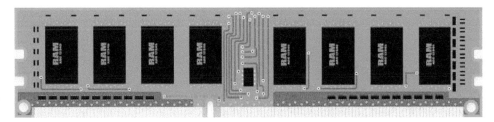

Figure 3.6: RAM.

You can think of a computer's memory as being made of lots of small storage boxes into which programmers can place information. Each storage box has its own unique address that can be used to access the information stored in that box. Memory addresses start at zero and increase sequentially up to the size of available RAM. When we declare a variable (see Figure 3.7) we do not have to concern ourselves with the specific

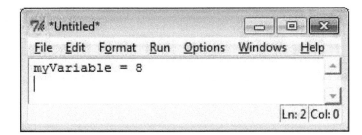

Figure 3.7: Declaring a variable in Python.

memory address where our data is to be stored as this is decided by the translator. We can assign a name, or identifier, to the data, which the translator will turn into a memory address on our behalf.

Constants

It is fairly common for certain literals to be used within your code. This could be for a specific constant value, such as PI, or to enumerate a set of error codes. Regardless of the reason behind these literals, they have one thing in common: their values will not change. The code sample below, written in C, shows how a constant can be declared and used. Once a constant has been declared, using the const keyword, it can be used in the same way a normal variable can. However, if you attempted to assign a new value to PI after the initial declaration then you would get an error.

```
const PI = 3.14;
float radius = 2;
float area = PI * radius * radius;
printf("the area of a circle with a radius of %f is %f",
radius, area);
```

Enumeration, where sets of items are each given a unique numeric identifier, can be set up with constants. Consider the following example of error codes used by the HTTP protocol.

```
const BAD_REQUEST = 400;
const UNAUTHORIZED = 401;
const PAYMENT_REQUIRED = 402;
const FORBIDDEN = 403;
const NOT_FOUND = 404;
...
```

A constant is a bit like a variable in the sense that it has an identifier and will store a value in memory, but it has one key difference; its value will not change. In many languages it is possible to define constants in such a way that a syntax error will be generated if the programmer attempts to change the value of a constant. However, not every language makes use of constants, with one notable language being Python. In this situation the coder just has to treat standard variables as if they are constants and not change their values. For this reason it is common for coding standards to be used by developers to ensure constants stand out from other variables. Common methods include making the identifiers all capitals, as shown in the examples above, or adding the letters CONST to the front of the identifier. It is also common to use underscores to separate words. For example, THIS_IS_A_CONSTANT.

It is good coding practice to set up constants for these literals. By using constants your code becomes more readable, as the meaning of the identifiers is much clearer than using a hard coded value. Also, although constants are not meant to change, over time some of them might be given different values – for example, if HTTP were given a new set of error codes. By using constants you only have to change the value at the start of the code rather than searching through the entire code base and changing every instance.

Scope and lifetime of variables

Once a variable is defined it will have a lifespan. For some variables, known as global variables, this could be the entire time the program is running. For others, known as local variables, this could be for a single function call. Scope refers to the time a variable is accessible and whether or not it is local or global.

Local variables

Local variables are those that can only be accessed by the subroutine they have been declared in.

This program (Figure 3.8) uses a subroutine to work out the value of adding two numbers together. It also uses the same variables to work out the addition and display it after the subroutine has run.

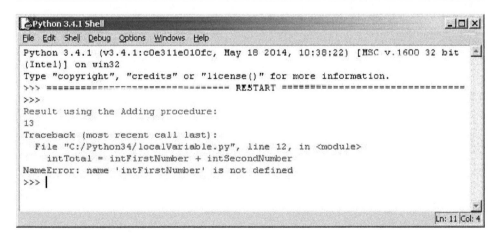

Figure 3.8: Local variables.

The code produces an error because the variables intFirstNumber and intSecondNumber are local to the subroutine 'Adding'. When they are called from the main block of code the computer can't find them.

Some languages, such as C, use a block level scope. This means that variables defined inside a block of code, such as a while loop, would not be available after the while loop ends. This level of local scoping can be difficult for some newer developers to get used to, and common coding standards suggest that all variables should be defined and initialised at the start of a function.

Global variables

Global variables are available to any subroutine throughout the program. The program below (Figure 3.9) is exactly the same as the previous example except that the variables, intFirstNumber and intSecondNumber, are declared as being global and are therefore accessible throughout the entire program.

```
*Python 3.4.1: localVariable.py - C:/Python34/localVariable.py*
File  Edit  Format  Run  Options  Windows  Help

def Adding():
    global intFirstNumber
    global intSecondNumber

    intFirstNumber = 5
    intSecondNumber = 8

    intTotal = intFirstNumber + intSecondNumber

    print("Result using the Adding procedure:")
    print(str(intTotal))

Adding()

intTotal = intFirstNumber + intSecondNumber
print("Result after using the Adding procedure:")
print(str(intTotal))
```

```
Python 3.4.1 Shell
File  Edit  Shell  Debug  Options  Windows  Help
Python 3.4.1 (v3.4.1:c0e311e010fc, May 18 2014, 10:38:22) [MSC v.16
00 32 bit (Intel)] on win32
Type "copyright", "credits" or "license()" for more information.
>>> ================================ RESTART ========================
==========
>>>
Result using the Adding procedure:
13
Result after using the Adding procedure:
13
>>>
```

Figure 3.9: Global variables.

This time the program runs successfully because the variables being called are global and they can be accessed from any point in the program.

Self-documenting identifiers, annotation and program layout

When developing code for real projects it is unlikely that you will be working alone. Most development happens within a team of developers, with each working on a different part of the code base. When working in a team it becomes necessary to read one another's code: this means that it is of vital importance that any code you write is easily understood. The way the code is laid out, how you express your ideas, your use of constants, naming identifiers and the way you annotate your code will make a big difference to how easy your code is to interpret. When different programmers do not interpret code correctly, they can inadvertently introduce bugs into the system.

One of the key ways to make code more maintainable is to add annotation in the form of comments. A comment will be ignored by the translator but will be useful to any other developer when reading over your code. In Python a comment is preceded by the # symbol while in Java and C++ // is used. The code below shows an example of a comment in Python.

```
# INPUT - radius : float
# OUTPUT - area of the circle : float
# Purpose - to find the area of a circle.
# Author - Adam Hamflett
def areaOfCircle(radius):
PI=3.14
  return PI * radius * radius
```

Adding comments to code can be a tedious process and most developers prefer to make their code self-documenting. Some coders only add comments to their code after the code has been completed, thus increasing the chance that some code will remain uncommented or of the comments not fully reflecting what the code does. Self-documenting code can help avoid this.

In order to make code self-documenting it must be readable and understandable enough to make comments unnecessary. In order to make code self-documenting, certain rules must be adhered to while producing your code. These rules are detailed below.

* Use meaningful identifiers by following naming conventions set out by the development team. Camel case, which is a common naming convention, is where words are concatenated together, with each new word starting with a capital (the first word may or may not); for example: myFirstVariable. An alternative method is snake case; for example: my_first_variable.
* Use indentation when nesting programming statements such as iteration or selection.
* Make use of constants where appropriate.
* Avoid using global variables.
* Consider the layout of your code and be consistent. If you always put a space after a variable assignment, x = 2 instead of x=2, then do that throughout the code.
* Ensure that your code is not bunched into one big block; ensure key blocks are separated by line breaks.
* Avoid adding unnecessary white space such as extra line breaks or tabs.
* Declare variables at first use rather than having them all at the start of the program.
* Within your chosen language, make use of error mechanisms such as exceptions and assertions.

```
def f(z):
  s = 0
  a = 0
  b = len(z) - 1
  while z[a] == z[b] and s < math.floor(len(z) /2)
    a = a + 1
    b = b -1
  if a >= len(z)/2: return True
  else: return False
```

Consider the poorly written code above. This code would need comments to make it more understandable by other developers. If you spend time reading the code and trying out some sample values, you might ultimately realise that the aim of the function is to find out whether the string passed to it is a palindrome or not. By refactoring, or restructuring, the code slightly and changing the identifier names, the code becomes a lot more readable.

```
def isPalindrome(wordToCheck):
  start = 0
  end = len(wordToCheck) - 1
  midpoint = floor(len(wordToCheck) /2
  while wordToCheck [start] == wordToCheck [end] and start <
  midpoint)
    start = start + 1
    end = end -1
  if start >= midpoint return True
  else: return False
```

There is a debate on whether or not code can be truly free of comments and thus be fully self-documenting. Most development teams make use of both strategies.

Program layout

Python is an unusual language in the sense that it uses indentation when creating while loops or other blocked statements. This forces the developer to layout their code explicitly. This is not the case for a lot of languages where you are not forced to layout your code. The poorly laid out code below is written in Javascript and taken from a simple online game . The code has been changed to make it more difficult to read.

```
function toggle(image, row, col){
if (playersTurn){
if (row == nimStack[col] && currentColSel == -1){
image.src = "rockAlt.png";
currentColSel = col; selectAmount = 1;
nimStack[col] --; imageList.push(image);}
if (row == nimStack[col] && col == currentColSel){
image.src = "rockAlt.png";
imageList.push(image);
selectAmount++;
nimStack[col] --;}}}
```

Although this code will work, maintaining it will be much more challenging. Looking at this code for the first time it will be difficult to work out what it is doing even though efforts have been made to use sensible variable names. Below is the exact same code laid out to be more readable. Although this code is out of context, and it may be difficult to fully understand what it is doing, hopefully you can see that paying attention to the layout can make the code much more readable.

```
function toggle(image, row, col){
  if (playersTurn){
    if (row == nimStack[col] && currentColSel == -1){
      image.src = "rockAlt.png";
      currentColSel = col;
      selectAmount = 1;
      nimStack[col] --;
      imageList.push(image);
    }
```

```
   if (row == nimStack[col] && col == currentColSel){
      image.src = "rockAlt.png";
      imageList.push(image);
      selectAmount++;
      nimStack[col] --;
   }
  }
}
```

Parameter passing

When a sequence of instructions is going to be repeated a number of times at different points in the same program it is often useful to put them in a separate subroutine. The subroutine can then be called at the relevant points in the program.

Imagine a very security-conscious online store that wanted you to re-enter your username and password after every stage of your purchase. The Pseudocode below describes the process. Notice that the same sequence of instructions is repeated three times, making the algorithm long and complicated.

```
username = INPUT "Enter username"
password = INPUT "Enter password"
IF checkLogin (username, password) == FALSE THEN
  OUTPUT "Access denied"
  EXIT
END IF
OUTPUT "Collect customer details"
username = INPUT "Enter username"
password = INPUT "Enter password"
IF checkLogin (username, password) == FALSE THEN
  OUTPUT "Access denied"
  EXIT
END IF
OUTPUT "Collect bank details"
username = INPUT "Enter username"
password = INPUT "Enter password"
IF checkLogin (username, password) == FALSE THEN
  OUTPUT "Access denied"
  EXIT
END IF
deliveryAddress = INPUT "Enter delivery address"
processOrder(username, password, deliveryAddress)
```

In comparison look at the pseudocode below, which uses subroutines to describe the same process. Every time the 'Security' instruction is encountered, execution jumps to the 'Security' subroutine and implements it. Notice how much simpler the process is; this makes it less error-prone and easier to modify. A change like this one could save you writing hundreds of lines of code. More importantly, if a bug is found in the subroutine then the fix only needs to be applied in one place. Functions, subroutines and procedures are the first step towards code re-use, as you can see in the example below.

```
SUB security()
  username = INPUT "Enter username"
  password = INPUT "Enter password"
  IF checkLogin(username, password) == FALSE THEN
    OUTPUT "Access denied"
    EXIT
  END IF
END SUB
security()
OUTPUT "Collect customer details"
security()
OUTPUT "Collect bank details"
security()
deliveryAddress = INPUT "Enter delivery address"
processOrder(username, password, deliveryAddress)
```

When programming a subroutine can be defined as 'a named block of code that carries out a specific task'. Most programming languages make use of two types of subroutine; functions and procedures.

Functions

A function is a subroutine that returns a value.

In the Python example (Figure 3.10) a function is created called funcArea. This function will take in two values (Height and Width) and return the area of a square of those dimensions.

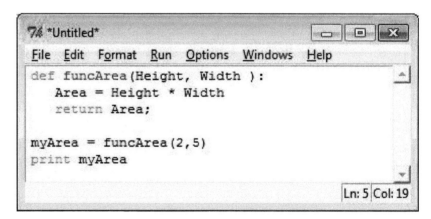

Figure 3.10: Functions in Python 2.

Line 1 creates the function, the word def (short for define) tells the computer that this is a subroutine. The next part, funcArea, is the name of the function and is used when you want to call the subroutine. You can choose any function name you like but using names that describe the purpose of the function makes your code easier to understand. The final part of the instruction is the *parameters* (Height, Width). This tells the computer that this function will accept two values that have been called Height and Width. Line 2 calculates the area of the square by multiplying the two values together. Line 3 is important as it returns the Area variable back to the program that called the function. Line 4 is interesting, as this is where the main program calls the subroutine. You can see the function name is used, funcArea, along with two numbers in brackets (2, 5). These values are called *arguments* and are the values that are passed to the subroutine. So Height becomes 2 and Width becomes 5. Finally, line 5 tells the main program to print out the number it got back when it called funcArea.

```
74 Python Shell                                         ___ ⊡ ✕
File  Edit  Shell  Debug  Options  Windows  Help
Python 2.7.3 (default, Apr 10 2012, 23:31:26) [MSC v.1500 32 bit (Intel)] on ▲
win32
Type "copyright", "credits" or "license()" for more information.
>>> ================================ RESTART ================================
>>>
10
>>> |
                                                     ▼
                                              Ln: 6 Col: 4
```

Figure 3.11: Function being run in Python.

Figure 3.11 shows the result of running the program. funcArea has been called with the values 2 and 5. These have been multiplied together and the result returned to the main program. Finally the result has been printed.

Procedures

Procedures are subroutines that don't return a value. They can display information to a user but they don't return any information back to the main program.

The example in Figure 3.12 shows a procedure being used to calculate the area of a square. Line one remains the same except that the name of the subroutine has been changed to procArea as a reminder that this is a procedure not a function. Line 2 also remains the same and simply multiples two numbers together. Line 3, however, is different; the result is displayed straight to the user and *not* returned to the main program as it was in the function. Line 4 simply calls the procedure with the parameters 3 and 6.

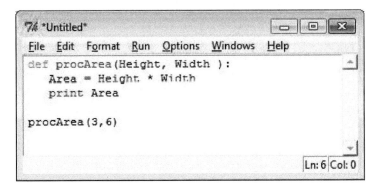

```
74 *Untitled*                                         ___ ⊡ ✕
File  Edit  Format  Run  Options  Windows  Help
def procArea(Height, Width ):                         ▲
    Area = Height * Width
    print Area

procArea(3,6)
                                                     ▼
                                              Ln: 6 Col: 0
```

Figure 3.12: Procedures in Python 2.

```
74 Python Shell                                         ___ ⊡ ✕
File  Edit  Shell  Debug  Options  Windows  Help
Python 2.7.3 (default, Apr 10 2012, 23:31:26) [MSC v.1500 32 bit (Intel)] on win32 ▲
Type "copyright", "credits" or "license()" for more information.
>>> ============================= RESTART =============================
>>>
18
>>> |
                                                     ▼
                                              Ln: 6 Col: 4
```

Figure 3.13: Running a procedure in Python.

Figure 3.13 shows the result of running the program. Execution begins on line 4 when the procedure is called and passed the values 3 and 6. The procedure then takes these values and calculates the Area of the square before displaying the result (18) to the user.

Parameters by value

Parameters are used to pass values in to a subroutine. This example procedure (Figure 3.14) uses two parameters, Height and Width. These parameters are used throughout the subroutine and are replaced by copies of values when the subroutine is called.

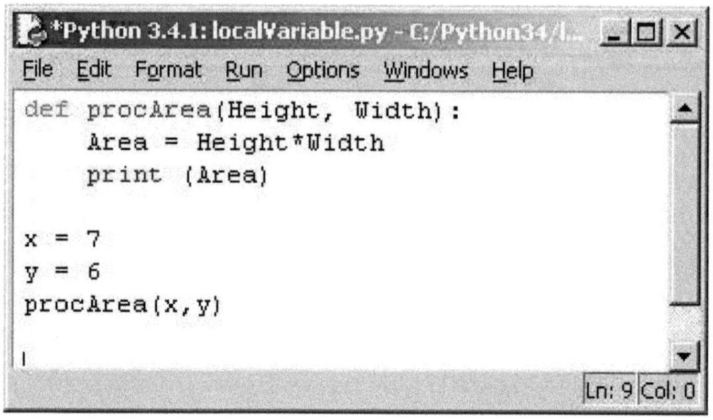

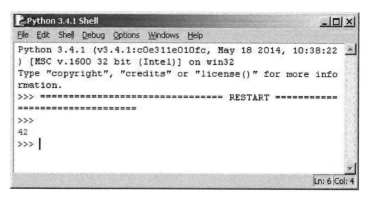

Figure 3.14: Procedures in Python 3.

For example, procArea(x,y) replaces the word Height with a copy of the value stored in x (7) and the word Width with a copy of the value stored in y (6) throughout the subroutine. The result is that the number 42 is displayed (Figure 3.15).

Figure 3.15: Procedures in Python 3.

Using parameters makes code easy to read and they should be used in preference to global variables whenever possible.

Parameters by reference

In the previous section you saw the result of calling procArea(x,y). This creates a copy of the variable x and a copy of the variable y and passes them in to procArea. This technique is often called pass by value or pass by copy.

An alternative way of passing parameters in to subroutines is to pass by reference; this means that rather than making a copy of a variable the subroutine is passed the address of the variable. The main difference is that when passing by reference any change made within the subroutine will also affect the variable outside the subroutine (much like a global variable).

In Python it is possible to pass parameters by reference. This will happen automatically if they are not primitive data types such as integers and strings. The code below demonstrates the difference between pass by reference and by value. The code below will output 10, 11 and then 10 again. The data inside myVariable has been copied, meaning that all changes to x do not impact myVariable at all. Primitive data types are therefore passed by value in Python.

```
def passByValue(x):
  print x
  x = x + 1
  print x


myVariable = 10
passByValue(myVariable)
print myVariable
```

Now consider a procedure which accepts and manipulates a list in Python. Lists are not primitive data types and therefore are not passed by value but by reference. This means that a pointer to the data is passed rather than creating a copy of it. The first time it prints it will display Bob and Sally. At the end of the passByReference procedure it will have had 'new data' added to the list and will therefore display Bob, Sally followed by new data. However, the print call immediately after the procedure call will also output the list with new data in it. This shows that the list has been changed inside the procedure and the impacts of that change exist after the procedure has ended.

```
def passByReference(l):
  print l
  l.append("new data")
  print l


myList = ["bob", "sally"]
passByReference(myList)
print myList
```

Pass by reference means that any changes to a parameter will impact the code which called the function. Programmers must be careful not to change data in lists or other data structures when coding their own functions unless they are aware of the consequences.

Recursion

A recursive function is one that calls itself until a base case is met. This often provides a succinct way to carry out the same operation a number of times.

The most common example of a recursive function is one that is used to calculate the factorial of a given number. The factorial of any given number can be calculated by multiplying together all the numbers beneath it. For example, the factorial of 4 (shown as 4!) can be calculated as $4 \times 3 \times 2 \times 1$ or 24. The factorial of 6 can be shown as, $6! = 6 \times 5 \times 4 \times 3 \times 2 \times 1$ or 720.

The calculation is carried out by repeatedly working out $n \times (n-1)$ then multiplying the result by the previous one. This operation is repeated until $n = 1$ (factorials don't use negative numbers or zero).

It is possible to solve this problem without recursion, although the solution is lengthier and less *elegant*.

Using recursion, a function to calculate the factorial of a given number might look like Figure 3.16.

```
def factorial(n):
    if n == 1:
        return 1
    else:
        return n * factorial(n-1)
```

Figure 3.16: Recursive function.

Line 2 recognises the base case. When n = 1 we know the answer will always be one so we stop calling the function and simply return the answer 1. Line 5 is the clever one. Each time it is executed, it returns n multiplied by the result of calling the factorial function with n − 1. As a result, if factorial(4) is called, the number 24 is printed out.

Figure 3.17 shows this in action. The function calls begin at the top and the green arrows show the values being entered each time the function is called. The blue arrows show how the result from each function call is passed back up the chain.

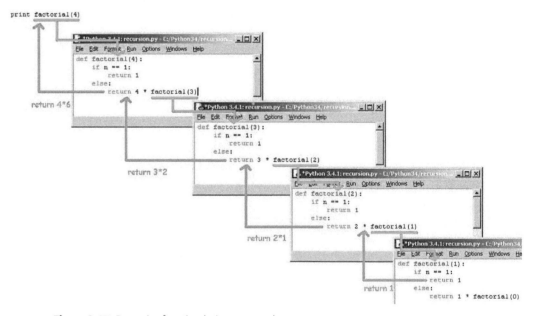

Figure 3.17: Recursive function being executed.

Mathematical operations

The table left shows all of the key mathematical operations used in programming expressions. Most of them will be self-explanatory apart from MOD and DIV which are more specific to programming.

MOD will divide two numbers together, but rather than giving the answer it will return the remainder. 8 MOD 3 will return the value of 2. This is because 3 will divide into 8 twice leaving a remainder of 2. Below is a set of examples demonstrating MOD.

17 MOD 10 = 7

27 MOD 10 = 7

65 MOD 2 = 1

78 MOD 5 = 3

Operation	Symbol
Addition	+
Subtraction	−
Multiplication	*
Division	/
Modulus	MOD (python uses %)
Integer division	DIV (python uses //)

DIV again divides two numbers but this time will only return a whole number. This number will always be rounded down. 38 DIV 10 will return the value of 3 as 38 ÷ 10 = 3.8 and DIV is only interested in the values to the left of the decimal point. DIV is known as integer division, as the result will always be an integer.

Validation and verification

Validation and verification are used to ensure any input provided by the user is as correct as it can be. Validation checks occur before data is committed to storage while verification occurs afterwards.

The key validation checks are:

- Character check (or type check) – Ensures that the input is of the correct data type. For example, all input is numeric or contains only specific characters.
- Length check – Checks the number of characters to ensure they do not go over a specific limit.
- Range check – Checks that numeric values are within a certain range.
- Format check – Ensures data conforms to a set a rules. For example, e-mail addresses must always contain an @ symbol.
- Existence (or presence check) – Ensures data exists.
- Check digit – Only available for specific input. See barcodes for more detail on check digits.

The key verification checks are:

- Double entry – Enter the data twice and then compare to ensure accuracy.
- Proof reading – A human will read over the input to manually check.

Big O notation

In order to explain **Big O**, pronounced 'Big-Oh', we need to take a short look at the order of **functions**. Consider the two **functions** in Figure 3.18:

$f(x) = 2x$

$g(x) = 4x + 1$

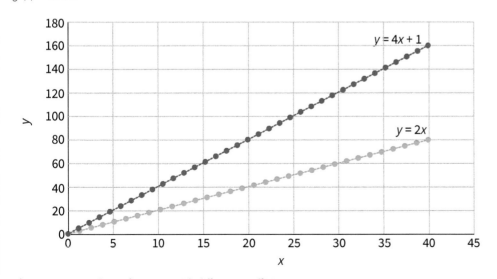

Figure 3.18: Two linear functions with different coefficients.

Both of these **functions** exhibit linear growth, even though $g(x)$ grows faster than $f(x)$.

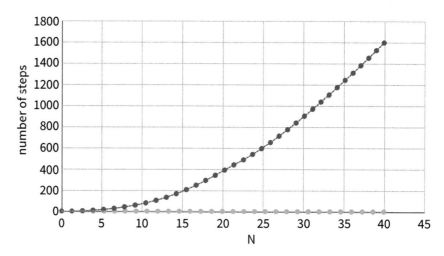

Figure 3.19: Chart showing how a linear and squared function grow in comparison to one another.

Comparing a squared **function** to a linear one (Figure 3.19), we can see that the squared **function** grows much faster. We can say that a squared **function** is of a higher order than the linear one. In fact, all squared **functions** are of a higher order than linear ones. This is independent of the **coefficients** used, as eventually a squared **function** will outgrow a linear one. $f(x)$ and $g(x)$ below show these **functions** in their more general form.

$$f(x) = ax + b$$

$$g(x) = ax^2 + b$$

Consider the two **functions** below. The **coefficients** for $f(x)$ were purposely made larger than those of $g(x)$. This way we can show that for some value of x we will get the result that $g(x) > f(x)$ and this can be clearly seen in Figure 3.20.

$$f(x) = 4x + 10$$

$$g(x) = 0.5x^2 - 10$$

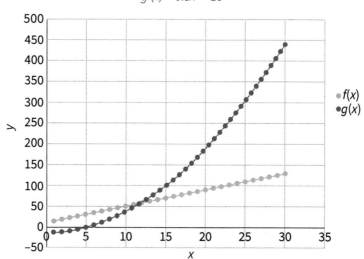

Figure 3.20: Chart showing how linear squared functions grow faster than a linear one regardless of the coefficients used.

Families of **functions** which share the same order can be classified using the **Big O** notation. That means that all linear **functions** can be generalised by the notation $O(n)$ and all squared **functions** as $O(n^2)$. The key families of **functions** which are used in computer science are listed in order below (and some are shown in Figure 3.21), from the slowest growth to the quickest.

O (1) Constant time

O (log n) Logarithmic time (note – logs are base 2)

O (n) linear time

O (n log n) Logarithmic time (note – logs are base 2)

O (n^2) squared time

O (n^3) cubed time

O (n^c) polynomial time

O (c^n) exponential time

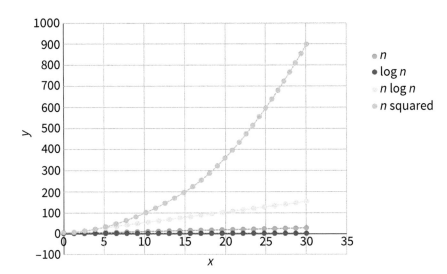

Figure 3.21: Chart showing different orders of functions and how they compare to one another.

We have already seen how a **function** can be derived to show the growth of an algorithm, based on the size of the input f (n). Consider a **function** which has its efficiency modelled by the **function** f (n) = 2n + 5. We can more simply write O (n), as the algorithm will grow linearly based on the input. A number of standard algorithms will be introduced in the next section and their efficiency examined using **Big O** notation.

Computing in context: NP-Complete problems

Most of the algorithms in this chapter have a time complexity which is, at worst, bounded by a polynomial function. These problems, for example sorting, form a set of problems which can be *solved* in polynomial time. There exists another set of problems, known as non-deterministic polynomial problems, where the solution can be quickly *verified* in polynomial time.

Non-deterministic polynomial problems (or NP) may or may not have an algorithmic solution to them which is bounded by polynomial time. The ones which do not are considered hard problems and form a set of problems called NP-hard. These are the hardest problems to solve and so far no one has found a general solution to one, although some special cases can be solved. A problem is considered to be NP-hard if there is a way to reduce or convert the solution into another NP-hard problem. This may seem confusing, but ultimately the definition is just showing that there is a link between all NP-hard problems and those problems are difficult to solve.

NP-Complete problems are ones which are both NP and NP-hard. NP-Complete problems are very common in computing, such as cryptography, and so far no one has been able to solve them in polynomial time. A one million dollar reward fund is offered by the Clay maths institute for anyone who manages to show that a NP-complete problem can be solved in polynomial time. However, the implications of solving NP-complete are vast. Cryptography only works because decrypting a file without the key is a NP-complete problem and would take a massive amount of computing time to achieve. Should a solution be found in polynomial time it would leave cryptographic methods used by every website in the world useless.

Sorting algorithms
Bubble sort

	32	12	56	3	31	76	45	49	64
Index	1	2	3	4	5	6	7	8	9

One of the easiest sorting algorithms to both understand and implement is bubble sort. It takes a list or array of items as input and produces a sorted list at the end (Figure 3.22). In order for the sort to work, the items within must be of a comparable type. So given two items, x_0 and x_1, it must be possible to test $x_0 > x_1$, $x_0 < x_1$, and $x_0 = x_1$. This might seem a trivial point to make, but it is crucial that we are formal in our definitions. For example, if you had a list {4, Fred, 8}, then sorting could not take place as Fred cannot (in any meaningful way) be compared to numbers.

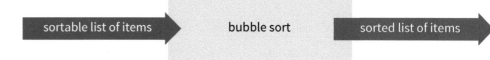

Figure 3.22: Input and output diagram for bubble sort.

Pseudocode

```
FUNCTION bubblesort(list)
  REPEAT
    swapped = false
    FOR n = 1 TO LEN(list)-1
      IF list[n-1] > list[n] THEN
        temp = list[n-1]
        list[n-1] = list[n]
        list[n] = temp
        swapped = true
      END IF
    NEXT n
  UNTIL NOT swapped
  RETURN list
END FUNCTION
```

Bubble sort revolves around two loops. The inner loop will always run $n - 1$ times, where n is the size of the list. This has the job of moving to the end of the list the largest value that has not already been moved, or is in the correct position. The outer loop will run if and only if no more values were swapped in the previous run of the inner loop.

Initial unsorted list

	32	12	56	3	31	76	45	49	64
Index	1	2	3	4	5	6	7	8	9

First run of inner loop

	12	32	3	31	56	45	49	64	76
Index	1	2	3	4	5	6	7	8	9

After the first run of the inner loop we did eight comparisons, or $n - 1$, and were left with the largest number in position 9. Each swap moved the larger numbers to the higher indices, a bit like bubbles rising to the top of a glass. In fact this is how bubble sort got its rather odd name.

Second run of inner loop

	12	3	31	32	45	49	56	64	76
Index	1	2	3	4	5	6	7	8	9

Third run of the inner loop

	3	12	31	32	45	49	56	64	76
Index	1	2	3	4	5	6	7	8	9

By the end of the third loop we end up with a sorted list. As the third loop required a swap, we need to run the inner loop once more.

Efficiency analysis of bubble sort

The inner loop for bubble sort will perform $n - 1$ comparisons every time it is run. The key to working out the efficiency for bubble sort is to find out how many times the inner loop runs. In the previous example the inner loop ran four times or $f(n) = 4(n - 1)$. Creating a general case, we end up with $f(n) = C(n - 1)$. However, based on the input, we could end up with a very different **coefficient** C for each invocation. Below are two lists which show the best and worst case scenarios for bubble sort. In the best case scenario the inner loop runs only once. This is because the list is already sorted, meaning that no swaps occur. In the worst case scenario, where the list is in reverse order, the inner loop must run eight times.

Best case scenario

	2	4	8	10	16	20	24	32	45
Index	1	2	3	4	5	6	7	8	9

Worst case scenario

	9	8	7	6	5	4	3	2	1
Index	1	2	3	4	5	6	7	8	9

First run

	8	7	6	5	4	3	2	1	9
Index	1	2	3	4	5	6	8	9	9

Second run

	7	6	5	4	3	2	1	**8**	**9**
Index	1	2	3	4	5	6	7	**8**	**9**

Eigth run

	1	**2**	**3**	**4**	**5**	**6**	**7**	**8**	**9**
Index	**0**	**1**	**2**	**3**	**4**	**5**	**6**	**7**	**8**

Generalising the best case scenario we get $f(n) = n - 1$ as the inner loop only runs once or $O(n)$. Generalising the worst case scenario gives us $f(n) = n(n-1) = n^2 - n$. Bubble sort has a time **complexity** of $O(n^2)$ as the outer loop, on average, will have to run more than once proportionally to the number of elements in the list.

Memory usage of bubble sort

Bubble sort is a very simple algorithm and makes little additional use of memory other than a few variables. Regardless of the size of the input, the additional memory footprint of bubble sort does not change. Therefore, as the memory usage is constant in both the best and worst cases, we can represent it as $O(1)$.

Python code for bubble sort

Figure 3.23 shows an example of Python code for a bubble sort.

```
1     import random
2     l = []
3     for f in range(1,3000):
4         l.append(random.randint(1,30000))
5
6     def displayfirstandlast(l):
7         for i in range(0,5):
8             print str(l[i]) + ",",
9         print "....",
10        for i in range(len(l)-6, len(l)-1):
11            print str(l[i]) + ",",
12        print ""
13
14
15    def bubbleSort(l):
16        swapped = True # to ensure loop runs once
17        while swapped:
18            swapped = False
19            x=1
20            while x<len(l):
21                if l[x-1] > l[x]:
22                    temp = l[x-1]
23                    l[x-1] = l[x]
24                    l[x] = temp
25                    swapped = True
26                x += 1
27        return l
28
29    displayfirstandlast(l)
30    bubbleSort(l)
31    displayfirstandlast(l)
32
```

Figure 3.23: Python code for bubble sort.

Insertion sort

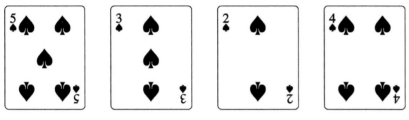

Figure 3.24: Input and output diagram for insertion sort.

Insertion sort (Figure 3.24) draws its inspiration from how humans sort cards in their hand when playing a game. Consider a hand of cards which are not in order (Figure 3.25).

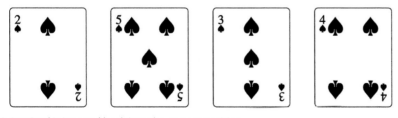

Figure 3.25: Unsorted hand of cards.

One approach to order cards that could be taken is to hold the cards in one hand and remove a single card with the other. That card can then be inserted into the correct position. This simple procedure is repeated until the hand is sorted. For example, the 2 of spades could be drawn by the player's right hand leaving the following situation (Figure 3.26).

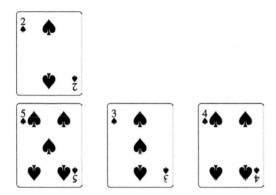

Figure 3.26: A single card removed ready to inserted back.

The 2 of spades can then be inserted into the correct position in the left hand by pushing all of the other cards to the right and placing the 2 of spades at the front (Figure 3.27). This simple example leads us to the fundamental principle of insertion sort where we remove a single item and place it back into the list. Like bubble sort and other sorting algorithms, insertion sort can only work on lists of items which are comparable to one another.

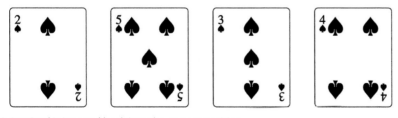

Figure 3.27: Card is inserted back into the correct position.

Initially we assume that the first item in the list is in the correct position, regardless of how true that may be, and refer to it as a sub-list of size 1. In insertion sort we guarantee that the sub-list is always sorted. This means we can insert other records into that list into the correct position, creating an ever growing sorted list until all items have been inserted. In the example below, the shaded boxes will show the progress of the sorted sub-list.

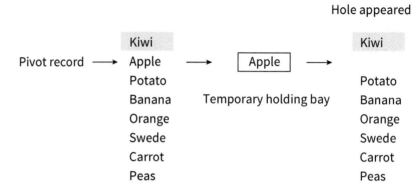

Figure 3.28: Item removed from the list ready for insertion.

Insertion sort will start with the second item in the list and place it into a temporary space or variable (Figure 3.28). This will produce a hole in the list allowing us to safely shift items around without losing data. In order to add the removed item into the sub-list, it is compared to the first item. If the value is less than the current record then all of the items below it are shifted along by one.

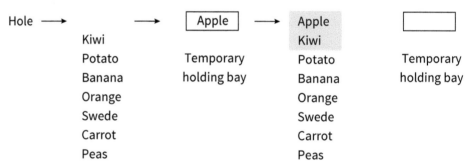

Figure 3.29: Top item is shifted down and the removed item inserted back in.

Apple is less than Kiwi so that means that Kiwi must be shifted along into the hole. Once the shift has happened then Apple can be inserted into the correct position creating a sorted sub-list of two items (Figure 3.29). The next item in the list becomes the current item and the algorithm is repeated (Figure 3.30).

	Apple	Apple	Apple
	Kiwi	Kiwi	Kiwi
Pivot record ⟶	Potato		Potato
	Banana	Banana	Banana
	Orange	Orange	Orange
	Swede	Swede	Swede
	Carrot	Carrot	Carrot
	Peas	Peas	Peas

Figure 3.30: Next step of insertion sort.

Potato will get inserted at the end of the sorted sub-list and no shifting needs to take place. The next item becomes the current item. A shift, when it takes place, requires more steps than if the item is just placed at the back of the sorted sub-list. This is important to note as it will impact the time **complexity** of the algorithm. This will then continue until the list is sorted.

Pseudocode

```
FOR p = 1 TO LEN(list)
  # remove the current item into a temp variable
  hole = list[p]
  z = p
  # keep shifting until we are at the end of the list
  # or found the point of insertion
  WHILE z >0 AND list[z-1] > hole
    list[z] = list[z-1]
    z = z - 1
  END WHILE
  # insert the item into the correct position
  list[z] = hole
NEXT
```

Efficiency and analysis of insertion sort

$L = \{x_0, x_1, x_2, x_3, \ldots x_n\}$ List of items to be sorted

$n = |L|$ The cardinality (length) of the list

$S = \{\text{sorted sub-list}\}$

Each item in L must be removed from the list into a variable, apart from x_0, which means that insertion sort must run the outer loop at least $n - 1$ times, where n is the size of the list. In order to insert a value back into the list, we must compare the item with each subsequent one to find where it must be inserted. The search starts from x_0 going to x_i, where i is the position we removed the item from. In the best case scenario we do not need to perform any shifts, as the list is already sorted, which means that only one comparison needs to be done for every iteration of the outer loop. This leaves us with a linear function $O(n)$.

Value	6	2	1	7	3	7	9	14	15
Index	1	2	3	4	5	6	7	8	9
x_i	x_0	x_1	x_2	x_3	x_4	x_5	x_6	x_7	x_8

To work out the time **complexity** of insertion sort for the worst case scenario, we must analyse the inner loop as it swaps values. During the first execution of insertion sort for the above list, we are checking to see if $x_0 > x_1$, or 6 is > 2, which means that we need to do one comparison leading to a shift. In order to make analysis of the algorithm easier, we shall only consider comparisons rather than considering swaps as well.

Value	2	6	1	7	3	7	9	14	15
Index	1	2	3	4	5	6	7	8	9
x_i	x_0	x_1	x_2	x_3	x_4	x_5	x_6	x_7	x_8

The second iteration, $x_0 > x_2$, leads to two comparisons, against x_0 and x_1. If p is the position we are currently looking at and the inequality $x_0 > x_p$ holds true then we need to perform p number of swaps. In the worst case scenario, which is where the list is in reverse order, we have to perform the maximum number of swaps each time the outer loop runs. The tables below show the stages of insertion sort for the worst case. The shaded columns show the number of comparisons made each loop.

Initial list

Value	10	9	8	7	6
Index	1	2	3	4	5
x_i	x_0	x_1	x_2	x_3	x_4

First run

Value	9	10	8	7	6
Index	1	2	3	4	5
x_i	x_0	x_1	x_2	x_3	x_4

Second run

Value	8	9	10	7	6
Index	1	2	3	4	5
x_i	x_0	x_1	x_2	x_3	x_4

Third run

Value	7	8	9	10	6
Index	1	2	3	4	5
x_i	x_0	x_1	x_2	x_3	x_4

Fourth run

Value	6	7	8	9	10
Index	1	2	3	4	5
x_i	x_0	x_1	x_2	x_3	x_4

The number of comparisons done on this list is $1 + 2 + 3 + 4 = 10$. Taking the generic case, we end up with the pattern $1 + 2 + 3 \ldots + n - 2 + n - 1$. Although out of the scope of this book, this pattern is that of triangular numbers. The sum of all triangular numbers $\sum_{k=1}^{x} k$ can be represented by the function $f(n) - \dfrac{n(n-1)}{2}$

Therefore, insertion sort's worst case scenario will be:

$$f(n) - \frac{n(n-1)}{2}$$

$$f(n) = \frac{1}{2}(n^2 - n)$$

$$\frac{1}{2}(n^2 - n) \quad \in O(n^2)$$

Space usage of insertion sort

Insertion sort is a very simple algorithm and makes very little additional use of memory other than a few variables. Regardless of the size of the input, the additional memory footprint of insertion sort does not change. Therefore, as the memory usage is constant in both the best and worst cases, we can represent it as $O(1)$.

Quicksort

So far the sorting algorithms considered perform poorly on larger sets of data, but are simple to implement and perform well for small sets of data. Quicksort performs much more favourably for larger sets of data, but is more complicated to understand and implement. Quicksort is a recursive algorithm which will apply itself to smaller and smaller sections of the list until the number of values being looked at is one. The basic steps of quicksort are:

1   Pick a single item from the list and call it the pivot x_p.
2   Reorder the list so all items which are less than the pivot are before it and all items which are larger come after. Once this operation is complete, the pivot will be in its final positon. This is known as the partition phase.
3   Perform steps 1 and 2 recursively on all items less than x_p and again on all items greater than x_p. Keep doing this until the number of items smaller or greater than x_p is one or zero.

Most of the work for quicksort happens in the partition phase and is summarised by the algorithm below. There is more than one way to perform the partition and the one described below is the most documented method.

1   Swap the pivot with the item in the rightmost positon of the list.
2   Record the position of the leftmost item in the list and store it in a variable storePosition.
3   For each item in the list (excluding the pivot)
    a   If the value of the item being looked at is less than the pivot
        i   Swap the item for the item in storePosition
        ii   Add one to storePosition
4   Swap the pivot for the item in storePosition.

In Pseudocode, this algorithm can be written as follows.

```
FUNCTION partition(array, left, right)
  pivot = pick random index
  pivotValue = array[pivot]
  Swap array[pivot] and array[right]
  storePosition = left
  FOR j=left TO right
    IF array[j] < pivotValue THEN
      Swap array[j] and array[storePosition]
      storePosition ++
    END IF
  NEXT
  Swap array[storePosition] and array[right]
  RETURN storePosition
END FUNCTION
```

	7	1	4	6	9	12	3	8	2
Index	1	2	3	4	5	6	7	8	9

The above partition algorithm, once a pivot has been chosen, will reorder the array so that all items less than the pivot will be on the left and items larger will be on the right. Numbers to the left and right may not be in numeric order, but they will match the property $x_{p-1} \leq x_p \leq x_{p+1}$. The best way to understand the above algorithm is to see a worked example.

When picking a pivot, a random index will be used, as the choice of pivot is not crucial to how the algorithm works, but it is crucial to the efficiency (which will be discussed later) of the algorithm. The pivot will be shown in red and values swapped in a lighter shade.

Step 1 – swap the pivot and the end of the list

	7	1	4	6	9	12	3	8	2
Index	1	2	3	4	5	6	7	8	9

	7	1	4	2	9	12	3	8	6
Index	1	2	3	4	5	6	7	8	9

By moving the pivot to the end of the list we are essentially moving it out of the way for the main loop of the algorithm. At no point do we want to compare the pivot to itself, as that makes no sense. Therefore moving it to the right and ensuring the loop ends before it gets there (right –1) we can prevent this from happening.

Step 2 – swap values if less than the pivot

	1	7	4	2	9	12	3	8	6
Index	1	2	3	4	5	6	7	8	9
StorePosition =	1		J =	2			

The first iteration will compare array[1] to the pivot, resulting in no swap as 6 is not less than 6. On the second iteration, however, a swap occurs as 1 is less than 7. The swap, array[j] and array[storePosition] is shown above. Once a swap occurs, storePosition is incremented by one. What is really happening is that storePosition is keeping track of where the last number smaller than the pivot was seen, or where the pivot must be placed after the algorithm runs. Larger numbers are then swapped so that their index is always greater than the store positon.

	1	4	7	2	9	12	3	8	6
Index	1	2	3	4	5	6	7	8	9
StorePosition =	2		J =	3			

	1	4	2	7	9	12	3	8	6
Index	1	2	3	4	5	6	7	8	9
StorePosition =	3		J =	4			

The next two iterations are shown above. Notice that all values in positions less than storePosition are lower than the pivot. This property holds true throughout the execution of the algorithm.

	1	4	2	3	9	12	7	8	6
Index	1	2	3	4	5	6	7	8	9
StorePosition =	4		J =	7			

Both 9 and 12 are not less than the pivot, so we move past them without any swaps. A new property has emerged, which existed before, but was not obvious. That is that all values between storePosition +1 and j have a value greater than the pivot.

Step 3 – Swap pivot for the item in storePosition

		1	4	2	3	6	12	7	8	9
Index		1	2	3	4	5	6	7	8	9
StorePosition =		5			J =		8			

Once the final step has occurred, all values less than the pivot now are to the left while all values to the right are larger. This array is not yet sorted. However, it will be after we perform the recursive steps.

Quicksort recursion

```
FUNCTION quicksort(array, left, right)
  IF left < right THEN
    P = partition(array, left, right)
    # quicksort lower values
    quicksort(array, left, p -1)
    # quicksort higher values
    quicksort(array, p+1, right)
  END IF
END FUNCTION
```

When the partition **function** runs, it will return the position of the pivot in the array after reordering has taken place. In order for the array to be ordered, quicksort must be recursively run on both the lower and upper sub-arrays. Looking back at our example, the partition function would return index 5. This means that we repeat the quicksort algorithm on the lower numbers, quicksort(1, 4) and the upper numbers, quicksort(6, 9).

		1	4	2	3	6	12	7	8	9
Index		1	2	3	4	5	6	7	8	9
StorePosition =		4								

Quicksort(array, 1, 4) – pivot index 3

Running partition on the lower numbers, taking index 3 as the pivot, produces the following reordering after the partition algorithm has been run, returning index 3. After the partition, as 0 is less than 3, we need to run quicksort twice more: quicksort(array, 1, 2) and quicksort(array, 4, 4). The next recursion of quicksort will be quicksort(array, 1, 2) as we always do the lower numbers first, regardless of whether we still have larger numbers to do. The full recursive tree can be seen in Figure 3.31.

	1	4	3	2
Index	1	2	3	4

	1	2	3	4
Index	1	2	3	4
StorePosition = 3				

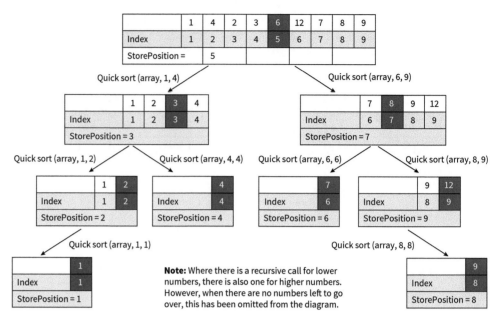

Figure 3.31: Full recursion tree for quicksort.

Time Complexity of quicksort

Quicksort's time **complexity** can be shown to be $O(n \log_2 n)$, which makes it the most efficient sorting algorithm seen here so far. Both insertion sort and bubble sort have a growth **function** of $O(n^2)$, which means that, as n gets larger, quicksort outperforms them more and more. In order to understand where $O(n \log_2 n)$ was derived from, we must first work out the time **complexity** for the partition **function**.

To work out the number of comparisons the partition function will perform, we can do a simple bit of arithmetic, right – left. The first time partition is called, it will be based on the full array, which means that its time **complexity** will be n. However, for subsequent calls, it will be based on the size of the partitions after reordering. This can be affected by the choice of pivot and the input.

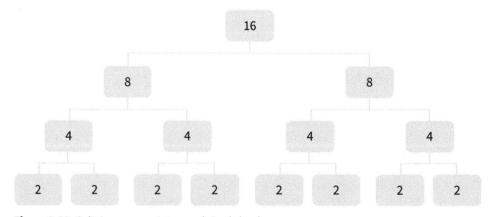

Figure 3.32: Splitting an array into equal sized chunks.

Consider the ideal scenario, where each partition is split equally, for an array of 16 items as shown in Figure 3.32. We would need to have 4 levels of recursion, including the initial invocation, in order to fully sort the list. Following the same pattern for 32 items, we require 5 levels of recursion as shown in Figure 3.33. In the general case, where the partition sizes are always halved on each invocation, we will need $\log_2 n$ levels of recursion.

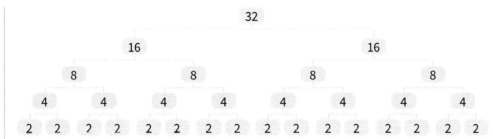

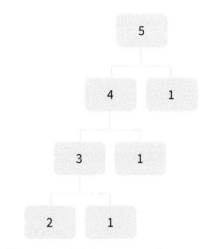

Figure 3.33: Splitting an array into equal sized chunks for an array with 32 elements.

At each level we will have many invocations of partition. However, at each recursive level, we will always perform n comparisons. If an array of size 8 is split into two equal chunks of 4, then partition will require 4 comparisons for each chunk. As we have $\log_2 n$ levels of recursion, each performing n comparisons, then the time **complexity** of $n \log_2 n$ is confirmed.

It will not always be the case that partition splits cleanly in half. As it turns out, on average partition will still lead to $O(n \log_2 n)$ unless we get the worst case scenario. In the worst case scenario, as shown in Figure 3.34, partition always splits the input so that one subarray has a size of one. We end up with n levels of recursion rather than $\log_2 n$. We still, at each level, need to do n comparisons. This leads us to a worst case time **complexity** of n^2.

Figure 3.34: Splitting an array where one chunk is always 1.

Space complexity for quicksort

As quicksort is a recursive **function**, it requires memory every time a **function** is added to the call stack. As quicksort uses a constant amount of memory, regardless of input size, for each **function** call, then we can work out the size requirements based on the number of recursive calls. With careful implementation, the number of calls on the stack can be limited to $\log_2 n$ even in the worst case scenario.

Search algorithms
Linear search

Figure 3.35: Input and output diagram for serial search.

A linear search (Figure 3.35) will, given an array and a search term, return the index of the first instance of that search term or −1 should the item not be found.

```
FUNCTION linearSearch(A, search)
  I=0
  WHILE I<LEN(A) and A[I] != search
    I++
  END WHILE
  IF I == LEN(A) THEN RETURN -1
  ELSE RETURN I
END FUNCTION
```

A linear search will start at the first index in the array and compare the search term to every item until that item is found or the end of the array is reached. The loop has an additional comparison which will cause the loop to exit either at the end of the list or when the item is found. If we have reached the end of the array, where I = LEN(A), then –1 is returned to signify an error.

The time **complexity** of a linear serial search will in the best case be scenario 1, if the item was found immediately. In the worst case, when the item is not found, it will take *n* comparisons. So we have to do between 1 and *n* comparisons, meaning that a linear search is $O(n)$.

The space **complexity** of a linear search is constant or $O(1)$.

Binary search

Figure 3.36: Input and output diagram for binary search.

Binary search (Figure 3.36) is a divide and conquer algorithm which requires the initial array to be sorted before searching. As the initial array is sorted, each item in the array has the property $x_{i-1} < x_i \leq x_{i+1}$. Initially binary search will look at the item in the middle of the array, x_m, and compare it to the search terms. This leads us to three possible scenarios:

$$\begin{cases} x_m = s & \qquad\qquad Return\ m \\ x_m < s & item\ is\ between\ 0\ and\ m-1 \\ x_m > s & item\ is\ between\ m+1\ and\ n \end{cases}$$

If the search term is smaller or greater than the middle value then we can discount half of the array immediately. For example, if the search term was 42 and the middle value was 21, then there is no point looking at any values to the left of the midpoint, as all values to the left are less than 21.

Pseudocode

```
FUNCTION binarySearch(A, search, left, right)
  mid = left + ((right - left) / 2)
  IF right < left THEN RETURN -1
  ELSE
    IF A[mid] > search THEN
      RETURN binarySearch(A, search, mid +1, right)
    ELSE IF A[mid] < search THEN
      RETURN binarySearch(A, search, left, mid-1)
    ELSE
      RETURN mid
    END IF
  END IF
END FUNCTION
```

	4	15	23	26	32	39	45	56	57
Index	1	2	3	4	5	6	7	8	9

Binary search is a recursive algorithm which, at each invocation, will divide the problem in half by discarding half of the array each time. Using the above array and the search term "56", we can invoke binary search by binarySearch(A, 56, 1, 9). Finding the midpoint is done using the calculation Mid = left + ((right – left) / 2). Substituting values gives us the following answer.

Mid = left + ((right – left) / 2)

Mid = 1 + ((9 – 1) /2)

Mid = 1 + 8 / 2

Mid = 5

This may seem overly complicated and you may wonder why we could not just use Mid − (right − left) / 2. To understand this we need to look at the next invocation of binary search. As 56 > 32, left becomes 6 and right remains 9. So we recursively call binary search with binarySearch(A, 56, 6, 9) giving us the array below. Red parts of the array will no longer be considered and the next midpoint is shown in magenta.

	4	15	23	26	32	39	45	56	57
Index	1	2	3	4	5	6	7	8	9

If we stuck with the (right – left) /2, or (9 – 6) / 2, this would gives 1.5 rather than 7.5. So, in order to find the correct midpoint, we need to add on the left.

Note that in the situation when the range of indexes is even and there is no clear midpoint, leading to a fractional result for the midpoint, a decision has to be made to either round down (floor) or round up (ceiling). It does not matter which one is used as long as the choice is consistent. Commonly rounding down is used.

Continuing with binary search, 45 is compared to the search term 56, which leads to the next invocation binarySearch(A, 56, 8, 9).

	4	15	23	26	32	39	45	56	57
Index	1	2	3	4	5	6	7	8	9

Mid = left + ((right – left) / 2)

Mid = 8 + ((9 – 8) / 2)

Mid = 8 + 1 / 2

Mid = 7.5

Using floor, this rounds down to 8.

Time complexity of binary search

Binary search is more efficient than linear search, but does have the disadvantage that the array must be sorted. Given a sorted array, binary search's growth **function** is $O(\log_2 n)$. Every time we recursively call binary search one comparison is made. Therefore the time **complexity** of binary search is solely based on the number of recursions.

Every time binary search is called, the range of values being considered will be halved. For example, if there are 32 elements in the array then the next call for binary search will consider 16 values. Taking this further, by halving the size for each call, the worst case scenario for an array of 32 items is 6 comparisons (Figure 3.37). For any n, the number of times we can halve a number until getting to 1 is $\log_2 n$. Therefore the time **complexity** of binary search, as only one comparison is done per recursive call, is $O(\log_2 n)$.

Space complexity

Every time binary search is invoked we need a constant amount of space to run the **function**. Thus the space **complexity** for binary search is directly linked to the number of recursive calls we must make, which gives us $O(\log_2 n)$.

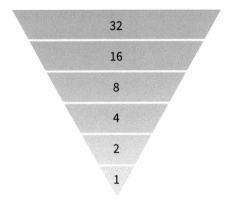

Figure 3.37: Pyramid showing how the problem is reduced for every call to binary search.

Shortest-path algorithm

Dijkstra's algorithm will find the shortest path between two **vertices** in a **graph**. The **graph** can be represented as an ordered pair, $G = (V, E)$ where $V = \{$**set** of all vertices$\}$ and $E = \{$**set** of all edges$\}$. In order to find the shortest path each **edge** must have an associated cost, that is if $e \in E$ then $|e|$ is the cost of that **edge**. To help clarify the above mathematical definitions we can consider the example **graph** in Figure 3.38. $a \in V$ is read as 'a is an element of the **set** of **vertices** V' and is one of the **vertices** in the **graph** below. That **vertex** has three edges, $\{a,b\}$, $\{a,d\}$ and $\{a,g\}$ which have the associated costs of $|\{a,b\}| = 7$, $|\{a,d\}| = 3$ and $|\{a,g\}| = 14$. The size of the lines is not representative of an edge's cost. The green circles in Figure 3.38 represents vertices and the lines represent edges.

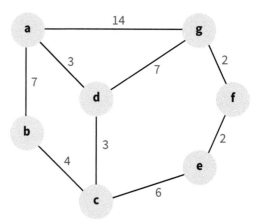

Figure 3.38: Example graph with weighted edges.

To understand what is meant by the shortest path, it worth defining what a path is by using the **graph** in Figure 3.38 as an example. Taking two **vertices**, c and g, there exists a path between them $p = \{c,e\}$, $\{e,f\}$, $\{f,g\}$ with a cost $|p| = 6 + 2 + 2 = 10$. A second path $q = \{c,b\}$, $\{b,a\}$, $\{a,g\}$ with a cost $|q| = 4 + 7 + 14 = 25$. Clearly $|p| < |q|$ meaning that the path p is shorter. Considering all possible paths, then p is the joint shortest path with $r = \{c,d\}$, $\{d,g\}$ having the same cost $|r| = 10$.

Considering the path between two **vertices**, we can assign costs to the intermediate nodes to help show the shortest path. That cost will be the smallest sum of all edges followed from the initial starting node to the current one. Adding these costs, shown in green, to the Figure 3.38, we get Figure 3.39.

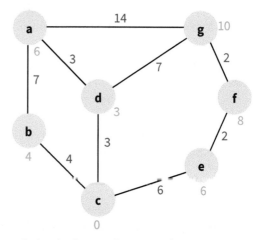

Figure 3.39: Example graph showing intermediate cost values.

There exist two possible values for the cost of **vertex** a: $|\{c,b\}| + |\{b,a\}|$ and $|\{c,d\}| + |\{d,a\}|$. The cost assigned to a **vertex** will always be the smallest sum, so as $3 + 3 < 4 + 7$ we assign the cost of 6.

Algorithm

1   Assign initial cost to each node of ∞ other than the starting node which is **set** to 0.
2   Add all **vertices** to a **set** of unvisited nodes and **set** the start node to be the current node.
3   For each unvisited neighbour, u, of the current node, c:
   a   Add $|c|$ to the cost of the connecting **edge** $|\{c,u\}|$.
   b   If the new cost is less than $|u|$ then replace the cost of u.
4   Remove the current node from the **set** of unvisited nodes.
5   **Set** the unvisited node with the smallest cost from the unvisited **set** and make that the current node.
6   Repeat steps 3 to 5 until we mark the destination node as visited.

Below is an example of this algorithm finding the shortest path from a to e.

Set up phase

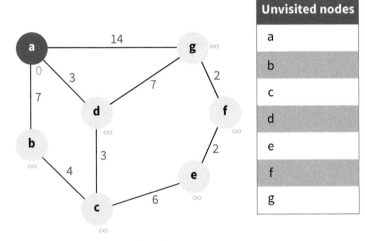

Figure 3.40: Set up stage for Dijkstra's algorithm.

All nodes are added to a **set** of unvisited nodes and the cost of infinity is added to every node except the starting node which has the cost of 0. The current node is the start node, highlighted in crimson (Figure 3.40).

Main loop

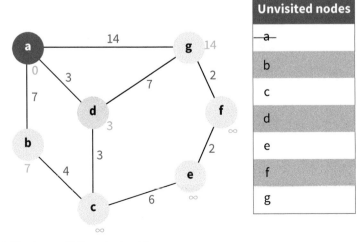

Figure 3.41: First loop of Dijkstra's algorithm.

Node *a* has three other nodes connected to it and their costs must be calculated.

$|b| = 0 + 7$

$|g| = 0 + 14$

$|d| = 0 + 3$

As $|d| < |b|$ and $|d| < |g|$ we **set** the current node to be *d*, as shown in pink (Figure 3.41). Node *a* has now been visited, shown in crimson, and can be removed from the unvisited **set**, shown as a strikethrough.

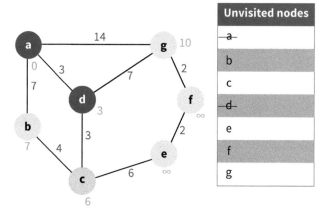

Figure 3.42: Second loop of Dijkstra's algorithm.

$|g| = 3 + 7$

$|c| = 3 + 3$

The cost of *c* is **set** to 6 as it was previously ∞. $|g|$ previously was 14, which is greater than the new calculated cost of 10. Therefore the cost of *g* is replaced with the new lower value. Node *d* is then **set** as visited and the next current node becomes *c*, as it has the lowest cost so far (Figure 3.42).

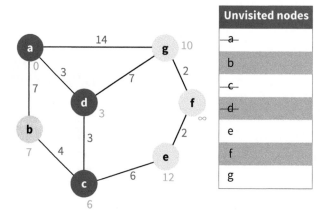

Figure 3.43: Third loop of Dijkstra's algorithm.

Node *b* has the lowest cost of all unvisited nodes, but does not have any connecting nodes which still remain in the unvisited node list. So we mark it as visited (Figure 3.43) and make no further alterations to the **graph**. The next node with the smallest cost becomes *g*.

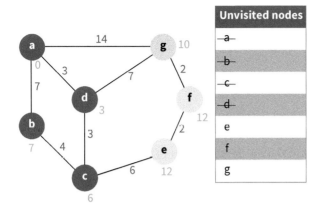

Figure 3.44: Fourth loop of Dijkstra's algorithm.

$$|f| = 10 + 2$$

In Figure 3.44 we have two nodes in the unvisited node **set** which have the same cost. It does not matter which one we pick as we will still get the same result overall. Even though picking e would the most logical choice, the graph indicates that f will be chosen, showing that the choice of node when costs are equal does not matter (Figure 3.45).

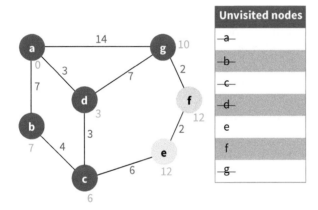

Figure 3.45: Fifth loop of Dijkstra's algorithm.

$$|e| = 12 + 2$$

Node e currently has a cost of 12, which is less than the new cost calculated above. Therefore no changes will be made. Node f is marked as visited and e becomes the next current node (Figure 3.46).

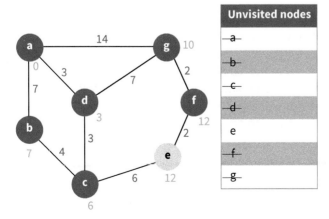

Figure 3.46: Final loop of Dijkstra's algorithm.

Finally node *e* can be marked as visited as there are no other nodes connected to it which exist in the unvisited **set**. The final cost was $|e| = 12$ which comprised the path {*a,d*}, {*d,c*} then {*c,e*}.

- G = **graph** to be searched
- S = source node
- D = destination node
- U = unvisited **set**

```
FUNCTION dijkstra(G, S, D)
  # set up phase
  S.cost = 0
  FOR EACH v in G
    IF v != S THEN
      v.cost = ∞
      v.previous = NULL
    END IF
    Add v to U
  NEXT
  # main loop
  current = S
  WHILE U NOT empty AND D is in U
    Remove current from U
    FOR EACH neighbour v of current IN U
      T = current.cost + length (current, v)
      IF T < v.cost THEN
        v.cost = T
        v.previous = current
      END IF
    NEXT
    current = min_cost(U)
  END WHILE
END FUNCTION
```

Time complexity

The time **complexity** for this algorithm is based on the implementation of the unvisited **set** and how finding the minimum cost within that **set** works. If the unvisited list is implemented as a simple linked list then the time **complexity** will be $O(|V|^2 + |E|)$ where V is the **set** of all **vertices**, E is the **set** of all edges and $|V|$, $|E|$ represent the number of items in those sets (the **cardinality**).

The main loop will run $|V|$ times as we have to visit each node to find out the shortest path. Also, if the unvisited **set** is implemented as a list, we would have $|V|$ comparisons in that **set** to find the minimum cost. This gives us $|V| \times |V| = |V|^2$. The inner loop is based on the number of edges and runs once for each **edge** in the **graph**. Although it is repeated for every node, suggesting it should be multiplied to $|V|^2$, we never look at every **edge** in each loop. Each **edge** only needs to be considered once per run of the algorithm.

By using more efficient ways of storing unvisited nodes the time **complexity** can be brought down to $O(|E| \log_2 |V|)$.

Sequence, selection and repetition

Sequence

Sequence simply means executing each instruction *once* in the order it is given.

For example, in the LOGO program in Figure 3.47 the turtle has followed each instruction in the order it was given to draw a square.

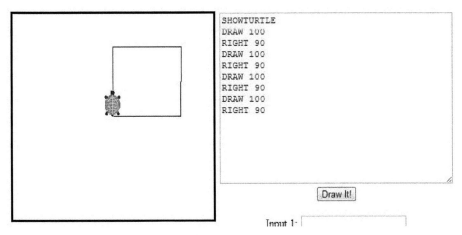

Figure 3.47: A turtle follows a sequence of instructions.

This principle of executing each instruction one after the other (top -> bottom, left -> right) is an important one and is used by most programming languages.

Figure 3.48 shows Python being used to display a sequence of messages. You don't need to understand Python to see that each instruction has been executed once in the order it was given.

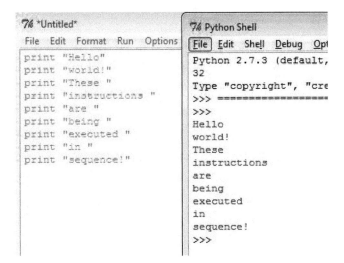

Figure 3.48: Python is used to display a sequence of messages.

Selection

There are times when you don't want every instruction to be executed. You want the hardware to select which instruction to execute based on some condition in the program or on input from a user.

For example. these flowcharts show what we want to happen when a user tries to log on to a computer with a username and password.

Figure 3.49 shows a sequence of instructions being used to perform this task. First the computer collects the Username then it collects the Password then it denies the user access then it allows the user access. Not much good as it will allow everyone access regardless of the username and password they give!

Figure 3.50 shows selection being used to perform the same task. First the computer collects the Username then it collects the Password. Next it checks to see if the Username and Password are correct and selects the next instruction to execute based on this. Much more useful!

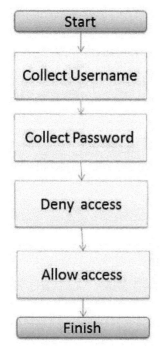

Figure 3.49: Sequence.

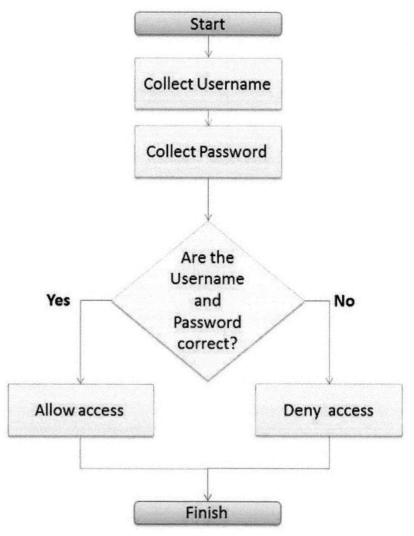

Figure 3.50: Selection.

Figure 3.51 shows the set of instructions needed to implement this task in Python. Line 1 asks the user to enter a Username then line 2 asks the user to enter a Password. Next, line 3 checks to see if the username they have entered is "Admin" and the password they have entered is "1234". Line 4 displays the welcome message if the criteria on Line 3 have been met. Line 5 signals that the next instruction will tell the computer what to do if the conditions on Line 3 have not been met. Line 6 displays the "Access denied" message but only if the conditions on Line 3 are not met.

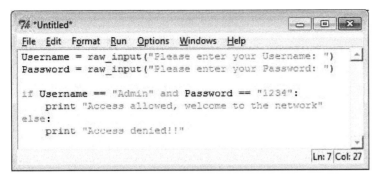

Figure 3.51: Using selection in Python.

Figure 3.52 shows the result of running this program. The first time the user gave the correct details, the second time they didn't and a different message is displayed as a result.

```
7% Python Shell
File  Edit  Shell  Debug  Options  Windows  Help
Python 2.7.3 (default, Apr 10 2012, 23:31:26) [MSC v.1500 32 bit (Intel)] on win
32
Type "copyright", "credits" or "license()" for more information.
>>> ============================== RESTART ==============================
>>>
Please enter the correct password: guessing
Please enter the correct password: who knows
Please enter the correct password: i dont know
Please enter the correct password: password
Please enter the correct password: 1234
>>> |
                                                              Ln: 10 Col: 4
```

Figure 3.52: Selection in action.

The most common branching construct for selecting which instruction to execute is IF ELSE statements.

IF ELSE statements

The example you saw in Figure 3.51 uses IF ELSE statements. They are pretty easy to understand.

IF this happens **THEN** do this **ELSE** do this.

But that is only useful if there are only two possible outcomes. What if we want to tell the user whether they got their username or their password wrong?

Figure 3.53 shows the use of ELSE IF statements to cope with this situation (abbreviated to elif in Python).

```
7% *Untitled*
File  Edit  Format  Run  Options  Windows  Help
Username = raw_input("Please enter your Username: ")
Password = raw_input("Please enter your Password: ")

if Username == "Admin" and Password == "1234":
    print "Access allowed, welcome to the network"
elif Username!= "Admin":
    print "Sorry, the Username you entered was incorrect"
elif Password!= "1234":
    print "Sorry, the Password you entered was incorrect"
                                                              Ln: 9 Col: 57
```

Figure 3.53: IF ELSE, ELSE IF statements.

Repetition

There are many times when you find yourself giving the same instruction repeatedly. Repetition is used to tell the computer's hardware to follow the same instruction a number of times or until a condition is met. Programming languages use loops to repeat an instruction.

Compare the sequence of instructions in *Figure 3.54* to those in *Figure 3.47*. The program in *Figure 3.47* uses nine separate instructions compared to just five in Figure 3.54 to complete the same task. It should be clear how the code in Figure 3.54 is working: it simply instructs the hardware to repeat the DRAW 100, RIGHT 90 instructions four times.

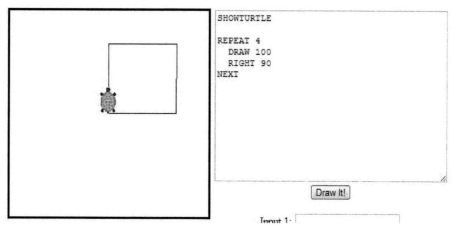

Figure 3.54: Repetition in LOGO.

Loops save having to repeatedly write out the same instruction, which in turn means you are less likely to make mistakes in your program. The ability to repeatedly carry out the same instruction and do it identically each time is one of the most powerful properties of computer systems.

Programming languages typically implement two different methods of repetition: FOR Loops and WHILE Loops.

FOR Loops

For loops execute an instruction (or sequence of instructions) a set number of times. Much like the REPEAT NEXT example in Figure 3.54.

Figure 3.54 shows an example of a FOR loop written in Python and Figure 3.55 shows the FOR loop being implemented.

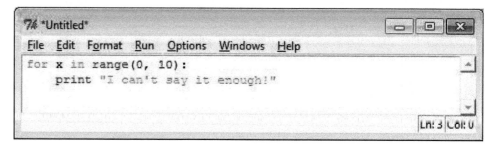

Figure 3.55: FOR loops in Python.

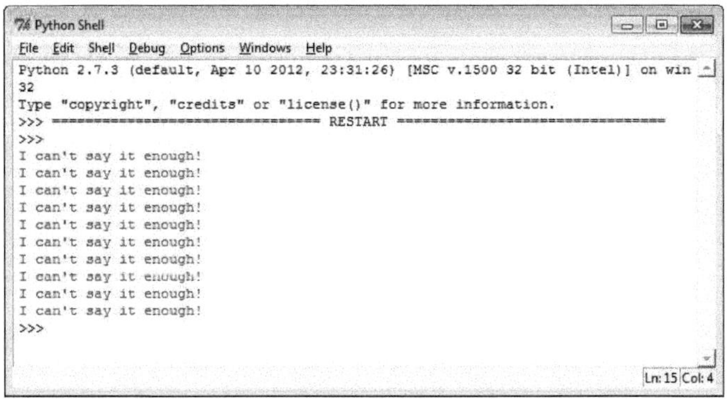

Figure 3.56: Running a FOR loop.

In Figure 3.55 line 1 tells the hardware to start with x as zero and increment it every time the instruction on line 2 is executed. It also tells the hardware that the instruction on Line 2 should be executed until x is equal to 10. Line 2 simply tells the hardware to print out a message. So x begins as zero and every time the message is printed it increases by 1. When x equals 10 the program stops printing messages.

The same code can be written in Pseudocode like this:

```
for x=1 to 10
  Print "I can't say it enough"
next x
```

WHILE Loops

WHILE loops are also used to repeat an instruction but whereas FOR loops execute instructions a set number of times WHILE loops repeat an instruction until a condition is met.

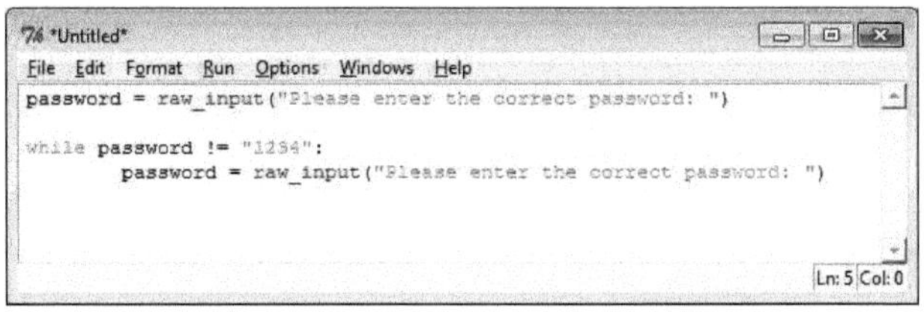

Figure 3.57: WHILE loops in Python.

Figure 3.57 shows a simple WHILE loop in Python. Line 1 asks the user to enter a password. Line 2 tells the computer to repeat the instruction on line 3 as long as the password entered by the user is not "1234". Line 3 is the same as line 1 and just asks the user to enter their password. Consequently the user will be prompted for their password repeatedly until they enter "1234". Figure 3.58 shows the result of running this program, notice that the instruction on line 3 of Figure 3.57 is repeated until the user enters the password "1234".

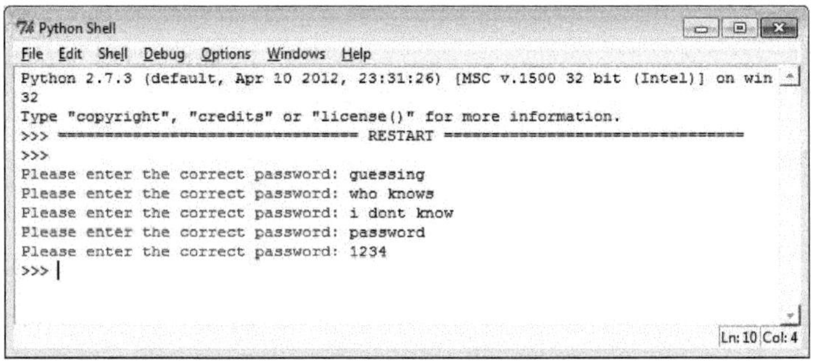

Figure 3.58: Running a WHILE loop in Python.

Although Python does not support it, there is another type of loop known as repeat until or do – while. This is where the condition is placed at the end of the loop rather than the start. By placing the condition at the end we ensure that the loop will always run at least once. That is not always the case with standard while loops.

```
x = 1
do
  print x
  x = x + 1
while x <10
```

Counts and rogue values

Counters are commonly used in iteration to keep track of the current position. This may be as part of the terminal condition or as a way to iterate over a list. In order to use a counter you need to set up a variable initialised to 0. Then every time a loop occurs, 1 is added to the counter. The code below shows how a counter can be used within a loop. Count is first initialised, then used as part of the condition and finally incremented within the loop. This code uses the counter to display the first 10 squared numbers.

```
count = 0
while count <=10
  print count, "squared is", count * count
  count = count + 1
end while
```

Counters may also be employed to keep track of something other than the number of iterations, for example counting how many students have passed their computing exams if the pass mark was 40. Looking at the code you can see we are employing two counters: count and position. Count is being used to calculate how many students have passed, while position is keeping track of where in the array we have reached.

```
array studentMarks[100]
count =0
position =0
while position < 100
  if studentMarks[position] >=40 then count = count + 1
  position = position + 1
end while
```

Counters can be used to terminate iteration but sometimes this straightforward approach will not work. Consider the situation where we have defined studentMarks to hold 100 students, but each year the number fluctuates between 20 and 100 students. How will we know how many marks to consider when doing an average? A way is needed to let the algorithm know that we have reached the last student.

Rogue values can be employed to solve this problem. Simply put, a rogue value is one which is so abnormal that it could never occur under normal circumstances. As such rogue values are a perfect way to signal the end of a list or sequence. For example, no one will get a negative mark in a test so –1 can be considered a rogue value. Therefore, if the studentMark array uses –1 in any index that does not store a mark then we can employ this knowledge to update our terminal condition.

```
array studentMarks[100]
total =0
position =0
while position <100 and studentMarks[position] != -1
  total = total + studentMarks[position]
  position = position + 1
end while
print total / position
```

studentMarks[position] != –1 will stop the loop as soon as –1 is seen in the array. So if we had 70 students, the value of studentMarks[69] would store the last student and studentMarks[70] would be –1.

Logical operators

The exact definition of logic is an area of controversy between computer scientists, philosophers and mathematicians but for our purposes you can think of logic as the use of logical operators to reason the outcome of a given argument.

Thinking logically simply means applying these logical operators consistently to *all* data you are given. It is important in computing, as computers have no creative thought process so will always produce identical output when given the same data and operation as input.

In computer science we think of logic as binary, with any logical operation having one of two outcomes: TRUE (1 in binary, 'Yes' on a flowchart) or FALSE (0 in binary, 'No' on a flowchart). For example, 4 > 5 would return FALSE because 4 is not greater than 5.

On this course you simply need to know the basic logical operators and recognise where to use them in your programs. Using these symbols to create and solve propositions is called Boolean Algebra. This is a fascinating area of mathematics at the very heart of computer science and it's well worth looking through the 'extra' reading section to find out more or refer back to Chapter 2.

Operator	Meaning	Example
>	Greater than	A>B will return TRUE if the value of A is higher than the value of B otherwise it will return FALSE.
<	Less than	A<B will return TRUE if the value of A is less that the value of B otherwise it will return FALSE.
<=	Less than or equal to	A<=B will return TRUE if A is the same as or smaller than B otherwise it will return FALSE.
>=	Greater than or equal to	A>=B will return TRUE if A is the same as or larger than B otherwise it will return FALSE.
!=	Not the same as	A!=B will return TRUE if A is not the same as B but FALSE if A is the same as B.

NOT	The opposite of	NOT(A) will return TRUE if A is FALSE and FALSE if A is TRUE.
EQUALS (usually ==)	The same as	A==B will return TRUE if A is the same as B otherwise it will return FALSE.
AND	Both statements must be true.	(A==1) AND (B==4) will return TRUE if A is 1 and B is 4, otherwise it will return FALSE.
OR	Only one of the statements needs to be true.	(A==1) OR (B==4) will return TRUE if A is 1 or B is 4. It will return FALSE only if A isn't 1 and B isn't 4.
XOR	The argument is false if both statements are true. The argument is false if both statements are false. Otherwise the statement is true.	A XOR B will return TRUE if A and B are different binary values, i.e. if A is TRUE and B is FALSE or if A is FALSE and B is TRUE.

Binary logic table

The table below shows the outcome of logical operators when given two binary inputs A and B.

A	B	OR	AND	XOR	>	<	<=	>=	==	!=
0	0	0	0	0	0	0	1	1	1	0
0	1	1	0	1	0	1	1	0	0	1
1	0	1	0	1	1	0	0	1	0	1
1	1	1	1	0	0	0	1	1	1	0

Implementing logical decisions in your programs

When, based on the result of the logical operation, the computer chooses which of a number statements to execute, this is called selection. Selection is also used during iteration to decide whether or not to repeat a set of instructions.

The most commonly used forms of selection are IF statements and SELECT CASE. You can read more about these in the Programming Techniques chapter. You can also read about the most common forms of iteration: FOR and WHILE loops. Reading about these constructs first will make the following examples much easier to understand.

Identifying the points in a solution where a decision has to be taken

Identifying the points in a solution where a decision has to be taken sounds difficult but is in fact very simple. All you need to do is draw a flowchart. When the flowchart is finished, anywhere you see a decision diamond is either going to be a loop or a decision in your final program. These constructs are the only ones that require logical operators to be used.

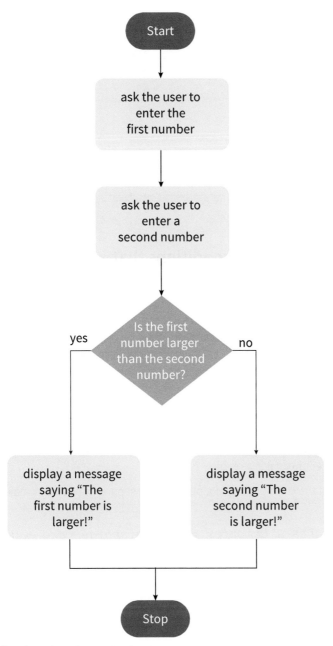

Start

ask the user to
enter the
first number

ask the user to
enter a
second number

Is the first
number larger
than the second
number?

yes   no

display a message
saying "The
first number is
larger!"

display a message
saying "The
second number
is larger!"

Stop

Figure 3.59: A flowchart describing a simple program.

For example, imagine you want a program that asks the users to enter two numbers and then tells the user which number was larger. The first thing to do is draw a flowchart, like the one in Figure 3.59.

By looking at the flowchart you can see that the logical decision is represented by the blue diamond. You can also see that it must be made after the two numbers have been entered, and even what should happen for each possible outcome. Converting the flowchart in to Pseudocode will show you which logical operators to use and where they should appear in the code.

```
          A == first number
          B == second number
IF A > B is TRUE then print "First number is larger"
    Otherwise print "Second number is larger"
```

From here it is easy to create a final program, shown in Figure 3.60:

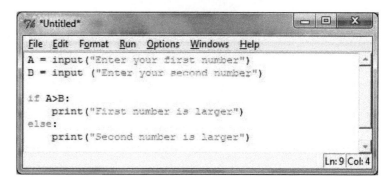

Figure 3.60: Final program.

Determine the logical conditions that affect the outcome of a decision

Determining the logical conditions that affect the outcome of a decision can be very easy or really difficult. It all depends on the complexity of the decision to be taken. The basic methodology is to take the rules and write them out in normal English, then you can rewrite the sentences using the logical operators wherever possible and get rid of any extra text you don't need. This process should leave you with a logical argument that is easily turned into selection or iteration. An alternative is to use a flowchart, but this tends to be more time consuming.

For example, Sarah wants to buy a new computer. She wants a computer with a graphics card and more than 8GB of RAM. She doesn't want a sound card and only wants either a Linux or Windows Operating System. Write a program that takes the specification of a computer and tells her if it is suitable.

Step 1: Write out the conditions again; put them on separate lines if this makes them easier to read.

> She wants a computer with a graphics card and more
> than 8GB of RAM.
> She doesn't want a sound card but does want either a Linux or
> a Windows Operating System.

Step 2: Rewrite the sentences using logical operators wherever possible and getting rid of any extra text you don't need. Don't forget to use brackets to make it clear which pieces of data the logical operations apply to.

> (GraphicsCard == TRUE) AND (RAM > 8GB) AND
> (SoundCard==FALSE) AND ((OperatingSystem = "Windows")
> OR (OperatingSystem = "Linux"))

Step 3: You should now be ready to write the logical decision as an IF statement,

```
IF (GraphicsCard == TRUE) AND (RAM > 8) AND
(SoundCard == FALSE) AND ((OperatingSystem = "Windows") OR
(OperatingSystem = "Linux")):
  Print("Specification meets all your criteria")
ELSE:
  Print("Sorry, that computer is unsuitable")
```

Another way to determine the logical conditions that affect the outcome of a decision is to use a flowchart (Figure 3.61). You can then write the logical operator next to each decision then combine them to give you the correct answer.

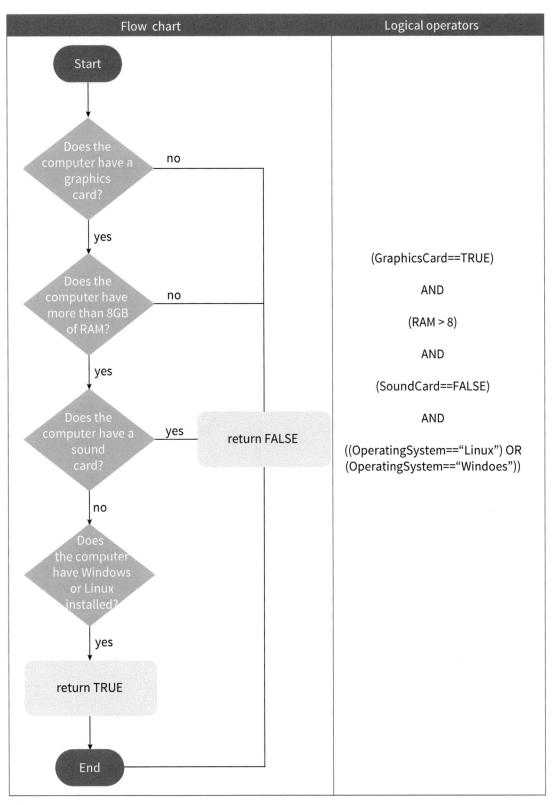

Figure 3.61: Flowchart.

Determining how decisions affect flow through a program

Determining how decisions affect flow through a program is also pretty simple to do once you have created a flowchart. Look at the example in Figure 3.62, it's easy to see how the flow (which instruction will be executed next) will be affected by the outcome of the decision.

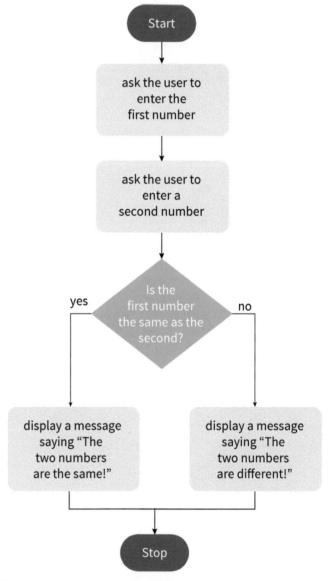

Figure 3.62: A flowchart describing a simple program.

Standard and custom functions

When programming a solution it is common to require code written by someone else. This could be to display text on the screen, play a sound, transmit a packet over the network or display a picture. Regardless of the task the programmer needs to do, it is likely that someone has already written code that you could take advantage of. This tends to come in the form of a library.

Library software is a collection of classes or functions that provide common services for programmers. Searching and sorting are two classic examples of services a library can provide. Libraries will be provided by experts in their fields, either as part of the programming environment (such as random numbers in Python) or installable (such as Pygame). These classes and functions have been carefully tested and written as efficiently as possible.

To use libraries inside your own programs you need to import them. This tells the translator that you wish to make use of these functions and defines which functions are available. It also provides a namespace enabling each library, including your own code, to use the same function names. Functions within a library are referenced through their namespace. The code below shows a library named 'time' being imported into Python. Access to the delay function is done through the namespace 'time'.

```
import time

print "hello"
time.delay(5)
print "world"
```

Some functions and classes provide such fundamental features that they are included as part of the main language, either as a standard library or as functions immediately available. These functions are known as standard libraries. In C, the standard functions come in the form of standard libraries such as STDIO (standard input and output). The C code below will take a number in using scanf, check if it is divisible by 2 and then display the result on the screen using printf. The standard library is accessed by the line #include <stdio.h>.

```
#include <stdio.h>

int main()
{
  int n;

  printf("Enter an integer\n");
  scanf("%d", &n);

  if (n%2 == 0)
    printf("Even\n");
  else
    printf("Odd\n");

  return 0;
}
```

In Python, there are a number of standard, immediately available functions which require no libraries to be imported. A few are listed in the table below.

Function	Purpose
len	Get the length of a string or list
chr	Converts a number into a character using ASCII
ord	Gets the ASCII value of a character

Data compression

In computing, 'compression' means reducing the amount of file space (bytes) that a given file takes up. This can be done in a number of ways but they all really do the same thing: remove unnecessary bits to reduce the overall number of bits in the file. In the past, compression was important because computer memory was expensive. Today, memory is much, much cheaper but compression remains important because of the volume of

Computing in context: 7-Zip

7-Zip is a piece of open source compression software that uses multiple compression and encryption algorithms to reduce the size and increase the security of files. As 7-Zip uses multiple compression algorithms, it is able to achieve very high compression ratios. Its website states that the authors were able to compress 15 684 168 bytes of Mozilla Firefox files into just 4 621 135 bytes, a compression ratio of 0.2.

information we transmit over networks. A smaller file size means fewer bits to transmit, so a faster transmission is achieved.

The level of compression is measured by its compression ratio. The compression ratio is the size of the compressed file divided by the size of the original. The ratio will be a number between 0 and 1; the closer the ratio is to 0, the tighter the compression. Different pieces of compression software, such as WinZip, WinRAR and 7-Zip, achieve slightly different compression ratios for different data sets.

The 256-bit encryption used also means that the compressed data can be transmitted securely across the internet.

You can find out more about the compression and encryption algorithms used by 7-Zip (and even see the code itself).

Lossy and lossless compression

As you might expect, there are many different compression algorithms. These all try to reduce the number of bits in a file and use a wide range of methods to do this. However, all these algorithms fit into one of two broad categories: lossy and lossless.

Lossy compression means that the file is compressed to a smaller size but some information is lost during the process.

Lossless compression techniques are able to reduce a file's size without losing any information.

Lossless compression may seem preferable to lossy compression, but if the lossy algorithm can provide a much better compression ratio and the lost data is not important, the choice may not be so clear cut. This is particularly true when compressing images: it may be possible to remove a huge amount of information without noticeably reducing the quality of the image.

Run length encoding for lossless compression

Run length encoding is a popular and widely used method of lossless compression. In some files a single character will be repeated many times in a row (this doesn't happen in spoken and written languages but will happen in many other situations, for example DNA sequencing).

Run length encoding replaces a sequence of repeated characters with a flag character, followed by the character itself and the number of times it is repeated. Using this method BBBBBBBBB would become $B9 (the $ is the flag) and so the file size is reduced from 9 bytes to 3, a compression ratio of 0.3. Any other characters that are not repeated would not be compressed and just included in the file as normal. So AAAAAANNNBBBBBBBBBUUBYE! would become $A6NNN$B8UUBYE, giving a compression ratio of 0.69! Notice that we don't compress sequences of letters shorter than four; this is because our notation for highlighting repeated characters is itself three characters long, so the pay-off between the time taken to compress and the compression ratio achieved makes it pointless.

Look at the bitmap images shown in Figures 3.63 to 3.66; many of the pixels are the same colour, which leads to long sequences of identical values. By using run length encoding it is possible to reduce the number of letters needed to represent the image from 64 to 34, a compression ratio of 0.53

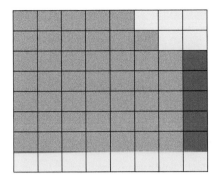

Figure 3.63: A simple image made from 64 pixels.

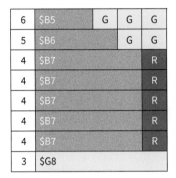

Figure 3.64: A simple image made from 64 pixels.

G	G	G	B	B	B	B	B	8
G	G	B	B	B	B	B	B	8
R	B	B	B	B	B	B	B	8
R	B	B	B	B	B	B	B	8
R	B	B	B	B	B	B	B	8
R	B	B	B	B	B	B	B	8
R	B	B	B	B	B	B	B	8
G	G	G	G	G	G	G	G	8

Figure 3.65: A simple image made from 64 pixels. The column on the left shows the number of bits required to represent each row.

6	$B5		G	G	G
5	$B6			G	G
4	$B7				R
4	$B7				R
4	$B7				R
4	$B7				R
4	$B7				R
3	$G8				

Figure 3.66: Run length encoding reduces the file size.

Dictionary coding for lossless compression

Dictionary encoding is another form of lossless compression. There are many different types of dictionary compression, but they all work on the same principle. A dictionary of commonly occurring sequences of characters is created. In the text these sequences are replaced by pointers to the relevant place in the dictionary. The references are shorter than the words they replace, so the file is reduced in size. Creating the dictionary is simply a case of scanning the document to find the most common words and assigning a reference to each.

Huffman Encoding

One of the easiest dictionary encoding methods to understand is Huffman encoding.

In the English language some letters are used far more than others. For example, in most large pieces of text it is likely that the number of As will be larger than the number of Zs. However, computers use the same number of bits to represent both A and Z, which can waste a lot of space. Huffman encoding uses a dictionary to store all the letters that occur in a piece of text. Each letter is then given a unique code, with the most commonly occurring letters being given a shorter code than less used ones.

For example, if we wanted to write the word GOOGLE using 8 bits for each letter, the word would take up 48 bits. But if we used the Huffman dictionary in Table 3.1 and replaced each bit sequence with its Huffman code, it would be just 14 bits, giving a compression ratio of 0.2.

The important thing to notice is that the most commonly used characters (G and O) have the shortest codes, which helps to maximise the file's compression.

Huffman code	Letter
00	G
01	O
010	L
011	E

Table 3.1: An illustration of Huffman encoding.

Compression algorithms will have a proportionally greater impact on longer pieces of text, as there will be more instances of repeated letters.

Comparing compression

When comparing compression algorithms you need to consider the following factors. It is important to note that it is not worthwhile comparing lossy with lossless algorithms, as lossy will always reduce the file size more than lossless.

Compression ratio: A ratio between the original file and the new compressed file.

Compression/decompression time: The amount of time it takes to compress or decompress a file. Sometimes size saving may be sacrificed for speed.

Saving percentage: A percentage measure of how much smaller the compressed file is to the original.

When comparing compression algorithms, you need to consider the scenario that it will be used in. If speed is critical or processing time is limited then you may opt for a simpler algorithm which may not compress as efficiently.

Test data

After code has been written it is crucial that it undergoes rigorous testing. Without testing there is a chance that the code, under certain circumstances, may not work as expected. Logic errors, where code produces the wrong result after execution, are difficult to spot when coding and can be even harder to solve. The more testing there is, the more robust the final solution will be. End users, although used to patches and updates, do not like software which crashes often or produces unexpected results.

In order to thoroughly test programs, it is important to come up with a good test strategy and decide what test data should be used. Tests must be repeatable, so that if a test fails, the coder can input the same data to help diagnose the issue. Without this ability to repeat a test, it can be very difficult to find and diagnose the bug. In order to come up with a good strategy for testing we first must consider what we mean by good test data. Tests should include normal, invalid and borderline tests. The table below describes and exemplifies the different types of test data. The examples will be based on the simple code below.

```
def maxNumber(a,b):
  if a > b:
    return a
  else:
    return b
```

Type of test	Description	Example
Normal	Values which would occur under normal running conditions.	maxNumber(5,10) maxNumber(9,98)
Invalid	Values which should not be accepted and must not crash the algorithm.	maxNumber("5",6)
Borderline	Values which are at the edge of acceptable ranges. Another way of thinking about borderline tests is to consider the conditions used within the code and test either side of these.	maxNumber(5,6) maxNumber(6,5) maxNumber(5,5)

When selecting test data it is important that you test a range of values. If you always test numbers under 100 in the maxNumber example, how do you know it will work for numbers greater than 100? This may be a trivial example, but the question is valid. Not all code examples are trivial and a common mistake developers make when alpha testing is not to try a range of normal values.

Invalid values should try and break any validation rules in place such as presence, range and length checks. When deciding on test data you should focus more on data which could appear in everyday use which is nethertheless still invalid. For example, if you were producing a system which calculated parking charges then a realistic invalid value may be 0 rather than text. 0 would be outside the range of accepted values, but it could potentially be entered.

Borderline tests tend to be most useful when dealing with range checks. Most logic errors tend to occur due to using incorrect conditions on while loops or if statements. This is why borderline tests are some of the most useful ones to include. Selecting this type of test data can be tricky and it requires you to understand how an algorithm works. In the maxNumber example any set of numbers which is less than or equal to one difference would be considered borderline.

Trace tables

When designing algorithms or trying to debug existing ones it is common to use a technique known as trace tables. To create a trace table, you need to list all of the variables which change (not constants) and write them as the columns. Each row will then store what assignments happen as the code is run. Reading through code and noting down values in a trace table is known as a dry run. It is also common to write down any parts of an array or string which are significant as columns. Consider an algorithm to work out if a word is a palindrome or not. A palindrome is a word which is spelt the same forwards and backwards such as Hannah or rotator. A sample algorithm for this problem is listed below.

```
word ← INPUT
start = 0
end = LEN(word) - 1
WHILE (word[start] == word[end] AND start != end)
  start = start + 1
  end = end - 1
END WHILE
IF start == end RETURN TRUE
ELSE RETURN FALSE
```

Before implementing this algorithm, we should perform a dry run. Trying the test data "Hannah" causes the algorithm to produce an error.

start	end	Word[start]	Word[end]
0	5	H	H
1	4	A	A
2	3	N	N
3	2	N	N
4	1	A	A
5	0	H	H
6	-1	Out of range	Out of range

The trace lines shown in green shown are correct, while the lines in grey should not have been executed and eventually result in an error. This shows that the previously defined algorithm is not correct for the **domain** {all words}. At most, when executing this algorithm, we should only compare half of the letters: after that we know that the word is a palindrome. Below is an improved algorithm which works for the palindrome "Hannah".

```
word ← INPUT
start = 0
end = LEN(word) - 1
WHILE (word[start] == word[end] AND start < FLOOR
(LEN(word) / 2))
  start = start + 1
  end = end - 1
END WHILE
IF start >= LEN(word)/2 RETURN TRUE
ELSE RETURN FALSE
```

This code works for "Hannah" and "Rotator". The trace table below shows it working for "Rotator". The line in grey will not actually be run as it is not necessary. Comparing a letter to itself will always be true, so there is no need to run the comparison. When running a word which has an even number of letters the loop will run once more than required.

start	end	Word[start]	Word[end]
0	5	R	R
1	4	O	O
2	3	T	T
3	2	A	A

When designing algorithms, it is important to do dry runs like this for a spread of values. For completeness, the trace table below shows that the word "prop" is not a palindrome. The line in grey shows where the `while` loop ends and as `start` is not greater than `LEN(word)/2`, it will return false.

start	end	Word[start]	Word[end]
0	3	P	P
1	2	R	O

Using dry runs to determine the purpose of code

Dry runs can also be used to determine what a section of unknown code does. To do this you simply need to select some test data and then perform the dry run as shown above. Consider the mystery code below.

```
def mystery(x):
  a = 2
  b = True
  if x <=a:
    b = False
  while a<x-1 and b == True:
    if x % a == 0:
      b = False
    a = a + 1
  return b
```

Ignoring the fact that this is not written with readability in mind, this code does perform a useful task. The first thing to consider is what form the input and output will take. The output, shown by the return, is clearly a Boolean value. The parameter x, which forms the only input, must be an integer. This can be inferred by the fact that it is being directly compared to the variable a which clearly contains an integer. As no casting has taken place this is a safe assumption to make.

Looking at the code more closely reveals that the first if statement is some form of validation rule. Numbers less than 2 will always return False. Therefore, there is no point performing dry runs on these numbers. To determine what test data to use requires us to read the code and make educated guesses on which test data will give us the most information. The rationale behind this is purely motivated by time. Performing dry runs on algorithms can be time consuming and anything we can do to cut the process down will be time well saved – especially in an exam situation. The trace table below shows the first sensible test run, where x = 3. We could have done a much larger number, say 59, but the resulting trace table would be large. Therefore, when selecting test data for a dry run, it is better to go for smaller values.

x	a	b	a<x–1 and b == True
3	2	True	False

When x is 3 our mystery function returns True. It may already be apparent to you what this code does, but let us make the assumption that it is still a mystery. One dry run will not always be enough. Taking a logical approach, it makes sense to do the next few numbers as well. These are shown below.

x	a	b	a<x–1 and b == True
4	2	True	True
	3	False	False

x	a	b	a<x–1 and b == True
5	2	True	True
	3	True	True
	4	True	False

x	a	b	a<x–1 and b == True
6	2	True	True
	3	False	False

x	a	b	a<x–1 and b == True
7	2	True	True
	3	True	True
	4	True	True
	5	True	True
	6	True	False

The table below summarises the results of our dry runs. When doing testing such as this, you should always have in the back of your mind, "what is this code doing?" As soon as you have worked it out you can try and predict the next value. After that point you should be confident that you know what the code does. Our mystery function has returned true for 3, 5 and 7 so the question is: what do these numbers have in common? It has to be something to do with checking if a number divides cleanly or not. Hopefully you have realised that this is how we check for prime numbers: 3, 5 and 7 are all prime. Our mystery function will determine if an integer is prime or not.

x	Result
3	True
4	False
5	True
6	False
7	True

Chapter summary

- Algorithms are a set of mechanical steps which will take a given input and deterministically produce an output.
- Pseudocode is a method of representing algorithms which is not language specific.
- Flowcharts are another method of representing algorithms in a diagrammatic format and tend to be used for smaller algorithms.
- Variables are programming constructs which use identifiers to store information in RAM.
- The key difference between constants and variables is that once a constant has been assigned a value it cannot change while the program is running.
- Local scoped variables will only exist in the code block where they were defined.
- Global scoped variables are available throughout the program.
- Self-documenting code is code which uses sensible identifiers, good layout and clear code to reduce the need for comments and other forms of documentation.
- Parameters provide input into procedures and functions; they become variables within the functions to allow the programmer access.
- Procedures do not return values while functions do.
- Passing parameters by value will create a copy of the value.
- Passing by reference means that if the parameter is changed then the original will also change.
- Recursions are functions which call themselves, a type of iteration.
- Validation occurs while data is being inputted into a computer system. The common validation rules are:
  - character check
  - length check
  - range check
  - format check
  - existence check
  - check digit.

- Verification occurs after the data has been inputted. The two main methods are double entry and proof reading.
- Big O is a method of comparing algorithms together and measures the growth in terms of time or space.
- The order of growth in Big O, from smallest to largest, is shown in the table below–

Algorithm	Time complexity	Space complexity
Bubble sort	$O(n^2)$	$O(1)$
Insertion sort	$O(n^2)$	$O(1)$
Quicksort	$O(n \log_2 n)$	$O(\log_2 n)$
Linear search	$O(n)$	$O(1)$
Binary search	$O(\log_2 n)$	$O(\log_2 n)$
Dijkstra **graph** search	$O(|V|^2 + |E|)$	$O(|E| \log_2 |V|)$.

- The main sorting algorithms are bubble sort, insertion sort and quicksort.
- There are two main search algorithms: linear search and binary search.
- Dijkstra's shortest path algorithm will find the shortest route in a given map if each edge has a weight.
- Sequence is the order in which programming statements are executed.
- Selection will choose one of two paths to follow based on a condition.
- Repetition or iteration will repeat a block of code until a condition is met. The three main types of iteration are for, while and repeat/until loops.
- Counters can be used to keep track of where in a loop we have reached and is commonly used as a method of stopping iteration.
- Rogue values can also be used to stop iteration by assigning an abnormal value to delimit a string of text or a list of data.
- Logical operators are used as part of conditions and will form part of a logical expression.
- Data compression will reduce the size of data. There are two types of compression; lossy, where data is lost so we get an approximation of the original data and lossless, where no data is lost.
- Run length encoding will replace strings of the same characters with a character count.
- Dictionary encoding will create a list of commonly occurring sequences and replace all occurrences with a shorter reference in the dictionary.
- Huffman encoding will use shorter binary values to represent letters which occur more frequently.

End-of-chapter questions

1   Explain the difference between logarithmic and exponential growth for a given algorithm.   [3]

2   A developer has been asked to create an app for a music festival that will create a high-score table based on the number of tweets each band has received. She was going to use quicksort to order the final output once all of the tweets had been added up. Explain why using quicksort would not be the best choice in this scenario.   [3]

3 A balanced binary tree is one that ensures that every level is as full as it can possibly be. Explain why searching a balanced binary tree has a worst-case time complexity of log *n* while searching a binary tree would have a worst-case time complexity of *n*. [6]

4 Look at the code below. State one local and one global variable.

```
X = 6
function example()
Y = 5
Z = Y * X
print (Z + Y + X)
end function
```
[2]

Further reading

Learn Python	Search for Python on codeacademy.com
Java IDE	search for IDE on netbeans.org
Notepad++ IDE	search for Notepad++
Visual Studio IDE	Go to visualstudio.com
Logic in computer science	search for Logic in Computer Science on Rice University's Computer Science page
Boolean algebra	Search for Boolean Algebra on Surrey University's Electrical and Electronic Engineering website
Predicate logic	Search for Predicate Logic on Old Dominion University's Computer Science website
Propositional logic	Search for Propositional Logic on Stanford University's Infolab website
File compression	Search for File compression on How Stuff Works

Chapter 4
Principles of programming

Learning objectives

- Explain the nature and relative advantages of different programming paradigms, and identify possible situations where they may be used.
- Describe the distinguishing features of different types of programming paradigms, including procedural, event-driven, visual and mark-up languages.
- Describe the role of an object-oriented approach to programming and the relationship between object, class and method.
- Describe the need for the standardisation of computer languages, and the potential difficulties involved in agreeing and implementing standards.
- Identify ambiguities in natural language and explain the need for computer languages to have an unambiguous syntax.
- Interpret and use formal methods of expressing language syntax: syntax diagrams and Backus-Naur form (extended Backus-Naur form is not to be used).
- Describe the differences between high-level and low-level languages.
- Identify and describe situations that require the use of a high-level or a low-level language.
- Identify and justify which type of language would be best suited to develop a solution to a given problem.

Programming paradigms

A programming paradigm is the fundamental structure and approach of a programming language. So far in this course you will have come across the procedural programming paradigm. Programs written in a procedural language will run from the start to the end sequentially unless a control statement, such as a loop or IF, is encountered. However, there are many other programming paradigms, some of which you may have come across without realising it. In this chapter you will be introduced to some of the more common paradigms.

Procedural

Languages that use the procedural paradigm work sequentially and are made up of a series of commands intended to be run one after another. They are made up of statements including variable assignment, selection (IF), iteration (loops) and procedures. Modularity is introduced through procedures, from which the paradigm gets its name.

Procedural languages are also known as imperative languages. Imperative languages use statements to change the state of the program. A program's state can be thought of as the values of its variables at any given moment. Programs written using an imperative language make use of assignment to change the state of their variables.

Procedural programming is the simplest programming paradigm so it is usually the first one that developers learn. There are a number of languages, including C and Python, which offer the opportunity to develop procedurally. Most algorithms are written in a linear fashion which means that they fit nicely with the procedural paradigm. However, not all problems, for example GUI based problems, can be best expressed in a linear algorithm and thus other paradigms might be better suited to solve them.

Visual

When first learning programming at school, it is likely that you will have started with a visual programming language. These make use of intuitive user interfaces to help build programs rather than relying solely on text. One of the first visual languages you are likely to have encountered is Scratch (Figure 4.1).

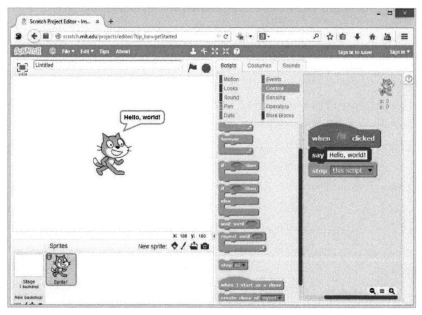

Figure 4.1: Visual programming language Scratch.

Scratch is made up of a series of characters that can have actions applied to them by dragging and dropping code blocks. Scratch makes use of the event-driven paradigm to allow the developer to program interaction. By eliminating the need to remember the syntax of a language, budding developers can spend more time considering the logic of the problem.

One downside of using visual programming languages is that they are not ideal for larger or more advanced problems. They are limited due to the fact that there is only so much screen space available. With most of it taken up by the user interface, there is not much room left for your code. Development time can also be longer as typing commands can be much faster for experienced developers. However, visual programming languages are great for starting to learn to code.

Event-driven

Programs that rely heavily on user interaction will normally be written using an event-driven paradigm. The essential premise is that a program will sit in a loop waiting for the user to perform an action. When an action occurs, a function (known as a listener) will run to process that action.

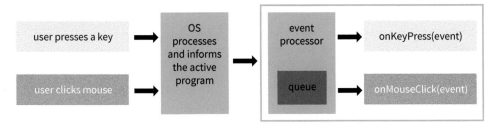

Figure 4.2: Flow of data when external events occur.

When a user interacts with an input device, the OS will process it in the usual way and then send then the event to the applications event queue (Figure 4.2). The event processor of the application will then process the event and send it to the relevant listener. Events themselves tend to take the form of an object (see OO programming later in this chapter) or some specialised data structure. Developers are responsible for creating the code for the listeners and selecting which ones they are interested in processing. The mechanism of the event processor is normally abstracted away from the developer.

The event processor, in the simplest form, will be a nested loop structure which uses either IF or select/case statements to direct the event to the correct listener. Pygame, a game library for Python, is event driven. A code sample below shows the event processor of a simple Pygame project. The outer loop will listen until the user asks the program to quit. The inner loop will iterate over the event queue and act upon the events that the program is interested in. The actual processing of the events occurs in the listener functions.

```
exitProgram = False
while not exitProgram:
  for e in event.get():
    if e.type == KEYDOWN:
      onKeyPress(e)
    elif e.type == MOUSEBUTTONUP:
      onMouseClick(e)
    elif e.type == QUIT:
      exitProgram = True
```

Event-driven programming requires the developer not to think of their code in a linear fashion but rather as a set of actions triggered by the user. Listener functions will not run one after another. Graphical user interfaces and games will always make use of the event-driven paradigm. It is fairly common for most modern languages to offer some form of event processing. For some languages, like Java and Python, there is more than one way to implement events.

Mark-up languages

Mark-up languages are not explicitly a programming paradigm but they are so prevalent in web technologies that they will be included here. Mark-up languages add commands, or mark-up, to a text document to offer meaning to the text. The commands give instructions to the program reading the file on how to interpret and display the text.

HTML

One of the most common mark-up languages is HTML. An example of HTML is shown below.

```
<html>
<body>
<h1> This is my web page </h1>
<p> This is my paragraph. </p>
</body>
</html>
```

The commands in HTML, known as tags, are surrounded by chevrons. Commands are opened, for example <h1>, so that any text that follows will have the command applied to it. Commands are then ended using a forward slash inside the tag, for example </h1>. In the above example the <h1> tag will instruct the browser that the text 'This is my web page' should be displayed as a heading.

XML

XML (eXtensible Mark-up Language) is another mark-up language that is commonly used in web applications. XML is used for structuring and marking-up data for storage rather than information for display. It looks very similar to HTML, but is meant to act more like a database. The developer is free to create their own tags and specify their own meaning to them. Developing your own tags is referred to as creating an XML schema. An example of XML is shown below.

```
<?xml version='1.0' encoding='UTF-8'?>
<news>
  <headline> Shock! Computing teacher spotted away from
  computer!</headline>
  <story> ........ </story>
</news>
```

Mark-up languages are commonly combined with other languages. The most common combination is JavaScript with HTML. JavaScript will process user interactions and offer a true programming environment while HTML will be used to format the output and the user interface.

Object-oriented programming

Most modern programming projects use the object-oriented paradigm, so it is important, once you understand the basics of procedural languages, to move on to object-oriented programming.

Object-oriented (OO) programming is known as OO or OOP and has gained popularity among the programming community. Most languages offer some form of OO support, including languages that were originally designed to be procedural. OO allows programs to be well structured and potentially offers the potential for reusable code, which is much sought after in programming.

Selection, iteration and assignment, along with identifiers and constants, all basic to procedural programming, are also available in the object-oriented paradigm. This makes moving from procedural to OO much more straightforward than it would be otherwise. One of the key differences, however, is that, in OO, procedures are replaced by classes, objects and methods, and the whole code is structured and designed differently. Classes and procedures both offer modularity of code, but classes allow the developer to produce more reusable code and relate their design more closely to reality.

Three characteristics define an OO language:

- encapsulation
- inheritance
- classes and objects.

Objects, classes and methods

In OO, code is developed around objects and classes. An object is a combination of data and the actions that can operate on that data. A class is the definition of an object; it embodies all the information needed to create and manipulate objects of a particular type (Figure 4.3). For example, there are many types of cars, which may differ, but fundamentally they share common descriptions and actions. If you saw a car coming down the road you would immediately classify it as a car before noticing the make and model. A car is an example of a class while a specific car, such as a Jaguar, is an example of an object.

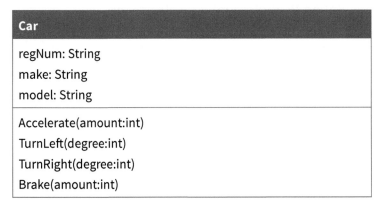

Figure 4.3: Class diagram for a car class.

A class has two main sections:

- a description (attributes)
- actions (methods).

Methods are fundamental to OO languages. A method is a piece of code that implements one of the behaviours of a class. For example, the car class could have the method 'TurnLeft'.

In order to identify an individual car, it must be described, and in OO this means creating an object. The process of creating an object is known as instantiation and the code below shows how an instance of the class car could be instantiated. The notation used in the Pseudocode below is common to many different OO languages. When an object is created, a blank version is generated on the heap (a large pool of memory) and a reference to it is returned. The keyword *new* is responsible for instantiating a class and allocating memory. Once instantiation has occurred, a reference to the object will be created, pointing to the location of that object in memory.

```
ford = new Car()
ford.regNum = 'YR99'
ford.make = 'Ford'
ford.model = 'Fiesta'
print ford.make, ford.model
```

To set an attribute of a class, you need to use the reference created during instantiation. Attributes are treated as variables within the object and are accessed by using a full stop between the object name and the variable. You can assign attributes or use them in other expressions exactly as you would any other variable. Accessing attributes is shown in the code above. Here we are setting up three attributes for our Ford car: the make, registration number and the model. The last line uses the print method to print two of these attributes as an example of how they can be used. It is important to note that setting the attribute for one object does not affect any other car object. All objects are distinct from each other, even if they share the same class.

Encapsulation

Encapsulation is the hiding of the implementation of a class and controlling access to its methods and attributes. Classes can hide how they work from developers using them in their programs. Anyone using the class needs only to understand the interface to the class, i.e. its methods and attributes.

Using encapsulation to implement data structures

One common use of OO programming that relies on encapsulation is the implementation of data structures, such as stacks. Here is some Pseudocode showing how a stack structure could be implemented in OO:

```
CLASS Stack
  start = -1
  list = []
  free = 0
  FUNCTION pop()
    oldstart = start;
    if start == null then
      return null;
    ELSE
      start = list[start].next
      list[oldstart].next = free
      free = oldstart
    END IF
    RETURN list[oldstart]
  END FUNCTION
```

```
FUNCTION push(value)
  temp = new Node();
  temp.data = value;
  temp.next = start;
  start = temp;
END FUNCTION
END CLASS
```

The pop() and push() methods are held within the class structure. The diagram in Figure 4.4 shows how the class will be presented to developers.

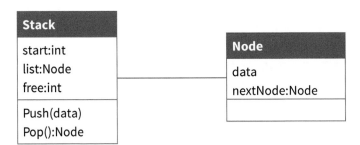

Figure 4.4: Class diagram for stack.

```
test = new Stack()
test.push('Bert')
test.push('Sally')
print test.pop()
print test.pop()
```

If this stack class was placed within a library file, developers would only need to import it in order to use its functionality.

Inheritance

In the real world, inheritance has a very specific meaning. We inherit genes from our parents, and in some cases money from relatives. The idea is that something is being passed down through some form of relationship. Inheritance, in OO, follows the same principle.

Consider the two classes shown in Figure 4.5.

Car	Van
Accelerate(amount:int)	Accelerate(amount:int)
Brake(amound:int)	Brake(amound:int)
CurrentGear():int	CurrentGear():int
Gearup()	Gearup()
Geardown()	Geardown()

Figure 4.5: Two classes which share common methods.

They are clearly different classes. A van is much larger than a car and has more storage space. However, they both have very similar operations. They accelerate, brake and turn. It makes little sense to write the same code twice, so the methods they have in common can be placed into a new class called RoadVehicles (Figure 4.6). This new class will contain all of the shared methods and attributes of both class Car and class Van.

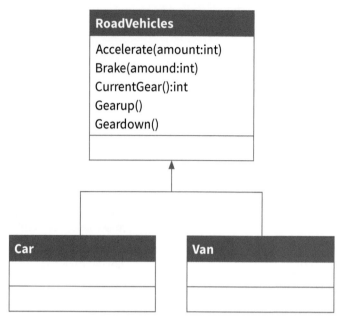

Figure 4.6: Example of how inheritance can be used to enable code reuse.

Car and Van now inherit from class RoadVehicles. They no longer define the shared methods themselves; rather, they inherit them from class RoadVehicles. RoadVehicles is said to be the superclass of both Car and Van, while Car and Van are subclasses of RoadVehicles. RoadVehicles is also a base class, that is, the first class within a hierarchy of classes. Subclasses can have methods of their own, which are specific to them. Consider the following classes.

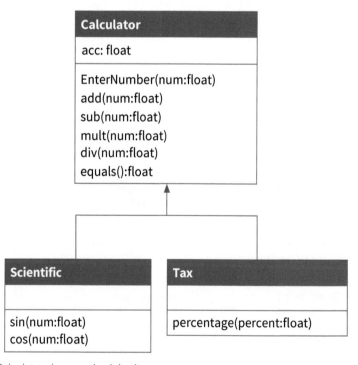

Figure 4.7: Calculator classes using inheritance.

The class diagram shown in Figure 4.7 shows a basic calculator superclass. All calculators, regardless of the type, offer these core services. Scientific calculators offer more services, such as sin and cos. Tax calculators might offer extra functionality such as percentages. These two types of calculator are subclasses, each having methods of their own.

Here is the Pseudocode for the Calculator and Scientific classes:

```
CLASS Scientific INHERITS Calculator
  FUNCTION sin(num)
    acc = Math.sin(num)
  END FUNCTION
  FUNCTION cos(num)
    acc = Math.cos(num)
  END FUNCTION
END CLASS
CLASS Calculator
    acc = 0
  FUNCTION enterNumber(num)
    acc = num
  END FUNCTION
  FUNCTION add(num)
    acc = acc + num
  END FUNCTION
  FUNCTION sub(num)
    acc = acc - num
  END FUNCTION
  FUNCTION mult(num)
    acc = acc * num
  END FUNCTION
  FUNCTION divide(num)
    acc = acc / num
  END FUNCTION
  FUNCTION equals()
    RETURN acc
  END FUNCTION
END CLASS
sci = new Scientific()
calc = new Calculator()
sci.enterNumber(45)
sci.sin(45)
print sci.equals()
calc.enterNumber(45)
```

The Scientific calculator class inherits all of the attributes and methods of the Calculator base class.

The Scientific class can use any method from the Calculator class. However, Calculator cannot use any of the methods from the Scientific class. Subclasses can inherit functionality only from their superclass. It is not a two-way process. In the code sample above, the line calc.sin() fails because 'calc' is an object of type Calculator, which does not have the sin() method.

Standardisation of computer languages
Why standards are needed
When hardware manufacturers create new devices, for example external hard drives, they must ensure that their devices are compatible with existing hardware. What use would an external hard drive be if you could not plug it into your computer? External hard drives are

connected using a USB (universal serial bus) connection available on all computers. USB is an example of a standard.

Standards are set up and developed for companies to use to ensure that their products will integrate with one another. Normally a consortium of interested parties will get together in order to develop the standard to ensure it meets the needs of their future products. The USB standard is currently being developed by the implementers' forum whose most notable members include Apple, Microsoft, Intel and Hewlett-Packard. Although these companies are direct competitors, it is important that the devices they produce can be integrated together. Imagine having to own an Apple Mac just to sync your iphone with itunes; this would limit the market for the iphone to Mac owners and would ultimately impact profits.

The importance of standards relates to interoperability of software and hardware. By implementing a standard you can have the confidence that your product will work as part of a larger system. Similar ideas exist for programming languages, but language standards are much less clear-cut. For example, different programming paradigms would require different standards.

Some languages, such as JavaScript and HTML, have very clear standards and are produced by the W3C (World Wide Web Consortium) as the need for interoperability is clear. Almost every modern device has a web browser, meaning that if there were no standard for web technologies, none of these devices would be able to access all web content.

In order for standards, such as HTML, to work effectively all browser manufacturers must follow them. This rarely is the case, although the situation is better than it used to be. Any web developer will know that you have to test and make changes to your code to ensure it will run on all web browsers. Code that renders fine in Chrome might look different when viewed in Internet Explorer. When companies implement software standards they may sometimes add their own additions or interpretations to try and get their products noticed.

The biggest issue with standards is that they only work when all interested parties can agree and implement them exactly as specified. Most companies will put their own interests first and will argue for their ideas to be the ones that everyone else implements. Factors which will negatively impact standardisation are differing end goals for a standard, different requirements based on future products, desire to be the company steering the standards group and inability to agree on core feature sets. Also, even when standards are agreed, if they are not prescriptive enough then their implementations may subtly differ leading to incompatibility. Web browsers displaying HTML is a case in point.

Software standardisation offers additional issues due to the inherent complexities of software. Complex systems tend to be based on very abstract ideas. These abstract ideas can be very challenging to tie down to a single set of standards. For example, if there was a de facto standard for defining iteration there would be a number of direct consequences. If all iteration were based on while loops and written in the format below then we would lose the flexibility of using FOR loops and REPEAT/UNTIL loops. These are both useful in different situations. Also, if we standardised the format of the while loop then this would directly impact how a language could be defined. A standard is not meant to restrict the developer. How software standards are to be implemented is not itself standardised, leading to variations in implementation.

WHILE CONDITION

CODE TO REPEAT

END WHILE

Ambiguity in natural language

$2 + 3 \times 4$

When calculating the result of the above calculation, there are two alternative interpretations. The first one, and the one which is correct, is where multiplication is done before addition giving an answer of 14. However, we could do the addition first leading to the answer 20. In Maths you learn about BIDMAS (brackets, indices, division, multiplication, addition and subtraction) that defines the order that operations are carried out. In computing we call this operator precedence. By using BIDMAS we can turn what was ambiguous to something which can only have a single interpretation.

Ambiguity in natural language means that a statement can be interpreted in more than one way. This can be difficult when dealing with day-to-day English, but for computers ambiguity is impossible to interpret. When defining programming languages it is essential that no ambiguity exist. If a computer, when interpreting a statement, is given two possible alternative paths then it will not be able to determine which one is correct.

IF = 5

THEN = 10

IF IF > THEN THEN PRINT 'Hello'

For example, you will have already learned that you cannot use keywords as identifiers. The code above is ambiguous, although a human could make sense of it. When the compiler sees the letters 'IF' on their own, it would have two options if the code above was valid. Is this an identifier or the start of an IF statement? The equals after it offers no further help, as we would have to decide if this was assignment or just an equality check. Ultimately the compiler would be unable to decide on which set of syntax rules to apply and would have to 'guess'. This leads to two possibilities: the guess is right or wrong. If it is right, the code will run as expected. If the guess is wrong then the code could produce bizarre logic errors and not behave as expected. There must never be a situation where coder and compiler infer different meanings from the same syntax.

Natural language processing is a major area of research in computer science, with the most notable being the development of chatbots to pass the Turing test. The Turing test is where a computer has to converse with a human in an intelligent way to trick them into believing they are conversing with a real human and not the chatbot. The test is set up so that the human will be either assigned a computer running natural language processing software or another human. Their task is to determine if they are indeed talking to another human or a machine. One of the more successful attempts was 'Eugene Goostman', a chatbot developed by Vladimir Veselov, Eugene Demchenko and Sergey Ulasen. In 2014 it fooled one third of the judges who chatted with it.

When processing language, humans will use the context of the conversation, our own memories, our beliefs and our common sense to interpret the conversation. If I said, 'winter is coming', some people will think about the changing seasons while others will immediately think about the book (and TV series) Game of Thrones (by George R. R. Martin). If the context of the statement was discussing the weather then the meaning becomes clear. If I was talking about what I watched last week then how my statement will be interpreted becomes linked to the person's knowledge of the book. Context and knowledge are incredibly difficult things for a computer to simulate accurately, which is why Eugene, even though he only managed to fool a third of judges, was considered to be a great achievement.

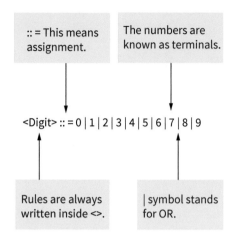

<Digit> :: = 0 | 1 | 2 | 3 | 4 | 5 | 6 | 7 | 8 | 9

:: = This means assignment.

The numbers are known as terminals.

Rules are always written inside <>.

| symbol stands for OR.

Figure 4.8: Diagram showing a digit rule.

Basics of Backus Naur form

Backus Naur form (BNF) is a way of writing down the grammar of a programming language. It defines rules that must be followed in order for source code to be syntactically correct. Rules for a programming language must not be ambiguous, as introduced in the last section.

The following IF statement is syntactically incorrect.

IF ELSE a > 10 THEN END IF a = 1

ELSE should never follow immediately after an IF. Syntax rules state that a comparison should follow such as a > 10. In order to enforce this syntax rule, the above IF statement could be written in BNF. Rules defined in BNF will tell the compiler what valid syntax will look like. Defining a rule for IF statements is complex so we will consider a simple rule, to define a single digit from 0 to 9 (Figure 4.8).

Reading it from left to right –

Let the rule **digit** be defined (or assigned) as being the terminal 0 or 1 or 2 or 3 or 4 or 5 or 6 or 7 or 8 or 9. Terminals cannot be evaluated any further and take the form of symbols, characters or digits. The | symbol represents OR (disjunction or choice). If terminals or non-terminals are next to each other then this is considered concatenation (conjunction), meaning they are joined together. Rules can be combined together by referring to the name of a rule within another. When a rule is used in this way it is known as a non-terminal. This is because we have to evaluate it before we can accept the syntax.

<Two_Digit_Number> ::= <Digit> <Digit>

The rule <Two_Digit_number> has been made up of a <digit> followed immediately by a second <Digit>. We already know that a <Digit> is a single digit number from 0 to 9. Rules can be evaluated (or tested) with specific values. Consider the number 54.

<Two_Digit_Number> ::= <Digit> <Digit>

<Two_Digit_Number> ::= 0 | 1 | 2 | 3 | 4 | 5 | 6 | 7 | 8 | 9 <Digit>

<Digit> is a non-terminal and must be evaluated further. By replacing <digit> with 0 | 1| 2 | 3 | 4 | 5 | 6 | 7 | 8 | 9 we reach a stage where we are left with terminals. 5 can be compared to one of these terminals so the first part of the rule passes. The second <digit> is evaluated in the same way.

<Two_Digit_Number> ::= 5 <Digit>

<Two_Digit_Number> ::= 5 0 | 1 | 2 | 3 | 4 | 5 | 6 | 7 | 8 | 9

<Two_Digit_Number> ::= 54

At this point we are out of input, meaning that the number 54 matches the rule and is accepted as valid input. However, the evaluation of 5A would not be accepted.

<Two_Digit_Number> ::= <Digit> <Digit>

<Two_Digit_Number> ::= 0 | 1 | 2 | 3 | 4 | 5 | 6 | 7 | 8 | 9 <Digit>

<Two_Digit_Number> ::= 5 <Digit>

<Two_Digit_Number> ::= 5 0 | 1 | 2 | 3 | 4 | 5 | 6 | 7 | 8 | 9

The input we have left is A, however this is not one of the available choices. This means that the input is not syntactically correct as it does not match the rules laid out in our simple grammar.

Recursion in BNF

So far, our grammar is not very practical; imagine being able to store numbers that can have up to 200 digits. We could define a rule for every possible set of digits as shown below.

<Two_Digit_Number> ::= <Digit> <Digit>

<Three_Digit_Number> ::= <Digit> <Digit> <Digit>

<Four_Digit_Number> ::= <Digit> <Digit> <Digit> <Digit>

This is clearly an impractical way of doing it. It is possible to define a single rule that can define any number of digits. Below is the recursive rule for a number of variable lengths of digits.

<Number> ::= <Digit> | <Digit> <Number>

What we are saying here is that we can either have a single digit or we can have a digit followed by another number. Consider the number 5983 and how the <number> rule would interpret it.

<Number> ::= <Digit> | <Digit> <Number>

<Number> ::= 5 <Number>

<Number> ::= 5 <Digit> | <Digit> <Number>

<Number> ::= 59 <Number>

<Number> ::= 59 <Digit> | <Digit> <Number>

<Number> ::= 598 <Number>

<Number> ::= 598 <Digit> | <Digit> <Number>

<Number> ::= 5983

First of all the 5 is evaluated. This is clearly a digit so it can match to either <Digit> or <Digit><Number>. As there is still more input left we cannot match to the first rule part of the disjunction. The second part is evaluated which then calls the <Number> rule for the digit 9. This recursion will continue until the end has been reached. The 3 matches the <Digit> on its own and as there is no more input the recursion ends.

Defining syntax

Let us take a simple assignment expression where V is a variable and <E> is an expression.

<A> ::= V = <E>

Anything in BNF which is surrounded by <> refers to a rule. So we need a rule for expressions. To keep things simple we will only use simple arithmetic expressions. L represents a literal.

<E> ::= <T> + <E> | <T> – <E> | <T>

<T> ::= <F> * <T> | <F> / <T> | <F>

<F> ::= <E> | V | L

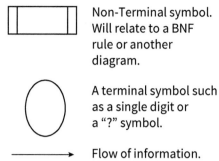

Non-Terminal symbol. Will relate to a BNF rule or another diagram.

A terminal symbol such as a single digit or a "?" symbol.

Flow of information. This is the path you must follow to use the rule.

Figure 4.9: Syntax diagram symbols.

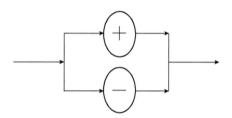

Figure 4.10: Disjunction.

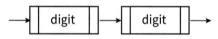

Figure 4.11: Concatenation.

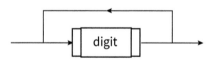

Figure 4.12: Recursion.

The extra rules allow us to implement operator precedence (i.e. * binds more than +). When all of the rules are in place a parser can then be constructed.

Syntax diagrams

Backus Naur is what most languages will be defined in, however syntax can also be defined in diagrammatic form. Syntax diagrams represent BNF rules in a more accessible manner. Although syntax diagrams are easier to understand for humans it is important to remember that a computer will not be able to use them. (Figure 4.9) shows the symbols used in syntax diagrams.

In order to build syntax diagrams, concatenation and disjunction will need to be represented. Disjunction can be demonstrated with the aid of the example below.

<sign> ::= + | –

The + and – are terminal symbols and so the circle symbol must be used. The two circle symbols are drawn on top of each other in order to show disjunction (Figure 4.10). Reading the diagram from left to right, there is a clear branch where the flow of the diagram can choose one path or another. Branches are how disjunction is represented in a syntax diagram.

Concatenation is just as easy. Consider the following rule.

<Two_Digit_Number> ::= <Digit> <Digit>

The rectangular symbol shows non-terminal symbols. To show two digits together they can be placed on the same line (Figure 4.11).

Recursion is much more straightforward in syntax diagrams than in BNF. To repeat a section of the diagram is simply a matter of drawing an arrow looping on itself. The diagram for the rule <number> is shown in Figure 4.12.

<Number> ::= <Digit> | <Digit> <Number>

As you can see there is no alternation in the diagram. This is because in BNF we need a termination clause. In the diagram this is unnecessary.

High- and low-level languages

Low-level languages reflect the design of the processor on which they are to run much more closely than their high-level equivalents. In high-level languages, a lot of the detail of memory addressing, assigning registers and accessing hardware is abstracted from the programmer; in low-level languages the developer has direct access to these. Each CPU architecture has an instruction set; low-level languages offer a direct one-to-one mapping between low-level commands and the machine code instructions in this instruction set. The most common low-level language is assembly code, which will be introduced in this section.

Conversely high-level languages hide the inner workings of how things like registers are assigned or where data should be stored in memory. Each line of high-level code could translate into multiple lines of machine code. Because a lot of the low-level details are hidden from the developer they are free to focus their attentions on developing algorithms. However, they must sacrifice closer control of the hardware in return. Table 4.1 shows some of the key differences between high- and low-level languages.

High-level languages	Low-level languages
Each line of code translates into multiple lines of machine code.	Each line of code translates into a single line of machine code.
Does not give direct access to registers or other CPU features.	Allows the developer to manipulate registers and the CPU directly.
Instructions are semantic and do not reflect the design of the processor.	Instructions are directly linked with the instruction set of the processor and are based on the design of the processor.

Table 4.1: Comparison of high- and low-level languages.

Machine code instructions

When code is written in languages such as Python or Visual Basic .NET, the code is readable and understandable by humans and is known as source code. Processors have no understanding of source code and cannot execute it directly unless it is translated into machine code. A translator is the name given to software that takes source code and converts it to machine code. Source code, written as a text file, allows software to be created without the need to understand the inner workings of the instruction set of the target processor. The programming language hides a lot of the complexities of the processor, such as memory addressing modes.

Each processor architecture (for example, ARM or x86) has its own set of instructions. The compiler must specify the target architecture before compiling, as the differing architectures are not compatible. Each line of source code can be compiled into many lines of machine code (Figure 4.13).

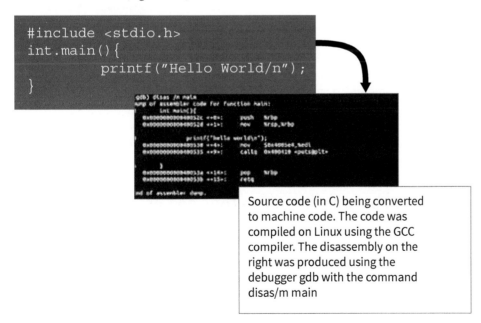

Source code (in C) being converted to machine code. The code was compiled on Linux using the GCC compiler. The disassembly on the right was produced using the debugger gdb with the command disas/m main

Figure 4.13: Source code being converted into machine code.

Structure of machine code

Machine code is the binary representation of an instruction, split into the opcode and the operand (the instruction's data). Assembly code uses text to represent machine code instructions, or mnemonics. Each processor architecture has a set of instructions that it can run; this is known as the instruction set. Table 4.2 shows the basic structure of an instruction:

Bits 1-6	Bits 7-16
Opcode	Operand

Table 4.2: Basic structure of an instruction.

The size of instructions differs from architecture to architecture and between different instructions. In the example in Table 4.2, the instruction is 16 bits in size. Every instruction available, in a given instruction set, will have a unique binary value known as the opcode. When an instruction is executed by the processor, it uses the opcode to determine which instruction to run. Table 4.3 shows an example instruction set, which is not based on any real-life processor and should be treated as an example only. Note that ACC stands for accumulator, a special purpose register.

Opcode	Assembly Mnemonic	Description
000 001	MOV	Moves a value to a register
000 010	ADD	Adds a value and stores in ACC
000 100	SUB	Subtracts a value and stores in ACC
001 000	MUL	Multiplies a value and stores in ACC

Table 4.3: Showing example machine code instructions and their respective opcodes.

Each opcode represents a different instruction and mnemonics are used to make development in Assembly language easier, because dealing with binary can get very complex. As an example, Table 4.4 shows a simple program that will perform the calculation (4 + 5) * 2:

	Opcode	Data	Value of ACC
MOV value 0 to ACC	000 001	0000 0000 00	0000 0000 0000 0000
ADD 4 to ACC	000 010	0000 0001 00	0000 0000 0000 0100
ADD 5 to ACC	000 010	0000 0001 01	0000 0000 0000 1001
MUL 2 to ACC	001 000	0000 0000 10	0000 0000 0001 0010

Table 4.4: Showing an example of how the computer sees the opcode and data as binary.

Some instructions take up more than one word. In the above example, the MOV instruction has two arguments, the first being the register to use. In this case ACC (accumulator) is represented by register 0. The value to move into ACC is stored in the second word. ADD and MUL both store the value to add or multiply in the data part of the instruction, which is known as immediate addressing. However, we could just as easily store it separately. Placing data in the second word of a double-word instruction allows the full 16 bits to be used, thus supporting larger numbers.

Relationship between machine code and Assembly code

Assembly code is the step above machine code, allowing the coder to write code using mnemonics, which represent machine code instructions. Each Assembly code instruction has a one-to-one mapping with a machine code instruction. This is unlike source code, which has a one-to-many mapping. When converting Assembly code to machine code you will use an assembler.

C language

Although Assembly code is the most obvious low-level language, there are others. The most notable example is C. C is different to Assembly code in that it can act as a high-level language as well. It needs to be translated and a single line of code can produce multiple lines of machine code. C also has the ability to run machine code directly and give direct access to memory through the use of pointers. C is therefore the language of choice for most applications requiring a low-level language, as it offers the best of both worlds.

 Tip

Machine code and Assembly code form the main focus of another part of the course and questions based on these topics may not appear in questions linked to the processor and the FDE cycle. However, the terms opcode and machine code are key in answering questions in this section successfully.

Applications requiring low-level languages

Due to the complexity and difficulty of writing in low-level languages, most programmers will prefer to develop in a high-level language. This means that most scenarios would be better implemented using a high-level language with one or more of the paradigms described earlier in this chapter. However, this does not mean that low-level languages are redundant. Some scenarios are much better suited to implementation in a low-level language. Table 4.5 shows a few examples, with justifications, of why low-level is more suitable.

Application	Why a low-level language is suitable
Device drivers	Device drivers need to be small and as efficient as possible. You need to be able to manipulate memory addresses in order to fully control the hardware.
Embedded software	Software which runs on simple devices such as a washing machine, modern central heating systems or any other device with a simple microprocessor. Software on these devices needs to be small and have direct access to the hardware. They commonly will only have a simple operating system.
Interfacing with custom hardware	This runs along the same lines as device drivers. If you create your own hardware, for example a robot, and connect it to a PC then you will effectively need to write software that can directly control it. This will require direct access to the connecting cable and the ability to manipulate control signals.

Table 4.5: Showing some of the possible applications of low-level languages.

Chapter summary

- There are many different programming paradigms, each with their own strengths and weaknesses.
- Procedural programming languages describe which steps to take to solve a problem and how to complete each step.
- Assembly language instructions consist of two distinct sections: operators, such as ADD or SUB, and operands, which are usually memory addresses.
- Visual languages allow code to be created through drag and drop. They are commonly used for learning programming by students.
- Event-driven languages will run functions depending on what events are happening in the system, normally triggered by the user.
- Software standards define how code should be written with regard to the structure, naming of identifiers and how modules are created. They may also define the specifics of how a language works, but leave the implementation up to other vendors.
- Examples of standards include HTML and JavaScript.
- Object-oriented languages describe the solution to a problem by creating objects that represent real-world entities.
- Classes are templates for real-world objects which have attributes and methods.
- Objects are instances of classes and represent a real-world object.

- Methods are actions that classes or objects can perform, for example SpinWheel().
- Attributes are properties of a class or object such as radius or colour.
- Classes can inherit attributes and methods from other classes. For example, a Car class might inherit the attributes and methods from a Vehicle class. In this example, Car would be a subclass and Vehicle a superclass.
- Backus Naur form (BNF) is a way of representing syntax as a context-free grammar. BNF contains a number of key elements:
  - the rule written as <rulename> ::=
  - concatenation: elements of the BNF are written next to each other
  - <IF> ::= IF <expression> THEN <statement>
  - disjunction: elements are separated by the | symbol and effectively offer a choice of options
  - <digit> ::= 0 | 1 | 2 | 3 | 4 | 5 | 6 | 7 | 8 | 9
  - recursion: allows rules to be iterative
  - <digits> ::= <digit> | <digit> <digits>.

🔍 End-of-chapter questions

1   Define the following object oriented terms:

   a   Class   [2]

   b   Object   [2]

   c   Inheritance   [2]

   d   Encapsulation   [2]

   e   Polymorphism   [3]

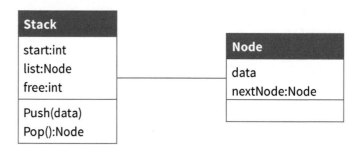

2   The class diagram above shows the abstract data type for a Stack.

   a   Show code to instantiate an object and assign it to a variable called "myStack".   [1]

   b   Add the data items "Football" and "Drawing" to this object.   [2]

   c   Using the keyword "print", write the code and show the output if the "pop" operation was run.   [3]

3 A sprite class has the following definition:

```
CLASS Sprite
  X : int
  Y : int
  moveLeft(amount : int)
  moveRight(amount : int)
  moveUp(amount : int)
  moveDown(amount : int)
END CLASS
```

a If you were developing a platform game, explain why you may
wish to use inheritance on this class. [4]

b Why would using polymorphism make rendering a single frame
in the game (drawing the screen) more efficient? [6]

4 A small business gives a product code to every item it sells. This product
code will always start with two letters followed by five numbers. Two BNF rules
have already been defined; <LETTER> which represents a single letter and
<DIGIT> which represents a single digit. Write the rule <PRODUCT> to represent a
product code for this company. [2]

Further reading

Mobile apps and object-oriented code	Search for Object-Oriented Programming in the Era of Mobile Development on informit.com
IOS dev centre	Search for Apple iOS developer centre
Android SDK	Go to developer.android.com
Introduction to object oriented-programming	Search for Object Oriented Programming Concepts on codeproject.com
LMC simulator (javascript)	Go to www.pcnict.co.uk/lmc/lmc.html
Introduction to X86 assembly	Go to c-jump.com/CSI77/CIS77syllabus.htm and search the page for Introduction to x86 Assembly

Chapter 5
System analysis

Learning objectives

A • Describe different appropriate approaches to analysis and design, including Waterfall and Agile.

• Describe the purpose of a feasibility study and the processes that an analyst would carry out during a feasibility study.

• Explain that proposed solutions must be cost effective, developed to an agreed time scale and within an agreed budget.

• Describe the different methods of investigation.

• Analyse a problem using appropriate techniques of abstraction and decomposition.

• Represent and interpret systems in an appropriate diagrammatic form, showing the flow of data and the information processing requirements.

• Describe the selection of suitable software and hardware to address the requirements of a problem.

• Describe the various methods of changeover: direct, pilot, phased and parallel. Identify the most suitable method for a given situation and its merits compared to other methods.

• Describe the use of alpha, beta and acceptance testing.

• Describe the nature and use of perfective, adaptive and corrective maintenance.

• Describe different procedures for backing up data.

• Explain how data might be recovered if lost.

A • Explain at which stage of the development each piece of documentation is produced.

- Describe the contents and use made of user documentation and maintenance documentation.
- Describe the components of maintenance documentation, including annotated listings, variable lists, algorithms and data dictionaries.

Introduction

Software is not cheap to build, mainly due to the high cost of developers and the time that projects can take to complete. Larger software systems, such as accounting systems for professionals, can take two or three years to make and involve hundreds of staff. Even games can take a lot of time and money to produce. For example, back in 1999 a game called Shenmue, produced by Sega for the Dreamcast games console, cost $47 000 000 to develop. Most of the cost of development goes towards paying for software developers and other staff rather than hardware. When dealing with massive projects, involving hundreds of people and millions of dollars, it is crucial that formal methods are followed to ensure that projects are developed with as few issues as possible. All software projects, to a greater or lesser extent, make use of the systems lifecycle. However, how they follow the lifecycle depends on the methodology chosen. In this chapter you will learn about the key phases of the systems life cycle as well as the key methodologies used in modern software development. It is important to note, at this stage, that there is no one methodology that is better than any other. Each methodology comes with its own set of merits and drawbacks, meaning that the one chosen should depend on the projects being attempted.

Approaches

Program development techniques cover the various approaches to the design, writing and testing of programs. Each approach has its own set of advantages and disadvantages, so a particular approach may be perfect for one project but completely inappropriate for another. Which approach to use is decided by the project manager and can have a critical impact on the successful implementation of the solution.

Systems lifecycle methodologies

Each of the lifecycle methodologies described here implements the systems lifecycle in a different way. This means that each has its own set of advantages and disadvantages that makes it suitable of different projects.

Waterfall

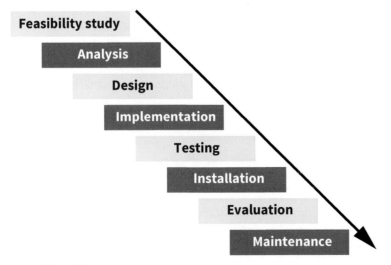

Figure 5.1: Waterfall model.

> **Tip**
>
> Exam questions can sometimes focus on the advantages and disadvantages of the Waterfall model, so make a point of highlighting these in your notes. Also, don't be afraid to draw diagrams of different methodologies (particularly spiral and Waterfall models) in your exam. These are often worth marks.
>
> To successfully answer exam questions on the systems life cycle you should be able to recommend a particular model over the others for a given project and justify your decision in terms of its relative advantages and disadvantages.

The Waterfall approach is probably the most famous incarnation of the systems analysis cycle. It was initially designed for use in manufacturing and engineering environments where the products being created were based around hardware rather than software. Since then, the Waterfall approach has been successfully employed across a range of industries and sectors. Its linear nature, and the fact that deliverables are produced at the end of each stage, made it popular in the early days of software engineering.

In the Waterfall approach the different stages are arranged in order, with each stage cascading down to the next (Figure 5.1). It is impossible to begin one stage of the development until the preceding one has been completed. This linear approach to development is both the biggest strength and the Achilles heel of the Waterfall approach.

Each stage in the Waterfall approach ends with a deliverable document, produced to inform the next stage. For example, at the end of the design stage the design documentation is produced, detailing exactly what is to be created during the implementation stage. These deliverables can be shown to clients or used internally within the company. It is very important that these deliverables are detailed and accurate, as it is possible that the team that builds the system will be completely different from the team who implement the project; both rely on the design documentation. At the end of each phase, some testing of the deliverables occurs to make sure that they meet the overall requirements of the project and that nothing has been omitted.

These deliverables constitute a major advantage of using the Waterfall approach, as they can be used to provide concrete deadlines, called milestones, for the project, which helps build client confidence. These regular deadlines also bring a level of discipline to a large project that can be lacking in some of the more flexible models and methodologies you will see later.

Computing in context: high profile failure of the Waterfall approach

In 2010, the American President Barack Obama set out to reform healthcare in the USA. He aimed to provide health insurance to US citizens who couldn't afford the expensive premiums charged by private healthcare companies and were therefore very vulnerable if they fell ill. An important part of the reforms was the creation of healthcare.gov, a federal website that was to serve as a marketplace where people could compare insurance plans, learn about the new subsidies and sign up for coverage. The federal portal was plagued with technical glitches from its rollout, including long sign-in wait times, log-in difficulties, insurance account creation problems, slow page loads and outages. One source claimed that of the 20 million people visiting the site, just half a million were able to access it.

Senior aides publicly blamed the Waterfall development approach for the poor quality of the site, believing that the project would have been much better implemented by the 'adoption of modern, incremental software development practices, like a popular one called Agile, already used in the private sector'.

Aside from the deliverables, the other main advantage of the Waterfall approach is that it forces developers to consider the requirements of the system thoroughly, rather than diving straight into programming. A detailed, thorough design reduces the possibility of mistakes later on. In addition, the model is relatively simple and easy to understand. This makes it attractive to clients who don't understand software development, as it helps them grasp long, technical projects.

However, despite its popularity, the Waterfall approach has some important disadvantages that make it unsuitable for certain types of project. In particular, the Waterfall approach is much less flexible than the alternatives you will see later on. Most importantly, following the Waterfall approach makes it very difficult for systems developers to react to changes or problems that crop up during any of the later stages. If a problem is discovered during the implementation stage, it may be necessary to go right back to the top of the Waterfall and revise the requirements.

It is also very difficult for software engineers or their clients to completely understand the requirements of a system at the start of development. It is common for the requirements of a project to evolve over the course of development, as the programmers grow to understand the area in which they are working and the client better understands what the software might be capable of. This problem is amplified by the length of time that the Waterfall approach can take to implement, it is perfectly feasible for the process to take so long that, by the time the project has been completed, the requirements have changed dramatically.

Summary: Waterfall approach

- The different stages are arranged in order, with each stage feeding into the next.
- No stage of the development can be begun until the preceding one has been completed.
- Each stage ends with a deliverable or handover document produced to inform the next stage.
- It is simple to understand and suitable for large projects where the requirements are clearly understood.
- It is very bad at reacting to changing requirements and is not suitable for projects where the requirements may not be fully understood at the start.

Agile

Agile methods were developed in the 1990s to provide a flexible alternative to the more structured development models, such the Waterfall approach, that were being used at the time. There are many different types of Agile development, but they are all based on the same founding principles outlined in the 'Agile Manifesto'.

Agile techniques value collaboration and people over processes and tools. There is a strong focus on providing programmers with the tools and resources they need, then trusting them to solve the problem set as efficiently as possible. Teams are trusted to organise and manage themselves, with a focus on regular meetings and interactions rather than the documentation-heavy approach favoured by the Waterfall approach.

This focus on collaboration is also extended to customers and clients. Agile programmers spend much more time meeting regularly with clients to discuss the system's development. This is radically different from the Waterfall approach, in which clients must rely on a few intensive meetings to negotiate contracts or finalise requirements.

Agile programmers favour using their time to produce software rather than detailed, comprehensive documentation. They prefer their projects to be judged on how well their software works, rather than how well its development has been documented. This means that they are able to deliver well-written software much faster than programmers working to more rigid developmental approaches. This avoidance of lengthy documentation, combined with the high level of client contact, allows Agile programmers to focus on responding to change rather than simply following a plan. One of the founding principles of the Agile methodology is that it is impossible to know all of a user's requirements at the start of a project, something that is hotly disputed by proponents of the Waterfall approach. All this means that Agile projects are able to quickly adapt to changes, for example, a competitor releasing a new product or a new operating system becoming available.

There are a number of different implementations of the Agile methodology, each sharing the tenets of the Agile Manifesto but implementing them in different ways. The most well known of these are extreme programming and Scrum.

- Extreme programming emphasises four areas of Agile development: communication, simplicity, feedback and courage. Communication means communication between individual programmers and teams as well as regular communication with clients and customers. Simplicity encourages programmers to adopt the most straightforward solution to a client's problems rather than providing an overly complex or unnecessarily detailed one. Opportunities for regular feedback are also built into the development process, with programmers often working in pairs; this is known as pair programming, with one developer coding while the other observes and offers advice.
- Like other Agile methods, Scrum focuses on regular iterations to create functional prototypes quickly. Scrum programmers focus on having fixed length iterations (for example, 30 days) called sprints. A Scrum project will be worked on by several teams at the same time, with each team focusing on a different piece of functionality. These teams will hold regular meetings, called scrums, to update each other on their progress and give feedback on any problems they have encountered.

Activity 5.1

One way to maximise marks on the exam is to have a mastery over the keywords used in each section. To this end, you should design and develop an app to support students in learning their keywords. Pick a methodology which is best suited and then use it to help develop the app. To make this more meaningful, you may wish to work in small teams of developers.

Activity 5.2

Use the internet to find a technology company that uses Agile development. What are they creating? Why do you think they have chosen this methodology?

Activity 5.3

Follow the Waterfall model to create a simple hangman game in Python. Analyse the problem then design a solution before coding your program. Evaluate the methodology you used: did it help or hinder your games development?

Summary: Agile approach

- Has various implementations including extreme programming and Scrum.
- Focus on communication, feedback, courage and simplicity makes it possible to develop very well-written programs quickly.
- Some Agile techniques, such as pair programming, are not popular among developers or managers and a lack of documentation and specific deadlines can lead to problems with customers who are unfamiliar with the approach.

Software projects and application systems

The purpose of an ICT development project is to create an application system, which is a combination of software and hardware, that meets the needs of a given set of users or purposes. Application systems (or systems for short) tend to be commissioned when there is a perceived need or when improvements to a current system are required. Take care to distinguish between application systems (which enable users to achieve some purpose) and systems software, which is the software that runs in the background on computers providing a base platform on which applications are run.

It is easy to think that new ICT systems always take an old manual system and automate it with ICT; however, this is increasingly not the case. Computing systems have been around for a long time. There are systems in use that were originally developed many years ago and are referred to as legacy systems. These systems use old technology and may be archaic by modern-day standards. They could be upgraded, but the cost of replacing legacy systems can run into the millions and so not all of them get replaced. Where the legacy system is retained, the company or organisation concerned might build a new front-end for it, that is, a new way of interacting with it, that uses modern technology, such as the world wide web.

Reasons to commission a new system could be company expansion, old systems being too slow compared to modern alternatives, lack of support for old software or a desire to capitalise on new technologies. Systems could also be built if a new business venture has been identified. There is always a reason for building a new ICT system and this reason is always business driven. It is worth mentioning, at this point, that building a new ICT system requires much more than programming skills; it also need business experts, analysts, project managers, testers, technical authors, marketers etc. The project team must include people who have a good awareness of business methods, people skills and creative problem solving.

Regardless of whether an existing ICT system is in place, some formal approaches will be followed in order to produce the system. When a new system, or an upgrade, is commissioned, a series of steps will be followed, known as the systems analysis cycle. Each project will go through several of the phases shown in Figure 5.2, but they do not have to use all of them. How the systems analysis cycle is implemented on a project is known as an approach, for example Waterfall or Agile approach, which will govern which phases are used and their relative importance.

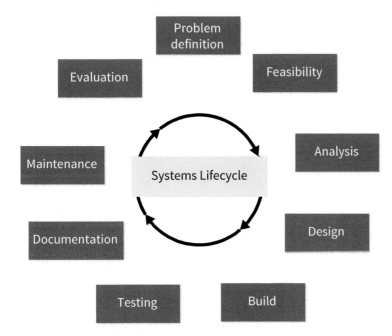

Figure 5.2: Systems analysis cycle.

Stakeholders

A stakeholder is someone, or a group of people, with a vested interest in the new system being built. They may be passive stakeholders, meaning that they will not be involved in the production of the system, or active stakeholders who have a part to play in the system to be built. Under normal circumstances, a new system involves two main companies: the company that requires a system to be built and the company that will produce it. We can call them the customer and the development company. In the real world this simple distinction cannot always be drawn, as there may be many other companies involved in the project: for example, the suppliers of hardware, possibly custom-built hardware; contractors providing specific technical skills not currently available in the development company; offshore development teams; and even legal representation. Some development companies outsource the work if they do not have the required technical skills or staff. Staffing on a large-scale project is expensive, with some software developers earning over £50 000 per year. Any cost saving that the development company can do, for example sending some of the development work offshore, will enable it to increase its profit margins. In any software development project, staffing is the single biggest cost.

Users

The user is not the same as the customer. The customer is the person who requires a new system, while the user is the person who will use it. It may seem an odd distinction to make, but it is important. Consider an ATM (automatic teller machine). The people who use ATMs are the general public. Apart from owning an account with the bank, they are not directly involved with it. So in this case the user is not the person who has initiated the new system. The bank has asked for the new system to be built and is therefore the customer.

It is crucial to consider the users, as they are the people who will be interacting with the system on a daily basis. If the system does not meet their needs, it will fail.

Programmers

Programmers, or developers, are the people building the system. They take information passed to them by the systems analysts and use it to develop the system. They rarely have direct involvement in the analysis or design of a system, but they do have a vested interest in the success of the project. They are usually the people who spot the more subtle problems with the new system and their input is invaluable to the systems analysts. It is common for a systems analyst to talk to the lead programmer during the whole of the systems analysis cycle, to get the thoughts and ideas of the programming team.

Project managers

Project managers have a critical role to play in the project. It is their responsibility to monitor progress and allocate resources to the project. There is normally a project manager on both the customer side and the developer side. The reason for this is straightforward: both parties want to ensure that there are no nasty surprises coming up, for example the project falling behind or new requirements needing to be introduced. The two project managers work very closely together.

In order for project managers to plan out the project successfully, they need to understand how well their teams work and what skills they have. It is normal for different members of staff to have different sets of skills and to be able to tackle certain problems or tasks at different rates. It is the project manager's job to ensure that they know as much as possible about their team. It is also important that they can produce realistic estimates for different tasks. That way, they can monitor the project and flag up any areas of concern quickly, before they become major issues.

Systems analysts

The role of the systems analyst is simple: to find out exactly what the customer wants. This is not as straightforward as it sounds. For a start, most customers are not sure exactly what they want at the start of the project, but have just a vague idea. As a result, analysts have to use their own experience and expertise to fill in the blanks that occur along the way. They are responsible for conducting fact finding and producing the requirements specification (more on this later) and they also suggest possible implementation methods for the proposed project. They monitor the project, along with the project manager, offering expert knowledge on the system to be built. The systems analyst is the first port of call for programmers if they have a problem with or a query on the requirements specification.

Problem definition

The problem definition phase documents the process of identifying what problems exist in a user's current system or defining what problems a new system could solve. A customer will identify, or have identified for them, either problems with their existing system or software to help them to expand their company, for example producing a mobile app. At this point, very little will be known about the system, other than that there is a perceived need for it. The development company will be called in to have an initial meeting. In this meeting it is critical for both the customer and the development company to discuss fully what is required, so that the customer is reassured that the development company can deliver what they require and the development company can decide whether they want to take the project on. It is common for customers to have an unrealistic view on what is required for the new system, so both parties must agree on the scope of the project at this stage. Unbounded projects are guaranteed to fail, as there is no way to differentiate what the customer required at the start and what they require six months down the line. Sometimes, when requirements are fluid, the development company may choose a methodology that allows them to change requirements quickly, such as Agile development.

It is important to remember that the analyst is a computer expert, but is not necessarily an expert in the customer's business; on the other hand, the customer is an expert in their own business, but not necessarily an expert in computers. This is why they must work together to pool information to ensure that the correct problems are solved in the correct way.

Feasibility study

A feasibility study establishes whether or not the project can be done, given the scope laid out during the problem definition phase. Also, it considers whether it is desirable for the developing company to proceed with the project. When embarking on a software project there must be confidence on both sides that the project can be delivered on time and within budget. If this is not the case, the customer may choose a different supplier or may become dissatisfied with the work and the development company could get a poor reputation as a result. In essence, if a project fails to meet the time and financial restrictions, it has failed. Even if a good working product is produced, when a project goes over budget people tend to focus on this fact. From the development company's point of view, if a project is unlikely to bring in much profit or might bring negative attention to their company, they may decide not to proceed.

When deciding on how feasible a new system will be, a number of factors must be considered. These are discussed below.

Economic feasibility

A project has a specific budget, which must include all the costs of the project, including:

- software licences
- hardware
- human resources/wages
- the development company's running costs.

Remember that profit is also an important consideration.

The hardware and software costs are fairly straightforward and are unlikely to change over the course of the project. Human costs are the most variable and account for the majority of the budget. Staffing costs are based on the number of people on the project, the amount they earn and the length of the project. This cost can vary considerably; for example, what happens if someone gets a pay rise or someone leaves and you have to get someone more expensive or a contractor? What happens if the project is delayed? It is important, therefore, to know up front which staff you will need and to have a good idea of the length of the project. It is also important to build in some flexibility, based on a risk assessment. Profit is also very important for a project; the development company will want to make a profit, not just enough to cover their costs. Economic feasibility considers the overall budget and the overall costs. It then decides if enough profit can be made to make the project worth doing. If the development company make a loss or just breaks even, it would not really be worthwhile taking the project on. Some development companies, if work is scarce, may take a project at cost or even at a slight loss.

Time feasibility

Late projects result in going over budget because of the cost of developers' wages. It is critically important that projects are delivered on time, as the developing company will make a negative impression if they cannot deliver when they said they could. Sometimes it is even more critical, as the customer could well have very pressing business reasons for a project to be delivered by a certain date. Failure to meet the deadline could lead to litigation.

In order to decide on how long a project will take, the project manager will have to estimate how long their developers will take to do the project. This requires a balancing act based on the cost, skill level and number of staff to bring onto the project.

Once the estimated length has been worked out, based on prior performance of the programming team, it is compared with the customer's deadline. If it can be done in the given time frame, the project can go ahead.

Technical feasibility

Can the project be done with the technical resources available? Some things are not possible or feasible with current technology. For example, accurate speech recognition is not reliable, nor is being able to do facial recognition in dark environments. This means that projects that have these requirements are not technically feasible. However, what is more likely to cause problems is if the development team does not have the technical skills needed to satisfy the requirements. For example, if you need an expert in SQL for the project, but do not have this resource, the project is either not possible or it will cost extra to buy in the expertise.

Every developer, when they join the company, fills in a skills audit to show what technologies they can work with. The project manager looks through this list when deciding whom to take onto the project. Therefore, if there is no one with the correct skill set available (or if they are already assigned to another project), the project cannot go ahead. Developers update their skills audit as they acquire new skills.

Political feasibility

Projects can sometimes have aspects that are politically sensitive or go against the beliefs of certain groups of people. Systems such as the NHS, tax credits, Olympic computer systems and animal testing come under the direct scrutiny of the general public and media. When these projects go wrong, the media will undoubtedly report on it and show the development company in a negative light. The development company needs to decide whether the potential positives outweigh the possible negative publicity.

Legal feasibility

Legal feasibility helps decide whether the project will be able to comply with all the laws that may affect it in the countries where it will be released. File sharing software, although legal in essence, has fallen foul of the law; companies producing or facilitating it have been sued. Napster, one of the first and most popular, was shut down for a long time as the courts decided that the company could do more to protect copyright. It then released a paid service, but it did not do very well as the company had already lost most of its user base to competitors. Legal feasibility needs to be taken very seriously as the effects can be very damaging for both the customer and the development company. Fines running into millions can be imposed if the software does not comply with the law. Also, some countries might ban the use of the software completely and could even pursue criminal action.

Analysis

Analysis is the process of finding out exactly what the system will entail by employing various fact finding methods. It is critically important that the result of the analysis is as complete as it can be, as incorrectly defined requirements can lead to big delays and escalating costs. At the end of analysis, the requirements specification is produced. This is a document that contains the exact requirements of the new system. The four main fact-finding methods used during analysis are:

- observation
- questionnaire
- document collecting
- interview.

These methods are not meant to be used on their own, but as a collective entity. It is impossible to gather a complete picture of the system by using only one method or talking to only one person. The key to success is to try to understand the business problem from the point of view of the company as a whole, rather than from an individual perspective.

Observation

Observation is where the analyst shadows employees of the customer for a period of time, making notes on how they do their job. They observe employees in their natural environment to see exactly how the business works. One of the biggest advantages of this method is that the analyst sees parts of the system that employees may not realise are important or consider important enough to discuss. Sometimes, some things that we do, especially when they are done every day, are so natural that we fail to notice them. An outsider notices these common actions and can include them in the new system, even if they were not part of the original problem definition.

Advantages	Disadvantages
Pick up parts of the system that are not immediately obvious to the customer.	Some people may feel threatened while being watched.
Confirm information gathered through different fact-finding methods.	There is no guarantee that some of the more subtle parts of the system will show up during the observation period.

Table 5.1: Advantages and disadvantages of the observation fact finding method.

Questionnaire

Questionnaires are quite a common method of fact finding, but can also be one of the most difficult. Designing a questionnaire requires knowledge of the system to be built and the range of people to whom the questionnaire can be sent. This prior knowledge is essential so that the questions can be targeted. It is also important to restrict the number of choices available for each question, as some people may give unexpected responses. This means that questionnaires can give only limited information about very specific parts of the system.

Using questionnaires can allow the analyst to get a lot of responses on a specific subset of requirements. As a questionnaire can be given to a lot of people, you will most likely get back a range of responses. For example, consider the idea that employees should use a touch-screen system or swipe card to gain entry to a secure area. This could be set up as a question and the analyst could then see what the users' responses would be. The analyst could then make the appropriate decision, backing it up with hard evidence.

Advantages	Disadvantages
Can be given to a large number of people at once.	Hard to create and design.
Can get a large number of different opinions.	Not all questionnaires sent out will be completed.

Table 5.2: Advantages and disadvantages of the questionnaire fact finding method.

Document collection

During document collection the analyst gathers any business documents that relate to the new system to be constructed. These include orders, invoices, financial records and any other document that is in use on a day-to-day basis. Documents in use in the current system are a good guide to what is required in the new system. Some key elements which could be inferred from analysis of existing documents are:

- The data they use and what will need to be stored by the new system.
- The analyst can get a very good understanding of the business process by following the trail of documents and seeing the flow of data from start to finish.

One advantage of document collecting is that documents cannot lie, distort or misrepresent information. This means that the information found in them can be trusted, unless someone has purposely gone out of their way to doctor the documents. Of course, they do not give a complete picture, but they do help support whatever picture the analyst has already built up. They also help the analyst build up a data dictionary. However, it is not always obvious how, why or when a document is created. This means that more information is required, which can provide new avenues of investigation for the other fact-finding methods.

Advantages	Disadvantages
Documents are reliable and show most of the data stored in the system.	Documents give a limited view of the system and do not say how they were created.
Document trails help support the analyst's picture of business processes.	Documents may contain sensitive information and there may be restrictions on seeing them.

Table 5.3: Advantages and disadvantages of the document collecting fact finding method.

Interview

Interviewing is normally where most analysts start, and they will pick some key stakeholders of the project (on the customer's side) and ask them targeted questions about the current and new system. A lot of information can be gathered in a very short space of time using this method. However, it is difficult to interview a large number of people because interviews are difficult to schedule and can be time consuming.

Human nature plays a major role in interviews as well, as not everyone is good at being interviewed and some people may be nervous or even mildly hostile to the analyst. They may also exaggerate what they do to try to impress the analyst or their superiors. Not everything they say can be trusted, so it must be verified by using other fact-finding methods.

Advantages	Disadvantages
Large amounts of information can be gathered and the analyst can respond to the person to query their responses.	Time consuming, so only a limited number of people can be interviewed.
Interviews produce detailed responses about key parts of the system.	Interviewees may not be fully truthful, so their responses need to be verified.

Table 5.4: Advantages and disadvantages of the interview fact finding method.

Requirements

A requirement is a specific feature of the new system and is recorded in a document called a requirements specification. Requirements can be broken down into the following key sections:

- Interface requirements
- Functional requirements
- Performance requirements

A very important point to make here is that a requirement must be measurable. That is, we must be able to say, without any doubt, that the requirement has been met or not met at the end of the project. This is important contractually so that the development company can be paid, but also to help keep the scope of the project. An ambiguous requirement could be interpreted by different stakeholders in different ways, which invariably leads to problems and potentially to conflict.

Interface requirements

The interface of a system is where the end-user interacts with it, whether by pushing a button or entering some data or viewing a report. In most cases, the interface of computer systems is mainly driven by software. However, many new systems also include a hardware interface. Consider a game such as Guitar Hero. The game comes with a software element, namely the game itself, and a hardware element, which is the custom controller. In this case, the interface requirements must take both the software and hardware interfaces into consideration.

Interface requirements depend on the end user and also the complexity of the new system. As such, it is imperative that detailed analysis has already been carried out on what the user may require. A common mistake is to confuse interface requirements with interface design. At this stage the development company is not worried about what the interface will look like or how the user will interact with it. The decision to have three or five buttons on the guitar is not important at this point. What we are interested in is the standard to which the interface must conform in order to be considered suitable by the end user. So Guitar Hero's interface requirements would be, for example, 'the hardware must be durable, with large accessible buttons suitable for use by people with less manual dexterity' or 'the software interface must be immediately accessible by a beginner gamer'.

Functional requirements

Functional requirements detail what the system will do and what key features it will have. An example of a functional requirement for Guitar Hero would be the scoring and combination mechanisms. Looking at a more work-based scenario, Microsoft Word® could be considered. Some of the functional requirements would be auto correction, word count, spell check and many of the other features. The requirements dictate what the features should do, not what they should look like. In fact, it is very common for features described to have no possible user interface. What the functional requirements focus on is simply what they need to achieve in order to be considered successful.

Performance requirements

Performance requirements cover such things as response times and throughput. They have to be specific, for example, 'the user interface must respond to a request from the user in a bounded time of x seconds'. Bounded, in this context, means a reasonable maximum time agreed by both the customer and the development company. An Adobe Photoshop performance requirement might be 'the user interface must respond in a reasonably bounded time no greater than 10 Ms'. The requirement is not 'everything will run fast', because a lot of what the system does is mathematically very complicated. It is therefore meaningless to say that actions such as resizing a very large image will occur quickly. What if a user runs it on a slower PC? Should it be required always to run at the same speed? Clearly that is unrealistic.

Performance is very important in a system, but the requirements set out must be clear, realistic and measurable. Failure to implement this could lead to differing opinions between the customer and the development company.

Requirements specification

Once information has been gathered, it is time to place all of the accrued knowledge into a single document, known as the requirements specification. This document then provides not only the basis for design, but also a fundamental reference for all of the other phases, most notably the evaluation phase.

In order to ensure that the requirements specification is correct, it is essential to follow a template. This template may vary from company to company and from methodology to methodology. Below is a sample template, adapted from the IEEE standard 830-1998:

- Introduction
- Purpose
- Scope
- Definitions and abbreviations
- References
- Overview
- Overall description
- Product perspective

- Product functions
- User characteristics
- Constraints
- Assumptions and dependences
- Specific requirements
- Interface requirements
- Functional requirements
- Performance requirements

Although, for the purpose of the course, it is not important to understand exactly how a requirements specification is written, it is useful to be aware of it. There are a number of key elements to the template that are necessary for understanding its purpose:

- *Purpose and scope*: Every project must have a scope. Putting it simply, if a project is unbounded, how will you know when you have finished? By stating exactly the expected outcomes and limitations of the new system, you can prevent misunderstandings over what the project can do. The purpose of the system is also crucial. If this is misunderstood by any of the stakeholders, there will be problems when it comes to sign-off.
- *Product functions and product perspective*: This describes where the system fits into the larger picture, or its role in the business.
- *User characteristics*: This is where the end user's experience of the system is documented. Remember that this is key when writing the user interface requirements. If you do not produce a system that is accessible by the end user, the system may not be used correctly and will ultimately fail.
- *Constraints*: These are the key boundaries and limitations to which the new system must adhere. They are related to the scope of the project and to the feasibility study.

Design

Design is the process of taking the requirements of a new system and deciding what the system will look like, how it will store data and how it will process that data. Design can only go ahead once the requirements specification has been completed. Each requirement then needs to be incorporated into the design. The design includes a number of areas:

- hardware and software choices
- data structure design
- input design
- output design.

Input

This is also known as the interface design (Figure 5.3). Interface design shows how information will be input into the new system and also how it will be displayed after processing. It does not describe how that information will be processed, nor does it look at the functional requirements other than to show interaction.

Output

Output design is carried out in a very similar way to input design. The first thing to think about is what triggers the output. Normally, an output design is triggered by something the user has done on an input screen. Figure 5.4 shows a simple example.

Figure 5.3: An input interface design.

Example GUI input design

Figure 5.4: Output example.

In this example an invoice output is triggered when a new order has been entered into the system. Triggers may include entering new data into the system, clicking on specific buttons or even the completion of a scheduled batch process. There are no hard and fast rules on what designates an output trigger, but there must always be one for every output designed. If a trigger cannot be identified, that output will never be seen.

Data structure design

Data structure design is fundamental to how a system will work. It dictates what data needs to be stored and how that data will be organised. This then has a direct impact on how the rest of the system will work. It is almost impossible to produce an input or output design without knowing exactly what data will be stored. The data structure design process tends to start with listing all the data that is required. This information will have already been gathered during analysis and placed into a data dictionary. A data dictionary stores every item of data, the size of that data, the type of the data and a comment to explain what that data means. Table 5.5 is an example:

Name of field	Data type	Data size	Description
Surname	Text	20 characters	The surname of a client
Forename	Text	15 characters	The forename of the client
DVD name	Text	30 characters	The full name of a DVD
DVD owner	Text	20 characters	The name of the client who owns the DVD

Table 5.5: Example data structure design.

Once the data dictionary is completed, decisions are made on how the data will be saved. This could be in a file or, in the case of a larger-scale system, an SQL database. If a database is used, normalisation must be carried out (see Chapter 14).

Analysing the problem using abstraction and decomposition

When tackling difficult problems computational methods can help make the problem easier to solve. In this section we will look at two of the most important methods, abstraction and decomposition.

Abstraction

When a solution is presented for a given computing problem, we say that we have a concrete solution for that problem. However, sometimes our solutions can be generalised so that they can provide part of the solution to other problems. For example, if I produced code that emails people who passed an online computing test, then it makes sense that the same code could be adapted to work with other tests. **Abstraction** is the process of separating concrete instances of a solution from the ideas that were used to solve them. For example, queues are used to store print jobs in a print manager as well as being used to determine the next process to run when using round robin scheduling. They both use the abstract idea of a queue.

When dealing with an abstract idea, the meaning behind the idea must be separated from the details of how it will work or be implemented. Abstraction for computer science can be split into two main parts:

- **Control abstraction** hides actions and programming control, such as if statements. The basic premise behind high-level programming languages is control abstraction – hiding the details of machine code from the developer.
- **Data abstraction** hides how bits are organised for primitive data types such as floating point or dates.

Abstract data types such as stacks and queues (not to be confused with primitive data types) are an example of abstraction. Only the operations performed on them and any constraints on the data type are defined. For example, a stack would define what push and pop do (see Chapter 1) while an ordered set would define that items must be held in a logical order.

One of the most important skills to cultivate for a developer is the ability to think in abstract terms. This allows you to consider the ideas behind an algorithm or a system without getting bogged down with the implementation details. When abstracting, it is possible to generalise in layers. Each layer will hide more of the key implementation details than the last.

Example: Abstraction layers

Abstraction is about generalizing the idea of how to solve a problem away from any specific implementation detail. Abstractions can be combined into multiple layers enabling more and more of the concrete implementation to be generalised.

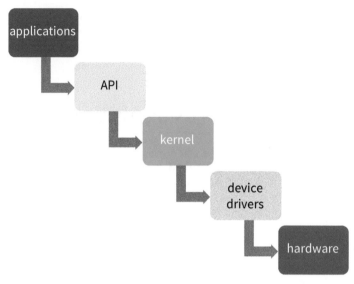

Figure 5.5: Abstraction layers for a typical operating system.

Figure 5.5 represents an example of abstraction layering for operating systems. Consider a simple application that opens a file and saves some text to it (see code below). The first abstraction is the idea of opening, writing and closing a file. The program makes use of some built-in Python functions. The details of how `'open'`, `'write'` and `'close'` work are hidden or abstracted, because the developer is not interested in how Python will perform these actions. The problem for the developer is not how to write a series of bits to the hard drive, but rather that the text "hello world" must be saved.

```
f = open("test.txt","w")
f.write("hello world")
f.close()
```

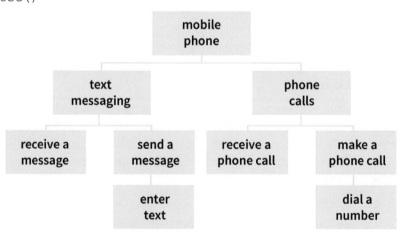

Figure 5.6: A simple stepwise refinement diagram.

Figure 5.6 is very simplistic but it illustrates the process of identifying the main components of a problem. Each box represents a different component and it is easy to imagine how each component could be coded as a separate procedure, for example, send_message(). Notice that components can contain other components which we call **sub-procedures**.

Once you have identified the component parts of a problem, the next step is to identify how you will structure your solution. The diagram that illustrates the components of the solution will probably be very similar to the one that identified the components of the problem. In many cases it will just be a case of creating a procedure to carry out each component of the problem.

Tip

If you are asked to break a given problem into its component parts, a good place to begin is by underlining the keywords in the question. The same mark scheme will be applied to every student taking the exam so the markers will want all the answers to be as similar as possible. As a result most of the components you'll be expected to list in your answer will probably be alluded to in the question.

As you have already seen, many components of a problem will be made up of other components. Just as many procedures can be combined to provide the solution to a larger problem, many sub-procedures can be combined to provide the solution of a larger, more complex procedure. It is not unusual to have a procedure that consists almost entirely of calls to smaller sub-procedures.

Large systems may be broken down into modules, which will comprise of multiple functions or classes. These then would be broken down further until we are left with modules that are small enough to define and implement easily. Most of the time, in an OO system, that would mean the point where you are producing a single class.

Representing systems in diagrammatic form

When representing systems in diagrammatic form you can use flowcharts, data flow diagrams or entity relationship diagrams (Figure 5.7). Each one can be used for different purposes and commonly they are combined to give a full overview of the systems.

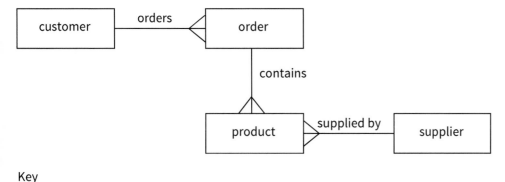

Key

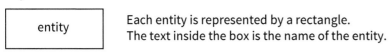

Each entity is represented by a rectangle.
The text inside the box is the name of the entity.

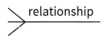

A relationship is shown as a line. The crows feet represents the cardinality of many. As such it is read one-to-many from the single point to the crows feet. The text is a description of the relationship.

Figure 5.7: Entity relationship diagram.

Entity relationship diagrams

Once the entities are known it is important to show how they will relate to one another. There are three main relationships:

- one-to-one
- one-to-many (see Figure 5.8)
- many-to-many.

Many-to-many links cannot exist and must be removed during normalisation. Once the entities are decided, and all many-to-many links are removed, then the task of drawing the diagram occurs. Consider the following tables.

Customer(CustomerID, Name)

Order(CustomerID, OrderNumber, ProductID)

Product(ProductID, Product, SupplierID)

Supplier(SupplierID, Supplier)

Customers can make more than one order. Each order can contain multiple products and finally each supplier can supply multiple products.

Entity relationship diagrams or ERDs provide a quick reference point for creation of a database. Also they provide an excellent way of working out which entities will be involved in a query. Most queries will span across multiple entities and as such we need to give careful thought to them.

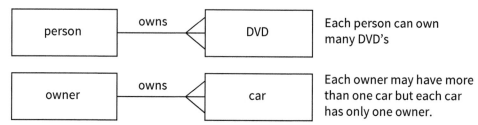

Each person can own many DVD's

Each owner may have more than one car but each car has only one owner.

Figure 5.8: One to many relationship in an entity relationship diagram.

Flow charts

Flowcharts are used in two ways. The first is to show the overall flow of the system, known as a system flowchart, and representing an algorithm. For more detail on the symbols used for flowcharts and how algorithms can be represented as a flowchart, see Chapter 3.

Systems flowcharts show the relationship between components and how data flows between them. The goal is to gain an overview of how data will pass through the system rather than looking at specific individual algorithms.

Data flow diagrams

Data flow diagrams, or DFDs, show how a system will process information. Two advantages DFDs have over flow charts are:

- FDs can be broken down into multiple levels
- they show the distinction of internal and external parts of the system.

There are three main symbols on a DFD (Figure 5.9):

External entities represent anything from outside the system to be modelled. This tends to be some form of human input but could be anything such as a sensor or another separate system. Sometimes other external entities need to be involved in a data flow and these should be represented on the diagram, such as letting the warehouse staff know that a new order has been made (Figure 5.10).

external entity

internal process

data store

Figure 5.9: The three main symbols on a DFD.

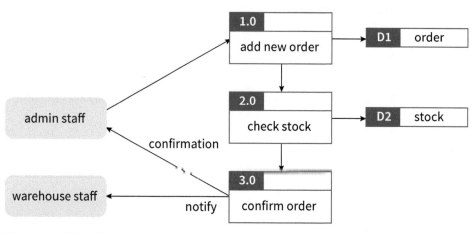

Figure 5.10: DFD with two external entities.

Internal process is where something is done with the input given. Add new order, for example (Figure 5.11), will save the order to the database as well as possibly validating the input. All processing that occurs will happen in an internal process.

A data store represents the database or anything else in which we can store data, such as a file.

It is common on DFDs to put return arrows only if data (other than confirmation that the transaction was successful) needs to be returned. The flow of data is shown via arrows. You can add a label to the arrow if you wish (Figure 5.10) to express something such as the type or nature of the data to flow. If the flow is obvious then it is better to leave it blank so that the diagram does not become cluttered.

The numbering system is very important and allows two things:

1   different levels of DFDs to be used
2   reference to the diagram if notes are going to be made.

Internal processes can be split into multiple levels that allow extra detail to be looked at. Consider the process of adding a new order. Looking at the validation could split this down.

Figure 5.11: An internal process.

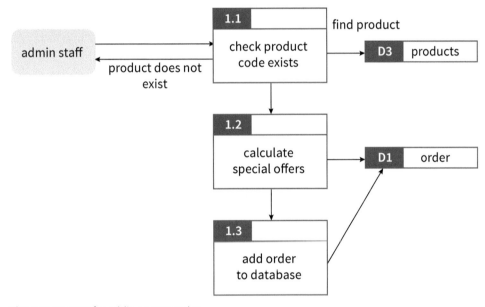

Figure 5.12: DFD for adding a new order.

Figure 5.12 shows that the add order process actually involves a number of steps, including an error response if an invalid product has been chosen. A new data source, products, has been added, which could have been overlooked if the process had not been broken down. The numbering is very important here. Each process starts with the number 1.x to show it is the breakdown of process 1. We call this a level 1 diagram. The original diagram is called a level 0 diagram. If we decided more detail was required for process 1.2 (Calculate special offers) then we would draw a level 2 diagram. The processes would then be numbered 1.2.1, 1.2.2, 1.2.3 and so on.

Building the system

Development is the planning, writing and testing of the software, and the creation and testing of any hardware required. It also includes the writing of the user documentation (see later in this chapter). It is usually the longest part of the process of creating new applications.

Approaches to software development are described later in this chapter.

Testing

Untested or poorly tested code tends to result in unstable applications and wrong output, leading to dissatisfied customers and users. Most developers find it very difficult to find bugs in their own programs, not because of the complexity of testing, but because they make subconscious assumptions and use their software in the way they assume others will. Other people may take a very different approach to using the software, which can result in them finding bugs or problems that the developer did not. This is why developers pass their code on to another person to test. There are a number of testing strategies that can be used and it is common to use more than one to test software. The better tested software is, the more robust it will be. Problems found later on in the systems analysis cycle are harder and more expensive to fix.

White box testing and unit tests

White box or glass box testing is where the structure of the code is being tested, and requires knowledge of how the code was developed. Every time you have a control statement, such as IF, you effectively create a new path through the system. Each path must be tested in order to be sure that the code will run as expected. These sorts of tests tend to be carried out by the developer, as they understand the code. They know what sort of values should trigger a certain path through the code. Consider the example shown in Figure 5.13.

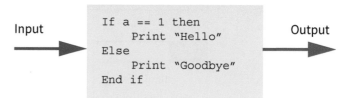

Two possible paths through this code

Figure 5.13: Example code with IF statement for white box testing.

There are two possible paths through the code: 'a equals one' and 'a does not equal one'. In order to check the code, the programmer needs to run two tests.

Programmers normally create some unit tests to ensure that the code they have written is working as expected. Unit tests run the code to be tested with various sets of input, usually using an automated script that can be run on a regular basis.

As most code within a large system is coupled with other parts of the code, it is entirely plausible that changes made by one developer can impact code written by another. Unit tests allow us to do fast regression testing (picking up bugs downstream) of existing code.

Unit tests are written by the developer under the guidance of the **methodology** being employed on the project. As a minimum, unit tests should use valid, invalid and extreme values to ensure that the code can cope.

Here is a simple function written in Python:

```
def findMaxNumber (listToCheck):
  max = listToCheck[0]
  for v in listToCheck:
    if v > max:
      max = v
  return max
print findMaxNumber ([5,1,9,5,3,10,14,3])
```

This is a simple test using a single set of values for the function 'findMaxNumber', but running the test will not guarantee that the code is correct for all values.

Below is a sample unit test for the function 'findMaxNumber'.

```python
import random
import unittest
def findMaxNumber(listToCheck):
  max = listToCheck[0]
  for v in listToCheck:
    if v > max:
      max = v
  return max
print findMaxNumber([5,1,9,5,2,10,14,3])


class findMaxUnitTest(unittest.TestCase):
  def setUp(self):
    print "set up unit test for findMaxNumber"

  def test_normalValue(self):
    # generate a list of numbers
    l = []
    for a in range(1,100):
    l.append(random.randint(1,100))
    # add the value 101 in the middle
    l.insert(50,101)
    # run test
    self.assertEqual(findMaxNumber(l),101)

  def test_invalid(self):
    l=["a", 13, "b"]
    # this should raise a type error
    self.assertRaises(TypeError, findMaxNumber,l)

  def test_empty(self):
    l=[]
    self.assertEqual(findMaxNumber(l), False)

suite = unittest.TestLoader().
loadTestsFromTestCase(findMaxUnitTest)
unittest.TextTestRunner(verbosity=2).run(suite)
```

Two of the tests failed to produce the required output. One caused a runtime exception, which was not expected, and the other failed to work as expected. Unit tests are a great way for the developer to do alpha testing in a systematic way and continue to test their code throughout the lifetime of the project. Unit tests will be run as part of automated quality assurance for the code to ensure that by changing one part of the system, other parts will not break. Ideally this would happen as often as possible, but that would be dependent on the complexity of the system, the number of tests to perform and the speed at which the tests run.

Unit tests are defined differently depending on the language chosen, but they normally make use of object-oriented programming (see Chapter 4). Most of the unit testing framework is based on inheriting the testing features of a base class, in Python's case the class 'TestCase'. Each test is allowed to set up data by overriding the 'setUp' method and tear down data by overriding the 'tearDown' method. Each test is defined by adding the text 'test_' in front of the method name.

Figure 5.14 shows the corrected code, which will pass the unit tests defined above:

```
def findMaxNumber(listToCheck):
    if len(listToCheck) ==0:
            return False
    max = listToCheck[0]
    for v in listToCheck:
        if not isinstance (v,int):
            raise TypeError("test")
        if v > max:
            max = v

    return max
```

```
test_empty (__main__.findMaxUnitTest) ... set up unit test for findMaxNumber
ok
test_invalid (__main__.findMaxUnitTest) ... set up unit test for findMaxNumber
ok
test_normalValue (__main__.findMaxUnitTest) ... set up unit test for findMaxNumb
er
ok

----------------------------------------------------------------------
Ran 3 tests in 0.000s

OK
```

Figure 5.14: Corrected code.

Black box testing

In black box testing (Figure 5.15), we do not have knowledge of the code and are testing the functionality of the program based on the requirements specification. We take valid, invalid and extreme input data and compare the output to what we expect should happen, based on the design and requirements specification. If the output is correct, the test will pass. We are not interested in which paths were followed to get to the result; what we are interested in is whether the code does what it is supposed to.

Figure 5.15: Black box testing diagram.

Black box testing is commonly done by people who are not directly involved in development and is carried out in a very systematic manner. For example, it is not acceptable just to play around with the software to see if it works. Testers use a test script, which enables them to test every element of the system and allows tests to be reproduced. Should a test fail, the developer will need to be able to reproduce the bug in order to fix it.

Alpha and beta testing

Testing is carried out in phases and by different people. The two most obvious phases are alpha and beta. These terms relate to alpha and beta builds of the software. Alpha builds tend not to be stable and may lack functionality or even not work in all circumstances. It is important that an alpha build is not given to the customer or users, as they may feel that this is the level of quality they will get once the system is complete. Alpha tests are always carried out by the developer or by their in-house testing team.

Beta builds are more complete and are created later in the development cycle. They should be more stable than alpha builds, since all of the main functionality has been already tested, but may contain bugs and problems. Beta builds are stable enough to give to the customer for beta testing. The customer carries out beta testing as if they were using the code in a live situation. All faults found are, of course, returned to the development team for correcting.

End user testing

End user testing is the last testing phase, and it occurs before the customer agrees to pay for the final system. The end user tests the system using real data. The goal of end user testing is for the customer to ensure that what the developer has produced meets the requirements specification and for the developer to prove that they have met the requirements so that they can be paid.

Documentation

During the life of the project a lot of documentation is produced. This includes the design documents, diagrams and the requirements specification. However, this is all internal documentation and is mainly of interest to the development company.

The focus of this phase in the development cycle is documentation for the customer and end user. Technical authors write user documentation, working alongside the developers and using the same design documents, chiefly the requirements specification. Writing good documentation is not easy, and this phase needs to happen in parallel with software development to ensure that it is completed at the same time. The documentation needs to be planned, designed and tested, and there are normally at least two rounds of commenting before final versions are ready.

User documentation

Every application system has a user interface, which enables the end user to interact with the system. The user will, in most circumstances, require training in order to use the system. So there may well be a training course, with an accompanying manual. In addition, there should be a full set of documentation for use after the training is completed. It will also be used for users who start to use the system sometime after its initial launch.

User documentation should be very carefully targeted towards the readers and their needs. There needs to be material suitable for the novice user (straightforward and avoiding technical terms). The user should be able to find out how to perform any task by consulting this document.

The user documentation could include some or all of the following, depending on the type of application system:

- step-by-step 'getting started' guides or tutorials for the main features of the system
- installation guide
- user guide focusing on user tasks
- reference manual
- online help, at the level of both individual controls, such as input fields, and at the task level
- error messages and trouble-shooting guide
- frequently asked questions (FAQs) detailing common questions and problems
- glossary.

Technical/maintenance documentation

If the new system is a bespoke product for a company, rather than an off-the-shelf product such as a database, there needs to be at least one person in the company who can ensure that it runs smoothly once it has been implemented. That person is normally ICT literate and has a good understanding of technical ideas and concepts. Their role is to ensure that the system is set up and configured correctly, and to ensure the smooth day-to-day running of the system. It is not likely to be someone who was involved in developing the system, but may have been involved during analysis.

To help technicians use the system, they have technical documentation produced by the developer. They need to know how the database was set up, how the system can be configured and what hardware is required to install the system. They also need access to the design documents and code so that they can get a deeper understanding of the system. Technical documentation includes:

- Any form of diagrams used in analysis and design.
- The data structure – What data structures have been used, database table designs and any other information about what data needs to be stored.
- Algorithm designs – Algorithms will normally be presented in Pseudocode or flowchart form.
- Annotated code listings – Code listings that abide by the coding standards set out by the development company. Normally self-documenting and/or annotated.
- Variable lists – Lists of the key variables listing their data types and purpose. More temporary variables, such as loop counters, would not be included.
- Data dictionary – This will describe all of the fields that need to be stored in the data structure including data type, size, relationship with other tables and a description.
- Design documents – Any relevant documentation from the design phase.
- Hardware and software requirements.
- Configuration guide and options – How the system can be configured, which could be through a menu system or by editing configuration files.

Implementation

Implementation (for bespoke systems) is the process of installing the new system at the client site and putting it into use. It occurs after the software and documentation have been produced by the development team. If the new system is a bespoke product for a company, implementation is carefully managed. It normally includes both hardware and software components.

There are a number of ways to manage the implementation of a new system and four of them are discussed below.

Direct Changeover

Direct changeover, also called the 'Big Bang' changeover, is the simplest option, but can be very dangerous and should only be used if there is no old system or if the old system is broken or unworkable; for example, releasing a mobile app where one did not exist before.

New systems invariably have problems, for example, bugs, lack of training or lack of understanding of the new system. Just swapping over to the system straightaway could mean a loss in productivity or, worse, if the new system fails completely, a complete shutdown of the business. Even though the system will have been tested, there is no guarantee that it will work as expected when using live data.

Phased Changeover

Big projects are normally split into many smaller chunks, known as modules. This is a natural part of systems analysis and forms the basis for implementation. This type of implementation works best with certain methodologies, such as rapid application design. Initially, only part of the new system is used, the rest still being based on the old system. As such, if there are problems with the first implemented component, the remainder can be delayed and the old system used until the problems are cleared. This does mean that the old and new systems must be able to work together, which is not always possible. If they are completely incompatible with one another, a phased approach cannot work.

The phased approach works best when a small company is upgrading an existing system or implementing a brand-new system. It is not suitable for companies with many different premises.

Pilot Changeover

Companies, especially larger ones, tend to have more than one business site. For example, Sainsbury's has literally hundreds of shops all across the country. Each one is likely to be doing a very similar, if not identical, job to the other shops. This is the perfect environment for a pilot changeover. In a pilot, just a small number of shops run the new system while the rest rely on the old one. That way, if the system is faulty or if there are problems, only a few shops will be affected. This is an ideal model for any business that has many similar branches. It is not suitable for companies spread across many sites, with each one doing something different, or for companies with only a small number of sites.

Parallel Changeover

If you cannot afford for the system to fail at any time, parallel changeover is usually the best method to use. In parallel changeover, the old and new systems are run at the same time, causing duplication of all tasks, while the new system is checked to ensure consistency. Thus, if one fails, there is a backup to take over immediately. This does mean that the employees will be doing double the amount of work. For every order that arrives, they need to enter and process it through two systems. This can become very tiresome and very inefficient, so it is highly undesirable to do this for too long. Parallel changeover is the safest type, but also requires the most work. It is best reserved for critical systems such as those used by banks, where the loss of even a single transaction could be catastrophic.

Maintenance

After implementation, a system is formally handed over to the customer, and then enters the maintenance phase. There are two aspects to maintenance covering two main ideas: fixing problems and adding new functionality.

The customer, at this stage, normally expects one of the following maintenance arrangements for bug fixes:

- The developing company will fix any problems for a period of time after the product has been released (a bit like a warranty for software). This will take the form of a rolling maintenance contract or an upfront payment.
- The developer will charge for every fix that is produced for the software rather than pay a maintenance contract. This can be thought of as a 'pay as you go' scheme.

Where new functionality is concerned, the customer normally expects the development company to provide updates, either free or paid.

Maintenance is rarely free. It is almost always paid for, even if the price is included in the original bid. The reason for this is that maintenance is very expensive for developers and requires a team of people working to support a product. We already know that problems found later on in the systems analysis cycle are harder and more expensive to fix. Clearly, all bugs found during maintenance have the potential to be costly to fix.

Because maintenance is so expensive, it is critical that it is well defined for both the customer and the developer. Problems and bugs can cause the system not to operate as intended, and range from simple spelling mistakes to serious issues with incorrectly defined requirements. Bug fixes do not add any extra functionality but merely ensure that the system meets the original specification.

Extra functionality should never be added unless the updates have been commissioned and have gone through the full systems analysis cycle. This is to ensure that the original functionality is not broken and that the customer does not get any nasty surprises.

There are three approaches to providing maintenance: adaptive, corrective and perfective. The approach is normally agreed in the contract between the customer and development companies. Due to changing circumstances this may change over time.

Adaptive maintenance

In adaptive maintenance the development company fixes bugs and also adds extra functionality to the system. It is common for systems to come in multiple versions, for example, basic, standard and professional. Customers can implement the basic version first, since it is likely to be available first, then upgrade to a higher level of functionality later. This way they can get something up and running quickly in order to support their business. New features tend to be added based on external needs. For example, recently the law changed to make companies more accountable for cookies. Complying with this requires adaptive changes to any web-based system.

Corrective maintenance

Corrective maintenance simply fixes problems as they arise to ensure that the system closely matches the original specification. Normally the customer will take out a support contract that asks the developer to work on corrective maintenance. Their mandate will be clear. They are to fix problems, without breaking the system or adding functionality.

Perfective maintenance

A perfect system is one that completely matches the original specification with no problems at all. There should be a direct mapping from requirements to implementation. So perfective maintenance is maintenance performed with the aim of achieving a perfect system. In order to make the system perfect, it will be necessary to fix all problems. If new or changed requirements are identified and agreed, the development company must also provide upgrades to implement them.

There should always be a current scope for the product and a way of describing what the perfect system should be. Perfective maintenance is expensive and very time consuming. It should only be used on very small systems or on critical systems. Systems such as air traffic control or nuclear power facilities fall into the latter category. Perfective maintenance also requires that performance is improved when possible. A perfect system is only as perfect as the testing carried out on it. So although you may fix all the bugs you encounter, this does not mean there are no more bugs left in the system.

Evaluation

Evaluation is contractually very important as it allows the development company and the customer to decide whether the project was successful. Evaluation is important to the customer because they must be sure that what they are buying is exactly what was specified in the requirements specification. However, evaluation is also important to the development company as it will determine whether they will be paid. To reduce arguments and the chance of litigation, there are a number of specific criteria that need to be considered before the system is designated a success, namely requirements, performance, usability, robustness and cost:

- *Requirements*: Does it meet the functionality set out in the requirements specification? It must meet every requirement in order for the system to be considered a success. This is why each requirement laid out in the specification must be objective and measurable. If a requirement can be interpreted in more than one way, there is a chance for conflict.
- *Performance*: Does it respond in a timely manner for the user? This can be subjective, so performance criteria are normally put in place to ensure that there are fewer areas of conflict. Certain complicated processes will be given a time frame in which they must respond, or defined to have progress bars. For example, a search of a database should not take longer than 30 seconds.
- *Robustness*: There is nothing worse than software that crashes all the time or is bug ridden. Robustness is a fundamental requirement for all systems. The level of robustness depends on the type of software to some extent. For example, if a word processor crashes it is annoying, but not critical, as users should be saving their work regularly. If an air traffic control system fails, the effects could be devastating.
- *Cost*: Has the project come in on or under budget? Systems that cost more than expected are rarely seen as successful. Extra costs are normally carefully negotiated and might have to be absorbed by the development company.
- *Usability*: It is crucial that the software produced is usable by the end users. This is dependent on the skill level of the end user as well as the nature of the solution. For example, a mobile app would tend to be menu based and be aimed at the novice user. Software to support a network administrator, on the other hand, could be command line based.

Program development techniques

Before looking at some of the approaches available to project managers, it is worth familiarising yourself with some of the more common program development techniques. Just as many different approaches use the same stages from the systems analysis cycle, there are a few key development techniques that are also shared by most approaches.

Incremental development

In incremental development, the entire system is designed before being divided into separate modules or subsystems. These modules are then programmed one after the other (Figure 5.16), with each module being designed in detail, implemented and tested before being added to the existing release.

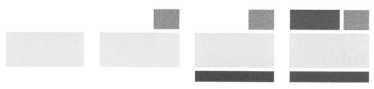

Figure 5.16: Incremental development example, showing how a sample program would be built under this approach.

This approach has a number of benefits. Software is generated quickly, so users get a chance to give feedback on the work so far. This in turn means that the development team can be more flexible and are better able to react to changing requirements, for example, the release of a new operating system. New functionality can easily be added to the existing product if the client decides they would like the software to do something extra. Development can also be carried out by specialists, and as modules can be created by different teams with different areas of expertise, they could even be written in different programming languages.

Incremental development also encourages very thorough testing, as each individual module is tested before its release using the methods described in this chapter, especially unit testing, meaning that the system is less likely to fail later on.

However, incremental development also has some inherent weaknesses. In order to be properly subdivided a problem must be well understood and the major requirements clearly defined, which isn't always possible at the start of a project. In addition, extensive integration testing needs to be carried out to ensure that the separate modules work well together, which requires very clearly defined programmatic interfaces.

Iterative development

Figure 5.17: Iterative development example, showing how a sample program would be built under this approach.

Iterative development models deliver a fully working system up front but then build on this functionality with every additional release (Figure 5.17). For example, Microsoft Word® has gone through many iterations since it was first released. Each release seeks to improve and extend the functionality of the last iteration.

Iterative development enables customers to experience the system from an early stage in development and to provide feedback on changes they would like to be made. The model also allows developers to spot problems early on and fix any bugs in the next iteration. Models based on iterative development work particularly well for large projects where the requirements are fully understood. However, projects can suffer if requirements are not substantively met by the initial release, as after this the focus is very much on refining existing functionality rather than adding new areas.

Prototyping

Figure 5.18: Prototyping development example, showing how a sample program would be built under this approach.

Prototyping seeks to combine the iterative and incremental development models by providing a cut-down version of the final product on which the client can give feedback. This initial prototype can then be improved or have extra functionality added to it in order to produce a next prototype. This cycle is repeated (iterated) until the client is happy with the final product (Figure 5.18).

Prototyping allows a system to be quickly built in order to demonstrate ideas and concepts to the customer. Used properly, prototyping can provide a high degree of flexibility and enable developers to react quickly to changing requirements. However, prototyping can also make projects difficult to manage, as there are few concrete deadlines and mission creep can set in, with developers constantly refining the product, adding less and less relevant functionality.

Backup

Backup is the process of copying files from main storage to a separate area. That way, if a file is deleted, the backup can be accessed in order to retrieve the lost file. Every organisation has a backup policy as it is very common for files to get deleted or lost. When creating a backup policy you need to decide:

- Where will the backup be stored?
- What will it be stored on?
- How often will the backup be taken?
- How long will a backup be kept?

When we backup our files at home we may use a memory stick or external hard drive. We may even use a CD or DVD to backup our files. A network will tend to use magnetic tapes or hard drives. The amount of data that needs to be backed up could range up to many terabytes (1TB = 1000 GB) which means that no DVD or single external hard drive could fit it all on. It certainly could not fit more than one version of the backup. It is common to have a server that is completely dedicated to backing up files.

A backup will take a long time and potentially it can take many hours to back up all of the files. In doing so it could slow down the network for a long time. This means that backups often occur at night when everyone has gone home so as not to adversely impact people's productivity.

The more often we run the backup the better. Unfortunately this means we need to have bigger and bigger capacity in order to do this. There is a trade off between how often we do a backup and how long we can keep the backup. Eventually we will need to delete old backups to make way for the new ones. It is common to have backups on the opposite side of the building in a fireproof box. This limits the chance of both the backup and the main server being destroyed by a fire. However, to keep it really safe it should be stored off site.

The biggest issue with this is the additional cost as well as the extra time it would take to make a full backup.

In order to keep the size of a backup small many organisations use an incremental backup policy, where only the files that have changed are backed up. The first backup will copy all files and then after that each subsequent backup will only copy over the files that have changed. This dramatically reduces the overhead of a backup and means that it can be done more often. For this to work there has to be a central network clock that all computers are synced to.

When restoring data the latest backup, which contains the file in question, would be accessed and restored. Restoring a file is simply the process of copying the file from the backup to wherever the file is needed. If it was an incremental backup then the process is slightly more complex as the changes to the file need to be amalgamated.

Chapter summary

- A stakeholder is anyone who has a vested interest in the development of a system. Common stakeholders include:
  - user
  - programmer
  - project manager
  - system analyst.
- Analysis of a computing system will include:
  - Problem definition: the current problems with the system will be investigated and initially agreed upon.
- Feasibility: an investigation to ensure that the project is feasible by checking the following factors:
  - Economic: Is there enough money to pay for the system?
  - Time: Can the project be done in the timescales allowed?
  - Technical: Is the technology and expertise needed to produce the system available?
  - Legal: Will the project comply with the laws of the countries it will be released in?
- Fact finding: gather information needed to accurately define the new system to be built, using the following methods:
  - observation
  - questionnaire
  - interview
  - collecting documentation.
- Requirements specification will be produced at the end of analysis.
- Design is based on the requirements specification and is broken down into input, output, processing and storage design.
- Testing is where the system is put through its paces to ensure that it has met the requirements and most of the bugs have been fixed.
- Part of the deliverables of a project include documentation:

- User documentation: a manual on using the system provided to the end user
- Technical documentation: information to allow the system to be maintained.
- When a project is implemented, one of the following methods is used:
    - direct
    - phased
    - pilot
    - parallel.
- Once the system has been deployed, it must be maintained through one of the following methods:
    - corrective
    - adaptive
    - perfective.
- When developing systems, different methodologies will be used to implement the systems lifecycle:
    - Program development techniques cover the various approaches to the design, writing and testing of programs. Some of the more common ones are:
    - Incremental development is where the entire system is broken down into modules which are designed, implemented and tested before being added to the final product.
    - Iterative development will provide a full system upfront but then build upon the functionality as time goes on.
    - Prototyping is where only a small number of features are implemented combining both incremental and iterative approaches.
    - Systems lifecycle methodologies are the different ways in which stages of the systems lifecycle can be combined and implemented:
    - The Waterfall model is a linear approach to the systems lifecycle where each phase is completed fully before moving on to the next.
    - Agile development is focused on producing software rather than documentation and places value on communication and collaboration. Team meetings are favoured over documentation.

End-of-chapter questions

1   Describe what happens during analysis and what document is produced at the end. [5]

2   Discuss how the Agile methodology can deal with changing requirements. [6]

3   Pick and justify which development methodology would be best suited for creating an app to support students choosing their GCSE options. [8]

4   In the Waterfall approach what is handed to the client at the end of each stage? [5]

5   When is it suitable to use the Waterfall approach? [2]

6   When is it not suitable to use the Waterfall approach? [2]

7   Agile development methodologies focus on what instead of the tons of documentation produced by the Waterfall approach? [1]

Further reading

Teach ICT system systems analysis	Search for The System Life Cycle at tech-ict.com
Manifesto for Agile programming	Go to agilemanifesto.org
Software development methodologies	Search for Software Development Methodologies at codeproject.com
Unit testing from extreme programming	Go to the unit tests within the rules section of extremeprogramming.org

Chapter 6
System design

A This chapter contains A Level content only

Learning objectives

- Discuss contemporary approaches to the problem of communication with computers.
- Describe the potential for a natural language interface.
- Describe the problems of ambiguity that can be associated with input that is spoken.
- Explain the need for a design review to: check the correspondence between a design and its specification; confirm that the most appropriate techniques have been used; confirm that the user interface is appropriate.
- Describe criteria for the evaluation of computer based solutions.

Introduction

This chapter focuses on how humans and computers interact and why this has become an important area of research. How we communicate with technology has changed dramatically in recent years. Some of the first human-computer interactions were only possible through switches, oscilloscopes and dot matrix printers.

Figure 6.1: The Nellie computer.

Nellie (Figure 6.1), a computer created in the late 1960s, was a computer owned by Forest Grammar School in Berkshire. Programs were loaded through punch cards or punch tape. Input was provided by flipping switches or using a keyboard. There was no visual display unit so output was provided in the form of printouts, or wave-forms on an oscilloscope. These interactions are summarised in the Figure 6.2.

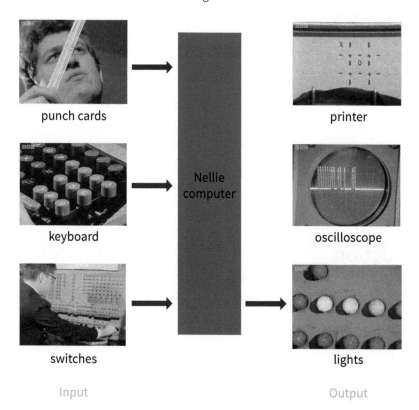

Figure 6.2: Diagram summarising the input and output of the Nellie computer.

Our interactions with technology are very different now to then. How we interact with computers is changing daily. Wearable technology, such as the Apple Watch or Microsoft Hololens are already available. The days of using a keyboard and mouse to interact with technology could be consigned to the history books.

Contemporary approaches to computer communication

Modern interaction between humans and computers is moving away from interfaces, such as keyboards and mice, to more tactile and intuitive methods. Some contemporary interfaces include the following:

- voice input
- touch screen
- force feedback
- virtual reality
- augmented reality.

Voice input

Using the human voice to control computing systems has been possible for some time. It started with simple fixed commands, as used with Microsoft Kinect. Using the Kinect, users could issue a small set of fixed instructions such as 'Xbox, pause'. The microphone on the Kinect would listen out for the trigger word 'Xbox' and then attempt to process the voice command after that. There are many more devices now which can be controlled using voice input, for example, a smartphone. The iPhone makes use of a system called Siri, Microsoft uses Cortana and Google uses Google Voice.

One of the key design goals for this software is to allow a greater use of spoken natural language. While the Kinect could only accept a small range of simple commands, Siri can respond to much more complicated instructions. You can ask Siri to set an alarm by saying 'set an alarm for 5 hours' time', for example. Siri then asks the user if they are sure and then sets the alarm. Both Google and Microsoft voice interfaces allow a similar set of instructions. However, not every command is understood and there are other issues the developers need to overcome.

Some of the issues the user may encounter are:

- The inherent complexity and ambiguity of natural language (see Chapter 4 for more information).
- Having to phrase a command in a different way because not all variations of the same command are understood.
- Accents. Not all accents are easily understood.
- Background noise. It is sometimes hard for software to distinguish voices from noise in the background.

Touch screen

Operating systems for mobile devices now use touch screens, normally capacitive touch, as the key form of input. On the other hand, most operating systems for desktop and laptop machines use smart touch pads or mice. Capacitive touch screens rely on the fact that the human body is an electrical conductor. When you press on such a screen, it distorts its electromagnetic field. The change of capacitance is then measured. This is then translated into x- and y-coordinates for the device.

Touch screens allow for the use of gestures, such as a swipe, to perform actions. Gestures such as pinching to make something smaller are intuitive to the user, and can be learned quickly, even by the really young. There are plenty of reports of children as young as two being able to interact with devices such as an iPad.

Touch screens require the user interface to be more menu-based and to use large icons. Anything which can be interacted with must be large enough for the average finger to accurately interact with. If user interface elements are too small and too close together then the device may not be able to accurately determine what had been selected. This is why a lot of websites have mobile versions to make it easier for the end user to interact with them.

Force feedback

One of the senses overlooked in most systems is touch. Haptic feedback gives the user a physical sense that an action has occurred by using subtle vibrations. For example, when you type on a touch screen it may give a small vibration to try and replicate the feeling of pressing a key down on a keyboard. Game consoles use force feedback in their controllers as an extension of the game. For example, when you crash your car or an explosion occurs, the controller will vibrate.

Many smartwatches use vibration to as an alert, as an alternative to sound: it feels as if someone has tapped you on the wrist. Some smart watches can even measure and transmit your heart beat to another smartwatch wearer who can feel your heart beat as vibrations on their wrist.

Virtual reality

By taking over as many of the user's senses as possible, and enabling them to navigate the new world in an intuitive way, the goal of Virtual Reality is to persuade the user that they are somewhere else. VR technology tends to take the form of a headset and sometimes special gloves and other peripherals. One example of VR technology which is in active development at the moment is the Oculus Rift.

Figure 6.3: Oculus rift.

The Oculus Rift uses two screens enclosed in a headset to give a stereoscopic view of the world (Figure 6.3). Each of our eyes sees the world slightly differently, which gives us our depth perception. The Rift shows slightly different images on each screen to simulate 3D. The device also includes 360 degree head tracking. This means that when you turn your head, the virtual world also changes.

PlayStation are also developing VR hardware in the form of Playstation VR (formerly Project Morpheus) (Figure 6.4). The key difference with Morpheus is that it makes use of motion tracking cameras on the PlayStation to monitor lights on the headset and the hand-held controller. This allows the PlayStation to track not only your head location but also how far you are moving, if you have ducked, and other motions.

Figure 6.4:

Augmented reality

Augmented reality (AR) takes the real world and lays digital information over it. This could use special eye-wear or a mobile phone camera to display a live feed with additional information. There are a number of applications which make use of AR interfaces, for example Star Chart for iOS (Figure 6.5).

The user holds their phone towards the night sky. The app overlays images of star constellations onto the image received via the phone camera. This is done by using a combination of GPS tracking (to know where you are in relation to the stars), the accelerometers (to know the orientation of the phone) and the compass (to know which direction you are pointing the phone in).

Microsoft Hololens is another example of augmented reality where users wear a headset with transparent eyepieces. Images are then projected onto to the eyepieces effectively overlaying what the user sees through the glass with computer-generated imagery. As well as augmented reality, the Hololens also contains cameras and motion sensors to detect the world around the wearer, allowing it to project onto real world objects such as a table or a wall.

System design validation

System design validation is a process of testing carried out during a systems lifecycle to ensure that the designed product meets the requirements. This will occur before implementation starts to make sure that what is being built is what was originally specified in the requirements. The earlier in the lifecycle of a project that problems are detected the better. The necessary fixes will then have less impact.

Part of the design review will be to bring the customer or users into the process to get their feedback. It is crucial to validate that the user interface is effective. It is common for a design prototype to be built in order for the user to try out the interface to get an idea of how it will work. The design prototype will not do any, or only basic, processing of the captured information. It really acts as a demonstration of the product so that the user interface can then be properly tested.

If there are issues found during the design stage this will mean that the system design will have to be updated. It could also result in a new or adapted prototype having to be built to ensure that the new design is valid. The feedback gathered from the design review will ultimately produce a more stable and effective interface.

With methodologies such as Agile (see Chapter 5), which take a more iterative approach, design validation will occur whenever a new design is created. Agile will make use of many smaller design reviews rather than a singular summative review for the whole project.

System design evaluation

Evaluation is contractually very important as it allows the development company and the customer to decide whether a project has been successful. Evaluation is important to the customer because they must be sure that what they are buying is exactly what was specified in the requirements specification. However, evaluation is also important to the developer as it will determine whether they will be paid. To reduce arguments and the chance of litigation, there are a number of specific criteria that need to be considered before the system is designated a success namely: requirements; performance; usability; robustness and cost.

Figure 6.5: Star chart.

Requirements	Does it meet the functionality set out in the requirements specification? It must meet every requirement in order for the system to be considered a success. This is why each requirement laid out in the specification must be objective and measurable. If a requirement can be interpreted in more than one way, there is a chance for conflict.
Performance	Does it respond in a timely manner for the user? This can be subjective, so performance criteria are normally put in place to ensure that there are fewer areas of conflict. Certain complicated processes will be given a time frame in which they must respond, or defined to have progress bars. For example, a search of a database should not take longer than 30 seconds.
Robustness	There is nothing worse than software that crashes all the time or is bug ridden. Robustness is a fundamental requirement for all systems. The level of robustness depends on the type of software to some extent. For example, if a word processor crashes it is annoying, but not critical, as users should be saving their work regularly. If an air traffic control system fails, the effects could be devastating.
Cost	Has the project come in on or under budget? Systems that cost more than expected are rarely seen as successful. Extra costs are normally carefully negotiated and might have to be absorbed by the developer.
Usability	It is crucial that the software produced is usable by the end users. This is dependent on the skill level of the end user as well as the nature of the solution. For example, a mobile app would tend to be menu based and be aimed at the novice user. Software to support a network administrator, on the other hand, could be command line based.

Chapter summary

- Common interface devices, including keyboards and mice, are still in widespread use but are starting to be superseded by other human-computer interaction methods.
- Voice input makes use of spoken language to allow interaction with a computer. It has a number of drawbacks:
- Commands have to be phrased in a specific way.
- Current software is not always able to judge the context or have the knowledge to answer the user.
- Accents or background noise can impact understanding.
- Slang will not always be interpreted.
- Touch screens are a feature of most new devices and can take advantage of gestures.
- Force feedback offers haptic feedback to the user which is adding a new dimension to human-computer interactions
- Virtual reality uses headsets to immerse the end user in an alternate world where they can interact by moving their bodies. Sensors track a user's movement and translate it into changes in the world the user is seeing.

- Augmented reality overlays details onto a live camera feed or projects onto glass. It will make use of sensors and other data to give the user a more immersive experience.
- New system design must be validated before being used to ensure that its implementation will match the requirements.
- Prototypes can be used to test out an interface design.
- Feedback in initial stages of a new design can be used to improve it before implementation.
- Evaluation allows the development company and the customer to decide whether a project has been successful. The key issues that need to be part of any evaluation are:
- Ensuring the requirements are met.
- Ensuring the system responds in an acceptable timeframe.
- Ensuring the product is robust.
- Review if the product was developed on cost and on time.
- Assess how useable the system is by the end user.

End-of-chapter questions

1 Describe one problem which arises when computers use voice input. [2]

2 Describe one contemporary interface which a gamer may use. [2]

3 Explain how augmented reality could be useful for a tourist in London. [4]

4 State the different factors which must be considered when evaluating a design. [5]

Further reading

How Siri really works	Search for How Apple's Siri really works at zdnet.com
HoloLens	Go to the HoloLens section of Microsoft's website
Design principles	Go to the Design Principles section of oodesign.com
History of augmented reality	Search for the History of augmented reality of pocket-lint.com

Chapter 7
Software engineering

Learning objectives

- Describe the types of software tool that have been designed to assist the software engineering process.
- Explain the role of appropriate software packages in systems analysis, systems specification, systems design and testing.
- Explain the role of Integrated Development Environment (IDE) tools in developing and debugging programs.
- Explain program version management.

Introduction

Software engineering is the term given to the process of developing software, including its testing, debugging, documentation and maintenance.

Software tools

Computer-aided software engineering (CASE) is the name of a software tool that provides a number of functions which assist with the design, development and testing of software.

Some of these functions include:

- providing a data dictionary
- a graphics/diagram production feature
- a code generator
- providing repositories of reusable code
- providing project management tool(s)
- incorporating version control
- carrying out report generation
- a prototyping tool.

Software packages

CASE tools can be split into three main categories (Figure 7.1)depending on what part of the lifecycle they are supporting. Upper CASE tools are used to support during analysis, lower CASE during development and integrated CASE are useful throughout.

Analysis and planning tools

The most obvious tool required in this section is one that helps to produce diagrams. These tools have templates, a range of system components, intelligent connectors and other useful functions. Flow chart creators, such as Gliffy, will focus on allowing the user to quickly generate diagrams (Figure 7.2). Features such as intelligent connectors speed up the diagram creation process and improve accuracy. Another commonly used CASE tool for diagrams is Microsoft's Visio.

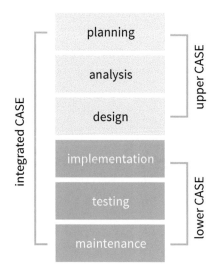

Figure 7.1: CASE tools categories.

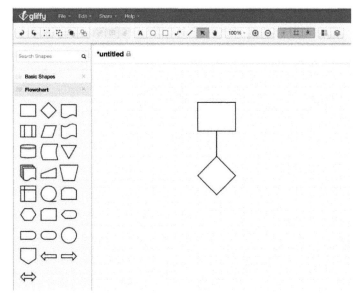

Figure 7.2: Gliffy flow chart tools.

Analysis is a very complex and involved process and it is not just diagrams where CASE tools can help. The results of fact finding and the recording of requirements must be managed carefully and checked. Tools such as CaseComplete (Figure 7.3) allow the recording and validating of requirements. In CaseComplete, requirements are recorded as use cases and described in detail. They can include test cases to validate that the requirements are correct.

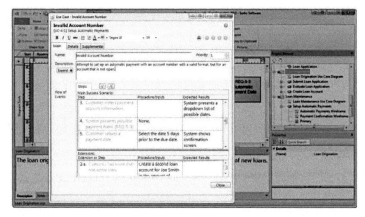

Figure 7.3: CaseComplete screenshot.

Lower CASE tools will also feature collaboration features so that different members of the team can access all of the resources. This makes management of what could be potentially hundreds of documents much more streamlined.

Design tools allow systems to be modularised ready for implementation. This goes beyond simply creating diagrams, but will look at how the code will be structured. Additionally, the user experience (or UX design) will have tools to help prototype interfaces. This type of design is sometimes known as wireframing as shown in Figure 7.4.

Figure 7.4: User experience design.

Finally, system testing can be supported though CASE tools and automated tests. Test plans and runs are recorded using these tools which can then link in with bug tracking software. A very popular free bug-tracking tool is Launchpad (Figure 7.5). This tool allows bugs to be reported, assigned and processed through the use of a web app. Launchpad also offers other features such as code reviews and translations.

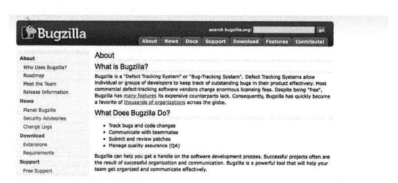

Figure 7.5: Launchpad showing bugs in Ubuntu (they may no longer be live bugs).

Integrated development environments (IDEs)

Development

Integrated development environments or IDEs are really just collections of tools that make a programmer's life easier. There are thousands of different IDEs, some are free, some cost money, some support many languages (some just one), but there is some functionality that is common to all.

Most provide simple colouring that highlights key words like `if` or `def`. They also provide automatic line numbering and some even draw lines to show which constructs (for example, IF and ELSE) match each other. All these simple tools help make code easy to read. Look at the examples below:

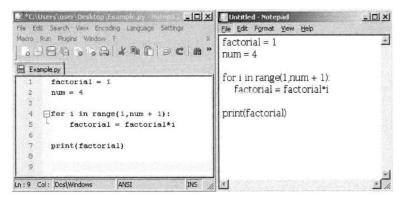

Figure 7.6: Example IDE.

The code on the left (Figure 7.6) is in the Notepad++ IDE so is coloured and numbered, with arrows indicating that line 5 is part of the FOR loop on line 4. The screenshot on the right shows the same code in a simple Notepad file. The code is identical and both would run but the example on the left is much easier to read, understand and debug. In Notepad++ you can even click on a variable and all the other instances of that variable will be highlighted (Figure 7.7), great for spotting mistakes in your code.

Complex IDEs can provide a great deal of functionality and most programmers have a favourite IDE. Your school or college probably provides an IDE for you to use in lessons but it is well worth looking through some of those in the Further reading section at the end of this chapter to find one that you like.

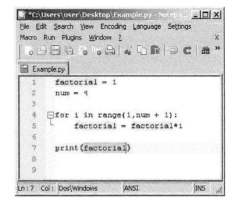

Figure 7.7: Highlighting variables in an IDE.

Debugging

As well as tools for helping to develop code, most IDEs also provide a range of tools that are useful for debugging (finding errors).

Automatic error checking

The example in Figure 7.8 is a simple program in Visual Basic that will print a series of message boxes when a button is clicked.

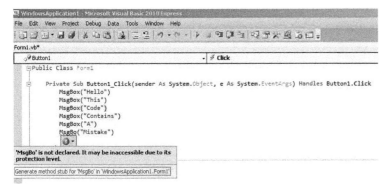

Figure 7.8: Error checking in an IDE.

On line 8 the keyword MsgBox has been misspelt. Before the code is even run the IDE has identified that it contains an error by underlining the keyword in blue and has provided an error message. Error messages in IDEs are notoriously inaccurate but they do at least show you where the error is likely to occur. Due to the way syntax analysis occurs it could be that more

Error: File exampleError.py; Line 3:
  SyntaxError: invalid syntax

Figure 7.9: Error message.

than one rule of the language is broken when the coder makes an error. In these situations the compiler will have to make a choice about which one to use. That may or may not be informative to the developer. For example, missing a bracket off in Python code will normally point the user to an error on the next line as shown in the example below (Figure 7.9).

```
text = 'hello'
text = text.lower(
print text
```

Error reports

On trying to run the program, the IDE then produces an error log explaining that the program cannot be translated and why. Notice that the error report tells the programmer the name of the file and the line number on which the error occurred as well as having a guess at what the error was (Figure 7.10).

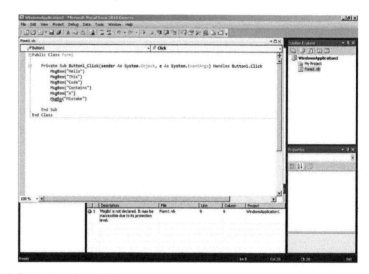

Figure 7.10: Error report in an IDE.

On large projects, detailed error reports like this can save programmers hundreds of hours.

Breakpoints

Breakpoints allow a programmer to stop the execution of a program on a specific line of code. This can be useful for finding out exactly where a logic error is taking place or checking the value of variables at a specific point in the code.

The screenshot in Figure 7.11 shows a breakpoint being placed on line 6. When the program reaches this line, execution will be halted.

```
Form1.vb
(General)
⊟Public Class Form1

⊟      Private Sub Button1_Click(sender As System.Ob
            MsgBox("Hello")
            MsgBox("This")
            MsgBox("Code")
            MsgBox("Contains")
            MsgBox("A")
            MsgBox("Mistake")

        End Sub
End Class
```

Figure 7.11: A breakpoint in an IDE.

During execution, when the computer reaches the breakpoint, execution is paused and the state of the program displayed to the programmer (Figure 7.12).

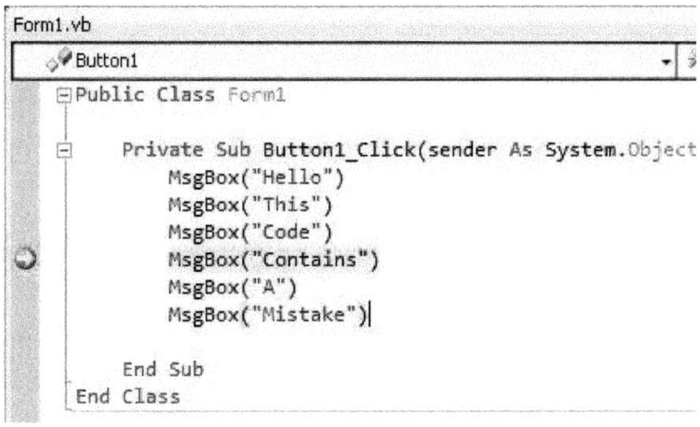

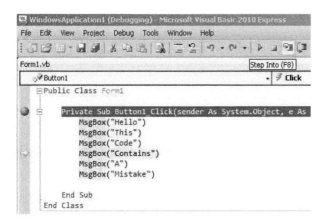

Figure 7.12: A program paused at a breakpoint.

Stepping through

Stepping through allows a programmer to execute each line of code, pausing to see the impact of that line after each step.

Figure 7.13: Stepping through in an IDE.

Different IDEs offer different ways of stepping through. In Visual Basic the easiest way is to place a breakpoint where you want to begin stepping through, run the program until it stops at the breakpoint and then click 'Step Into' to execute each line. In the screen shot in Figure 7.13, you can see that stepping through began on line 2 and has now reached line 6.

Program version management

During development, large amounts of code will be produced in multiple files. This code will be compiled together in order to produce the final program. As there are numerous people working on the code base at any given time, formal methods must be employed to manage changes. Version management CASE tools will ensure that changes are carefully controlled through the use of a process of checking in and out code.

When a file needs to be edited, it can be checked out by a developer. When code is checked out, no one else can edit the file and they will be informed who has the code and when it was checked out. When the changes have been made, the code will be checked back in. When code is checked in, a new version will be made. This means that the code before and after will be recorded. In the diagram in Figure 7.14, three versions of the same file exist with version 3 marked as the current file.

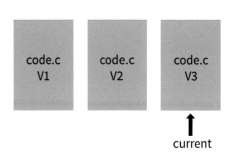

Figure 7.14: Three versions of the same file.

When checked in, each change is recorded so that changes can be rolled back. Rolling back a change means that one or more versions of the file will be discarded to go back to a more stable version. Also, the differences between versions can be shown, to see exactly what new code has been added. This is crucial if a bug has been introduced.

When a project milestone is reached, all files can be typically 'tagged' with that milestone. That way specific stable builds of the software can be released without impacting new development. Beta builds tend to be released in this way.

Also, versioning allows software to branch. When software branches a milestone is created, but two new code repositories are set up. This allows, for example, the easy creating of trial and pro versions of software without impacting the code they have in common. A popular version control system is the open source Git, as shown in the screenshot in Figure 7.15. In some projects, new features are developed in their own branches in order, then merged back to the master branch once ready. This way developers can have more autonomy over the feature in question without worrying about impacting other developers.

Figure 7.15: Screenshot of GIT – open source version control system.

 Chapter summary

- Software development can be supported by using CASE tools; Computer-aided software engineering.
- Analysis and planning tools enable the developer to create diagrams quickly (for example using UML – Unified Modeling Language), validate requirements and collaborate on every part of analysis.
- Design tools allow mock-ups of software to be produced for verification purposes.
- Test plans and bug repositories have CASE tools, which help large-scale projects keep track of which tests were run and what bugs were produced.
- IDEs offer additional tools to the developer, such as debugging, coding frameworks and the ability to manage larger code projects.
- Version management will monitor changes to code and will manage how code files are merged back into the master branch to avoid conflicts.

End-of-chapter questions

1   State what CASE stands for in software development.   [1]

2   Name one CASE tool for analysis or planning.   [2]

3   State two features of a modern IDE.   [2]

4   Describe how program version management is used during the development of software.   [3]

Further reading

What is version control?	Search for What Is Version Control? on the OSS Watch website
GIT basics	Search for Git Basics on git-scm.com
CASE tools	search for CASE Tools on the Tutorials Point website
PyCharm – example IDE	search for PyCharm on jetbrains.com

Chapter 8
Program construction

Learning objectives

- Describe the function of translation programs in making source programs executable by the computer.
- Describe the purpose and give examples of the use of compilers, interpreters and assemblers, and distinguish between them.
- Describe the principal stages involved in the compilation process: lexical analysis, symbol table construction, syntax analysis, semantic analysis, code generation and optimisation.
- Distinguish between and give examples of translation and execution errors.

Introduction

Translation programs

We use the term 'translators' to cover all the types of software that convert code from one form to another. Compilers, interpreters and assemblers are all types of translators.

Compilers

Compilers convert source code written in a high-level language, such as Small Basic, Java or C++, into machine code. A compiler produces a standalone executable file which can be released to others without the need for further compilation. A program is compiled once, but can be run many times. Compiled code protects the intellectual property of the developers, unless they release the source code themselves under an open source licence. When code is compiled, it will be targeted at a specific platform and CPU instruction set. Programs compiled for Mac OS X will not run on a Windows computer, nor will programs compiled for x86 processors run on ARM-based ones. If software is to be ported to other systems and operating systems, it needs not only to be recompiled, but also most likely changed, as software for different environments tends be coded differently.

Interpreters

An interpreter handles the job of translating code very differently from a compiler. Instead of producing a single executable, it translates each line of code into machine code, line by line. The interpreter takes the first line of the source code, translates it and executes it before moving on to the next. Any machine code produced while the interpreter is running is not saved, meaning that the interpreter must interpret the code every time the user wishes to run it. Interpreters are commonly used for a number of languages, including BASIC, Lisp, Prolog, Python, JavaScript and Scheme. In order to be able to run an interpreted language, you must have an interpreter installed on the system. One of the key design goals is that an interpreted language can be run on any system, as long as an interpreter has been installed. There are a number of key advantages and disadvantages of using interpreters.

Advantages

- Source code has to be written only once and then it can run on any computer with an interpreter.
- You can easily inspect the contents of variables as the program is running.
- You can test code much more efficiently as well as being able to test single lines of code.
- Code can be run on many different types of computers and OSs, such as Macs, UNIX, LINUX and PCs.

Disadvantages

- You must have an interpreter running on the computer in order to be able to run the program.
- As source code must be compiled each time, interpreted programs can sometimes run slowly.
- You have to rely on the interpreter for machine-level optimisations rather than programming them yourself.
- Developers can view the source code, which means that they could use your intellectual property to develop their own software.

Compilers and interpreters are contrasted in the Table 8.1:

Feature	Compiler	Interpreter
Source code	Hidden from other developers and users. Intellectual property protected.	Shown to all developers and users. Intellectual property risk.
Multiple platforms	Compiled code will only run on CPUs which have the same instruction sets. Also the OS has to match.	Will run on any platform from the same source code base. An interpreter is required to run.
Distribution	Executable files can be easily distributed on CD or over the internet.	Systems need to be set up before the code can be run. This can include installing library files as well as the interpreter.

Table 8.1: Contrasting compilers and interpreters.

Intermediate code

Virtual machines, as a computational concept, have been around for a long time. In essence, they represent a generic computer residing within the (physical) computer that is running it. That computer is referred to as the host, while the OS run by the virtual machine is known as the guest. In this section we look at process virtual machines, which virtualise a single application only. Process virtual machines act as interpreters for generic machine code instructions known as intermediate code.

Process virtual machines, referred to as VMs from now on, run intermediate code that has previously been compiled. Source code is compiled into intermediate code to prevent the incompatibilities that exist when trying to run compiled code on different CPU architectures or OSs, but intermediate code retains some of the advantages of compiled code. This generic intermediate code cannot be run by a CPU directly and is merely an abstraction rather than a real instruction set. In order to run the code, it must be interpreted by a VM. One example of a programming language that is both compiled and interpreted is Java (Figure 8.1).

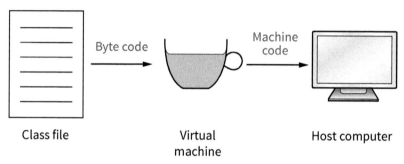

Figure 8.1: Java.

Java is a popular programming language originally created by Sun Microsystems, but now owned by Oracle. Java source code is written in much the same way as in other programming languages and bears some comparison, in syntax at least, to C++. Once the source code has been produced, it is compiled into intermediate code (known as byte code in Java), which is a pseudo-executable file (known as a class file). Byte code must then be interpreted by the Java VM when the program is run. This means that for any Java program to run, the Java VM must be installed first.

The host system will not be able to run the intermediate code (byte code) held in the class file directly (Figure 8.2). It would be like someone speaking Russian to you (unless you happen to speak Russian). In order for that person to be understood, their speech would have to be translated by an interpreter. The process VM has the job of translating Java byte code into machine code. As well as managing the translation of intermediate code to machine code, the VM has to trap OS library calls. So when the byte code tries to open a window, the VM makes some system calls to your OS to open a window on its behalf. This applies to any library call, from opening a file to any other library-related task. Libraries will vary wildly from OS to OS, so this additional functionality is crucial.

Process virtual machines manage their own threads and have their own memory management system. This provides a fully sandboxed environment for the software to run in, which has a main advantage of offering extra security features, such as restrictions on accessing the hard drive or other system resources.

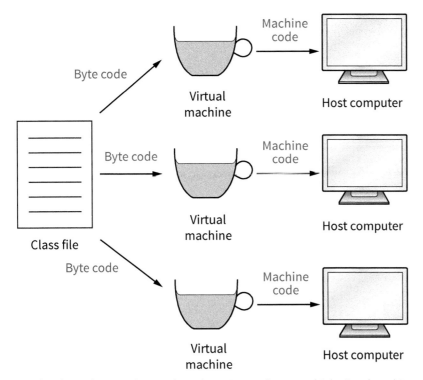

Figure 8.2: This shows the same byte code as Figure 8.1 running on multiple virtual machines.

The Java code (top part of Figure 8.3) would be compiled into byte code (the bottom part of Figure 8.3). Byte code does not run on any known computer and requires a Java virtual machine to run it. Intermediate code acts in the same way as normal machine code, but is not architecture specific.

Java is an example of a programming language that is both compiled and interpreted. First of all, source code is compiled into intermediate code (for example, Java byte code) and then interpreted by a VM. There are number of advantages of doing this:

- Code can be run on many different host OSs without the need to recompile.
- Intellectual property is protected as source code is not released.
- Code can be optimised by both the compiler and the interpreter.

Assemblers

In the early days of computing, programmers wrote machine code directly. But they quickly realised that writing binary machine code was not a good way to write complex programs. To make low-level programming more manageable, they designed a language called Assembly.

Assembly code is a step above machine code, allowing the coder to write code using mnemonics that represent machine code instructions. Each Assembly code instruction has a one-to-one mapping with a machine code instruction. This is unlike source code, which has a one-to-many mapping. Machine code is a binary representation of an instruction that can be run on a specific CPU architecture. Writing machine code directly in binary would be very time consuming and prone to errors. When converting Assembly to machine code you use an assembler, which is a form of translator. Converting Assembly code into machine code is known as assembling, rather than compiling, owing to the different structure of Assembly code compared to other programming languages, meaning that an assembler has to do less work than a compiler.

```
outer:
  for (int i = 2; i < 1000; i++) {
      for (int j = 2; j < i; j++) {
          if (i ÷ j == 0)
              continue outer:
      }
      System.out.printin (i):
  }
```

```
0:      iconst _ 2
1:      istore _ 1
2:      iload _ 1
3:      sipush 1000
6:      if _ icmpge      44
9:      iconst _ 2
10:     istore _ 2
11:     iload _ 2
12:     iload _ 1
13:     if _ icmpge      31
16:     iload _ 1
17:     iload _ 2
18:     irem
19:     ifne    25
22:     goto    38
25:     iinc    2, 1
28:     goto    11
31:     getstatic        #84: System.out.PrintStream:
34:     iload _ 1
35:     invokevirtual #85: //Method printin:
38:     iinc    1, 1
41:     goto    2
44:     return
```

Figure 8.3: Disassembled exemplar byte code.

Opcode	Data
10010011	11001010

Table 8.2: Machine code instruction.

Opcodes and Data

A machine code instruction is split into two main parts, the opcode and the data (also known as the operand, or operands). Table 8.2 shows how a 16-bit instruction could be split. An opcode is a specific binary value that represents a single instruction from the processor's instruction set. In order for the instruction to be executed correctly, it requires data, the second part of the machine code instruction. Sometimes the data is split over multiple bytes, meaning that the next set of bytes fetched to the CPU will actually be the data from the last instruction, rather than the next instruction to be processed. Also, machine code instructions differ from architecture to architecture, so an ADD instruction on an x86 processor may look completely different from the ADD instruction on an ARM processor. The binary values used are not the same on different architectures, which is one of the key reasons why programs written for one architecture will not run on another.

Mnemonics

Assembly languages assign a mnemonic to each opcode in order to make Assembly code more human readable. It also makes use of labelling and other features to make low-level coding simpler for the developer. Some example mnemonics are:

- ADD – adds numbers together.
- MOV – moves data from register or memory to another location.

- SUB – subtracts numbers.
- JMP – jumps to a memory address and starts executing at that point.

Assembly code also uses labels to represent variables and memory addresses.

Assembly for x86 processors

So far we have been considering Assembly and machine code in the general sense, but from this point forward we consider the x86 Assembly language. This chapter is not designed to teach you Assembly, but rather to give you an idea of how Assembly is structured and written. To get a better understanding of writing Assembly code, try developing LMC (Little Man Computer) code.

The example code in Figure 8.4 will first move (mov) the value 1 into the accumulator referenced as ax and then add 5 to it. This code makes use of immediate addressing. x86 Assembly makes use of hexadecimal values rather than decimal. Note that although 1 and 5 in hex are the same as 1 and 5 in decimal numbers, this will not always be the case. Both of the instructions above have two operands in the data part of the instruction and these are encoded as part of the instruction when assembled.

```
mov ax, 1
add ax, 5
```

Figure 8.4: Example code.

Translating assembly to machine code

Assembly code has a one-to-one mapping between the mnemonic instructions of the language and their binary code equivalents. This means that translation may seem almost trivial, but this is not the case. Owing to the inclusion of variables and labels, there is still a lot of work to be done and a two-phased approach must be taken. In the first phase, labels are converted into memory addresses and stored in a symbol table. Symbol tables in assembly work differently from those used during lexical analysis (covered later) and should not be regarded in the same way. The second phase of assembly involves converting the mnemonics into their binary representations and combining them with the binary representations of the data.

Symbol table

When a label or variable is encountered during assembly, an entry is made in the symbol table. This maps the label or variable to a memory address. Variables map to a memory location that will be used to store its value, while labels map to the exact position of the instruction that it needs to jump to. Consider the example of a machine code program (Table 8.3) and the resultant symbol table (Table 8.4):

Address	Mnemonic	Op1	Op2
0	mov	count	10
1	mov	ax	0
2	loop: add	ax	count
3	sub	count	1
4	CMP	count	0
5	JNE	loop:	

Table 8.3: Machine code program.

Symbol	Address
count	6
loop	2

Table 8.4: Symbol table.

The Assembly code on the left performs the calculation $10 + 9 + ... + 1$ and stores the result in the ax register. Next to each line of code is the instruction's memory address. A symbol table (shown on the right) is produced as the assembler works through its first phase. In order to store the count in memory, an address has to be set up, for example the first available memory address after the program. This decision about assigning the memory addresses to variables is up to the assembler. When a label is encountered, the memory address of where it was defined is placed in the symbol table; in the above example that would be address 2. Once the symbol table has been produced, as shown above, the assembler goes over the code and replaces every variable or label with the memory address stored within the table. Here (Table 8.5) is the same program with the symbols replaced:

Address	Mnemonic	Op1	Op2
0	mov	[6]	10
1	mov	ax	0
2	add	ax	[6]
3	sub	[6]	1
4	CMP	[6]	0
5	JNE	[2]	

Table 8.5: Machine code program.

Note that memory addresses (not immediate values) are represented by surrounding them with square [] brackets.

The compilation process

Compiling is a complicated process and requires a large amount of processing time. To make the task simpler, compiling is separated into a number of phases. Each phase produces something for the next phase to work on. Some of the tasks that the compiler must perform are:

- lexical analysis (parsing source code)
- syntax analysis
- checking types
- generating machine code
- sequencing code blocks
- allocating registers
- optimising.

Some of these operations have been simplified for the A-Level course and the key phases that will come up on the exam can be summarised in Figure 8.5.

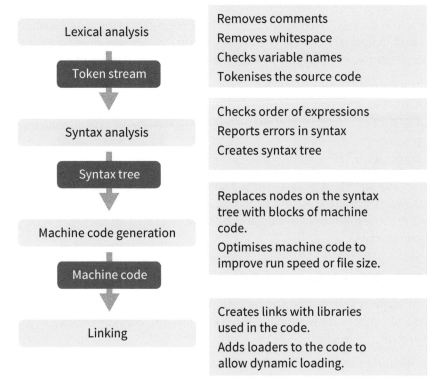

Lexical analysis	Removes comments Removes whitespace Checks variable names Tokenises the source code
Token stream	
Syntax analysis	Checks order of expressions Reports errors in syntax Creates syntax tree
Syntax tree	
Machine code generation	Replaces nodes on the syntax tree with blocks of machine code. Optimises machine code to improve run speed or file size.
Machine code	
Linking	Creates links with libraries used in the code. Adds loaders to the code to allow dynamic loading.

Figure 8.5: Key stages in compilation.

Lexical analysis

When a compiler receives source code, it parses it and decides whether each line contains keywords, variables, constants or anything else accepted by the language. It converts the source code into a token stream. A token is a numeric representation of a keyword or identifier. Identifiers, such as variables and function names, must be treated independently. Each token represents a different identifier and if that identifier is seen again, the same token is used. As a token is just a single number, extra information about it, such as the name of the identifier, is stored in a symbol table. Lexical analysis makes use of spaces, newlines or atomic values to separate tokens. Atomic values are core parts of a language, such as operators or keywords. The compiler removes anything deemed unnecessary, such as comments and white space (tabs, newlines etc.). Anything that does not match the pattern for a keyword, operator, literal (a hard coded value) or identifier is flagged up as an error. The lexical analysis phase does not check the syntax or the order of keywords and operators; it simply prepares the code for syntax analysis.

The lexical analyser does not pick up typing mistakes. The example shown here should read: IF YES=1 THEN PRINT "moo", but it has been mistyped:

```
IFFY ES=1 THEN PLINT "moo"
```

The lexical analyser would not pick up IFFY and PLINT as errors, but assume they were identifiers. Both IFFY and PLINT are perfectly acceptable identifier names, but where they are placed is clearly wrong.

Lexical analysis will not pick up any errors in the ordering of expressions.

```
IF 1=A PRINT THEN "moo"
```

Again this code would be accepted by the lexical analyser, even though the order of the expression is invalid. As long as each atomic part of the code matches an identifier, literal or keyword, lexical analysis will accept it.

In order to tokenise source code, which is the key design goal of the lexical analyser, it reads each individual character and then tries to match it to something it recognises. For example, the expression 2 × 3 + 4 would be converted to a stream of tokens such as:

- NUMBER <2>
- MULTIPLIES
- NUMBER <3>
- ADD
- NUMBER <4>

A token would normally be represented as a number, which would be assigned by the lexical analyser through the use of a symbol table. To make the process a bit more human friendly, the above token stream is represented by words. This is an informal way of representing tokens.

```
a = 10
b = 20
b = (a + b) / 2
print a,b
```

Figure 8.6: Python.

Regular expressions

The lexical analyser searches through the code looking for specific patterns of letters, numbers and symbols. These are called regular expressions. Consider the following lines of Python code (Figure 8.6):

In this code you can see examples of variables, assignments, operators and keywords. In order to tokenise this code there needs to be a regular expression for each. Figure 8.7 shows what these regular expressions would look like. At first they may seem confusing, but they are in fact very straightforward. For example, suppose variables must be made up of lowercase or uppercase letters only.

A lexical analyser recognises identifiers, keywords, operators and literals, and each one has its own regular expression. These are then applied to the source code to generate the stream of tokens as shown in Figure 8.8.

Token	Regular expression
print	print
variable	[a-z]|[A-Z].$^+$
assignment	=
operator	+|-|$^+$|\

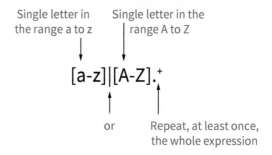

Single letter in the range a to z — Single letter in the range A to Z

$$[a\text{-}z]|[A\text{-}Z].^+$$

or — Repeat, at least once, the whole expression

Figure 8.7: Simple regular expressions representing common tokens.

Symbol	Description	Example	Possible input
.	Represents any character, digit or symbol	.at	cat hat mat bat zat 3at
*	Repeats the symbol immediately to the left. Can be empty.	ab*	a ab abb abbb abbbb
[a-z]	Range of characters. Accepts a single character in the range specified inside the [] brackets.	[a-c]$^+$	abc aabbcc caba bbaabbccaaa
[^a-z]	Character is NOT in the range specified in the [] brackets.	[^a-c]$^+$	uyd hythytd popodd qqwtyuw
a|b	A choice between two or more items.	+|-$^+$	+ - -- --- ----

Figure 8.8: Example regular expression operators.

Regular expressions can be represented as diagrams known as automata or state machines. Although we will not look at automata in any great detail, it is useful to know that they can be converted directly from regular expressions. When developing a lexical analyser, a finite deterministic automaton is created for each expression and combined to enable the analyser to make the right choice of token at any given point during parsing. This forms the internal representation of the language in the compiler.

Each circle represents a state of the analyser, each line a transition between states, and the text on each line shows which transitions are legal (Figure 8.9). Normally each transition (each line) represents a single letter rather than a group. Groups of characters have been added to make the diagram more compact and readable. One issue we currently have is that at the moment we have no idea which automaton to use if we see the input 'p'. It could be 'print' or it could be 'pad' – one is a keyword and the other is an identifier. Because we need to know about future input, we call this a non-deterministic finite automaton, or NFA. A parser cannot be written based on an NFA because for every given input we could potentially have more than one transition to take. In order to create a lexical analyser we must convert the non-deterministic automaton to a deterministic automaton. How this works is outside the scope of A-Level Computer Science, but is well documented on the web for the interested reader.

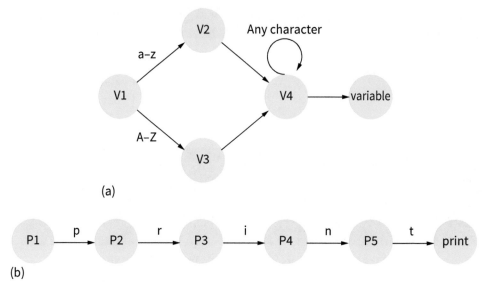

Figure 8.9: Finite deterministic automata for print keyword.

Symbol table

A token may have a value, for example a variable name, procedure name or constant. In addition, the language may also define some tokens to represent keywords and operators. Both language-defined tokens and user-defined tokens must be stored in the symbol table. Identifier names can be made up of many characters and are descriptive in order to help the developer. A compiler does not need to make use of long names to help it understand the code, and by replacing long identifiers with a simple token it can reduce the amount of work to be done by the syntax analyser. Each element of the code is replaced with a token that will provide an index to the symbol table. The symbol table stores:

- an index or identifier
- the name of the token
- data type
- scope and restrictions.

Comments and white space are removed at this stage. Spaces, carriage returns and comments are simply there to aid the programmer and have no relevance to the compiler. Indentation aids readability but is irrelevant to a **compiler**. Consider the following code snippet:

```
1 IF A > 5 THEN A = A * 2
2 ELSE A = A * 3
3 A = A + 2
```

This code produces the following tokens.

IF VARIABLE GREATER_THAN THEN VARIABLE EQUALS

VARIABLE MULTIPLIES LITERAL ELSE VARIABLE EQUALS

VARIABLE MULTIPLIES LITERAL VARIABLE EQUALS VARIABLE

PLUS LITERAL

It will also produce the following symbol table (Table 8.6):

Token code	Type	Lexeme
1	IF	-
2	Variable	A
3	>	-
4	Literal	5
5	THEN	-
6	=	-
7	*	-
8	Literal	2
9	ELSE	-
10	Literal	3
11	+	-

Table 8.6: Example symbol table after lexical analysis.

The code and symbol table would produce the following token stream:

1 2 3 4 5 2 6 2 7 8 9 2 6 2 7 10 2 6 2 11 8

When an error is found during compilation, it will be returned to the developer via translator diagnostics. During lexical analysis, the errors found will be due to incorrect identifier naming. For example, consider the statement 1Var = 10. Looking at this as a human, we can guess that the developer wanted a variable called '1Var' and to assign the value 10 to it. However, the lexical analyser does not have such an easy task reading this and it would not match the correct regular expression. When a number is the first part of an expression, the lexical analyser has to make a choice between a number and an identifier.

A simple identifier that would allow numbers at any point in a regular expression would be [0–9a–zA–Z] .+, while a regular expression for integer literals could be [0-9] .+.

Now consider the expression 123 = 50. According to the regular expression we have written so far, '123' could be either a variable or a number. At this point the lexical analyser has a choice to make, which can result in ambiguity and incorrect compilation. We could say that because there is an equals sign after it, we should match to an identifier. However, the number 123, anywhere else in the code, would then always match to an identifier. Effectively we have an ambiguous set of regular expressions and this would lead to code being misinterpreted and some very complex bugs to fix. It is common that languages do not accept a number as the first part of a variable definition. A common (simple) variable definition would look like:

[a-zA-Z][0-9a-zA-Z].+

With this definition, the lexical analyser would report an error for 1Var through translator diagnostics.

Activity 8.1

```
1    %{
2         lineNumber = ;
3    %}
4
5    letter [a-zA-z]
6    digit [ - ]
7    id {letter}({letter}|{digit})*
8    number {digit}+
9    %%
10   { } printf("<IF>");
11   ^{id} {dispNewLine(); printf("<ID>");}
12   {id} printf("<IF>");
13   ^{number} {dispNewLine(); printf("<NUMBER>");}
14   {number} printf("<NUMBER>");
15   [^a-zA-Z0-9 \t\n]+ printf("the rest is \\%s\\",yytext);
16   %%
17   dispNewLine(){
18     printf("%d : ", lineNumber++);
19   }
```

Note – This must be done on Linux (any Debian based system like Ubuntu).

1 Install the lexical analyser flex using **sudo apt-get install flex**

2 Enter the code shown above and save the file as exampleLex.lex

3 Run the lex command to produce the C source code for the l**exical analyser.**

> **lex -t exampleLex.lex > exampleLex.c**

4 Compile the scanner using **gcc. gcc exampleLex.c –o exampleLex -ll**

5 Run your scanner by executing the command **./exampleLex**

6 Try a number of lines of code to see what happens. See if you can work out which rules are being run. Press CTRL-D to exit.

7 Edit example.lex to include more keywords and operators such as brackets and maths. For each change you make, you must regenerate the source (run lex) and then compile (gcc).

8 The ldd command in linux will show what libraries a program currently uses. In order to view which libraries are linked you must find the binary executable (not rely on the $PATH environment variable). Enter the command **cd /bin** to navigate to a directory containing some common linux binary files.

9 Enter the command **ldd echo**

10 Research what each of the libraries do for the echo command. A library tends to have the extension. so

11 Navigate to the folder /usr/games folder by using the command **cd /usr/games**. List the contents of this directory using the **ls** command.

12 Run **ldd** on any file in this folder. Why do you think there are so many extra library files? What do some of these extra ones do?

Syntax and semantic analysis

Once a string of tokens has been generated, the syntax analyser part of the compiler checks whether the sequence of tokens is in an acceptable order. Here are two token streams:

VARIABLE EQUALS CONSTANT

CONSTANT EQUALS VARIABLE

The first is acceptable, the second is not.

The compiler will understand all of the rules of the language. Just as there are rules that must be followed in English, programmers must also follow the rules of the programming language they are using. If they do not, they will be faced with a syntax error. A syntax error occurs when the tokens passed to the compiler do not match any rule stored within the compiler. Once syntax has been checked to be 100 per cent correct, the compiler can construct an abstract syntax tree.

Semantic analysis tries to imply meaning to the code that has been read in during syntax analysis (the semantics of the code). One of the most important elements of semantic analysis is to determine type checks and any inconsistencies that may occur. This is doubly important for languages that are not strongly typed (languages which do not insist you specify a data type, such as string or integer, when the variable is defined).

Consider the situation where we have two variables, one containing an integer and the other a string. Attempting to add these two directly will cause a syntax error, as they are different types and there is no automatic way to convert an integer to a string or vice versa: the code is semantically incorrect. To make it work, the coder should cast (convert) one of the variables to the data type of the other.

Abstract syntax trees

As the code is being parsed, a tree data structure is created, known as the abstract syntax tree, which is passed on to the next phase of compilation. Abstract syntax trees are unambiguous data structures that can be guaranteed to be syntactically correct and only readable in one way, which prevents issues with precedence. Figure 8.10 shows the expression 2×3 as an abstract syntax tree.

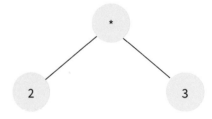

Operators are considered to be the root of a sub-tree and numbers are considered to be operands; in Figure 8.10 the operator *operates on the two operands, 2 and 3. We describe the two operands as children of the root.

Figure 8.10: $2 * 3$ (2×3) as an abstract syntax tree.

Consider a more complicated example, $2 \times 3 + 4$.

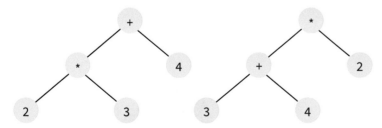

Figure 8.11: $2 * 3 + 4$ ($2 \times 3 + 4$) as an abstract syntax tree.

Which operation should happen first? Should the * be done first or should the + be done first? The two trees (Figure 8.11) show the two different ways in which this code could be interpreted. However, if you read the trees, it is clear what is meant and there is no room for ambiguity. The first tree adds 4 to the sub-tree $2 * 3$, while the second multiplies the sub-tree $3 + 4$ by 2. Trees are unambiguous, unlike source code, which must rely on operator precedence to achieve the same goal. Removing the ambiguity in the code simplifies code generation.

Machine code generation

Machine code generation occurs once the abstract syntax tree has been created and checked against the rules of the language. It is important to understand that there is no point in generating machine code if the program has any syntax errors. In order to do code generation the compiler will perform three tasks:

- Convert elements of the abstract syntax tree into machine code.
- Allocate registers to minimise memory access.
- Optimise the machine code to improve efficiency.

Machine code templates

Machine code generation is done by mapping parts of the abstract syntax tree to blocks of machine code. You can think of these blocks as machine code templates. Consider a simple line of code:

A = 2 + 3

Regardless of the values within the tree, we know that we need to perform an assignment and an addition. These are both common tasks in programming and machine code templates can be easily assigned. Code mapping is done by finding common abstract syntax tree patterns and matching them to blocks of machine code. This pattern-matching process keeps going until the whole tree has been mapped. In the Figures 8.12 and 8.13 two patterns have been identified and could have the following assembly code instructions mapped to them.

As machine code makes direct use of general purpose registers then part of the role of machine code generation is to allocate registers. Registers are temporary fast memory located in the CPU which are used during the execution of machine code instructions and the fetch, decode and execute cycle. When machine code instructions are to be run they first need to be fetched from memory, decoded to understand which operation to perform and finally executed. All three stages of the FDE (fetch–decode–execute) cycle require specific registers to accomplish the task.

There are a limited number of registers in a single CPU which means that it is not possible to assign a unique variable to a single register. This means that registers must be recycled as a program executes. Machine code generation, at a given point within the generated code, must decide what registers are assigned to which instructions. The exact mechanics of how this occurs is beyond the scope of A-Level, however it is a difficult problem

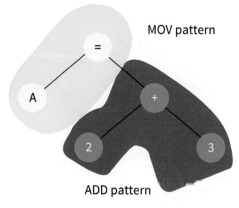

Figure 8.12: Matching parts of a syntax tree.

```
MOV #LABEL, ACC
```
Matches VAR =

```
MOV ACC, 0
ADD #ID1
ADD #ID2
```
Matches ID + ID

The final machine code from the previous abstract syntax tree would be:

```
MOV ACC, 0
ADD 2
ADD 3
MOV #A, ACC
```

Figure 8.13: Replacing parts of the syntax with machine code blocks.

and is considered to be an NP complete problem (nondeterministic polynomial time). NP complete, which is explained in Chapter 3, essentially means that solving the problem cannot be done in a reasonable time. To stop compilation from taking an exponential amount of time to complete, a best guess for register allocation is used which may or may not provide the most efficient generated code.

Optimising machine code

Most programmers write code very inefficiently and as programming languages become more high-level, programmers can become less adept at making their code efficient. Most programmers do not even know, or care, that their code is inefficient. Many compilers perform a number of optimisations for the developer. One way to speed up a program is to limit the number of jumps it has to do. A linear program with no jumps always runs faster than a heavily procedural program. IF statements, loops and procedure calls are inherently slow owing to the fact that they reset the FDE cycle, and should be used with some degree of caution. Any break in the flow of the code always carries a speed penalty.

Some short procedures can be turned into inline procedures. What this does is to copy and paste the contents of the inline procedure whenever it is called, thus reducing the need for jumps. Another way to optimise code is to make use of extensions to the CPU's functionality, such as 3D optimisation. These instructions may only be available on certain CPUs and as such the compiler will have to know which ones are available on a given CPU architecture. Overall, the goal of optimisation is to make the machine code run more efficiently.

Translation and execution errors

A translation error, such as a syntax error, occurs when a program is being compiled. An execution error, also called a runtime error, occurs when a program is running. Examples of execution errors include:

- division by zero
- reading past the end of file
- stack overflow/request more memory than available
- overflow of data type (for example, integer too big)
- trying to access an out-of-range array element.

173

Chapter summary

- Translators take source code and turn it into machine code. There are three main types: compilers, assemblers and interpreters.
- Interpreters will read, translate and execute the code line by line.
- Intermediate code is produced by a compiler but requires an interpreter to run. It allows code to be both compiled and interpreted to provide the benefits of both.
- Machine code instructions are made up of an opcode and operand.
- Assembly language uses mnemonics where each one represents a single machine code instruction.
- Assemblers will take a two-phase approach:
  - phase one – turn symbols into memory addresses and store this in a symbol table
  - phase two – convert assembly mnemonics into machine code.
- Compilers perform the following phases:
  - lexical analysis – removes comments and white space before producing a token stream
  - syntax analysis – checks the order of expressions using the token stream
  - machine code generation – matches parts of the syntax to machine code; it will optimise the generated machine code
  - linking – links the generated machine code to library software; it will add loaders to the code to enable dynamic library linking.

End-of-chapter questions

1   Explain the purpose of a virtual machine (VM) when using a programming language which is both compiled and then interpreted by a virtual machine.   [6]

2   There are a number of stages which must be followed when compiling code. For each of the stages below, explain their purpose and what they produce.

   a   Lexical analysis   [3]

   b   Syntax analysis   [3]

   c   Machine code generation   [3]

Further reading

Building a compiler – Lexical and syntax analysis	Search for The Compiler I: Syntax Analysis on the Hebrew University of Jerusalem's Computer Science department website

Chapter 9
Economic, moral, legal, ethical and cultural issues relating to computer science

Learning objectives

- Describe social and economic changes occurring as a result of developments in computing and computer use, and their moral, ethical, legal, cultural and other consequences.
- Describe the role of codes of conduct in promoting professional behaviour.
- Describe the possible effects of computers on the nature of employment in the computing industry and wider society.
- Explain how current legislation impacts on security, privacy, data protection and freedom of information.

Introduction

The advent of the computer has had an enormous impact on many areas of our lives. Law and order is one area that has been particularly affected by computer technology, with criminals using computers to facilitate their illegal activities, and crimes being committed that didn't even exist fifty years ago.

The use of computers also raises a number of ethical issues, including the use of computers in the workplace, artificial intelligence and automated decision-making, environmental impact and censorship.

Computer-related laws

Combating cybercrime (crime involving computers) is a complex and difficult task. Technologies evolve at a staggering rate and policing them requires officers to have a high level of technical proficiency. One of the biggest problems in policing computer use is the speed at which technology has developed, compared to how long it takes to draft and enact legislation prohibiting or restricting their use. This section will introduce you to some of the laws that have been introduced or updated to cope with the influx of new offences. The information contained in this chapter has not been checked by a lawyer and in no way constitutes legal advice.

Data Protection Act 1998

Computers enable companies to store vast amounts of information in a very small physical space. This data can also be transferred instantly across huge distances and between countries with different legal systems. This new technology has led to many problems, not least that private, personal data can be sold on to third parties (such as advertisers or insurance companies). Poorly protected data can be stolen by cybercriminals and poorly maintained data can quickly become out-of-date.

The advent of cloud computing, in which companies and individuals store all their data online rather than on their own computers, has compounded the problem. Some companies that facilitate information transferring and storage over the internet could be storing your information in another country or even on another continent, often without your knowledge.

The Data Protection Act 1998, was introduced largely to deal with these problems. It gives individuals the right to know what data is stored about them and who is storing it. It even gives people the right to see any data a company is storing about them and have it amended if necessary.

Types of data

One of the first issues tackled by the Data Protection Act 1998 was the question of what constitutes private information. For example, is your name personal, private information? To clarify these issues, the Act places information into two categories: personal data and sensitive data. Personal data concerns living people and tends to be information that is more widely available. Sensitive data includes details that you may not want to be widely known (Table 9.1).

Personal data	Sensitive data
Name	Ethnic origin
Address	Religious views
Date of birth	Political opinions
	Sexuality
	Criminal records

Table 9.1: Personal and sensitive data.

The eight principles of data protection

The of the Data Protection Act describe how those storing data must behave if they are to abide by the law.

1 Personal data shall be processed fairly and lawfully.

This means that those collecting and storing your personal data must have legitimate grounds for collecting and using it. It also prevents them from using the data in ways that have an adverse effect on you.

When collecting data, companies must be transparent about how they intend to use the data, and give individuals appropriate privacy notices. Finally, companies must handle people's personal data only in ways they would reasonably expect and ensure that they do not do anything unlawful with the data.

Example

A bank records information about companies that hold corporate accounts with the bank, including information about individuals who hold shares in those companies. It collects and holds this information to comply with its duties under anti-money-laundering regulations.

Unless the bank had obtained their prior consent, it would be unfair to use this information to send marketing material to the individuals concerned, inviting them to open personal accounts with the bank.

2 Personal data shall be obtained only for one or more specified and lawful purposes, and shall not be further processed in any manner incompatible with that purpose or those purposes.

The second principle means that those collecting your data must be clear from the outset about why they are collecting your personal data and what they intend to do with it. If they change what they want to do with the information, they must inform you and get your approval.

Example

A GP discloses his patient list to his wife, who runs a travel agency, so that she can offer special holiday deals to patients needing recuperation.

Disclosing the information for this purpose would be incompatible with the purposes for which it was obtained.

3 Personal data shall be adequate, relevant and not excessive in relation to the purpose or purposes for which they are processed.

The third principle states that companies hold only personal data about an individual that is sufficient for the purpose for which they are holding it. It also prohibits them from storing more information than they need for their stated purpose.

Example

An employer holds details of the blood groups of all its employees. Some of them do hazardous work and the information is needed in case of accident. For the rest of the workforce, though, such information is likely to be irrelevant and excessive.

4 Personal data shall be accurate and, where necessary, kept up-to-date.

This fourth principle means that companies must take reasonable steps to ensure the accuracy of any personal data they obtain. In practice, this means that they are responsible for ensuring that any data they are storing is up-to-date.

Example

A journalist builds up a profile of a particular public figure. This includes information derived from rumours circulating on the internet that the individual was once arrested on suspicion of dangerous driving.

If the journalist reports that the individual was arrested, without qualifying this statement, he or she is asserting this as an accurate fact. However, if it is clear that the journalist is reporting rumours, the statement is accurate – the journalist is not asserting that the individual was arrested for this offence.

5 Personal data processed for any purpose or purposes shall not be kept for longer than is necessary for that purpose or those purposes.

This is one of the simpler data protection principles. It means that companies must delete information that is no longer needed for the purpose for which it was originally collected.

Example

Images from a CCTV system installed to prevent fraud at an ATM machine may need to be retained for several weeks, since a suspicious transaction may not come to light until the victim gets his or her bank statement.

However, images from a CCTV system in a pub may only need to be retained for a short period because incidents will come to light very quickly.

6 Personal data shall be processed in accordance with the rights of data subjects under this Act.

In addition to the eight data protection principles, the Act also gives certain rights to data subjects:

- The right to access a copy of the information comprising their personal data.
- The right to object to processing that is likely to cause, or is causing, damage or distress.
- The right to prevent processing for direct marketing.
- The right to object to decisions being taken by automated means.
- The right in certain circumstances to have inaccurate personal data rectified, blocked, erased or destroyed.
- The right to claim compensation for damages caused by a breach of the Act.

The sixth principle of the Act upholds these rights.

Example

A man is refused a job in the construction industry and discovers that this is because the prospective employer checked his name against a blacklist maintained by a third party. The blacklist consists of the names of people who are regarded as unsuitable to be employed in the construction industry because they are trade union activists. The man writes to the person who maintains the blacklist, asking for his name to be removed as it is denying him the opportunity to gain employment.

In these circumstances, the person who maintains the blacklist would have great difficulty in establishing any legitimate basis for processing the man's personal data in this way – because the assessment of 'unsuitability' lacks justification, and because the individuals concerned were not told that their names had been placed on the blacklist. In any event, the man can show that he is suffering damage due to this processing and that this is substantial as it could continue to prevent him getting a job.

Figure 9.1 is a mind map summarising the first six principles of the Data Protection Act.

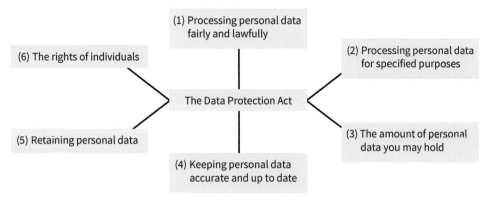

Figure 9.1: Mind map.

7 Appropriate technical and organisational measures shall be taken against unauthorised or unlawful processing of personal data and against accidental loss or destruction of, or damage to, personal data.

The seventh principle means that companies must have appropriate security and be able to prevent the personal data they hold being accidentally or deliberately compromised. This includes physical security, such as locked doors and windows, as well as cyber-security, such as firewalls and storing data in an encrypted format.

Example

A government employee leaves an unencrypted CD containing benefit claimants' details on a train. As a number of basic security precautions have been ignored, the Data Protection Act has been breached.

8 Personal data shall not be transferred to a country or territory outside the European Economic Area unless that country or territory ensures an adequate level of protection for the rights and freedoms of data subjects in relation to the processing of personal data.

The eighth principle is more complex than it first appears. Although companies must avoid transferring data outside the EEA, they can do so if those receiving the data abide by any relevant equivalent legislation (such as the EU-US Privacy Shield between the European Union and the United States).

Example

A university wishes to transfer its human resources department to East Asia, as data processing is cheaper to carry out. As the data being processed could be of a personal nature, the institution would be in breach of the Act.

Key roles in the Data Protection Act 1998

There are three key groups of people mentioned in the Act:

* *The Information Commissioner* is the person whom parliament has empowered to enforce the Act.

- *The data controller* is a person or company that collects and keeps data about data subjects (people).
- *The data subject* is someone who has data about them stored by a third party.

Exemptions from the Data Protection Act 1998

Not all organisations and people need to abide by the Act all of the time. There are specific exemptions for records relating to on-going criminal investigations and matters that could affect national security. Data kept for domestic (personal) reasons, such as a private address book, is also exempt.

Example

A taxpayer makes a data subject access request to HMRC for personal data it holds about her in relation to an on-going investigation into possible tax evasion. If, by disclosing the information that it has collected about the taxpayer, HMRC could prejudice its investigation, it could refuse to grant the subject access. For example, a reason to refuse the request may be that granting access would make it more difficult for HMRC to collect further evidence.

If, however, the taxpayer does not make the data subject access request until some years later, when the investigation (along with any subsequent prosecution) has been completed, it is likely that HMRC would have to comply with it.

Here is a list of useful exemptions.

With this in mind, the government introduced the Patriot Act 2001 to increase the powers of law enforcement agencies. The Act's full name is 'Uniting and Strengthening America by Providing Appropriate Tools Required to Intercept and Obstruct Terrorism Act of 2001'. It contains ten provisions, one of which enables courts to order internet service providers (ISPs) and companies with their headquarters in the United States to hand over information held on their servers anywhere in the world.

It is thought that the Act could be used by US courts to overrule UK and EU data protection legislation, with the result that many companies are now very wary of storing commercially sensitive information on US servers.

Computer Misuse Act 1990

The Computer Misuse Act 1990 was passed in response to a rising level of computer crime and the inability of existing legislation to properly punish those responsible. The Act is lengthy but the four main offences are outlined below.

Section 1: Unauthorised access to computer material

Someone is guilty of this offence if they use a computer to secure access to any program or data held electronically if the access is unauthorised and they know this at the time.

The intention to gain unauthorised access need not be directed at any particular program or data; a program or data of any particular kind; or a program or data held in any particular computer.

Anyone found guilty of an offence under this section of the Computer Misuse Act can face up to 12 months in prison in England and Wales or six months in Scotland. They may also be fined up to a maximum of £5000.

Computing in context: the Patriot Act 2001

Following the attacks on the World Trade Center, September 11th 2001, the US government felt that it was necessary to update its anti-terror legislation to deal with the increased threat from terrorists and organised crime.

This section of the Act is important, as it was the first time that hacking had explicitly been made illegal in the UK. Simply accessing someone else's computer system without their permission is punishable by a prison sentence, even if nothing is taken.

Section 2: Unauthorised access with intent to commit or facilitate commission of further offences

Someone is guilty of an offence under this section if they commit an offence under section 1 ('the unauthorised access offence') with the intention of committing a criminal offence or facilitating the commission of a criminal offence by others.

The Act defines further offence as meaning any activity that is against the law and makes no distinctions between the intention to commit the crime immediately and the intention to commit it at a later date. Importantly, someone could be found guilty of breaching this section of the Act even if they were unsuccessful or it can be proved that they could never have been successful.

Breaching this section of the Act can lead to a prison sentence of between one and five years, or a substantial fine.

An example of this might be if you were to hack into a bank's computer with the intention of transferring millions to your own bank account. You could be prosecuted under this section even if the bank's security measures meant that you could never have achieved your aim.

Section 3: Unauthorised acts with intent to impair the operation of computer, etc.

Someone is guilty of an offence under this section of the Act if they carry out any (knowingly) unauthorised act in relation to a computer with the intention of impairing the operation of the computer. This section also specifically covers any attempt to hinder others' access to programs or data held on a computer. Someone can, in fact, be found guilty under this section of the Act, even if they did not intend to damage the computer, if their conduct was reckless and therefore likely to lead to damaging the computer.

Breaching this section of the Act can lead to a prison sentence of between one and ten years or a substantial fine.

Section 3a: Making, supplying or obtaining articles for use in offence under section 1 or 3

Someone would be found guilty under this sub-section of Section 3 if they were to create, adapt, supply or offer to supply any materials with the intention that they be used to commit a crime. This sub-section also makes it an offence to obtain these tools with a view to passing them on.

Computing in context: the Computer Misuse Act 1990

In February 2014, Lauri Love, a 28-year-old British man living in Suffolk, was accused of breaking into Federal Reserve computers. Love allegedly tried to secretly infiltrate the New York Federal Reserve Bank's computer servers in order to steal non-public information and then post that information on the internet.

According to the indictment in October 2012: 'Mr Love used his unauthorised access to locate and steal certain confidential information residing on the Federal Reserve servers, including the names, e-mail addresses, and phone numbers of users of the Federal Reserve computer system. Mr Love then disseminated that information publicly by posting the information to a website that previously had been hacked and that he controlled.'

Love was accused of breaching the system to steal 'massive quantities' of confidential data, resulting in millions of dollars of losses.

A 2013 US Department of Energy audit report on Mr Love's activities found that personal information on 104 000 people could have been taken. It estimated the fallout of this to have cost the United States at least $3.7 million (£2.2 million), including $1.6 million spent on establishing a call centre to deal with people affected by the data breach. Mr Love is accused of working with at least three other people, who have not been named, to breach the security of the US military, the US space agency (NASA), the Environmental Protection Agency and FBI computers.

He was arrested by officers from the UK's National Crime Agency (NCA) under the Computer Misuse Act and is currently fighting extradition to the United States.

Copyright, Designs and Patents Act 1988

The Copyright, Designs and Patents Act 1988 was not introduced specifically to deal with crimes facilitated by technology. However, the ability of computers to create and distribute thousands of electronic copies of films, books, games and software means that the Act often has to be applied in cases relating to the use of computers.

Copyright law gives the creators of artistic and creative works the right to choose how their material is used. This includes digital artefacts such as games and application software as well as more traditional works such as films, music, dramatic productions, sculptures and books.

Copyright is an automatic right and arises whenever an individual or company creates a work. This means that there is no need to put a copyright symbol on your work. Anything you create is automatically copyrighted to you. Copyright isn't infinite; it lasts for a set period of time. For literary, dramatic, musical and artistic works and films, this is 70 years after the creator dies. For sound recordings, it is 50 years from when the work was first released.

Computing in context: Copyright, Designs and Patents Act 1988

In 2013, UK ISPs were forced by the UK courts to begin blocking access to two sites.

The blocks were imposed after the Motion Picture Association (MPA) won a court order compelling ISPs to cut off the Movie2K and Download4All websites. The MPA, which is the international arm of the Motion Picture Association of America, went to court, arguing that the two websites broke the UK's Copyright, Designs and Patents Act. Both the websites let people download or stream copies of recently released movies that had been ripped from DVDs.

The UK's largest ISPs, BT, Virgin, TalkTalk, Sky and EE, are all believed to have complied with the order and stopped their customers reaching the sites.

The British Phonographic Industry (BPI) is believed to be seeking to block many more sites, as it circulates a list of 25 domains it says are involved in pirating popular music. Included in the list are sites such as Grooveshark, Isohunt, Filestube and Monova.

Offences under the Copyright, Designs and Patents Act 1988

Under the Act it is an offence to do any of the following without the consent of the owner:

- Copy the work, for example, burning another copy of Windows to give to a friend.
- Rent, lend or issue copies of the work to the public, for example, making your music collection available to listen to for free online.
- Perform, broadcast or show the work in public, for example, show your favourite film to a large group of people without a special broadcast licence.
- Adapt the work. There are exemptions to this, but basically you can't take an existing piece of software, change some icons and sell it on.

Exemptions from the Copyright, Designs and Patents Act 1988

You can, however, do some things with copyrighted works without permission:

- Use works for educational purposes where no profit is being made.
- Replicate works in order to criticise or report on them.
- Copy and lend works (applies only to libraries, but they need a specific licence to operate).
- Record broadcasts for the purposes of listening to, or viewing, at a more convenient time: it is not illegal to record programmes from iPlayer or similar catch-up systems with the intention of watching them tomorrow.
- Produce a backup copy for personal use.
- Play sound recordings for a non-profit-making organisation, club or society.
- Make a copy of a computer program in order to study and test it to find out how it works.

Sanctions

Sanctions that can be handed down under the Act are wide ranging and depend on the seriousness of the offence committed, but anyone caught breaching the Act could be sentenced to up to two years in prison and receive a large fine. They may also be liable to pay for any damages caused to the holder of the copyright.

Regulation of Investigatory Powers Act 2000

The Regulation of Investigatory Powers Act 2000 was created to make provision for the interception of communications. It particularly focuses on electronic surveillance, the legal decryption of encrypted data and the interception of electronic communications by the security services, the Secret Intelligence Service and the Government Communications Headquarters (GCHQ). Under the Act, they can intercept e-mails, access private communications and plant surveillance devices.

The Act has been controversial since its inception, earning itself the nickname 'the snoopers' charter'. The government argues that it is necessary to allow law enforcement agencies to keep up with the increasingly technologically advanced techniques being used by criminals and terrorists. However, human rights and privacy campaigners are concerned by the lack of oversight and the wide range of the Act's provisions, many of which they feel could be open to misinterpretation. These groups were further alarmed in 2002 when the government requested that a much wider range of government bodies (including local councils and job centres) be given these powers. The request was eventually withdrawn following growing opposition, but the Act remains controversial.

Computing in context: Regulation of Investigatory Powers Act 2000

In March 2009, the government came under increasing pressure to reform the Regulation of Investigatory Powers Act 2000 (RIPA) after it became known that local councils were using the anti-terror legislation to gather information on minor misdemeanours, such as dog fouling and littering.

A survey of more than 180 local authorities found that:

- 1615 council staff have the power to authorise the use of RIPA
- 21 per cent (or 340) of these staff are below senior management grade
- RIPA powers have been used 10 333 times in the past five years.

Just nine per cent of these authorisations have led to a successful prosecution, caution or fixed-penalty notice.

Provisions of the Act

There are ten main provisions in the Act. It:

1 Regulates the circumstances and methods by which public bodies may carry out covert surveillance.
2 Lays out a statutory framework to enable public authorities to carry out covert surveillance in compliance with the requirements of the Human Rights Act 1998.
3 Defines five broad categories of covert surveillance: directed surveillance (includes photographing people); intrusive surveillance (includes bugging); the use of covert human intelligence sources (informants and undercover officers, including watching and following people); accessing communications data (record of e-mails sent, telephone calls made); and intercepting communications (reading the content of e-mails, listening to calls).
4 Allows the secretary of state to issue an interception warrant to examine the contents of letters or communications on the grounds of national security, and for the purposes of preventing or detecting crime, preventing disorder, public safety, protecting public health, or in the interests of the economic well being of the United Kingdom. This is the only part of the Act that requires a warrant.
5 Prevents the existence of interception warrants, and any and all data collected with them from being revealed in court.
6 Allows the police, intelligence services, HM Revenue and Customs (and several hundred more public bodies, including local authorities and a wide range of regulators) to demand telephone, internet and postal service providers to hand over detailed communications records for individual users. This can include name and address, phone calls made and received, source and destination of e-mails, internet browsing information, and mobile phone positioning data that records the user's location. These powers are self-authorised by the body concerned, with no external or judicial oversight.
7 Enables the government to demand that someone hands over keys to protected information; and makes it a criminal offence to refuse to supply actual encrypted traffic or refuse to disclose an encryption key.
8 Enables the government to force ISPs to fit equipment to facilitate surveillance.

9 Allows the government to demand that an ISP provides secret access to a customer's communication.

10 Makes provisions to establish an oversight regime, creates an investigatory powers tribunal and appoints three commissioners.

Ethical issues

In the past 30 years, computers have revolutionised the world we live in. We can communicate instantly with people thousands of miles away, we can copy in seconds documents that used to take weeks to type up, and access vast amounts of information from anywhere in the world. These advances have led to huge changes in the way we are educated, do business, work and even date. However, no change this seismic could be without controversy and we have also seen growing concerns about personal privacy. Whether you think the introduction of computers is a good or a bad thing probably depends on how you have been affected by them, but one thing is for certain: there is no going back!

Computers in the workplace

One of the places where computers have had the biggest impact is in the workplace. When you finish school, the chance of your going into a job where you don't need to use computers is minimal. Computers would not have been introduced into the workplace if they didn't have benefits for someone. One of the biggest benefits (for some people) has been their cost-effectiveness. Consider the case of car manufacturing. Not so long ago, cars were made 100 per cent by hand; each piece of metal, wood and plastic had to be cut and fitted by trained specialists. It took years to train a master craftsman who could consistently produce excellent work and make sure that all your customers received a car that they were happy with. Of course, even the best craftsmen and craftswomen can have bad days and no one can cut metal into the same shape by hand with 100 per cent accuracy every time. Workers also require holidays, days off and lunch breaks, as well as sickness and maternity leave. You might spend years training someone only for them to go and work for a rival manufacturer. Finally, of course, if you couldn't provide the working conditions that they wanted, they might go on strike, costing you lost orders and lost customers.

These days, all but a handful of modern car manufacturing plants use robots. These are expensive to buy initially but they can work 24 hours a day, 7 days a week and 365 days a year. Robots don't need lunch breaks, sick leave or holidays and, crucially, every piece of metal they produce is identical to the previous one and the next one. Robots don't join unions to demand better pay and conditions and won't leave you to work for a competitor. These qualities have meant that computers have replaced people in the vast majority of manufacturing sectors, from ship building and mining to car manufacture. While these sectors now employ far fewer people than they did previously, outputs are generally higher than they ever were. This has been great if you own a factory or want to buy a cheap, reliable car, but has meant redundancy (often for life) for people who previously occupied skilled, reliable jobs.

Of course, it's not only industrial workers who have lost their jobs because of the introduction of computers. Consider all the secretaries, typists and office workers whose roles are now redundant. Computers can scan documents, use speech recognition to take dictation, and even check for spelling and grammatical errors. Computers can scan, in seconds, documents it would take days to type up, even by a skilled typist using a modern word processor with all the advantages it offers, such as easy correction of errors, spell checking and so on. Databases, spreadsheets and effective search algorithms mean that companies no longer need huge pools of secretaries to file and retrieve client records. Think back to the last time you posted a piece of mail to someone. Compare this to the number of e-mails or text messages you have sent today and it's obvious that the number of postal workers required to deliver letters must have reduced significantly since the advent of computers. However, even in a single industry such as the postal service, the picture is blurred. As people buy more and more goods online, the requirement for package delivery is increasing and, with it, the need for postal workers.

In services such as teaching, where the introduction of computers has opened up a world of opportunities without costing a significant number of jobs, people are still concerned. Teachers are worried about their digital literacy skills: if they can't use the new e-register system, will they be fired? In addition, learning to use and integrate new systems can create extra work, which people might not want to do.

Of course, it's not all bad for employees. Computers can automate mundane, repetitive jobs, leaving people free to focus on more interesting, creative tasks, while learning how to use new technology can lead to more qualifications and better pay. In addition, think of all the new jobs directly and indirectly created through the use of computers: systems analysts, programmers, IT technicians and website designers. Many commentators believe that computers have created more jobs than they have ever removed. Using computers also opens up a world of flexible working. Employees can often work from home and deliver their work over the internet. This cuts down the cost of commuting and childcare for employees while allowing employers to save money on office space and resources.

Ultimately, the ethical arguments about computers in the workplace often come down to a conflict between owners and shareholders seeking higher profits, consumers who want cheap reliable products and workers who simply want reliable, well-paid jobs. Table 9.2 summarises some of the advantages and disadvantages of computers in the workplace.

Advantages	Disadvantages
New jobs have been created.	Some jobs have disappeared completely.
Computers speed up the repetitive, boring parts of jobs, leaving people free to do the creative, interesting parts.	People worry about not being able to use new systems.
Computers are cheaper to run, so have led to a reduction in the cost of manufactured goods.	Learning new systems can take time.
Repetitive jobs, such as copying documents or stamping metal, are carried out more reliably by computers.	New computer systems can be expensive to install.

Table 9.2: Advantages and disadvantages of computers in the workplace.

Code of conduct

When you join a company, enrol at school or sign up to any online system, you have to agree to some terms and conditions. These, amongst other items such as privacy, cover your code of conduct. This is a series of clear guidelines that the individual must adhere to when using the service. A lot of services will state that by the physical act of signing up you agree to abide by the code of conduct. However, schools and companies tend to get each employee to sign something. That way, should any illegal or immoral activity take place, the organisation or school can denounce it as being against their code of conduct.

The code of conduct in schools tends to govern what the student is allowed to do on the school system. This tends to be focused around only using the resources for school work and not for gaming or social media. Additionally, the school may enforce a filter which students are prohibited from bypassing. Companies on some levels may be less strict, but will have much stricter consequences for a breach. In school, you may get a detention or a few weeks of no internet. A company, on the other hand, may terminate your contract.

Code of conduct may include the following aspects –

- Privacy – How the individual may be monitored when using the service.
- Damage – Both physical damage to equipment and computer misuse.
- Access levels – What you may or may not have access to.
- Copyright infringement and protection of assets – Ensuring that the service is not used to breach copyright and that company assets are kept secure.

Artificial intelligence and automated decision making

Artificial intelligence means intelligence that has been built into a computer program, enabling it to perform tasks normally undertaken by humans. Alan Turing, English mathematician, wartime code-breaker and pioneer of Computer Science, developed the Turing Test to decide whether a computer could be deemed intelligent. The test involved an analyst putting the same question to a computer and a person. If the analyst could not distinguish which of the answers was supplied by a human, the computer could be said to be intelligent.

Recent developments in computing, especially powerful processors and cheap storage space, have meant that the creation of true artificial intelligence is coming closer to being a reality. However, these developments raise a huge number of ethical concerns. Imagine a car crash between two driverless cars where someone is killed: who is liable? Is it the programmer, the owner or the manufacturer? Should children and the elderly be allowed to control them? Should such cars have to obey current road rules, such as speed limits?

What about medical robots? IBM's Watson system is currently being programmed to diagnose medical diseases. Doctors and surgeons are required to remember a huge amount of information, work long hours and make life-or-death decisions. A computer would have no problem retaining everything it was told and it wouldn't get tired or hungry. But would you want it to make a decision on whether to operate on a patient?

Robots are already widely used in the military. In November 2012, the US Department of Defense tried to establish guidelines around minimising failures and mistakes for robots deployed to target terrorists. Military robots are not affected by human emotions such as passion or revenge, and so would not make decisions clouded by these feelings. Military robots (particularly drones) have already seen widespread service, in the last few years, in the fight against terrorism. At the moment, drones are controlled by humans, who have the final choice over whether to fire a weapon. However, it is not hard to imagine simply fitting some image recognition software to a drone and letting it decide what to shoot. Who would take responsibility for civilian casualties, in the event of such an incident? How would families get justice?

Think about robots in general (not just drones). If they are intelligent, do we have a right to demand that they clean our clothes, print our documents or calculate our taxes? Should machines with artificial intelligence be allowed to create new machines with even greater intelligence? Should they be allowed to vote? Many people argue that these issues should be addressed before we develop our technology any further.

Computing in context: Driverless cars

Automobile manufacturers and other companies have been experimenting with driverless cars for some time, and they have been legalised in certain US states. The benefits are obvious: no speeding motorists, no crashes because the driver fell asleep and no collisions with stationary objects. Very elderly and very young people could reach their destination safely without the need to pass a test. However, drivers also need to make ethical decisions as well as directional ones! Most drivers will brake to avoid hitting a rabbit, as long as it won't endanger their passengers or fellow motorists. Most of the same drivers would brake much harder to avoid hitting a cat or dog. The balance between not hitting an animal and not harming your passengers is a complex ethical decision, probably based on the individual, the animal involved and who the passengers are. Another example: three small children are crossing a road; two run straight out while the third waits to check if it is safe. If braking wasn't an option, should the driverless car swerve to avoid the two children in the road and risk hitting the one on the pavement?

What about legislation? If a driverless car does kill one of the children who ran in front of it, should the occupant be fined or jailed? What about the programmer or company that developed the car? Should you be allowed to use a driverless car if you are under the influence of alcohol or drugs?

These are all problems that need to be addressed before driverless cars become widespread. Remember, just because something is technologically possible does not mean that it is ethically neutral to do it.

Artificial intelligence and automated decision making

Advantages	Disadvantages
Computers won't react differently based on their mood or lack of sleep.	Computers are unable to make ethical decisions.
Computers can retain a huge amount of information.	Computers are not responsible for their actions, so seeking compensation for mistakes is difficult.
Given the same inputs, a computer always produces the same outputs, offering consistent advice.	Computers are only as good as their algorithms, which are created by people.

Table 9.3: Advantages and disadvantages of artificial intelligence and automated decision making.

Environmental effects

The environmental impact of computers is a complex issue. Many companies are trying to improve their environmental footprint (and their reputations) by going 'paper-less' or 'paper-light'. This approach relies on using e-mails and cloud storage to share information and store documents, which in turn means using less paper. This saves trees and is just one of the ways that companies use computers to soften their environmental impact.

Computers are also being used in the fight against climate change. Computer models and simulations can be used to predict weather and climate patterns, modelling the effects of different initiatives and developments to see which will have the greatest impact.

Computing in context: coltan

Most people have never heard of coltan and yet it is a key component in almost every electronic device they own. Coltan (short for columbite–tantalite and known industrially as tantalite) is used in capacitors to store charge, and 80 per cent of the world's known coltan reserves are in eastern Congo. However, only about one per cent of the metal sold on the open market is Congolese. The reality is that most of Congo's coltan is sold illegally and the revenue, instead of going towards the country's development, is helping to fund an on-going civil war. The coltan mines in the east are controlled by various armed groups, with civilians, including children, recruited as forced labour. The mortality rate in these mines is high.

The mining by the rebels is also causing environmental destruction. In particular, endangered gorillas are being massacred or driven out of their natural habitat as the miners illegally plunder the ore-rich lands of the Congo's protected national parks.

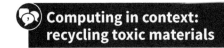

Computing in context: recycling toxic materials

Properly recycling broken computers is a complex and expensive task. Many computers end up simply being dumped in less developed countries where they cause untold environmental damage.

This is particularly a problem in West Africa, where thousands of discarded computers from Western Europe and the United States end up every day. They are placed in massive toxic dumps where children burn them and pull them apart to extract metals for cash. The people who break open these computers regularly suffer from nausea, headaches and respiratory problems. However, it's not just the human cost that is concerning; fumes from burning old computers create air pollution and many of the chemicals leak into the ground, contaminating local water supplies.

However, the issue of new technologies and the environment isn't as simple as it seems. Computers are complex devices and often contain rare metals and minerals that need to be mined from the ground. In fact, a ton of mobile phones contains more gold than a ton of gold ore. Computers often contain toxic chemicals that need to be disposed of when consumers decide that they want the latest device. Devices are assembled in huge factories with all their associated environmental costs. Of course, they also require electricity to operate, the vast majority of which is produced by burning fossil fuels. Every server, hub and network switch relies almost entirely on burning fossil fuels to operate. Anti-virus company McAfee™ recently reported that the electricity needed to transmit the trillions of spam e-mails sent every year is equivalent to powering two million homes in the United States and generates the same amount of greenhouse gas emissions as that produced by three million cars. Of course, electricity costs money and many large companies are keen to reduce their power consumption and switch to green energy. Google was among the first internet companies to take action to at its data centres. It is trying to promote efficient computing and seeking to increase its use of renewable energy.

Environmental impact

Advantages	Disadvantages
Computers can replace paper documents, saving trees and processing.	Computers are made up of rare chemicals that need to be mined.
Computer networks can be used to send products (such as films or music) that would otherwise need to be shipped in lorries and planes.	Computers are made up of toxic chemicals that are often not properly disposed of.
	Computers use electricity, most of which comes from burning fossil fuels.
	Computers require a great deal of intensive manufacture to create, all of which requires burning fossil fuels.

Table 9.4: Advantages and disadvantages of computers on the environment.

Censorship on the internet and offensive communications

Cheap, unrestricted access to the internet has meant that people can access new ideas and share thoughts with people they would never otherwise have met. Online communities are often referred to as 'communities of interest' because they allow people to connect based on a common interest. In the past a person's community was limited by geography to those who lived nearby. These days, with the internet, people can find communities with similar interests, such as cat animations or a particular political view.

This unrestricted access to information has sparked a huge debate between those who seek to control what people can access and those who think access to knowledge is a basic human right.

Those who seek to suppress information range from controlling governments to governments trying to protect intellectual property by compelling ISPs to block access to illegal download sites. There is also a great deal of support for internet censorship from religious and other groups who seek to prevent people from accessing material they deem inappropriate, such as pornography or alternative religious views. On the other side of the debate are human rights and privacy campaigners who argue that everyone should be able to access any (legal) material.

One of the factors weighing in support of those who would like the internet to be free of censorship is the composition of the internet itself. The internet predominantly uses the packet switching protocol TCP/IP, which makes it harder for governments and other pressure groups to intercept information. The internet also enables people to distribute new methods for protecting information (for example, encryption algorithms) very quickly and once these are released, it is impossible to prevent their use. Of course, this by itself is not enough to prevent censorship of the internet, and many governments have successfully blocked access to material they deem inappropriate. Even when material is not being explicitly blocked, many government agencies such as GCHQ in the UK and the NSA in the United States are known to be monitoring a huge amount of electronic communications.

The debate around internet censorship moves at a phenomenal pace and you should make sure that your own knowledge is as up to date as possible; it is, after all, a topic that directly affects your day-to-day life. The 'Computing in context' boxes below outline some of the landmark cases and events in the internet censorship debate.

Computing in context: the UK's internet filter

The arguments surrounding the restrictions are complex and well worth reading about. In simple terms, those in favour of the debate argue that easy access to pornography (particularly extreme pornography) is damaging to children. The National Society for the Prevention of Cruelty to Children (NSPCC) found that almost a quarter of 11 and 12-year-olds had been distressed by an experience online in the past year. It said that, of these, 18 per cent felt upset or scared for weeks afterwards. With pressure mounting to implement a UK internet filter, the UK Prime Minister, David Cameron, stated that, "Web firms have a moral duty to act but have not been doing enough to take responsibility."

Those against the censorship argue that such a filter harms free speech and would be impossible to implement properly, leading to restricted sites being accessible and non-restricted sites being banned. These groups also argue that it is up to parents to inform themselves and monitor their children's internet access, rather than relying on a 'nanny state' to do it for them. The major objection to the filter was that once it is possible to filter one website (say extreme pornography), it is trivial to filter others (for example, an anti-government website). Soon after the filter was implemented, these groups had their fears confirmed when sites about sex education and music piracy were also blocked.

 Computing in context: wikiLeaks and Bradley (later Chelsea) Manning

In March 2011, the US Army charged Private Bradley Manning with 22 counts relating to the unauthorised possession and distribution of more than 720 000 secret diplomatic and military documents. The most serious charge was that of 'aiding the enemy', a treasonous act that carries the death sentence in the United States. He was found guilty of 20 counts, six of them under the Espionage Act of 1917, but was acquitted of aiding the enemy. He was sentenced to 35 years. Private Manning told the court he had leaked the documents to spark a public debate in the US about the role of the military and about US foreign policy.

Manning downloaded the classified documents (among them was video footage of an Apache helicopter killing 12 Iraqi civilians) to a blank CD, which he hid in a music album case. Manning passed the documents to wikiLeaks, a website with a reputation for publishing sensitive material. At the time, wikiLeaks was run by Julian Assange, an Australian with a background in computer network hacking who released tens of thousands of documents obtained by Manning relating to the war in Afghanistan. The website then went on to disclose thousands of sensitive messages (written by US diplomats) and military records from the Iraq war, causing embarrassment to the US government.

Soon after releasing the documents, Amazon (which hosted many wikiLeaks servers) withdrew its services, soon followed by every DNS, which provided the wikileaks.org domain name. WikiLeaks responded by mirroring its site in 14 different countries, making it almost impossible to shut it down, despite US calls for wikiLeaks to be pursued with the same urgency as other suspected terrorist organisations.

WikiLeaks remains controversial, with some believing that it carries out important tasks, exposing government abuses of power and informing the public of what is being done in their name. However, others are outraged and see it as harmful to national security.

 Computing in context: Phil Zimmermann and PGP

One of the most important tools against internet censorship and invasion of privacy is access to strong, free encryption technology. It doesn't matter if your government is collecting your e-mail if they don't know what it says or where it is going. Similarly, there is no point in attempting to prevent people accessing websites if all the content is heavily encrypted.

Historically, encryption was only really relevant to military and diplomatic communications. However, in the information age, where huge amounts of our personal information and communications are stored online, cryptography becomes essential for maintaining our privacy. Capturing billions of e-mails and scanning them for keywords to find the ones you are interested in is also trivial compared to the effort required to do the same for traditional letters. Unfortunately, true encryption is very difficult and before 1990 had been almost exclusively in the hands of governments and their intelligence agencies.

In 1991, American computer scientist and privacy campaigner Phil Zimmermann created an encryption program called Pretty Good Privacy (PGP) and released it for free on the internet. PGP is based on existing public–private key encryption (see Chapter 17 for more detail), but also includes a range of other techniques, such as digital signatures. The important things are that it is simple to use, free, and provides a high level of encryption. It was soon being used around the world.

The US government was not amused, to say the least, since it includes encryption software in its list of military technologies (alongside tanks and cruise missiles). As a result Zimmerman was accused of being an international arms dealer, became the subject of a grand-jury investigation and found himself pursued by the Federal Bureau of Investigation (FBI).

Like all the issues surrounding internet censorship, the debate about people's right to encryption technologies continues. On the one hand are those who point out that these technologies can be used by criminals and terrorists to hide their activities. On the other hand are those who point out that encryption is vital for protecting the rights of repressed peoples and the privacy of everyone who communicates using the internet.

Source: Simon Singh (2002) *The Code Book: The secret history of codes and code-breaking* (London: Fourth Estate).

Advantages and disadvantages of unrestricted access to the internet

Advantages	Disadvantages
People can share and access information that would be very difficult for them to obtain without the internet.	Automated filters make it easy for governments to monitor millions of citizens.
People can spread news of atrocities and corruption very quickly, ultimately helping to bring those responsible to justice.	Computer networks are ultimately owned by governments and large corporations that can control the knowledge to which people have access.
	It is easy to disseminate false information or unconfirmed rumours.
	People can access vast amounts of illegal information and products such as extreme pornography.

Table 9.5: Advantages and disadvantages of unrestricted access to the internet.

Monitoring behaviour

The ability of governments to collect communications information and use this to monitor the behaviour of its citizens is another area where technology is causing controversy. In 2013, Edward Snowden released classified files that showed the US and UK governments were collecting vast amounts of information without people's consent in the name of national security.

Computing in context: Edward Snowden

On 9 June 2013, 29-year-old Edward Snowden revealed himself as the source of one of the biggest leaks in Western intelligence history. Snowden had been an intelligence analyst working as a contractor for the NSA. He used his position (and passwords provided unwittingly by his colleagues) to access classified material and leak it to the world.

Snowden began leaking information by e-mailing the columnist Glenn Greenwald, from the Guardian newspaper, insisting he install PGP encryption software on his laptop. Once they could communicate securely, they arranged to meet in Hong Kong to exchange information.

Snowden's initial leak contained around 20 documents, most of which were stamped 'Top Secret'. At a glance, it suggested that the NSA had misled Congress about the nature of its domestic spying activities, and quite possibly lied. Greenwald described the documents as 'unbelievable', and 'enough to make me hyperventilate'.

To date, Snowden's leaks have revealed that the NSA and GCHQ are using a secret program known as PRISM to collect foreign communications traffic from the servers of nine leading US internet companies, namely Microsoft, Google, Yahoo, Facebook, PayTalk, YouTube, Skype, AOL and Apple. Of particular concern to UK citizens was the amount of internet traffic being monitored by the UK's security service GCHQ, up to 600 million communications every day.

Snowden has also revealed that the NSA and GCHQ are using apps such as Google Maps and Angry Birds to record people's locations, websites visited and contacts. In addition, the NSA was shown to be monitoring the location of 5 billion mobile phones around the world. It was also revealed that it had used these capabilities to spy on foreign leaders and diplomats at the 2009 G20 summit. The most recent leaks have highlighted the NSA's plans to develop a quantum computer capable of breaking all forms of encryption currently in use.

UK and US government reaction to the leaks has been extreme, including detaining Greenwald's partner without charge for nine hours and confiscating all his electronic devices. In one particularly sinister response, the Guardian's London offices were raided and all the hard drives in the building destroyed. Of course, the action had little impact as copies of the leaked files exist on servers around the world.

Many people consider Edward Snowden to be something of a hero. Currently hiding in Russia, he was recently elected Rector at Glasgow University and runs regular VoIP and Twitter sessions explaining his motives for leaking such highly classified material. It's worth noting that some of the government activities he has highlighted may turn out to be illegal, and all are controversial. Others are disgusted by his conduct and say that, by revealing US and UK intelligence capabilities to the world, he is harming national security.

The intelligence community argued that this information was a vital and effective tool for monitoring the behaviour of people who might pose a threat to those around them. However, many people are against this kind of mass surveillance and monitoring believing that it gives the state too much power.

In 2013, Fusilier Lee Rigby was murdered outside Woolwich army barracks. During an inquiry into his death, it was revealed that his murderer had discussed his intention to kill a soldier on Facebook but this information had not been passed on to the security services. The security services were already aware of the killer and it is possible that had they known of his Facebook exchange they could have taken action to prevent the murder. This case underlines the difficulty in striking the right balance between the need of the state to protect its citizens and the needs of citizens to be protected from the state.

Analysing personal information

You have already seen how computers can use databases to store vast amounts of information and complex searching algorithms to quickly select the information they need. These properties can be combined to allow companies and governments to collect huge amounts of information and analyse it for their own purposes.

Store cards can be used to track which products you purchase and tailor the advertising leaflets sent to your home. E-mails can be searched for key phrases that might reveal potential criminal or terrorist leanings. There is a wealth of publicly available information that political parties use to target regions where they may be able to make the marginal gains that will help them win the next election.

Some people find this level of analysis invasive but many others find it very useful. If your local food store can stock food and drink that they think you are most likely to want then they won't lose stock to wastage and you are more likely to find the brands that you want.

Computing in context: Mosaic

Mosaic is a postcode-orientated information system. It takes data from a range of sources like the electoral roll, census and the DVLA, and uses this information to make predictions or assumptions about people who live in a particular area. Mosaic is used by political parties to target voters, department stores to decide what to stock in their shops and even travel agents to decide which holidays to market in a given area.

Upon being given any postcode in the country, Mosaic is able to make predictions about likely consumer habits and lifestyles. This information is very detailed, covering favourite products, media platforms consumers are likely to respond to, even most likely names. This information is very valuable to a range of businesses; not least retail chains, who want to ensure that their shops stock items local people want to buy. Mosaic can even tell you which other areas of the UK have a similar consumer profile; useful if you have a successful retail business and are looking to expand.

More and more political parties are also getting in on the act. The information provided by Mosaic can be used to highlight key types of voters in marginal constituencies. For example, if you know that voters in a particular postcode are sympathetic to your ideas and might be persuaded to vote for your candidate, you could focus resources on that area rather than others where the chance of success is much lower.

Piracy

Piracy has long been a problem for film and record producers but the advent of digital technology, in particular computer networks, has led to an explosion in the amount of pirated material available. Computers make it simple to instantly copy and share copyrighted works and almost impossible to track those who are committing the crime. With so many people accessing copyrighted material for free on the internet, many otherwise law-abiding people simply do not view it as a criminal offence.

Computing in context: the Pirate Bay

The Pirate Bay is a website that provides links and torrent files which enable peer-to-peer file sharing using BitTorrent.

The site was founded in 2003 by Gottfrid Svartholm and Fredrik Neij. The site made it easy to access thousands of copyrighted works and police estimated that the owners made around £109 000 a year through advertising on the website. Since 2009, many ISPs have been ordered to block access to the website, though the site is still easily accessible via proxies established by supporters all around the world. In 2009, the site owners were prosecuted for 'assisting in making copyright content available', found guilty and fined nearly £4 million, as well as being sentenced to one year in prison.

The cost of piracy is difficult to gauge but the Motion Picture Association of America estimates that piracy costs the US movie industry around $20.5 billion (£13.3 billion) per year. However, others question these figures; if someone watches a film they have downloaded illegally but would never have gone out and bought, has the film industry actually lost any money?

You have already seen some of the penalties for piracy in the section on Copyright, Design and Patents Act 1988, as well as how creative industries are joining with governments and ISPs to try and block access to pirated material. The difficulty is the sheer number of people who indulge in piracy. It is costly to track down and prosecute individual file sharers, many of whom are children and teenagers without any means of paying a fine.

Layout, colour paradigms and character sets

To people from different cultures, the same piece of information can mean many different things. There are many examples of brands that failed when they translated their famous slogans in order to target an overseas market; a quick search online for 'slogan translation mistakes' will reveal many examples where poor translation impacted on a product's success. This is particularly a problem if you are marketing a product or providing a service using a medium as international as the internet.

Layout

Even something as simple as website layout will be interpreted differently by different cultures. For example, English speakers read left to right. Therefore, websites built for these audiences tend to have important navigation items (like home buttons) on the left, text tends to be left aligned and the largest, most important articles appear on the left-hand side of the page. Arabic speakers, however, read right to left and websites built for this market tend be completely the opposite; text is right aligned, important articles appear on the right of the page and logos and home buttons appear on the top right rather than top left. If you want your product to sell in the Middle East then you need to ensure that your target audience finds your website as easy to read and navigate as possible. Simply translating the content of the page may not be enough.

Colour paradigms

Colours are particularly prone to cultural interpretation. This is important to know if you have one website that you are using to target lots of different markets. In Western Europe, for example, the colour pink is commonly associated with femininity. In Japan, however, there is no such distinction and in Thailand pink is simply the colour of Tuesday. Yellow in Western Europe can have connotations of caution, alarm or even cowardice but in China it is considered a royal or imperial colour and is seen as being particularly masculine. Of course, cultural interpretations of colour are liable to change over time and may not have a particular grip on the cultural psyche. Use the 'Further reading' section at the end of this chapter to find out more about the cultural associations applied across different cultures.

Character sets

You may already be familiar with the two most common character sets ASCII and UNICODE. ASCII uses 7 bits to represent 128 different characters. This is fine for the English language but is nowhere near enough if you want your product to be translated into Japanese or Arabic. This is one of the major reasons behind the prevalence of UNICODE on the internet. UNICODE compensates for its larger file size by making it possible to represent hundreds of thousands of characters.

However, simply being able to properly display the characters used by your target audience isn't enough. The way in which even simple information, such as a person's name, is recorded varies hugely between different cultures. Imagine you have created a website and want your users to register before they are given access to the content. In England, it is traditional practice for a person to have a single given name (e.g. Charlotte) perhaps a middle name and a surname they have inherited from their father. So a form, which requires the user to enter their first name and surname with an optional field for middle name is reasonably likely to be successful. However, what happens when someone from China wants to sign up for your site? In China, names are typically split into three parts, for example, Mao Ze Bao. The final word Bao is actually the given name, the first word Mao is the family name and the middle name is a generational name, which is also shared with siblings, so the same field layout is obviously not appropriate. In Iceland, a person's surname is generally just their father's name with 'sson' added to the end of the name for a son or 'sdóttir' for a daughter. It would be very unusual to call someone by their surname as it has no cross-generational significance and is very unlikely to be unique. If you want to appeal to all these groups a general 'full name' field is probably going to be more suitable, or even just 'family name', or 'given name'. It's also important that your database field lengths are able to cope with the number of characters entered. Many people assume that some cultures or countries (for example, Spanish) have longer names than others but there are so many variations within these that it is impossible to make any useful generalisations. A good rule of thumb is to aim for slightly over the average and then add ten per cent; so we could say that a first name field should be able to hold up to 20 characters.

Activity 9.1

Join Twitter and follow technology correspondents from major news outlets. Re-tweet anything you are sent that involves technology and the law.

Activity 9.2

Find a recent case where someone has been jailed for their use of technology. What laws were used to prosecute them?

Chapter summary

- The Data Protection Act sets out how those who collect personal and private data may use it. It also covers where this information can be sent and how long it can be kept for.
- The Computer Misuse Act makes it illegal to access a computer without consent as well as establishing the penalties for doing so.
- The Copyright Design and Patents Act sets out who has the right to make money from a particular creative work and how long those rights last.
- The Regulation of Investigatory Powers Act sets out the rules that govern how the UK government can collect information on its citizens.
- Computers have had an enormous impact on almost every work place imaginable. Some see this impact as a negative one costing jobs and reducing wages. Others see it as a very positive one that has created whole new industries.
- Advances in artificial intelligence have given rise to the prospect of automated decision making. Many are happy that impartial machines will make decisions formerly made by fallible humans; others are dismayed by the idea that a computer could make life-or-death decisions.
- Computers have made it easier to publicise the environmental impact of the actions of industries and individuals. But computers themselves require huge amounts of electricity and rare minerals to create and maintain.
- The internet has provided a wonderful forum for debate and free exchange of ideas. However, some governments view this freedom of expression as a threat and seek to censor it.
- Computers allow us not only to hold vast amounts of personal information, but also to analyse it to spot trends and patterns. For some this is useful, for others it is a serious invasion of privacy.
- Piracy and offensive communications began long before the invention of the computer but the advent of the internet means that it is quicker and easier than ever before to distribute offensive and illegal materials.
- The internet has made the world a much smaller place. This presents a unique set of challenges to those who are trying to communicate with everyone in this vast global marketplace.

End-of-chapter questions

1   The Data Protection Act 1998 contains eight principles, what are they?   [8]

2   What is the purpose of the Computer Misuse Act 1990?   [2]

3   In the context of computer-related laws, what does RIPA stand for?   [1]

4   Which piece of legislation is used to prosecute those who illegally download music?   [1]

5   Who is responsible for enforcing the Data Protection Act 1998?   [1]

Further reading

Data Protection Act 1998

Computer Misuse Act 1990

Copyright, Designs and Patents Act 1988

Regulation of Investigatory Powers Act 2000

Patriot Act 2001

Sebastian Thrun, *Google's driverless car*, TED

Kristi Essick, *Guns, Money and Cell Phones*, The Industry Standard Magazine, Global Issues, June 2001

Caroline Sourt, *The Congo's Blood Metals*, The Guardian, December 2008

Richard Wray, *Breeding toxins from dead PCs*, The Guardian, May 2008

James Chapman, *Blocks on internet porn to begin in new year: 20million families will have to make a Yes or No choice on access to filth*, The Daily Mail, November 2013

Laurie Penny, *David Cameron's internet porn filter is the start of censorship creep*, The Guardian, January 2014

Jane Wakefield, *Wikileaks' struggle to stay online*, BBC, December 2010

Ed Pilkington, *Bradley Manning may face death penalty*, The Guardian, March 2011

Profile: Private First Class Manning, BBC, April 2014

Timeline of Edward Snowden's Revelations, Al Jazeera

Chapter 10
Hardware and communication

Learning objectives

- Identify and describe the hardware and communication elements of contemporary computer systems and how they are connected.

- Identify and describe the main components of computer architecture, including von Neumann architecture.

- Identify and describe contemporary architectures.

- Describe different types of memory and caching.

- Describe and explain parallel processing.

- Describe and explain the limiting factors to parallelisation.

- Calculate the runtime of given tasks as a result of parallelisation and evaluate the effect of parallelisation.

- Describe the fetch-decode-execute cycle, including how data can be read from RAM into registers.

- Write simple programs in assembly language and demonstrate how these programs could be executed.

- Describe the use of contemporary methods and their associated devices for input and output.

- Explain the use of these methods and devices in contemporary computer systems and their suitability in different situations.

- Describe and differentiate between voice input for command and control systems, vocabulary dictation systems for general input, and voice print recognition for security. Discuss the suitability of each system in different situations.

- Compare the functional characteristics of contemporary secondary storage devices.

- Explain fragmentation and its consequences and describe the need for defragmentation.

- Describe networks and how they communicate.

- Explain the importance of networking standards.

- Describe the importance and the use of a range of contemporary protocols including HTTP, FTP, SMTP, TCP/IP, IMAP, DHCP, UDP and wireless communication protocols. Explain the role of handshaking.

- Identify and describe applications where connecting a portable device to a network is required.

- Describe the hardware required to make a wireless connection and explain how this might be achieved using contemporary wireless technologies.

Introduction

At the centre of all modern computer systems is a device referred to as the central processing unit (CPU), microprocessor or simply the processor. The processor is the brain of the computer; it carries out all the mathematical and logical operations necessary to execute the instructions given to it by the user. It is one of the most expensive parts of a computer system and upgrading a computer's processor remains one of the best ways of increasing a computer's performance.

Today, processors can be found in anything from smartphones and tablets to washing machines and microwaves.

As you might expect, processor designs are extremely complex and the way they are constructed (their architecture) changes rapidly. Innovations in specialist materials and improved design techniques are utilised to make them faster and more efficient.

To create a processor's architecture, specialists will first design the necessary circuitry. Silicon discs are then produced by melting sand, refining it and finely slicing the resulting crystal. Next, the circuit diagrams are transferred to the silicon discs, resulting in the creation of thousands of tiny transistors; these are joined together using copper to create small integrated circuits. Finally, these are packaged with the pins necessary to connect the processor to a computer's motherboard. This process takes place in a 'clean room', which is a very controlled and sterile environment. The smallest amount of dust could ruin the silicon.

This is a very basic overview of the manufacturing process used to create CPUs. It is well worth using the *further reading* section at the end of this chapter to find out more.

A processor is made up of a number of key parts, which work together to execute instructions. However, the processor requires software to perform any action and in this chapter you will learn about machine code, assembly code and their relationship with high-level programming. You will also explore how the processor transfers instructions from main memory to the processor.

Components of a processor

A processor is a small and complex device. Internally, the processor is made up of a number of key components, which include the Arithmetic Logic Unit, Control Unit and Registers (Figure 10.1). Each component does a different job. This type of processor is used in the von Neumann architecture, which will be discussed later in this chapter.

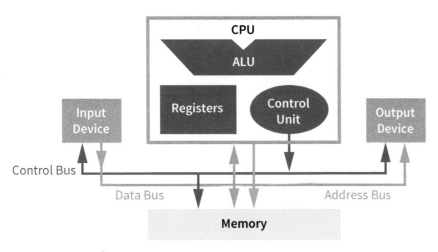

Figure 10.1: Overview of a computing system.

Arithmetic logic unit

The arithmetic logic unit (ALU) is responsible for calculations and logic operations. Calculations include floating point multiplication and integer division, while logic operations include comparison tests such as greater than or less than. The ALU also acts as a conduit for input and output to and from the processor.

Control unit

The control unit (CU) is a key part of the processor. It manages the execution of machine code by sending control signals to the rest of the computer. Control signals are sent via a control bus to connected devices, such as hard drives or the graphics card. Part of the CU's job is to synchronise instructions by using the processor's internal clock. This process will be based on the clock speed. An instruction will take one or more 'ticks' of the clock, known as clock cycles.

Registers

A register is a small block of memory used as temporary storage for instructions as they are being processed. The register runs at the same speed as the processor. A processor contains many registers; some are reserved for specific purposes while others are used for general purpose calculations. Machine code instructions can only work if they are loaded into registers.

General purpose registers are used as programs run, to enable calculations to be made, and can be used for any purpose the programmer (or compiler) chooses. Special purpose registers are crucial to how the processor works. Values are loaded in and out of registers during the execution of a process. Some of the key special purpose registers are:

- Program counter (PC)
- Memory address register (MAR) and memory data register (MDR)
- Current instruction register (CIR)
- Accumulator (ACC)

Program counter

The program counter (PC) stores the address of the next instruction to be executed.

Programs need to be loaded into memory by the operating system in order to function. As memory is referenced using memory addresses, the start of any given program has a specific memory address. It is not possible to know in advance where exactly in memory a program will be loaded, as this is managed by the operating system. Each instruction of the program is assigned an address in memory. The PC initially contains the address of the first instruction of the program, not the actual instruction.

As the process is run, the instruction to which the PC is pointing is loaded into the memory address register (MAR) so that it can be fetched from memory into the processor, and the PC is incremented so that it points to the address of the next instruction. The value added to the PC is calculated from the size of the instructions for the given instruction set.

Sometimes the value of the PC changes as the result of an instruction being executed. This tends to be when a JUMP instruction is run; JUMP is used to provide the functionality of procedures, IF statements and iteration.

Memory address and memory data registers

Currently running programs are stored in memory, which means that they must be loaded into registers. This process is known as fetching and makes use of two special registers, the memory address register (MAR) and the memory data register (MDR). The MAR contains the address of the instruction or data to be fetched. The fetched instruction or data is stored in the MDR. Because fetching instructions from memory can be a slow process, the processor always tries to fetch one instruction ahead of the one it is currently working on. So, while one instruction is being executed, the next one is being fetched. This process of looking ahead is known as pipelining.

Current instruction register

Once an instruction has been fetched, it is copied into the current instruction register (CIR) for executing. As the instruction in the CIR is being decoded and executed, the next instruction is being fetched into the MDR.

Accumulator

Any instruction that performs a calculation makes use of the accumulator (ACC). Many instructions operate on, or update, the ACC. If a subtraction instruction is run, it performs the subtraction using the data part of the instruction and stores the result in the ACC. Calculations take a step-by-step approach, so the result of the last calculation is part of the next. In a certain computer system, an instruction set may use the ACC as part of the calculation. Only one value needs to be given in the data part of the instruction. This is shown in Table 10.1 below:

Instruction	ACC
Initial value	0
ADD 4	4
ADD 2	6
SUB 1	5

Table 10.1: Table showing how the value of the ACC changes when instructions are executed.

Memory and caching

For a program to work, it loads instructions and data from main memory (random access memory or RAM) by using the Fetch-Execute cycle. As memory runs a lot slower than the processor, the processor is likely to have to wait for main memory to fetch data, which results in wasted clock cycles. The overall efficiency of the computer system is reduced, as a lot of time is wasted because of the speed mismatch between the memory and the processor (this is called the von Neumann bottleneck). Cache memory helps to solve this problem by acting as a 'middle man' between the processor and the memory.

Data and instructions that are used regularly are copied into the cache and when the processor needs this data, it can be retrieved much faster than if it were stored in RAM. The processor always tries to load data from the cache, but if the data it needs is not there, it is copied over from RAM. If the cache is full, the least used data in the cache is thrown out and replaced with the new data.

There are a number of algorithms that can be used to ensure that the cache contains the most regularly used data. This is a lot easier than you might expect, owing to the 80/20 rule. Programs tend to spend most of their time in loops of some description, which means that they will be working on the same instructions for a lot of their execution time. The 80/20 rule states that 80% of a program's execution time is spent in only 20% of the code. This proves to be fairly accurate in most cases.

When the processor requests data that is not in the cache, this is referred to as a cache miss. If a system has a high incidence of cache misses, the overall speed of the system will be substantially reduced. Whichever algorithm is employed to manage cache, the primary focus is to minimise cache misses.

Cache memory size is smaller than main memory owing to its high cost. It is categorised by different levels that describe its speed, size and how close it is to the CPU:

- **Level 1** cache is extremely fast but relatively small, and is usually embedded in the CPU.
- **Level 2** cache often has a higher capacity than Level 1, and as a result operates more slowly. It may be located on the CPU, dedicated to single or pairs of cores, or located on a separate chip, to avoid being slowed down by traffic on the main system bus.
- **Level 3** cache works to improve the performance of Level 1 and Level 2 cache and is typically shared by all cores of a processor.

Most modern computers share the same critical problem as a result of using the von Neumann architecture. Because of the speed mismatches between memory, secondary storage and the processor, most of the processor's time is spent idle. This is known as the von Neumann bottleneck.

Parallel processing

The classic von Neumann architecture uses only a single processor to execute instructions. In order to improve the computing power of processors, it was necessary to increase the physical complexity of the CPU. Traditionally this was done by finding new, ingenious ways of fitting more and more transistors on to the same size chip.

However, as computer scientists reached the physical limit of the number of transistors that could be placed on a silicon chip, it became necessary to find other means of increasing the processing power of computers. One of the most effective means of doing this came about through the creation of multi-core systems (computers with multiple processors).

One of the most common types of multi-core system is the parallel processor. They tend to be referred to as dual-core (two processors) or quad-core (four processors) computers.

Computing in context: von Neumann bottleneck

John von Neumann was a Hungarian-American mathematician, born in 1903. He is widely considered to be one of the fathers of modern-day computing. He also made many contributions to areas of mathematics such as game and operator theory.

In 1945, while consulting for an engineering group developing the EDVAC computer, von Neumann released a paper entitled 'First draft report on the EDVAC'. To give the report context, it is important to understand the EDVAC computer and generally how computing was achieved in the 1940s. The majority of computing systems in use today are based on the von Neumann architecture, named after him.

In parallel processing, two or more processors work together to perform a single task. The task is split into smaller sub-tasks (threads). These tasks are executed simultaneously by all available processors (any task can be processed by any processor). This hugely decreases the time taken to execute a program, but software has to be specially written to take advantage of these multi-core systems.

All the processors in a parallel processing system act in the same way as standard single-core (von Neumann) CPUs, loading instructions and data from memory and acting accordingly. However, the different processors in a multi-core system need to communicate continuously with each other in order to ensure that if one processor changes a key piece of data (for example, the players' scores in a game), the other processors are aware of the change and can incorporate it in their calculations. There is also a huge amount of additional complexity involved in implementing parallel processing, because when each separate core (processor) has completed its own task, the results from all the cores need to be combined to form the complete solution to the original problem.

This complexity meant that in the early days of parallel computing it was still sometimes faster to use a single processor, as the additional time taken to coordinate communication between processors and combine their results into a single solution was greater than the time saved by sharing the workload. However, as programmers have become more adept at writing software for parallel systems, this has become less of an issue.

Advantages	Disadvantages
More instructions can be processed in a shorter time because they are executed simultaneously.	It is difficult to write programs for multi-core systems.
Tasks can be shared to reduce the load on individual processors and avoid bottlenecks.	Results from different processors need to be combined at the end of processing, which can be complex and adds to the time taken to execute a program.
	Not all tasks can be split across multiple processors.
	Concurrency introduces new classes of software bugs.

Table 10.2: Table showing the advantages and disadvantages of a parallel computer.

Runtime calculations

You may be required in an exam to explain the limiting factors of parallelisation in parallel processing in terms of runtime. Programs written specifically for parallel processing may have a certain portion of code that cannot be parallelised.

In the following example, a program has a runtime of 5 hours when using a single core processor. If 80% (4 hours) of this program can be parallelised, then clearly a multi-core processor will reduce the runtime required. However, regardless of the number of cores used to execute this program, the minimum runtime cannot be less than the time taken to execute the non-parallelised 20% (1 hour). The remaining 20% will still be processed sequentially.

Amdahl's law is used to calculate the minimum runtime of executing a program on a certain number of threads:

$T(n) = T(1)\ (B + \frac{1}{n}(1 - B)$

Where:

- $T(n)$ = time taken on n threads
- n = number of threads
- B = fraction of the algorithm that is sequential

As in the single-core example above, Amdahl's law demonstrates that with one thread ($n = 1$), the runtime of executing the program is 5 hours:

$T(n) = T(1)\ (B + \frac{1}{n}(1 - B)$

$T(1) - 5 \text{ hours} \times (0.2 + \frac{1}{n}(1 - 0.2)) - 5 \text{ hours}$

However, using Amdahl's law to calculate the runtime in a quad-core processor with four threads ($n = 4$), you get:

$T(n) = T(1)\ (B + \frac{1}{n}(1 - B)$

$T(4) - 5 \text{ hours} \times (0.2 + \frac{1}{4}(1 - 0.2)) - 2 \text{ hours}$

Note that even with an infinite number of threads, the runtime of executing the program cannot be less than 1 hour.

Fetch-decode-execute cycle (FDE)

When instructions are to be executed by the processor, they must be loaded into the processor one after another, via a process known as the fetch-decode-execute cycle (FDE). In the previous section, you were introduced to a number of special purpose registers used during the FDE cycle and in this section you will see how they work together. It is important to remember that a single processor can only execute a single instruction at a time from the current instruction register. By using a large number of registers, the whole process can be made more efficient using a system called pipelining. Figure 10.2 shows a summary of the registers involved in the FDE cycle.

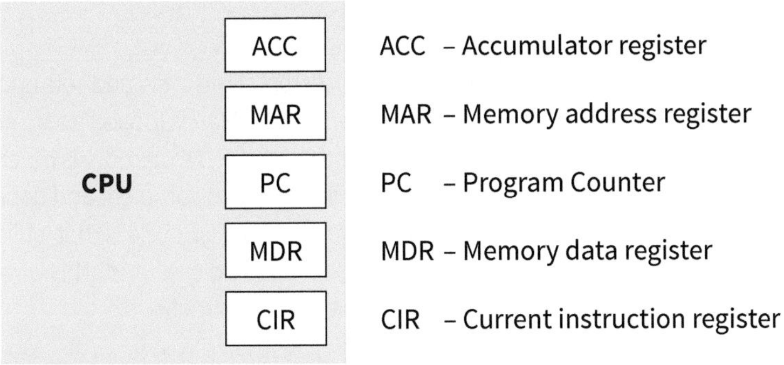

Figure 10.2: Specialist registers used during FDE cycle.

In Figure 10.3, the address stored in the PC is 0092. The first part of the cycle is to fetch the next instruction for processing. The PC is copied over to the MAR and then the PC is incremented. Most programs will run serially, unless a control instruction such as a jump is encountered, so by incrementing the PC it is highly likely that it will be pointing to the next instruction to be fetched.

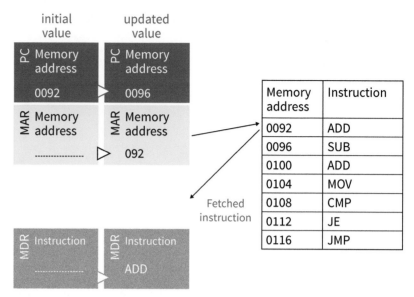

Figure 10.3: The content of registers change during FDE cycle.

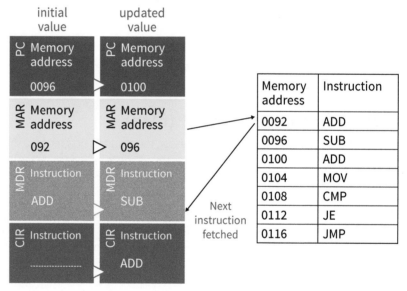

Figure 10.4: Registers during the second stage of the FDE cycle.

Figure 10.4 shows how the registers are altered in the first step of the cycle and sets up the fetch part of the cycle. In order to fetch, the address found in the MAR is looked up in memory and the contents of that memory address are loaded into the MDR. As memory is much slower than the processor, the fetch could take a number of clock cycles to complete and depends on whether the data is found in cache memory. An advantage of the FDE cycle is that while one instruction is being fetched, the previous one is being decoded and executed. This is why it is necessary to have separate registers for fetching and executing instructions.

In order for the processor to execute the instruction after the fetch, it must decode the **opcode** part of the instruction. The contents of MDR are copied over to the CIR. From here the instruction can be decoded and then executed, and as this is happening the next instruction can be fetched. Figure 10.5 shows what the registers look like during the second stage of the FDE cycle. As the first instruction, ADD, is being decoded, the second one is being fetched while the PC is pointing to the third. That way, the processor is always trying to be one step ahead of itself in order to make most efficient use of memory and clock cycles.

The cycle is designed to perform as many actions of the processor concurrently as possible, thus improving the overall speed of execution.

In nearly any program, at some point a control instruction that will force a jump from one instruction to another that is not in sequence will be encountered. The most common such instruction is a jump. A jump breaks the FDE cycle and forces it to start again from scratch, because the next instruction that has been fetched, the next one in sequence, is not the next instruction that should be executed. Consider the instruction JE 0092 (jump if equal to address 0092) and the CMP command has returned true for equality (Figure 10.5). Executing this instruction will cause a break in the linear flow of the program and will update the PC to be 0092.

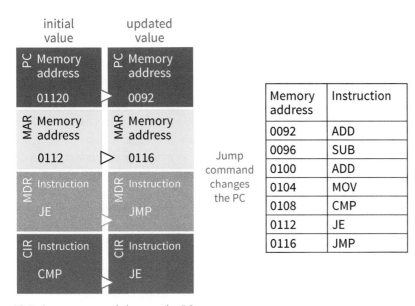

Figure 10.5: Jump command changes the PC.

Jumps slow down the processor by losing the benefits of pipelining. When programming in Assembly, or when a compiler optimises code, it is important to limit the number of jump commands.

Processor speed

Processor speed is measured by the number of clock cycles that the processor can perform in a second and is measured in hertz (Hz). A clock cycle is one 'tick' of the CPU clock. During a clock cycle the processor can fetch, decode and execute a simple instruction, such as load, store or jump. More complex instructions take more than one clock cycle.

It is easy to calculate the amount of time it takes to run one cycle for any speed of processor. The calculation for a 2 gigahertz (GHz) processor is shown in Figure 10.6:

The number 2 000 000 is obtained by converting GHz to Hz.

$$Frequency = \frac{1}{Time}$$

$$Time = \frac{1}{Frequency}$$

$$Time = \frac{1}{2097152}$$

$$Time = 4.768 \times 10^{-7}s$$

Figure 10.6: Calculating the time taken to complete one clock cycle on a 2 Ghz CPU.

> ## Tip
>
> You may be asked to calculate clock speed in the exam.

Processors are getting to the point where it is hard to increase speed. When the number of clock cycles per second is increased, the transistors within the processor have to switch faster, which generates more heat. Unless the heat is drawn away from the processor, it can easily overheat. A processor can reach temperatures in

Figure 10.7: Heat sink and fan alongside a processor.

excess of 300 degrees Celsius, which is hotter than an oven, in a matter of seconds. If you open up a desktop PC, you will see a large heat sink and fan attached to the processor (Figure 10.7), which has the job of pulling all of this heat away from the processor. You should never run a system without a heat sink as this could cause permanent damage to both the processor and the motherboard. It would also pose a severe fire risk.

Processor manufacturers, such as AMD or Intel, try other methods to increase the performance of their CPUs. This can include increasing the number of cores (processors) in the CPU, making existing circuitry more efficient, or developing new instructions. In order to make a fair comparison of these processors, they should be subjected to controlled tests. An excellent place to see benchmarks of different processors is http://www.cambridge.org/links/kwse6059.

Assembly language programming

In some computer systems, there is a simple architecture designed to help you understand the concepts of machine code and instruction sets. An example of this is the Little Man Computer (LMC). The LMC has a very limited selection of instructions, shown in Table 10.3 along with their opcodes. An xx in the opcode refers to the data part of the instruction (if required – not every instruction needs data). For example, in order to add, you first need to know what you are adding. To keep things simple, the LMC has only two registers, ACC and PC. Data and instructions are stored in memory locations known as mailboxes; this is an exact simulation of a standard von Neumann-based computer. Conceptually, a mailbox represents one single byte of memory.

Opcode	Name	Data	Explanation
1xx	ADD	The number to add	It will add a value from a mailbox to the current value of the ACC
2xx	SUB	The number to subtract	It will subtract a value from a mailbox from the current value of the ACC
3xx	STA	Stores a value into a mailbox	Will take the contents of the ACC and store it in a mailbox
5xx	LDA	Loads a value from a mailbox	Will take a value from a mailbox and store it in the ACC
6xx	BRA	Line number to 'jump' to	Unconditional branch. Will jump to the given instruction number
7xx	BRZ	Line number to 'jump' to	Branch if zero. Will only jump if the ACC is zero
8xx	BRP	Line number to 'jump' to	Branch if positive. Will only jump if the ACC has a positive value. NB: Zero is classed as a positive number
901	INP	Input from the user	Will input a value and store it in the ACC
902	OUT	None	Will output the contents of the ACC
xxx	DAT	Address of a variable	Used at the end of the program to declare any variables used

Table 10.3: Table showing the instructions available in the LMC.

Mailboxes can be referred to directly, or indirectly, through the use of labels. A label is a text symbol that represents a mailbox, making coding in LMC easier. When a label is used to represent a mailbox, the LMC assembler assigns a suitable mailbox as the code is assembled.

The simple LMC program in Figure 10.8 will add two numbers input by the user. Each line of the code is converted into an LMC machine code instruction and stored in a single mailbox. Line 1 is converted to '901', which is stored in mailbox 0. Line 2 stores the value in the accumulator in mailbox 6, which is represented by the LMC code as the label FIRST. The fully assembled code is shown in Table 10.4.

Pos	0	1	2	3	4	5	6
Value	901	306	901	106	902	0	12

Table 10.4: Table showing an LMC program and its mailboxes.

A more complicated LMC program can be seen in Figure 10.9. This program will display the numbers from 1 to 10, but could easily be updated to perform actions on any sequence of numbers. Assembly code, regardless of **CPU** architecture, does not have control statements such as IF or WHILE. Instead, the flow of execution is changed by conditional jump commands. In LMC, jumps are referred to as branches. It is possible to represent any programming control statement through branches and jumps.

Branches allow decisions and loops to be coded in LMC. Figure 10.10 is a diagrammatic representation of the LMC code to add the numbers 1 to 10. The line **BRA LOOPTOP** does an unconditional jump back to the top of the loop. **BRP ENDLOOP** breaks out of the loop once the ten numbers have been added. BRP will only branch if the value in the accumulator is positive, which is why 10 is subtracted from the current count. Initially count will be 1, so 1 minus 10 will result in a negative number. One gets added to the count and we branch unconditionally. This continues until count becomes 10, as zero is considered to be a positive number. Rather than having a command that loops only if the accumulator is negative, you can use simple maths to remove the need for the command entirely.

```
0       INP
1       STA    FIRST
2       INP
3       ADD    FIRST
4       OUT
5       HLT
6  FIRST DAT   0
```

Figure 10.8: Sample LMC program to add two numbers together.

```
0
1              LDA   ONE
2              STA   COUNT
3              OUT
4  LOOPTOP     LDA   COUNT
5              ADD   ONE
6              OUT
7              STA   COUNT
8              SUB   TEN
9              BRP   ENDLOOP
10             BRA   LOOPTOP
11 ENDLOOP     HLT
12 ONE         DAT   1
13 TEN         DAT   10
14 COUNT       DAT   0
```

Figure 10.9: Sample LMC program to display the numbers from 1 to 10.

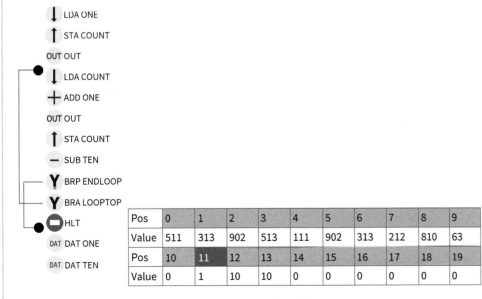

Pos	0	1	2	3	4	5	6	7	8	9
Value	511	313	902	513	111	902	313	212	810	63
Pos	10	11	12	13	14	15	16	17	18	19
Value	0	1	10	10	0	0	0	0	0	0

Figure 10.10: Diagram showing the LMC code required to add the numbers 1–10.

Activity 10.1

Using an LMC simulator enter the following code.

```
0              LDA  ONE
1              STA  COUNT
2              OUT
3    LOOPTOP   LDA  COUNT
4              ADD  ONE
5              OUT
6              STA  COUNT
7              SUB  TEN
8              BRP  ENDLOOP
9              BRA  LOOPTOP
10   ENDLOOP   HLT
11   ONE       DAT  1
12   TEN       DAT  10
13   COUNT     DAT  0
```

Run this program to ascertain its purpose. Once you understand it, write the code out in a high level language or in pseudocode.

Consider the following high-level code below:

```
1   x = 0
2   total = 0
3   while x < 10
4        total = total + x
5        x = x + 1
6   end while
7   print total
```

Rewrite this code using the LMC simulator.

Input and output devices

Input devices allow interaction with a computing system. This could be through a standard interface, such as a mouse or keyboard, or through more advanced interfaces such as Microsoft's Kinect games controller. Once data has been captured by an input device, it must be processed by software before information can be given back to the user.

Optical character recognition (OCR)

Optical character recognition (OCR) converts printed media into editable text documents using a scanner. OCR empowers the user to change sections of text on a printed document. It also means that old books, for example, can be digitised, allowing them to be published in new formats for new markets such as e-readers.

OCR is a post-processing step that occurs after a document has been scanned. It performs pattern matching by scanning the image for shapes it can recognise as letters, numbers or symbols. This is done by comparing the binary data to an internal database of known character shapes. When a binary shape is found in a document, OCR transforms it (resizes and rotates it) until it matches a known shape from the database. If no match is found, that shape is skipped.

It is very easy for a human to read text off a document, but very complicated for a computer to do it. This is why OCR will sometimes get it wrong, so the resulting document must be proofread.

Optical mark recognition (OMR)

Optical mark recognition (OMR) is based around a predefined form, which has areas where someone can mark multiple choice responses (Figure 10.11). The form has specific parts for someone to fill out by putting a thick black mark on them. A special reader then reads in this form in order to detect the dark marks and note their position on the page. As the form is predefined, the scanner knows what option the user has selected. If two marks are made in the same section, the reader accepts only one of the answers, most likely the first one. Also, if the mark does not cover the whole of the circle, the reader may miss it. This type of input is used for multiple choice exams and registers, as they can be automatically marked and processed. It is not suitable for any form of written communication.

Figure 10.11: A typical input sheet for an OMR reader.

Magnetic ink character recognition (MICR)

Magnetic ink character recognition (MICR) uses a combination of ink containing iron oxide and specific fonts so that data written using this ink can be read by a specialist MICR reader. Normal ink does not contain iron oxide, so only the MICR ink will be picked up by the reader, effectively ignoring everything else. This means that regardless of what is written over the magnetic ink, it can still be read by the device.

This is almost exclusively used for cheques because of the high cost of the reader (Figure 10.12). The cheque number and account number are written on the bottom of each cheque using magnetic ink. This can be very quickly read in by the reader, so cheques can be processed quickly by the banks. One of the key benefits of MICR is that it does not have to rely on OCR, which can be problematic.

Figure 10.12: A standard bank cheque. Notice the number in electronic ink along the bottom.

Touch screens

Touch screens are very popular in most modern computing devices, especially since the release of Windows 8, the first major desktop operating system focused on providing a touch screen interface. Many laptops, desktops and the majority of mobile phones have a touch screen interface. Car entertainment, satellite navigation devices and printers often use touch screens. There are two types of touch screen, Resistive and Capacitive. Both versions send the X and Y coordinates of the touch to the operating system when a touch is registered. It works using a grid system, with the screen being split up as shown in Figure 10.13. The Y-axis increases in value going down rather than up, which is different from what you may be used to in mathematics.

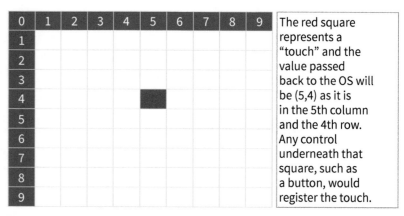

The red square represents a "touch" and the value passed back to the OS will be (5,4) as it is in the 5th column and the 4th row. Any control underneath that square, such as a button, would register the touch.

Figure 10.13: A touch screen grid.

Resistive touch screens are much cheaper and are made up of two thin transparent sheets. When these sheets touch each other, a voltage is recorded at that position. A certain amount of pressure is needed to make the sheets touch, which is why this type of touch screen is known as resistive. These screens do not provide as sharp an image as capacitive screens, nor do they allow for multiple touches.

Capacitive touch screens allow for a much sharper image and for multiple touch points to be recorded simultaneously, making them superior to, and more expensive than, resistive touch screens. Capacitive touch screens make use of the fact that the human body can conduct electricity: when you touch a capacitive screen you change the electric field of the area you touched. This change in field registers as a click and sends the X and Y coordinates back to the operating system. One downside, apart from the expense, is that you cannot make use of a capacitive screen when wearing gloves or using items such as a pen, as they do not conduct electricity.

Voice input

Voice input can be used to issue spoken commands to a computer system via a microphone, and the computer will try to interpret the commands and carry them out. An example of this may be a user asking a computer to increase the volume on a media player. Voice input is different to vocabulary dictation as there is a set amount of commands that the computer is able to carry out.

Vocabulary dictation

Vocabulary dictation can be used to input data into a computer system, where a user will speak into a microphone and the computer will try to change the spoken words into typed text. Vocabulary dictation is a popular interface as it is natural for people to communicate in this way. Specialist vocabularies are available with additional words for particular types of users, such as medical and financial users.

Table 10.5 shows some of the common advantages and disadvantages of voice input and vocabulary dictation:

Voiceprint recognition

Voiceprint recognition is the process of capturing a person's voiceprint then digitising and storing this data on a computer system. Voiceprint recognition is often used in security systems, where a person may attempt to gain entry to a high security room. When entry is attempted, the voiceprint of that person is again captured. The two data items are compared, with entry being allowed if there is a match.

Advantages	Disadvantages
• Speech input can be much faster than keyboard input • No need to learn to type • Less danger of RSI • Reduces typing mistakes such as spelling/hitting wrong key • Keyboard takes up room on the desk/space on a small touch screen • Users with a disability that prevents typing can use speech input • Hands-free advantages – can multi-task • Users find talking more natural than typing.	• Background noise interferes with speech recognition • The software may not cope with all accents of the same language • A user with a speech impediment, sore throat or cold may not be understood • Users with a disability that prevents speech would need to find a different method for input • Difficult to keep data input private as people can hear what you are saying • Words that sound the same (heterographs, such as 'too' and 'two') may be incorrectly interpreted.

Table 10.5: Advantages and disadvantages of vocabulary dictation.

Secondary storage

Computing systems that need to save information will have some form of storage device. Magnetic hard drives (HDD) are very common in desktop and laptop PCs, but increasingly solid state drives (SSD) are being used. Tablet computers, smartphones and some modern laptops or desktops make use of SSDs as their secondary storage device.

Storage devices in a computing system commonly store:

• the operating system and utilities
• user applications
• user documents and files.

Magnetic storage devices

A hard drive is a high-capacity storage medium, common in most modern PCs. Hard drives are used to store the operating system, software and user data. As hard drives have a fast transfer rate and a fairly fast access time, they provide a good compromise between storage capacity, performance and cost. Their speed does not come close to the speed of memory, the CPU or even SSDs.

Hard drives are a magnetic medium and store data on a hard drive platter (Figure 10.15). Data is read and saved using an arm that has a special read/write head at the end. As the disc spins, the arm travels across the disc. Each sector of the platter can store data and the movement of both the disc and the read/write head means that every sector on the hard drive can be reached. In order to read or write data, a small magnetic flux is introduced on the disc. The oxide on the hard drive platter remembers this flux. Data is then encoded using standard binary techniques, with the flux able to store either a 1 or a 0.

The faster the platter spins, the faster data can be read from the disc. This speed is measured in revolutions per minute, or RPM. A common speed for hard drives is 7200 RPM, but it can vary. Every minute that a 7200 RPM hard drive is in use, the platter will have spun 7200 times. Hard drives can run at 15 000 RPM, but these are expensive and

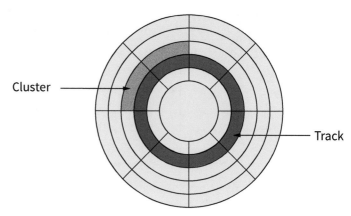

Figure 10.15: Hard drive platter.

tend to be used in servers rather than in home PCs. Laptops sometimes use slower drives to conserve power.

As hard drives provide a pivotal role in a PC, it is essential that they are well maintained. Hard drives do not last for ever and will develop errors over time. These errors are managed by the hard drive and the operating system; however, if there are too many errors, performance can be compromised. Also, these errors can lead to data corruption.

Flash storage devices

SSDs are becoming more popular in modern computing systems and use flash memory to store data rather than magnetic discs. They use a special type of memory that can retain its state once power has been disconnected. It is known as EEPROM or **e**lectronically **e**rasable **p**rogrammable **r**ead-**o**nly **m**emory. SSDs tend to have better performance than hard drives, but also tend to be more expensive and have lower capacity. Performance is increased due to the lack of physical motion. There is no spinning disc or moving read head and thus the time it takes to find data on an SSD is reduced.

Memory sticks and memory cards, such as SD (secure digital), use solid state technologies. They all have the same advantages and disadvantages as SSD drives.

Optical drives

Optical drives work by using lasers to store data by burning microscopic indentations into a disc such as a CD. This pattern of indentations is created in a spiral pattern, starting from the middle. Indentations and their absence create pits and lands (Figure 10.16), which are used to store binary data. A laser is aimed at the disc and reflected back, which can cause interference with the original laser. This change in interference is how the optical device can tell the difference between a pit and a land. DVD-ROM uses the same techniques to store data, but the data is stored on two layers. Two lasers of differing wavelength are used to read data from the two layers. Pits and lands are stored closer together, meaning that the laser's wavelength must be shorter.

Optical media tend to be used to store multimedia information or programs, for example DVD movies and music CDs. Software such as Microsoft Office is often distributed on this type of media. The capacity, cost and size of these media make them suitable for storing high-definition data.

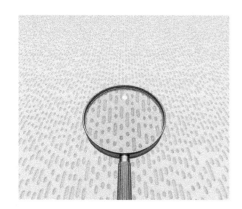

Figure 10.16: Pits and lands on the surface of a CD.

Blu-ray follows the same principles but uses a laser with a much smaller wavelength. The laser has a distinctive blue colour, which is why it is referred to as Blu-ray. With a smaller wavelength the pits and lands can be much closer together, allowing more data to be stored.

CD-R and DVD-R can store multimedia or user data onto CDs or DVDs. When a CD or CD-R is created, it cannot be modified. As such, it is useful for creating a permanent backup over time. As CDs are physically small, they will not take up too much storage space. Rewritable CDs and DVDs exist; they allow the user to write to them many times but are expensive and slow when compared to memory sticks and memory cards.

Contemporary storage devices

Storage systems for enterprises

Most of the storage devices considered so far are mainly intended for use by small systems or individual end users. Storage requirements for enterprises, however, are much more demanding. When you have over a thousand people trying to access the same set of files at the same time, some serious hardware is needed. A simple hard drive will not be sufficient.

In order to provide scalability and performance, multiple drives that can be brought together to act as a single drive will be needed. Building a custom network-attached storage device (NAS) can be very expensive. It is better to bring many disparate devices together and treat them as a single drive. This is known as virtual storage. Before we look at how virtual storage works, it is important to understand a few of the key technologies used for large-scale storage.

Redundant array of independent discs – RAID

Redundant array of independent discs (RAID) is one of the most common technologies that run behind the scenes. It can be used with both SSD and HDD and allows multiple drives to be brought together as a single drive. NAS devices will commonly support multiple drives and be in some form of RAID.

A RAID array can be in one of the following modes:

- *RAID 0 Striped*: this provides improved performance and additional storage. However, it does not provide any fault tolerance, so any errors on the discs could destroy the RAID.
- *RAID 1 Mirrored*: each disc provides the same information, which provides some fault tolerance. As data is repeated, read speed is increased (because it can be read from any disc), but write speed is decreased (because all discs must be updated).
- *RAID 3–6 Striped parity*: this requires at least three discs in the array. As well as fault tolerance it provides parity checks and error correction. The parity information is stored on a single drive, so the other drives can continue working when one of the drives fails. The lost data can be calculated using the parity data stored on the parity drive. This configuration involves sacrificing storage space to increase redundancy.

Common uses of storage devices

CD-ROMs and DVD-ROMs

CD-ROMs and DVD-ROMs are used to install software and store multimedia. Rewritable versions are expensive and slow and rarely used for backup.

Flash memory drive and portable hard drives

Flash memory drives are used to transport files from one place to another. Portable hard drives (whether magnetic or SSD) are external devices that function in exactly the same way as internal drives. They usually have a plastic or metal enclosure and normally connect to the computer through a USB cable.

Fragmentation and defragmentation

Files stored on computer systems can, over time, become fragmented. This means that they are split and stored on different parts of the disc. If a file is fragmented, it takes longer for the disc heads to move between parts of the file, which slows the process of loading it.

Defragmentation is the process where files are physically re-arranged on disc so that they are no longer fragmented and the parts of each file are stored together. This improves the speed of accessing data from disc.

Unlike magnetic storage devices, SSD uses direct access to data so there would be little point in defragmenting an SSD as there would be no improvement in read times as there's no physical read head to move. As a result, defragmentation may perform "trim" commands which may slightly improve the speed of future write operations. As SSD is currently made out of NAND based flash memory, which has a limited lifespan, the defragmentation process may shorten its lifespan.

Networks

Most computing systems are connected to some form of network, most commonly the internet. Computers may be connected through wired or wireless links. At its most basic, a computer network is a collection of interconnected computers that have the ability to communicate with one another.

The importance of networking standards

What underpins all communication is the idea of protocols. No matter what data is being sent or how the various devices in the network are connected, a set of protocols is required to ensure that both the sender and the receiver understand one another.

Types of network

Not every service or task a user wishes to perform will be done on a single computer. Networked computers can share files, offer services (such as email) and communicate with each other. Even when two PCs share a printer, a network is involved. The biggest network in the world is the internet.

When services are distributed over a network, you have a **distributed** system. A distributed system, in essence, is where computers work together by sharing services with one another in order to provide a complete system. In a distributed system, it is important to remember that both processing and data are distributed.

Networks differ in size depending on where they are located. At home, you will most likely have a small network. This is referred to as a local area network (LAN). Schools have a bigger network than at home, with many more computers connected together. Even though the size of a school network is large when compared to a home network, it is still referred to as a LAN. Local refers to the computers being near each other geographically rather than the number of computers connected to the network.

The internet is a worldwide communications infrastructure, which means that you can access websites, or more specifically web servers, in any country in the world. As the geographical distance between computers on the internet is very great, the internet constitutes a wide area network (WAN).

LANs are inherently more secure than WANs. In a LAN setting, all networked devices are likely to be under the control of a small group of network technicians, whereas WANs involve many different people. As data travelling over WANs is likely to travel over many different networks owned by many different people, there is a much higher risk of data being intercepted. This form of threat, known as a man-in-the-middle attack, means that unencrypted data could be stolen or altered. This is why you should be careful about what information you send over the internet and why you should also make sure that you only use sites that encrypt your personal data before sending.

Structures for networked services

Two common structures for networks are client–server and peer-to-peer.

Client–server structure

Most distributed systems work on the client–server model (Figure 10.17). Services, such as file storage, are made available on servers to which clients connect in order to access the services. Web servers, which host websites over the internet, are among the most common. Clients use web browsers to access the webpages held on the server.

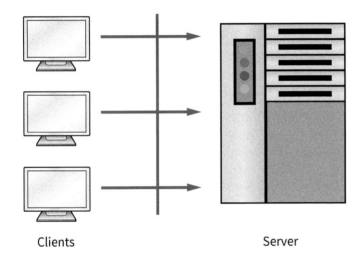

Clients	Server

Figure 10.17: Client-server model.

Servers are also known as centralised computing, as services and processing power are held at a central point on a network rather than using the distributed model, where resources are spread across a set of peers.

Clients and servers make use of a request–response model. Clients request a service or resource from the server. The server responds either with a security challenge or with the requested resource. If the server fails for any reason, the service cannot be provided by that server.

Peer-to-peer networks

In a peer-to-peer network, each computer, or peer, has the same status as the others. No computer acts as a server, meaning that peers must work together to fulfil the required task. One of the most common uses of peer-to-peer networking is file sharing. A file required by a number of peers is downloaded in parts. Initially each peer downloads parts of the file, known as leeching, until they have enough of the file to start sharing. Other peers on the network then start downloading the parts of the file from the peers that have already downloaded them, until each peer has full access to every part of the file. As soon as a peer has the whole file, it becomes a seed and continues to share the file until that peer is taken out of the network. Peer-to-peer networking allows very large files to be downloaded efficiently without the need for a powerful server.

Peer-to-peer technology can also be used to share the processing load for complicated calculations. This form of peer-to-peer networking is known as distributed processing. Difficult problems that require extensive processing time are split up into smaller chunks and these chunks are shared with peers. Each peer then solves part of the problem and returns the result to the peer that is responsible for consolidating and coordinating the calculations. Examples of distributed projects can be found at http://www.cambridge.org/links/kwse6061.

Protocols

When talking to someone who does not speak English as their first language, you may have difficulties being understood. At some point you will have to make a decision to aid communication. Maybe they speak a little English so you decide to use simple English, or maybe you speak a little of their language. It might be possible to mime what you want to say or even to try to draw or use symbols. If you're lucky, you might have a translator handy who could act as a go-between. However you decide to communicate, you will have needed to make a conscious choice of the communication style and decide on a set of rules to govern future communication. Computers, when they transmit data, can do so in many different ways. As such, it is crucial that each computer not only follows a set of rules, but ensures that both sides use the same ones. In computing, a set of rules that governs communication is known as a **protocol**.

In the early days of computers, there were many different ways of doing exactly the same job. This problem became very apparent when computers started to become networked. At that time, there were two main ways of communicating over a network, IPX (internetwork packet exchange) and TCP/IP (Transmission control protocol/nternet protocol). It is not possible for a computer using IPX to communicate with another computer using TCP/IP without making use of special hardware to translate, known as a bridge. IP addresses take the form of four sets of numbers ranging from 0 to 255, while IPX uses a 32-bit hexadecimal address. This is why the choice of protocols is so important: if each computer knows exactly how data should be sent over the network, when it arrives the computer will know exactly how to process it.

Protocol stacks

There are many different tasks that need to be carried out when sending a packet over a network. How will the packet get there? How will the packet be formatted? Does the packet need to arrive in a specific order? What happens when an error is introduced during transmission? Owing to all the work that needs to be done, it is not practical to place all of it into a single protocol, so a number of protocols are chained together and known as a protocol stack.

Protocol stacks have many advantages:

- Separation of logic so problems in a single protocol can be dealt with in isolation.
- Protocols at different parts of the stack can be swapped out.
- More flexibility when choosing what properties you want your network to have.

The TCP/IP protocol stack is a prime example.

The TCP/IP protocol stack

The TCP/IP protocol stack, which is the protocol suite used in most modern network transmission, is named after the two of the protocols it contains, although it also contains other protocols. Figure 10.18 shows the four key layers of the TCP/IP stack:

Tip

A classic exam question is to define a protocol and then explain why they are used in stacks.

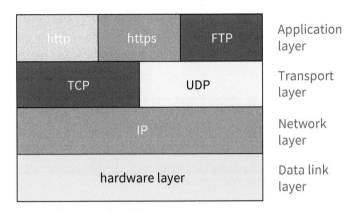

Figure 10.18: TCP/IP protocol stack.

At each layer, apart from the bottom layer, there is a choice of which protocol to use. Each choice provides a different service, which will provide different properties for the packet being sent.

The top layer has a large number of options and is sometimes referred to as the presentation or application layer. Protocols used in this layer are very specific to applications. For example, HTTP (hypertext transfer protocol) is used to transport the HTML of webpages, while FTP (file transfer protocol) is used to send simple files over a network. The transfer protocol used at layer three depends on the application that is running. Having this choice of layer three protocols means that it is very easy to add new protocols without having to change any of the existing structure.

This is possible because there is a common interface between layer three and layer two. So HTTP and FTP create a packet differently, but they set it up in a way that any of the layer two protocols will understand. Each protocol offers different services, but always formats packets so that they can be understood by the other layers. The service access point (SAP) is where protocols will communicate with each other (Figure 10.19) and is generic, so that any protocol can be swapped out without affecting the other protocols in the stack. That way, the application chooses the service it requires, without having to tailor the data for a specific protocol. It is important to note that protocols at both ends of the network must match, otherwise the packet will not be understood.

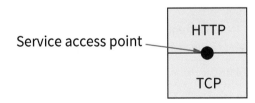

Figure 10.19: SAP.

Figure 10.20 shows how elements of the TCP/IP protocol stack communicate. The principle applies equally to other protocol stacks. Each protocol in the stack communicates along the logical communication lines. Each protocol considers that it communicates directly with its counterpart on the destination machine, and it does so by adding data to a packet's header for its counterpart to read. However, what actually occurs is that information is passed down each protocol, with data being added to the packet's header as it goes, before being placed on the network hardware, which transports it. At the destination, the packet is passed back

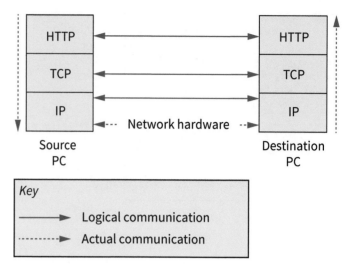

Figure 10.20: Packets travel through different layers of the stack.

up the protocol stack, with each protocol removing a part of the header. The actual path that a packet will travel is denoted by the dashed line in Figure 10.20.

HTTP

Hypertext transfer protocol (HTTP) allows resources, such as images or text files, to be transmitted over the network. Each item is identified using a, a uniform resource locator (URL), and is transmitted over port 80. HTML pages, which are stored as text files, are downloaded using HTTP along with any resources identified within. The web browser then interprets the HTML code and displays the webpage. HTTP is a stateless protocol, meaning that each HTTP request is independent. No data is recorded between requests. This makes interactive websites and web apps more difficult to program, which is why other technologies, such as sessions and AJAX, are becoming common on websites, as they overcome this shortcoming of HTTP.

When an HTTP request is sent, it is structured in the following way:

- Initial line
- Header line 1
- Header line 2 ...
- Optional message.

The initial line is different if this is a request to, or a response from, the server. When a request for a resource is sent to the web server, it might look like the line below:

```
GET /path/to/file/index.html HTTP/1.0
```

GET instructs the server to send a file, which is pointed to by the path, which is the URL with the host name taken off. The last part refers to which version of the HTTP protocol should be used. The server may respond with an error code, should a problem arise when it tries to send the resource back. Some of the more common error codes include:

200 – OK!

404 – File not found

302 – Resource has moved

500 – Server error

Header information is sent, which includes information about the browser and other general purpose information that will be used by the server. A lot of this information is used for statistical purposes by the web server, such as recording the most common browser type. The message is the data to be sent back, which will be the contents of the file.

FTP

File transfer protocol (FTP) works on an interactive model and is used when copying (uploading or downloading) a file from one location to another via the internet. FTP remembers information about the state of the connection; that is, each subsequent request makes use of information sent in previous requests. FTP uses port 21.

A common FTP conversation may look like this:

>> OPEN ftp.example.com

<< Which account do you want to access

>> USER bert

<< That account requires a password

>> PASS mypassword

<< welcome

>> CD mydirectory

<< DIR changed

>> LIST

<< Contents of directory myfile.txt

>> RETRIEVE myfile.txt

<< File sent

SMTP

The simple mail transfer protocol (SMTP) is an internet standard for electronic mail (email) transmission. SMTP by default uses TCP port 25 and the protocol for mail submission is the same, but uses port 587. Mail servers use SMTP to send and receive mail messages. Client mail applications, on the other hand, normally use SMTP only for *sending* messages to the server for relaying. For receiving messages, IMAP or POP are used.

IMAP

The internet message access protocol (IMAP) is a protocol used for transferring emails between computer systems via the internet. The IMAP protocol is generally used for email retrieval and storage as an alternative to POP. The IMAP protocol, unlike POP, allows multiple clients to connect to the same mailbox simultaneously.

DHCP

The dynamic host configuration protocol (DHCP) is a standardised network protocol used on internet protocol (IP) networks for assigning dynamic IP addresses to devices on a network. With DHCP, computers request IP addresses and networking parameters automatically from a DHCP server, reducing the need for a network administrator or a user to configure these settings manually.

TCP

The transmission control protocol (TCP) provides reliable and error-checked streams of packets over a network and is the core transport protocol for HTTP. Each set of data sent using TCP, known as an octet, contains a **checksum** generated using cyclic redundancy checks (CRC). A sequence number is also included, so that the stream of packets can be reorganised in the correct order at the destination. Port numbers, both source and destination, are included, so that the packet can be correctly routed to the corresponding application.

In order for a packet to be accepted, an acknowledgement field is included in TCP. This is simply the highest sequence number of the last accepted packet. This enables the source to resend data should packets get lost or damaged.

UDP

The user datagram protocol (UDP) provides an unreliable communication channel with a minimal level of features. There is no error checking, ordering of packets or resending of lost packets. UDP is commonly seen as a fire-and-forget protocol. At face value, this may not seem very useful, but UDP has a number of advantages. As it does not use any checksums or ordering, less data has to be sent with each packet, which makes better use of the bandwidth. Also, as there is less processing involved, data will be passed back to the application much faster. Applications that require data fast, but are not concerned about losing data along the way (such as video conferencing applications), are better served by UDP.

IP Address

In order for computers to talk to one another, each one must have a unique address, known as an IP address (internet protocol address). An IPv4 address is made up of a set of four numbers of up to three digits, ranging from 0 to 255, such as 192.168.0.1. When data is transmitted over a network, the IP address of both the sender and the receiver must be included. The destination IP address is needed to ensure that each packet can be routed to the correct destination. The source IP address must be included so that information can be sent back. Most networking communication takes the form of a request and a response, so without the source IP the response could not be sent back to the correct destination.

Computing in context: Running out of IP addresses

Each device connected to the internet must have a unique IP address. This uniqueness applies across the world, not just in a single country, which raises a massive problem: there are a limited number of IP addresses available. Version 4 of the internet protocol (IP), which uses four bytes to represent a single address, has a maximum of 4 294 967 296 or 2^{32} unique addresses. This value may seem huge, but considering that the world population is about 7.15 billion (7 150 000 000), not everyone on the planet can be connected at the same time using this version. Matters are made much worse by the fact that an individual may be using multiple devices connected to the internet at the same time, and every computer at work or at school must also have an IP address; it is easy to see how the number of addresses can run out.

This problem has been known for some time and steps have been taken to enable more devices to be connected:

- *Dynamic IP addresses*: Most devices connected to the internet do not have a fixed IP address, known as a static address, but rather a dynamic one. When a device connects to the internet, an IP address is assigned to it by the internet service provider (ISP). ISPs have a set of addresses assigned to them, which they use for their clients. A request is sent to a DHCP (dynamic host configuration protocol) server, which assigns an IP address. By issuing IP addresses on demand, they can be recycled.
- *Network address translation (NAT)*: Private LAN networks can share a smaller number of external IP addresses to connect to the internet by using network address translation, also known as IP masquerading. Each private LAN has an internal IP address range, allowing it to use as many IP addresses as needed. When connecting to the internet, these addresses must be translated to the external IP address. A router holds a table of these IP address translations so that responses can be returned to the sender. This effectively allows an entire LAN, such as a school might have, to share a single IP address. Modern home routers also use NAT to allow a single IP address to be shared by all connected devices.

NAT works by changing the TCP/UDP port numbers of the source IP address. In Figure 10.21, three PCs in a private LAN each have their own IP addresses. When they connect to the internet, these addresses are translated using NAT into the external IP, with each PC having a unique port number. When the result comes back, NAT uses the unique port numbers to translate the address back to the original private IP.

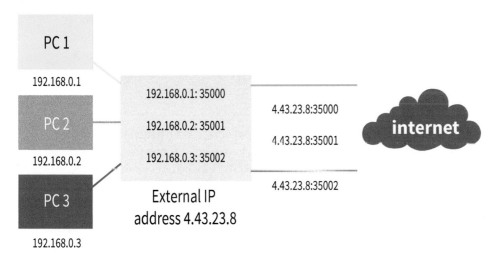

- *IP version 6*: IP addresses specified in this chapter are in accordance with version 4 of the IP protocol. There exists a version 6, which uses 16 bytes per address rather than four. This gives a maximum IP address range of $2128 = 3.4 \times 10^{38}$. This may seem like an obvious solution, but the problem is that devices that use version 4 do not work with version 6. A lot of the internet's infrastructure would have to be replaced, which is very difficult as no one person or organisation owns the internet or has influence over each router. Thus, version 6 rollout is very slow.

Activity 10.2

This task requires you to use Linux. This can be done by installing a Linux distribution of your choice, using a Raspberry Pi or using a virtual machine. The commands listed below will not work on a Windows PC.

1   Run the command ifconfig and write down the MAC address and the IP address of your current computer.

2   Run the command dig www.pwnict.co.uk +short. What does this command do?

3   Install traceroute (sudo apt-get install traceroute).

4   Run the command traceroute www.pwnict.co.uk. Explain the output of this command.

5   Run the command netstat -tp. Explain the result of this output.

Read over the tutorial for programming sockets in Python. A socket is a programming term for making and using a network connection.

Tip

A lot of the theory of handshaking is covered in this chapter. Make sure, where relevant, to make use it in your answers. The exam will normally focus on handshaking for communication over a cable rather than a network.

Handshaking

In order to set up a communication link, both devices need to agree on a set of protocols to use. This must occur before a single byte of data is sent and is known as handshaking. The handshaking signal is sent from one device to the other and is acknowledged by the second device. It is entirely possible that the second device disagrees with the choice of protocols, so either another set must be chosen or communication will fail.

Networking hardware

In order to connect computers together into a network, certain hardware is required. There is a massive range of hardware solutions for networking and the ones described in this chapter are the main ones.

Network interface card

In order for a PC to connect to a computer network, it needs a special piece of hardware called a network interface card or NIC. This hardware is responsible for placing packets onto network cables in the form of electronic signals, or bursts of light if the cable is optical. NICs produce electric signals based on the physical protocol being used on the network, one of the most common data transmission systems being Ethernet. NICs tend to be built into most modern motherboards, so extra hardware is not needed. Home networks make use of Ethernet and twisted pair cables, also known as CAT5.

Wireless interface cards, or WICs, are needed if the connection to the network is wireless. Most devices have WICs built onto their motherboards, with the exception of desktop PCs. Wireless networks make use of the 802.11.x protocol rather than Ethernet. Again, this is a physical protocol and uses electromagnetic waves to transmit data.

Hub

A hub allows more than one computer to be interconnected in a network by connecting them all into one central device or hub. When using a hub, each computer uses a single cable to connect to the hub, which ultimately creates a path between each computer. If a single cable breaks, it affects only the computer connected to the hub by that cable rather than the entire network. When a packet is sent to a hub, it will broadcast the packet to all other computers connected to the hub. A single hub, depending on the size, can have up to 48 PCs connected. If 48 computers were connected to a single hub, then, when a packet arrived, that packet would be repeated to all 48 connected computers. Internally, hubs are bus networks, with the bus being inside the hub.

Hubs work well for small networks with low network traffic, but the more PCs are connected, the more traffic will be generated, increasing the number of packets colliding or getting corrupted. Bandwidth is an issue with hubs, so it is not advisable to have too many devices connected to a single hub, nor is it sensible to chain them together. However, they are much cheaper than switches or routers, which means that they do have a part to play in most networks. A common approach is to use a hub to connect a small number of devices together, for example one room in a school, and then connect the hub to a switch so that some level of routing can be achieved.

Switch

Switches, unlike hubs, perform routing of packets from one port to another. A port on a networking device is the physical RJ45 connector for a networking cable, as shown in Figure 10.21. When the packet arrives, the switch determines the port on which the destination address exists; this process is known as routing. In order to ensure that packets are sent to the correct destination, a picture of the network must be built up in the form of a table.

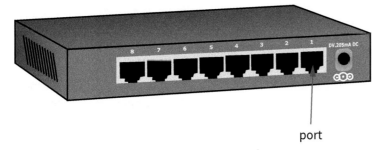

port

Figure 10.21: Network hub.

Switches perform routing at the MAC (media access control) level rather than at the IP level. MAC addresses are hard-coded into each device by the manufacturer, and take the format of 12 hexadecimal values. Every MAC address is unique, and while IP addresses can be changed, MAC addresses cannot. When a packet arrives at a switch, the switch looks at the packet's MAC address and forwards it on to the correct port. Initially the switch does not know which port a specific device is connected to, so it has a blank routing table. In this scenario the switch broadcasts a discovery packet to ascertain which port, if any, that networked device is on. When a device receives a discovery packet, it responds, allowing the switch to make a note of the port the reply came back on. A sample table (Table 10.6) is shown below:

Port number	MAC address
1	00:00:AE:3B:09:FF
2	00:00:4B:BC:00:E1
3	00:1A:D7:B6:CA:F2

Table 10.6: Table showing the MAC address of devices connected on various ports of a switch.

Router

Routers perform a very similar job to switches: they route packets to the correct port. Like a switch, they have an internal representation of which devices can be found on each port through the routing table. However, there are differences between the devices and they are used for very different purposes. Routers are used to connect different segments of a LAN together and allow access to the outside networks such as the internet.

Routers perform routing on IP addresses rather than MAC addresses. Sections of a network, known as sub-domains, can be assigned similar IP address ranges, which provide the router with more information to help it direct the packet. When connecting different parts of a LAN or WAN together, a router ultimately has to deal with more devices than a switch does. This is why routers tend to have a more powerful processor and are more expensive. Routers are necessary when connecting to any WAN, which is why the device you may use at home is a router.

Wireless interface card

A wireless interface card (WIC) connects to a wireless access point (WAP). A WAP is a device that allows wireless devices to connect to a wired network using Wi-Fi or similar standard. A WAP has a maximum number of devices that it can support and a physical broadcast range where connections are possible. It is possible to detect a wireless network by sitting outside a company's premises, which is why security on a wireless network is a top priority.

Wireless networks use encryption and require a special key in order to stop unauthorised people accessing the network. Home routers normally offer wireless connection and tend to have security set up by default. This is intended to protect data sent over the router, but the level of protection is only as strong as the encryption methods used. Some wireless security protocols, such as WEP, can be cracked very easily by a determined hacker. WPA2 is one of the more secure wireless protocols available at present.

Wireless networks minimise the amount of cable needed when setting up the network, but are more error prone. Distance from the router, interference from other devices and even bad weather can impact the speed and quality of connection. When a wireless signal is low, packets may contain errors and the data will need to be resent.

There are two main wireless technologies in use at the time of writing, 802.11 and Bluetooth. Both have their uses, but only 802.11 is used for networking. Bluetooth is used for connecting external devices, such as wireless handsets, to other devices.

Chapter summary

- A CPU is made up of the following components:
  - ALU – arithmetic logic unit
  - Registers
  - CU – control unit.
- Machine code instructions are written in binary and are made up of an opcode and data.
- Little Man Computer a is simplified architecture used to help learners understand the basics of low-level programming.
- The fetch–decode–execute (FDE) cycle will fetch instructions from memory to be run on the CPU. During the cycle the following registers are used:
  - MAR – memory address register, which stores the address of the instruction to fetch
  - MDR – memory data register, which stores the data or instruction once fetched
  - PC – program counter, which stores the address of the next instruction to fetch
  - CIR – current instruction register, from where the instruction will be decoded and executed.
  - ACC – accumulator, which is used to store the results of a calcultion
- Cache is fast memory that sits between memory and the CPU. It is used to help remove the impact of the von Neumann bottleneck.
- Processors, to improve the throughput of instructions, perform parts of the FDE cycle concurrently, which is known as pipelining.
- A multi-core system is a common architecture where processors have more than one core, allowing multiple processes to be run concurrently.
- Parallel systems are made up of multiple processors which can perform multiple operations concurrently. Code must be written in such a way as to take advantage of any parallelism.
- Random-access memory (RAM) stores the currently running programs, operating systems and user files.
- Read-only memory (ROM) stores the boot-up software required to initialise the hardware, load settings and initiate the operating system (OS).
- Input devices provide data for processing and come in the form of scanners, optical character recognition, optical mark recognition, barcodes, magnetic ink recognition, touch screens and sensors.
- Storage devices store data and programs when the computer is powered down. The main types of storage device are:
  - magnetic – back-up tape and hard drives
  - optical – CD, DVD and Blu-ray
  - solid state – solid state hard drives, memory sticks and secure digital (SD) cards.
- Redundant array of independent discs (RAID) arrays are used in servers and for more data-critical systems. They allow multiple drives to be connected together to form a single drive.
- RAID arrays can provide fault tolerance in the form of mirroring and parity bits.
- Storage area networks (SAN) can connect numerous different types of storage device as a single device.
- Virtual storage will abstract the type of storage device in a SAN, allowing devices to be added and removed without having to administer the individual devices.

- Networks rely on the use of protocols and standards to ensure that communication between devices can occur even if those devices were produced by different companies.
- Client–server-based architecture is where a powerful computer (known as a server) provides functionality to the rest of the network (a service). This can include providing files, websites or databases.
- Peer-to-peer networks have no server; rather each computer has the same status as the other. These networks are commonly used for file sharing.
- Error detection ensures that packets arrive at their destination without corruption. Common error detection methods include:
    - parity bits: adding additional bits to make the number of ones odd or even, depending on the type of parity chosen
    - echo: packets are returned from the destination and then compared by the sender
    - checksum: calculations are performed on the packet generating a checksum that is sent with the packet; this calculation is repeated and the checksums compared.
- Protocols are a set of rules that govern communication.
- Handshaking is a process that devices undertake when a connection is set up. This is where the set of protocols to be used is agreed.
- Protocol stacks allow the separation of logic for each protocol, enabling different parts of the stack to be swapped.
- Transmission control protocol/internet protocol (TCP/IP) stack is the most common protocol stack used in networking.
- Hypertext transfer protocol (HTTP) is used for the transmission of webpages and webpage components. HTTP uses port 80.
- HTTPS (secured) is a secure version of HTTP and communicates over port 443. Certificates and the secure sockets layer (SSL) protocol are used to secure communication.
- File transfer protocol (FTP) uses port 21 and allows files to be transmitted.
- The transport layer of TCP/IP uses either TCP or UDP:
    - TCP provides a streamlike communication with error detection, ordering of packets and confirmation that packets have been received.
    - UDP (user datagram protocol) is a fire-and-forget approach with minimal protections.
- IP is a network layer protocol that provides routing. It uses the end-to-end principle where each node is considered to be unreliable and therefore each node is asked to perform routing.
- Common networking hardware includes:
    - network interface card: allows a computer to connect to the network
    - hub: connects multiple computers and packets are broadcast to all connected devices
    - switch: allows multiple devices to be connected and provides routing by media access control (MAC) address
    - router: connects different networks together and uses IP addresses for routing; commonly used to connect to the internet.

End-of-chapter questions

1   Explain the purpose of each of the following items of networking hardware.

    a   Hub   [2]

    b   Switch   [2]

    c   Router   [2]

2   Describe, using specific protocol examples, the TCP/IP protocol stack.   [8]

3   Describe how the FDE cycle is used by the CPU and how pipelining can be
    used to make the process more efficient.   [8]

Further reading

OSI model (reference model for networking)	Search for the OSI model on tech-faq.com
Warriors of the net (video introduction to networking)	Go to warriorsofthe.net
HTTP protocol (request fields definition)	Search for HTTP request fields on w3.org
Microsoft introduction to TCP/IP	Search for Introduction to TCP/IP on the Microsoft TechNet website
Socket programming introduction in Python	Search for Python Sockets on codingtree.com

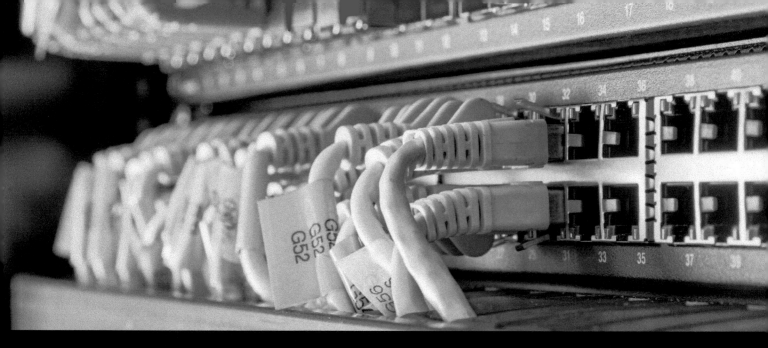

Chapter 11
Data transmission

Learning objectives

- Describe serial and parallel transmissions, their advantages and disadvantages.
- Describe simplex, half duplex and full duplex transmission methods.
- Explain the need for multiplexing and switching.
- Describe, using appropriate network protocols such as TCP/IP, the typical contents of a packet.
- Explain network collision, network collision detection and how these collisions are dealt with.
- Describe methods of routing traffic on a network.
- Calculate data transfer rates on a network.
- Calculate lowest cost routes on a network.
- Describe the internet in terms of a world-wide communications infrastructure.

Introduction

When data is transmitted, whether over a network or not, it is sent in the form of a packet. A data packet is split into three main parts: the message, a header and a footer (Figure 11.1).

Header	Message	Footer

Figure 11.1: Packet structure.

A packet has a maximum amount of data that it can transmit, defined by the protocol currently in use. Protocols enforce and provide services to enable data transmission and govern the rules that apply. As packets are limited in size, a large file needs to be split into multiple packets. Each packet, therefore, contains only part of the original file. For example, if a file is 36 MB in size and the maximum packet size is 10 MB, the file must be sent in four separate packets (Figure 11.2).

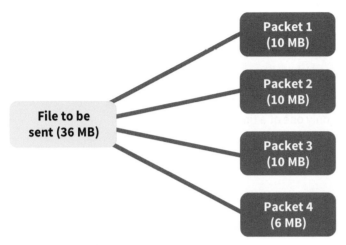

Figure 11.2: Files are made up of multiple structures.

A packet can be thought of as being like an envelope, with critical information about the destination and sender written on the outside of it. Information required to transmit the packet to the correct destination, such as source and destination IP address, must be added to the header. Each protocol employed during the transmission of data adds information to the packet's header or footer. Exactly how this process works is looked at later in this chapter.

Serial and parallel transmission

Data can be transmitted using serial or parallel transmission. Serial connections always send one bit after another in order. Parallel, on the other hand, can send more than one bit at the same time. Serial and parallel are independent of duplex mode (see below), meaning that you can have combinations such as serial full duplex or parallel simplex.

 Tip

Duplex mode and parallel or serial transmission are not just related to networking. Any cable transmitting data has a duplex mode and uses either parallel or serial communication. When answering questions on data transmission, it is important to know how each mode works.

Simplex, half duplex and full duplex transmission

When a network is set up, the parties involved need to decide how data will transmitted between computers; in other words, which protocol is to be used. They must also decide which duplex mode to use. There are three main duplex modes (Figure 11.3): simplex, half duplex and duplex (or full duplex).

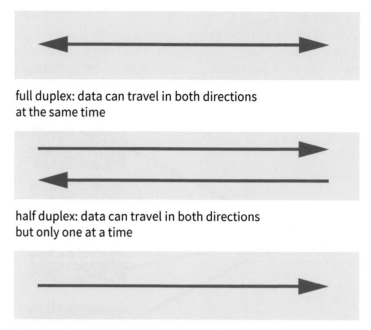

full duplex: data can travel in both directions
at the same time

half duplex: data can travel in both directions
but only one at a time

simplex: data can travel in only one direction

Figure 11.3: Types of duplex mode.

Simplex data connections send data in only one direction, so no return packets are allowed. Satellite connections for TV use simplex mode, as satellite dishes can only receive data from a satellite – they cannot send messages back. Full duplex, or just duplex, makes use of separate cables to send data back and forth. A twisted pair cable, such as CAT5, could have two pairs used for uploading and two for downloading (Figure 11.4). That way, packets travelling in opposite directions do not interfere with each other. Half duplex makes full use of all cables when transmitting data, but flow can switch direction based on communication need. As packets can travel in either direction along the same line, sometimes there are collisions when two packets are sent along the same line in different directions. When this happens, the data is lost and must be sent again.

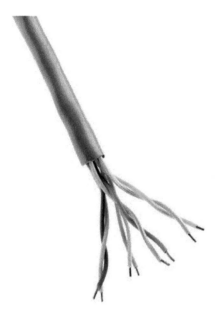

Figure 11.4: CAT5.

Multiplexing

Data transmission speeds can be increased using multiplexing. Multiplexing is a method where several independent data sources are combined and sent along a single route to a single destination. Several data streams can be combined and transmitted over the same wire.

Packet and Circuit Switching

A large network, such as the internet, can be an incredibly large collection of interconnected networks (Figure 11.5). There are so many connections that it will be possible for a packet to find more than one way to reach its destination. This is very similar to our road system. There are many different ways to get from one place to another. Some ways are quick, some are slow and some are just plain silly (for example, going from Reading to London via Birmingham). One of the key benefits of having multiple routes is that if one route is down, because of road works or traffic, alternative routes can be found. Networks have the exact same properties and packets can have a choice of how they are routed. Packet and circuit switching are two methods of sending packets across a network with multiple paths.

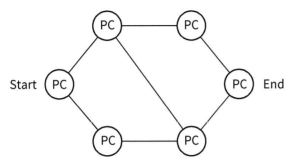

Figure 11.5: The internet.

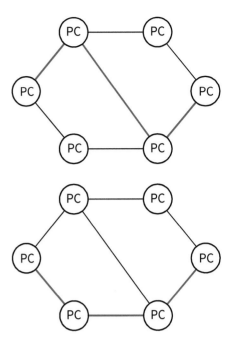

Figure 11.6: Routes of a single packet.

Because of all of the links, the internet is very resilient to broken lines or faults. If one line is broken, another one can be used. One issue with having so many paths is that a route needs to be worked out in order to get from one PC to another. A single packet can travel down the network in a number of different ways. Two of those ways are shown in Figure 11.6 (links travelled are shown in bold).

In circuit switching, a path across the network is set up in advance and all packets are then sent in order down the same route. The route cannot be used by any other traffic during that time. All packets, on arrival, will be in order, but the circuit is vulnerable because if any part of the route is broken, the whole circuit will fail. When a link fails, a new circuit has to be set up before further communications can take place, which could cause problems. One of the most common uses of circuit switched networks is our phone network. When a number is dialled, a circuit is set up so that voice data can pass. If that link breaks, the conversation has to end and the number be redialled. Another issue is that bandwidth can be wasted, as once a connection has been established, no other device can use the circuit until it is free. This is why you get an engaged tone when someone is on the phone when you happen to ring. If the link is being utilised well, this may not be so much of an issue, but this is rarely the case. Lost bandwidth in a networking context can lead to slower services overall.

Packet switching allows packets to take independent routes through the network. Each packet decides on its own route, which will be determined by which lines are available and how heavy the current load is.

Communication using packet switching is much more resilient to failed links, as, if one route is brought down, packets can independently seek alternatives. Communication is not broken. However, packets may not arrive in order, meaning that extra processing is required to reassemble the final message. Each packet has to be labelled with an order number and the destination PC has to keep track of packets until a specific batch of packets have arrived in order. This is handled by a protocol called sliding window. Bandwidth can be used more efficiently, as no part of the network is reserved. Every link can be shared by multiple connections.

Communication networks
Typical contents of a packet

A network packet is a formatted unit of data carried by a packet-switched network. When data is formatted into packets, the bandwidth of the communication medium can be better shared among users than if the network were circuit-switched.

> **Tip**
>
> When considering questions on packet and circuit switching, you will normally have to explain the differences. These are to do with the order of packets, how the routes are set up, how resilient they are and their use of bandwidth.

Two different types of data are contained within a packet, namely the control information and actual data. The control information provides the data needed for the network to deliver the actual data. In a typical TCP/IP packet, the control information includes:

- source and destination addresses
- order number of packet
- control signals
- error control bits.

Typically, control information is found in a packet's header and trailer, with the actual data in-between.

Network collisions

On a network, data collision is a natural occurrence where two sets of data are detected simultaneously. The two transmitted packets are discarded when a collision is detected. A computer waits a short, random, time before attempting to send the discarded packet again.

Routing traffic on a network and calculating route costs

When data is transferred over a network, a process called *routing* determines the path each data packet takes and ensures that packets are delivered to their destination as quickly as possible. Each route is determined using a routing table, which stores the different paths along which data can be sent. These tables are constructed in the memory of specialist network components such as routers, switches, bridges, firewalls and gateways.

In order to make the best use of network resources, the best path is chosen by calculating the lowest cost routes. In Figure 11.7, node A is sending a packet to node B. Assuming that the traversal of a node costs 0, the packet could be sent directly from node A to node B and the cost of this would be 6. However, there is a lower cost route for transferring a packet from node A to node B. The packet could be sent from node A to node C, which would yield a cost of 3, and then sent from node C to node B, which would yield a further cost of 2, totalling a cost 5. This would be the desired path for transferring a packet from node A to node B.

Destination	Cost	GoTo
A	0	A
B	5	C
C	3	C
D	7	C
E	11	C

Table 11.1: Cost to travel from different nodes on the network in Figure 11.7.

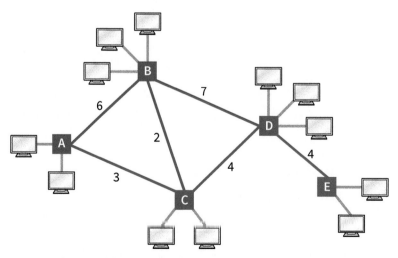

Figure 11.7: A sample network linked via routers.

You may be asked in the exam to produce a forwarding table for a node by calculating the lowest cost routes on the network. Table 11.1 is an example of a forwarding table for node A:

For each destination it shows the total cost and which node to go to first.

Data transfer rates on a network

Bandwidth is not a measure of speed as many people think, but a measure of how much data can be fitted onto a cable at any point in time. High bandwidth means that there is more room for data than there is with a low-bandwidth connection. Data still flows at the exact same speed along that cable. Broadband companies are notorious for misleading customers on this point, and they advertise bandwidth as speed. A 1 Mbit/s connection means that every second, 1 Mbit can be passed down the cable. A 10 Mbit/s connection sounds as if it is ten times faster, but if you only sent 1 KB of data down a 1 Mbit/s or a 10 Mbit/s cable, it would take exactly the same amount of time for that packet to arrive. So if all you do is browse simple web pages, such as BBC News, there is no need to pay for a higher-bandwidth connection.

Bit rate is another way of expressing bandwidth and is used to describe software's data transfer requirements. High bit rate connections are required when a large amount of data must be sent in a short period of time. Video conferencing needs to send a lot of data, which must arrive in a timely manner otherwise the video will stutter. In order to have a high-quality, stutter-free video stream, a high bit rate is required. When basic texts, such as Word documents or simple web pages, are going to be sent, a low bit rate is more than enough. In any given scenario, the bit rate requirements can be decided. Higher bit rate connections are more costly and are only advisable if the need is great enough.

In order to understand bit rate, it is useful to consider the differences between a dual carriageway (with one lane in each direction) and a motorway. Both have the same speed limit of 70 miles an hour. Let us assume that, on a busy day, all lanes are being used all of the time and that all cars travel at 70 miles an hour. Although this example is a little crude, it is not hard to see that the motorway would allow more traffic through over a period of time than the dual carriageway would. Packets on a network behave in a very similar fashion, in the sense that every packet travels at the same speed along a cable. The speed of a packet is determined not by the bit rate, but by the speed of electricity (or light if it is an optical cable). A single packet can travel no faster than this limit, and as such bit rate is not a measure of the speed of connection. As in the motorway example, you can increase the amount of data sent at a given time, which will ultimately lead to more packets arriving at a destination within a given timeframe. Bandwidth is the measurement of how much data can be sent in a given timeframe.

 Tip

Bit rate and bandwidth can be thought of as representing the same thing. There are technical differences, but this is not covered in the exam.

Below is a table (Table 11.2) of example applications and an indication of whether a low or high bit rate would be advisable:

Application	Low or high	Reason
Sending a text-based email	Low	Emails tend to be only a few kilobytes in size.
Streaming a video conference	High	Video sends a lot of data per second, depending on the quality of the video.
File server	High	File servers have a lot of requests for files arriving and need to process them fast. The higher the bit rate, the shorter the amount of time needed to send each file.
Browsing the web	Low	Most webpages, even those with rich multimedia content, tend to be small in size. They do send a lot of data out, but it tends to be spread out over a period of time. Also, your connection is limited to the speed of the web server you're connecting to. One exception to this is if the website makes heavy use of video.

Table 11.2: Bit rate required for various common tasks on the internet.

The Internet

The internet is a world-wide communications infrastructure of interconnected packet-switched networks. These networks use the standard internet protocol, TCP/IP, and are linked together using wired, wireless and fibre-optic technologies. They consist of a number of specialist hardware components, such as routers, gateways, bridges and switches, and a system of software layers.

The internet provides the infrastructure to access a range of information resources and services via the World Wide Web (WWW). It is worth noting that the WWW is not the same as the Internet; the WWW is only a major feature of it. The internet also provides the infrastructure for non-WWW applications, such as email and file sharing, for example.

Chapter summary

- When data is transmitted over a network it is broken down into packets. Each packet will have a header and footer attached which is generated by the protocols employed to transmit that packet.
- Duplex mode signifies which direction packets can travel at any given time:
  - duplex (or full duplex): both ways at the same time
  - half duplex: both ways but not at the same time
  - simplex: one direction only.
- Bit rate is the measure of how much data can be transmitted in a second. Measured as Mbps, or Megabits per second.
- Packet switching is where each packet will take an independent route through a network.
- Circuit switching is where all packets will follow the same route.

End-of-chapter questions

1   Explain the following data transmission modes.

    a   simplex   [2]

    b   duplex   [2]

    c   parallel   [2]

2   A set of bytes have been sent across a network using an error correcting code.
0101 1111 **0**
1100 1001 **0**
1110 1000 **1**
0110 0111 **1**
0100 1001

    a   Explain, using an example in the data above, how parity bits
        are calculated.   [2]

    b   One of the bits is wrong. Which bit contains the error and describe how
        this error correcting code works.   [2]

3   Describe two differences between packet and circuit switching.   [8]

4   A given network connection was measured to have a data transfer rate
of 3 Mbit/s (megabits per second). How long will it take to send
5 Mb (mega byte) of data?   [2]

Chapter 12
Data representation and data types

Learning objectives

- Explain the terms bit, byte and word.

- Describe and use the binary number system and hexadecimal notation as shorthand for binary number patterns.

- Describe how characters and numbers are stored in binary form.

- Describe standardised character sets.

- Describe the following different primitive data types: Boolean, character, string, integer and real.

- Describe the storage requirements for each data type.

- Apply binary arithmetic techniques.

- Explain the representation of positive and negative integers in a fixed-length store using both two's complement, and sign and magnitude representation.

- Describe the nature and uses of floating point form.

- State the advantages and disadvantages of representing numbers in integer and floating point forms.

- Convert between real number and floating point form.

- Describe truncation and rounding, and explain their effect upon accuracy.

- Explain and use shift functions: logical and arithmetic shifts. Interpret and apply shifts in algorithms and programs.

- Describe the causes of overflow and underflow.

Introduction: Representation of data as bit patterns

Bit, byte and word

In order to allow the processing and storage of data on computer systems, data must be converted into binary format. This is because computer systems can only process and store **B**inary dig**IT**s, also known as bits.

A single bit is represented as either a 1 or 0. These bits are grouped together to represent information that is more meaningful, from small integers to complex graphics and programs. Specific groups of bits are given names. For example, a group of 4-bits is called a nibble and a group of 8-bits is called a byte (B).

Table 12.1 shows the names given to bytes grouped together:

	Symbol	Values		
Byte	B	8 bits	2^0 B	1 B
Kilobyte	KB	1024 B	2^{10} B	1024 B
Megabyte	MB	1024 KB	2^{20} B	1 048 576 B
Gigabyte	GB	1024 MB	2^{30} B	1 073 741 824 B
Terabyte	TB	1024 GB	2^{40} B	1 099 511 627 776 B
Petabyte	PB	1024 TB	2^{50} B	1 125 899 906 842 624 B

Table 12.1: Prefixes used when representing units of size and how many bytes they represent.

A word is a group of bits that can be manipulated as a single unit by the CPU. The size of a word, also known as the word length, usually consists of 16, 32, 64 or 128 bits. Large word sizes mean that the computer system can transfer and manipulate larger groups of data than a computer system with a smaller word size, which generally means faster operation.

Describe and use the binary number system and the hexadecimal notation as shorthand for binary number patterns

In the exam, you will need to be familiar with three different counting systems: denary, binary and hexadecimal.

The most common counting system used in our everyday lives is the denary counting system (**Base 10**), which uses the digits 0, 1, 2, 3, 4, 5, 6, 7, 8, 9 to represent denary numbers.

The denary number 257_{10}, for example, means 2 'hundreds', 5 'tens' and 7 'units', as illustrated in the denary place value table (Table 12.2).

1000	100	10	1
	2	5	7

Table 12.2: 257 split into columns.

Binary

In the binary counting system (**Base 2**), the digits 0 and 1 are used to represent binary numbers.

The binary number 10100111_2 uses a group of 8 bits, as illustrated in the binary place value table (Table 12.3).

128	64	32	16	8	4	2	1
1	0	1	0	0	1	1	1

Table 12.3: The number 167 in binary.

In this example, the binary number 10100111_2 is a binary representation of the denary number 167_{10} ($128_{10} + 32_{10} + 4_{10} + 2_{10} + 1_{10}$).

Hexadecimal numbers representing binary numbers

In the hexadecimal counting system (**Base 16**), the digits 0, 1, 2, 3, 4, 5, 6, 7, 8, 9 are used to represent 0–9 and then the characters A, B, C, D, E and F are used to represent 10–15.

The hexadecimal number, $A7_{16}$, is illustrated in the hexadecimal place value table (Table 12.4).

The hexadecimal number $A7_{16}$ is a hexadecimal representation of the denary number 167_{10}, as

A 'sixteens' and 7 'units' give a total of one-hundred and sixty-seven (remembering that $A_{16} = 10_{10}$, and so 10_{10} sixteens $= 160_{10}$.)

Binary numbers can be quickly converted into hexadecimal numbers, and vice-versa, which is why hexadecimal notation is used as shorthand for binary numbers.

Hexadecimal numbers are more convenient for humans to use. Imagine a telephone conversation where you would read out the binary number "10100111_2". Mistakes are likely to be made and so it would be much easier to say "$A7_{16}$" and convert the number back into binary at the other end.

Therefore, to summarise the three different counting systems denary, binary and hexadecimal, Table 12.5 may be used.

4096	256	16	1
		A	7

Table 12.4: The number 167 as hexadecimal.

Denary$_{10}$	Binary$_2$	Hexadecimal$_{16}$
0_{10}	0000_2	0_{16}
1_{10}	0001_2	1_{16}
2_{10}	0010_2	2_{16}
3_{10}	0011_2	3_{16}
4_{10}	0100_2	4_{16}
5_{10}	0101_2	5_{16}
6_{10}	0110_2	6_{16}
7_{10}	0111_2	7_{16}
8_{10}	1000_2	8_{16}
9_{10}	1001_2	9_{16}
10_{10}	1010_2	A_{16}
11_{10}	1011_2	B_{16}
12_{10}	1100_2	C_{16}
13_{10}	1101_2	D_{16}
14_{10}	1110_2	E_{16}
15_{10}	1111_2	F_{16}
16_{10}	10000_2	10_{16}

Table 12.5: Comparison of denary, binary and hexadecimal values.

Converting between the three different counting systems

Converting denary to binary is a simple operation. In this example, you will convert the denary number 121_{10} into a binary number.

Begin by writing a table like this one, with the binary values along the top:

128	64	32	16	8	4	2	1

Next, find the largest number in your table that you can subtract from your number, leaving a positive result (or zero). Perform the subtraction and place a 1 in the column corresponding to that number. Here, 64_{10} is the largest number that can be subtracted from 121_{10}, and so $121_{10} - 64_{10} = 57_{10}$:

128	64	32	16	8	4	2	1
	1						

You repeat this operation over and over again until you are left with 0.

In this example, the largest number you have that fits into 57_{10} is 32_{10} ($57_{10} - 32_{10} = 25_{10}$), so your table becomes:

128	64	32	16	8	4	2	1
	1	1					

The largest number you have that fits into 25_{10} is 16_{10} ($25_{10} - 16_{10} = 9_{10}$), so your table becomes:

128	64	32	16	8	4	2	1
	1	1	1				

The largest number you have that fits into 9_{10} is 8_{10} ($9_{10} - 8_{10} = 1$), so your table becomes:

128	64	32	16	8	4	2	1
	1	1	1	1			

Finally, the largest number you have that can be subtracted from 1_{10} is 1_{10} ($1_{10} - 1_{10} = 0_{10}$), so your table becomes:

128	64	32	16	8	4	2	1
	1	1	1	1			1

Now you've reached 0, you just need to fill in the gaps in your table with 0s and the conversion is complete.

128	64	32	16	8	4	2	1
0	1	1	1	1	0	0	1

So because $64_{10} + 32_{10} + 16_{10} + 8_{10} + 1_{10} = 121_{10}$, 121_{10} in denary is 01111001_2 in binary.

Converting back is even easier! If you are given a binary number such as 10101001_2, all you need to do is write out your table, put your 1s in the correct column and add together the values:

128	64	32	16	8	4	2	1
1	0	1	0	1	0	0	1

So 10101001_2 in binary is 169_{10} in denary ($128_{10} + 32_{10} + 8_{10} + 1_{10}$).

To convert a denary number to hexadecimal, simply convert it to an 8-bit binary number. Then split your 8-bit binary number into two 4-bit sections and convert each of these to hexadecimal.

For example, to convert the denary number 31_{10} to hexadecimal you would first convert it to a binary number:

128	64	32	16	8	4	2	1
0	0	0	1	1	1	1	1

Then split this 8-bit binary number into two 4-bit sections:

128	64	32	16
0	0	0	1

8	4	2	1
1	1	1	1

Change the headings of your first 4-bit section:

8	4	2	1
0	0	0	1

8	4	2	1
1	1	1	1

Finally convert each of these 4-bit segments to hexadecimal:

8	4	2	1
0	0	0	1
1			

8	4	2	1
1	1	1	1
F			

So 31_{10} in denary is $1F_{16}$ in hexadecimal:

256	16	1
0	1	F

Storage of characters and character sets

Binary numbers can also be used to represent different characters, such as letters, digits, spaces, punctuation marks and other symbols.

Character sets work by mapping each character to a unique binary number. They are important, as characters can be represented differently by different computer systems and so an agreed convention allows for accurate data exchange.

Table 12.6 shows the 7-bit American Standard Code for Information Interchange (ASCII) character set for the 95 printable characters. The other 33 are non-printable control characters, for example, DEL.

Denary	Binary	Character	Denary	Binary	Character	Denary	Binary	Character
32	100000	*space*	64	1000000	@	96	1100000	`
33	100001	!	65	1000001	A	97	1100001	a
34	100010	"	66	1000010	B	98	1100010	b
35	100011	#	67	1000011	C	99	1100011	c
36	100100	$	68	1000100	D	100	1100100	d
37	100101	%	69	1000101	E	101	1100101	e
38	100110	&	70	1000110	F	102	1100110	f
39	100111	'	71	1000111	G	103	1100111	g
40	101000	(	72	1001000	H	104	1101000	h
41	101001	)	73	1001001	I	105	1101001	i
42	101010	*	74	1001010	J	106	1101010	j
43	101011	+	75	1001011	K	107	1101011	k
44	101100	,	76	1001100	L	108	1101100	l
45	101101	-	77	1001101	M	109	1101101	m
46	101110	.	78	1001110	N	110	1101110	n
47	101111	/	79	1001111	O	111	1101111	o
48	110000	0	80	1010000	P	112	1110000	p
49	110001	1	81	1010001	Q	113	1110001	q
50	110010	2	82	1010010	R	114	1110010	r
51	110011	3	83	1010011	S	115	1110011	s
52	110100	4	84	1010100	T	116	1110100	t
53	110101	5	85	1010101	U	117	1110101	u
54	110110	6	86	1010110	V	118	1110110	v
55	110111	7	87	1010111	W	119	1110111	w
56	111000	8	88	1011000	X	120	1111000	x
57	111001	9	89	1011001	Y	121	1111001	y
58	111010	:	90	1011010	Z	122	1111010	z
59	111011	;	91	1011011	[	123	1111011	{
60	111100	<	92	1011100	\	124	1111100		
61	111101	=	93	1011101	]	125	1111101	}
62	111110	>	94	1011110	^	126	1111110	~
63	111111	?	95	1011111	_			

Table 12.6: ASCII values.

You can see from the table above that the character 'A' is stored as the binary number 1000001_2, the character 'B' is stored as the binary number 1000010_2, and so on.

The problem with the 7-bit ASCII character set is that it is only able to represent 128 different characters. To accommodate different languages and other special characters, computer systems need to be able to store more characters than this.

As most modern computer systems have a 16-bit, 32-bit, 64-bit or 128-bit word length, this provided an opportunity to extend the 7-bit ASCII character set to an 8-bit character set. The original 7-bit character-mapping was left intact, but additional characters where added after the first 128 characters, for example, the character '£' is mapped to the binary number 10011101_2 (157_{10}). However, this still only allows the representation of 256 different characters.

UNICODE

Languages like Japanese, Arabic and Hebrew all have a much larger alphabet than English. To get around this problem, UNICODE was invented. UNICODE uses up to four bytes to represent each character (depending on the version). This means that it can represent up to 110 000 different characters – more than enough to cope with most of the world's languages.

Data types

In the exam, you will need to be familiar with the following primitive data types and their storage requirements:

Data Type	Description	Examples	Typical storage requirements
Character	A single letter, digit, space, punctuation mark or various other symbols	A, c, 4, @	• 1 byte for the ASCII character set • 4 bytes for the Unicode character set
String	A group of characters	"Computer science" "WJEC Eduqas"	Number of characters multiplied by: • 1 byte for ASCII • 4 bytes for Unicode
Boolean	TRUE or FALSE	1 or 0	1 bit, e.g. • 1 = True • 0 = False
Integer	Positive or negative whole numbers	12, –18, 0	2 bytes (allows storage of integers up to and including 65 535)
Real **(sometimes called Float)**	Fractions or numbers with decimal points	15.6, –12.75, 28.3, 0.12	The storage requirements depend on the size of the mantissa and exponent. This is typically the size of the word length of the computer system.

Table 12.7: The main data types of a computer.

The storage requirements for each data type can vary depending on the implementation of the programming language and word length of the computer system.

Representation of numbers as bit patterns

Binary can also be used to represent negative numbers (−1, −2, −3 and so on). There are two ways in which this can be done and you will need to read the exam questions carefully to be sure which method you should be using.

Sign and magnitude

Sign and magnitude is the simplest way of representing negative numbers in binary.

MSB							LSB

The Most Significant Bit (MSB) is simply used to represent the sign: 1 means the number is negative, 0 means it is positive. So to represent -4_{10} in an 8-bit binary number you would first write out the 4_{10} in binary...

MSB							LSB
128	64	32	16	8	4	2	1
0	0	0	0	0	1	0	0

...then change the MSB to a 1:

MSB							LSB
128	64	32	16	8	4	2	1
1	0	0	0	0	1	0	0

Creating 10000100_2. In another example, -2_{10} would be 10000010_2 in the sign and magnitude notation. This notation isn't used very often as it harder to do calculations as different bits mean different things; some represent numbers, others represent signs. There are also two representations for 0: +0 and −0.

Two's complement

Two's complement is a much more useful way of representing binary numbers, as it allows for simpler binary arithmetic.

The easiest way to show a negative number using two's complement is to write it out as a positive number using the usual binary method. Then, starting at the right-hand side, leave every bit up to and including the first 1 alone, but invert all the bits after this.

For example, to show -86_{10} in binary, first write 86_{10} as a binary number:

128	64	32	16	8	4	2	1
0	1	0	1	0	1	1	0

Then start at the right-hand side and leave everything alone up to and including the first 1:

128	64	32	16	8	4	2	1
0	1	0	1	0	1	1	0

Finally invert everything after this, so all the 1s become 0s and vice versa:

128	64	32	16	8	4	2	1
1	0	1	0	1	0	1	0

So -86_{10} in binary is 10101010_2 in two's complement notation.

Another method of showing a negative number using two's complement is by flipping all the bits and adding 1.

Adding and subtracting of binary numbers

Once you can represent positive and negative numbers using binary, the next step is performing arithmetic operations such as addition and subtraction on them.

Binary addition

Binary addition is fairly straightforward. Just remember these simple operations:

Operation	Result
0 + 0 =	0
0 + 1 =	1
1 + 1 =	10
1 + 1 + 1 =	11

To add together two binary numbers, just arrange them above each other in a table. This table shows the number 42_{10} above the number 18_{10}:

128	64	32	16	8	4	2	1
0	0	1	0	1	0	1	0
0	0	0	1	0	0	1	0

Then add together the corresponding bits using the operations shown in the previous table, making sure that you start at the Least Significant Bit (LSB):

						1	
0	0	1	0	1	0	1	0
0	0	0	1	0	0	1	0
						0	*0*

You can see in this table that the first operation $(0 + 0)$ has produced a 0. The second operation $(1 + 1)$ has produced 10; notice that you record the 0 but carry the 1 to the top of the next column so that the third operation is $1 + 0 + 0 = 1$:

						1	
0	0	1	0	1	0	1	0
0	0	0	1	0	0	1	0
0	*0*	*1*	*1*	*1*	*1*	*0*	*0*

So our final result is 00111100_2 or 60_{10}. You know this is correct because you can check your answer: $42_{10} + 18_{10} = 60_{10}$. In an exam, it's tempting just to work out the answer in denary and then write down the binary equivalent of this number. Avoid this temptation, as most of the time examiners won't give marks unless they can see your working.

Binary subtraction

Binary subtraction is the same as binary addition except that you convert the number to be subtracted into negative binary (using two's complement) before adding them together. This works because $4_{10} - 2_{10}$ is the same as $4_{10} + (-2_{10})$.

For example, if you want to calculate $68_{10} - 33_{10}$ in binary, the first thing you do is write the binary number for 68_{10}:

128	64	32	16	8	4	2	1
0	1	0	0	0	1	0	0

Then you work out what -33_{10} is in binary using two's complement and write this beneath it:

0	1	0	0	0	1	0	0
1	1	0	1	1	1	1	1

Finally you add them together using the same operations as for binary addition:

	1			1	1	1		
	0	1	0	0	0	1	0	0
	1	1	0	1	1	1	1	1
1	0	0	1	0	0	0	1	1

(Notice that the final 1 would be carried off the end of the final eighth bit and is just ignored.) So the answer is $00100011_2 = 35_{10}$ and you know this is correct because $68_{10} - 33_{10}$ is 35_{10}.

Describe the nature and uses of floating point form

Representing numbers in floating point form allows a greater range of positive and negative numbers, including real numbers, to be stored in the same number of bits. It is called floating point because the number of digits is fixed but the decimal point floats around.

Convert between real number and floating point form

To show your understanding of floating point notation in an exam, you may be required to convert a real number into floating point form. The following example uses an 8-bit signed mantissa and a 4-bit signed exponent to convert the real number 5.625_{10} into floating point form. The size of the mantissa and exponent can vary and so it is important that you read exam questions carefully and use the structure given.

Step 1: Convert the integer and fraction parts of the number into binary using a base 2 table where the denary numbers above one are doubled (as usual) and the denary numbers below one are halved:

Mantissa (8-bit)							
Sign	4	2	1	$\frac{1}{2}$ 0.5	$\frac{1}{4}$ 0.25	$\frac{1}{8}$ 0.125	$\frac{1}{16}$ 0.0625
0	1	0	1 .	1	0	1	0

So 5.625_{10} $(4_{10} + 1_{10} + 0.5_{10} + 0.125_{10}) = 0101.1010_2$. As the number being represented is a positive number, the sign bit is a 0.

Step 2: Move the binary point to the left so that the number is *normalised*, i.e. in the format $\texttt{Sign-bit.1}_{...2}$. As you are converting a positive number, the desired format is $0.1_{...2}$. For each shift, add 1 to the exponent.

Mantissa	Exponent
0101.1010_2	0
010.11010_2	1
01.011010_2	2
0.1011010_2	3

And so the normalised Mantissa is:

Mantissa							
Sign	$\frac{1}{2}$ 0.5	$\frac{1}{4}$ 0.25	$\frac{1}{8}$ 0.125	$\frac{1}{16}$ 0.0625	$\frac{1}{32}$ 0.03125	$\frac{1}{64}$ 0.015625	$\frac{1}{128}$ 0.0078125
0 .	1	0	1	1	0	1	0

Step 3: Convert the exponent into a 4-bit binary number.

Mantissa								Exponent			
Sign	$\frac{1}{2}$ 0.5	$\frac{1}{4}$ 0.25	$\frac{1}{8}$ 0.125	$\frac{1}{16}$ 0.0625	$\frac{1}{32}$ 0.03125	$\frac{1}{64}$ 0.015625	$\frac{1}{128}$ 0.0078125	Sign	4	2	1
0 .	1	0	1	1	0	1	0	0	0	1	1

So the final normalised floating point representation of the denary number 5.625_{10} is 0.10110100011_2.

One way of checking your answer is by using the formula **Value = Mantissa $\times$ 2$^{\textbf{Exponent}}$**:

$$\textbf{Mantissa} = 0.5_{10} + 0.125_{10} + 0.0625_{10} + 0.015625_{10} = 0.703125_{10}$$

$$\text{Exponent} = 2_{10} + 1_{10} = 3_{10}$$

$$\text{So Value} = 0.703125 \times 2^3 = 5.625_{10} \quad \checkmark$$

Normalisation

The precision of floating point binary depends on the number of bits used to represent the mantissa.

For example, in denary arithmetic 67849 could be 0.67849×10^5 with 5 digits for the mantissa or 0.06785×10^6 with 4 digits (not counting the leading zero) for the mantissa.

In order to achieve the most accurate representation possible with the number of bits available for a mantissa, the number should be written with **no leading 0s.** Normalisation is the process of removing these leading 0s and getting your mantissa in the form of $0.1..._2$ for positive numbers.

You may also be asked to convert a floating point number into denary. The floating point number 011100000101_2 is an example that uses a 6-bit signed mantissa and a 6-bit signed exponent.

Step 1: Calculate the denary value of the mantissa and exponent using the structure given.

Sign	$\frac{1}{2}$ 0.5	$\frac{1}{4}$ 0.25	$\frac{1}{8}$ 0.125	$\frac{1}{16}$ 0.0625	$\frac{1}{32}$ 0.03125		Sign	16	8	4	2	1
0 .	1	1	1	0	0		0	0	0	1	0	1

Once again the sign bit of the mantissa is 0, which indicates a positive number.

The denary value of the mantissa is 0.875_{10} $(0.5_{10} + 0.25_{10} + 0.125_{10})$, the denary value of the exponent is 5_{10} $(4_{10} + 1_{10})$.

Step 2: Calculate the denary value of the floating point number by using the formula:

$$\textbf{Value} = \textbf{Mantissa} \times \textbf{2}^{\textbf{Exponent}}$$

$$\text{So Value} = 0.875 \times 2^5 = 28_{10}$$

Alternatively, you can calculate the denary value of the floating point number by moving the binary point five places to the right:

Mantissa	Move • right
0.11100_2	–
01.1100_2	Once
011.100_2	Twice
0111.00_2	3 times
01110.0_2	4 times
$011100._2$	5 times

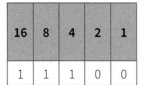

Sign	16	8	4	2	1	$\frac{1}{2}$ 0.5
0	1	1	1	0	0 .	0

This method also demonstrates that the answer is 28_{10} $(16_{10} + 8_{10} + 4_{10})$.

In order to represent very small numbers, it is possible to have a negative exponent and move the decimal point to the left. This is achieved by storing the exponent as a two's complement binary number. The floating point number 01110110_2 uses a 5-bit signed mantissa and 3-bit signed exponent.

Sign	Mantissa				Exponent		
	$\frac{1}{2}$	$\frac{1}{4}$	$\frac{1}{8}$	$\frac{1}{16}$	Sign	2	1
	0.5	0.25	0.125	0.0625			
0 .	1	1	1	0	1	1	0

Step 1: Convert the exponent to denary: in this example 110_2 becomes -2.

Step 2: Move the decimal point left two places.

Mantissa	Move • left
0.1110_2	–
0.01110_2	Once
0.001110_2	Twice

Step 3: Calculate the denary value of the mantissa.

Sign	$\frac{1}{2}$	$\frac{1}{4}$	$\frac{1}{8}$	$\frac{1}{16}$	$\frac{1}{32}$
	0.5	0.25	0.125	0.0625	0.03125
0 .	0	0	1	1	1

So the floating point number $0111011_2 = 0.21875_{10}$ ($0.125_{10} + 0.0625_{10} + 0.03125_{10}$)

Negative floating point numbers

The same method can be used to deal with negative numbers, but this time by representing the mantissa using two's complement. The following example uses a 5-bit signed mantissa and a 3-bit signed exponent to convert the real number -0.25_{10} into floating point form.

Step 1: Convert the integer and fraction parts of the number into binary using a base 2 table.

Mantissa (5-bit)				
Sign	2	1	$\frac{1}{2}$	$\frac{1}{4}$
			0.5	0.25
0	0	0 .	0	1

So $0.25_{10} = 000.01_2$.

Step 2: Using two's complement, convert the mantissa to a negative binary number by inverting everything after the first 1.

Mantissa (5-bit)				
Sign	2	1	$\frac{1}{2}$	$\frac{1}{4}$
			0.5	0.25
1	1	1 .	1	1

Step 3: Move the binary point to the left so that the number is normalised, e.g. in the format `Sign-bit.1...₂`. As you are converting a negative number, the desired format is $1.\dots_2$. For each shift, add 1 to the exponent.

Mantissa	Exponent
111.11₂	0
11.111₂	1
1.1111₂	2

And so the normalised Mantissa is:

Sign	$\frac{1}{2}$ 0.5	$\frac{1}{4}$ 0.25	$\frac{1}{8}$ 0.125	$\frac{1}{16}$ 0.0625
1 .	1	1	1	1

Step 4: Convert the exponent into a 3-bit binary number.

Sign	Mantissa				Exponent		
	$\frac{1}{2}$ 0.5	$\frac{1}{4}$ 0.25	$\frac{1}{8}$ 0.125	$\frac{1}{16}$ 0.0625	Sign	2	1
1 .	1	1	1	1	0	1	0

So the final normalised floating point representation of the negative denary number -0.25_{10} is 1.1111010_2.

You may also be asked to convert a negative floating point number into denary. The floating point number 1.0101010_2 is an example that uses a 5-bit signed mantissa and a 3-bit signed exponent.

Sign	Mantissa				Exponent		
	$\frac{1}{2}$ 0.5	$\frac{1}{4}$ 0.25	$\frac{1}{8}$ 0.125	$\frac{1}{16}$ 0.0625	Sign	2	1
1 .	0	1	0	1	0	1	0

Step 1: Using two's complement, convert the mantissa by inverting everything after the first 1.

Sign	$\frac{1}{2}$ 0.5	$\frac{1}{4}$ 0.25	$\frac{1}{8}$ 0.125	$\frac{1}{16}$ 0.0625	Sign	2	1
0 .	1	0	1	1	0	1	0

Step 2: Convert the exponent to denary. In this instance the exponent is 2.

Step 3: Move the decimal point two places right.

Mantissa	Move • right
0.1011_2	–
01.011_2	Once
010.11_2	Twice

Mantissa (5-bit)					
Sign	2	1		$\dfrac{1}{2}$ 0.5	$\dfrac{1}{4}$ 0.25
0	1	0	.	1	1

So the floating point number $1.0101010_2 = -2.75_{10}$ ($-2_{10} + 0.5_{10} + 0.25_{10}$) – don't forget it's a negative!

Advantages and disadvantages of representing numbers in integer and floating point forms

The advantage of storing numbers in integer form is that they are stored completely accurately. The disadvantage is that there is a limited range of numbers that can be represented using the bits available to you.

The advantage of representing numbers in floating point forms is that a greater range of positive and negative numbers can be stored in the same number of bits.

The disadvantages of using this method are that:

- numbers aren't normally stored completely accurately
- they require more complex processing
- there is no exact representation of zero.

Describe truncation and rounding, and explain their effect upon accuracy

Truncation

Truncation is the method for dealing with a situation where there are not enough bits to represent all of the number to be stored. The extra bits are simply left out at the end, for example 0.0101101_2 would be stored in 4 bits as 0.010_2.

Original fractional number							
Sign		$\dfrac{1}{2}$ 0.5	$\dfrac{1}{4}$ 0.25	$\dfrac{1}{8}$ 0.125	$\dfrac{1}{16}$ 0.0625	$\dfrac{1}{32}$ 0.03125	$\dfrac{1}{64}$ 0.015625	$\dfrac{1}{128}$ 0.0078125
0	.	0	1	0	1	1	0	1

Truncated fractional number				
Sign		$\frac{1}{2}$ 0.5	$\frac{1}{4}$ 0.25	$\frac{1}{8}$ 0.125
0	.	0	1	0

There is a truncation error of 0.0001101_2. The impact of this may be more obvious when converted to denary, where the original number was 0.3515625_{10} and the truncated number is 0.25_{10}.

This means an absolute error of:

Absolute error = Original number − Truncated number = 0.1015625_{10}

And a relative error of:

Relative error = Absolute error/Original number = $0.2888889 \approx 28.9\%$.

Rounding

This is similar to truncation but tries to get a little closer to the original value. This is the method normally used in mathematics, where in decimal, if the first number to be left out is five or more the previous digit is increased by one. For example, 0.175 would become 0.18 (stored to two decimal places).

In binary, if the bit after the last bit to be represented is a 1, the previous bit is increased by 1. From the truncation example above, 0.0101101_2 would therefore be stored as 0.011_2. The rounding error is 0.0000011_2, which would mean that the rounded representation is more accurate.

Original fractional number								
Sign		$\frac{1}{2}$ 0.5	$\frac{1}{4}$ 0.25	$\frac{1}{8}$ 0.125	$\frac{1}{16}$ 0.0625	$\frac{1}{32}$ 0.03125	$\frac{1}{64}$ 0.015625	$\frac{1}{128}$ 0.0078125
0	.	0	1	0	1	1	0	1

Rounded fractional number				
Sign		$\frac{1}{2}$ 0.5	$\frac{1}{4}$ 0.25	$\frac{1}{8}$ 0.125
0	.	0	1	1

There is a rounding error of 0.0000011_2, which may be more obvious when converted to denary, where the original number was 0.3515625_{10} and the truncated number is 0.375_{10}.

This means an absolute error of:

Absolute error = Original number − Rounded number = -0.0234375_{10}

And a relative error of:

Relative error = Absolute error/Original number = $-0.0666666_{10} \approx -6.7\%$

This is a much smaller error than with the truncated example above!

There can also be a loss of accuracy when a denary number is stored using floating point representation. In a computer system with an 8-bit signed mantissa and a 4-bit signed exponent, the closest possible representation of the denary number 6.9_{10} is:

	Mantissa							Exponent			
Sign	$\frac{1}{2}$ 0.5	$\frac{1}{4}$ 0.25	$\frac{1}{8}$ 0.125	$\frac{1}{16}$ 0.0625	$\frac{1}{32}$ 0.03125	$\frac{1}{64}$ 0.015625	$\frac{1}{128}$ 0.0078125	Sign	4	2	1
0 .	1	1	0	1	1	1	0	0	0	1	1

This can be proved by calculating the denary value of the floating point number:

$$\text{Denary value: } 0.8595_{10} \times 2^3 = 6.875_{10}$$

This means an absolute error of:

Absolute error $= 6.9_{10} - 6.875_{10} = 0.025_{10}$

And a relative error of:

Relative error $= 0.025_{10}/6.9_{10} = 0.00362319_{10} \approx 0.4\%$

The floating point system used could be modified to allow a more accurate representation of 6.9_{10} by adjusting the mantissa to use more bits. This could be done by re-allocating one bit from the exponent to the mantissa or by inferring one of the two bits on either side of the binary point and using the freed up bit to store one more significant digit in the mantissa.

Shift functions

Logical and arithmetic shifts

There are two main types of shift function, namely the logical shift and the arithmetic shift. Shift functions involve moving the bits within a register to the left or to the right.

A logical shift operation shifts each binary digit left or right and the vacated bits are replaced with 0's.

The following example performs right logical shifts to the binary number 00101011_2.

128	64	32	16	8	4	2	1
0	0	1	0	1	0	1	1
→ One Right Logical Shift							
0	0	0	1	0	1	0	1
→ Two Right Logical Shifts							
0	*0*	0	0	1	0	1	0

Alternatively, logical shifts can be performed to the left on the binary number 00101011_2.

128	64	32	16	8	4	2	1
0	0	1	0	1	0	1	1
← One Left Logical Shift							
0	1	0	1	0	1	1	*0*
← Two Left Logical Shifts							
1	0	1	0	1	1	*0*	*0*

Arithmetic shifts are similar to logical shifts, but can be distinguished by what happens to the bits that are shifted out of the register at each end and what replaces the vacated bit(s).

When arithmetic shifts are performed to the right, the sign-bit retains its current value. For instance, in the following example, a right arithmetic shift is performed on the two's complement binary number 10100110_2, which has a negative denary value of -90_{10}.

Sign	64	32	16	8	4	2	1
1	0	1	0	0	1	1	0
→ One Right Arithmetic Shift							
1	1	0	1	0	0	1	1

You will note that the new denary value of this two's complement binary number is -45_{10}. The effect of carrying out an arithmetic shift right is to divide the number by two. If you carry out a further right arithmetic shift, then the number will be divided by two again (the original number will have been divided by four).

Sign	64	32	16	8	4	2	1	
1	1	0	1	0	0	1	1	
→ Two Right Arithmetic Shifts								
1	*1*	1	0	1	0	0	1	~~1~~

Note that you have lost a *1* off the end of the register. This has introduced an accuracy error, as the new binary number equates to the denary number -23_{10} (whereas -45_{10} divided by $2 = -22.5_{10}$). This is because the register is not large enough to accurately store the result.

Left arithmetic shifts can also be carried out similarly to a logical shift, where the vacated bits are replaced with 0's. In the following example the two's complement binary number 00010010_2 is shifted left.

	Sign	64	32	16	8	4	2	1
	0	0	0	1	0	0	1	0
	← One Left Arithmetic Shift							
~~0~~	0	0	1	0	0	1	0	*0*

The original binary number represents 18_{10}. When one left arithmetic shift is applied, the result is 36_{10}. A left arithmetic shift is the equivalent of multiplying by two.

Overflow and underflow

Overflow

In the example above, the sign-bit 0 is replaced with another 0. However, problems can arise when the sign-bit is replaced with a different value. For example, a left arithmetic shift is carried out on the two's complement binary number 01100110_2, which has a positive denary value of 102_{10}.

Sign	64	32	16	8	4	2	1
0	1	1	0	0	1	1	0
← One Left Arithmetic Shift							
θ 1	1	0	0	1	1	0	*0*

This has produced an overflow error, as the new denary value of this binary number is -52_{10}. This is because the register is not large enough to accurately store the result, which should be 204_{10} (102_{10} multiplied by 2).

Overflow errors also occur with binary addition.

					1		
1	0	1	0	1	0	1	0
1	0	0	1	0	0	1	0
1 0						*0*	*0*

The result of this addition needs 9 binary digits, but there are only 8 available for the answer, leading to an error.

Underflow

Underflow occurs when an answer is too small to be represented and is stored as a zero. This generally occurs with small fractional binary numbers. For example, the smallest positive number that can be stored in the following 8-bit register is 0.0078125_{10}.

Sign	$\frac{1}{2}$ 0.5	$\frac{1}{4}$ 0.25	$\frac{1}{8}$ 0.125	$\frac{1}{16}$ 0.0625	$\frac{1}{32}$ 0.03125	$\frac{1}{64}$ 0.015625	$\frac{1}{128}$ 0.0078125
0 .	0	0	0	0	0	0	1

If a right arithmetic shift were carried out on this number, the result would produce an underflow error, where the number is too small to be accurately represented and is stored as zero.

Sign	$\frac{1}{2}$ 0.5	$\frac{1}{4}$ 0.25	$\frac{1}{8}$ 0.125	$\frac{1}{16}$ 0.0625	$\frac{1}{32}$ 0.03125	$\frac{1}{64}$ 0.015625	$\frac{1}{128}$ 0.0078125
0 .	0	0	0	0	0	0	0	*1*

Chapter summary

- File sizes are measured using magnitudes of bytes, from smallest to largest; byte, kilobyte, megabyte, gigabyte, terabyte and petabyte.
- Binary is base 2 and can be used to represent numbers; every column can be determined by the formula 2^n, where n is the column number starting at 0.
- Hexadecimal is base 16 and uses the letters A–F to represent values 10–15.
- Characters are encoded by giving each of them a number. That number can then be converted into binary.
- ASCII uses 7 bits to store characters while Unicode uses 16 bits. Unicode can be used to represent symbols from other languages such as Japanese.
- The key data types are character, string, Boolean, integer and real.
- Two's complement and sign-magnitude are methods of storing negative numbers in binary. Both use the most significant bit to represent negative numbers. 1 always means negative.
- Binary addition uses *carries* if the result of the addition is greater than 1.
- Binary subtraction is easier if you convert the number to be subtracted into a negative two's complement number.
- Floating point numbers are made up of a mantissa and an exponent.
- Normalised floating point numbers will always start with either 01 or 10.
- Overflow is when a number is too large for the number of bits being used to represent it.
- Underflow is when a number is too small for the number of bits being used to represent it.

End-of-chapter questions

1 A 16-bit machine code instruction contains a 6-bit opcode and a 10-bit operand as shown in below. Bit shift can be used to read the operand by moving it to occupy the most significant bit.

Data	1	0	0	1	1	1	0	1	1	0	1	1	1	0	0	0
index	0	1	2	3	4	5	6	7	8	9	10	11	12	13	14	15
	Opcode						Operand									

    a Which bit shift should be used? [1]

    b Apply the bit shift you suggested in part (a) to the above instruction. [1]

2 A byte is represented in sign-magnitude.

1	0	0	0	1	1	0	0

    a What number does this represent in denary? [1]

    b What is the largest and smallest value which can be stored using 8-bit in sign-magnitude? [2]

    c Explain, using an example, why sign-magnitude is problematic when adding two bytes together. [3]

3 Convert the following values from hexadecimal to denary.

    a   F4   [1]

    b   DA   [1]

    c   88   [1]

4 Convert the following values from octal to hexadecimal.

    a   431   [1]

    b   76   [1]

    c   54   [1]

5 A floating point number has a 4-bit mantissa and a 4-bit exponent.

1	0	0	0	1	1	0	0
Mantissa				Exponent			

    a   Convert the above floating point number into denary.   [2]

    b   If the exponent was reduced to 3 bits, what impact would that have on the numbers it could represent?   [2]

    c   What is wrong with the floating point number shown below?   [2]

0	0	0	1	0	0	0	1
Mantissa				Exponent			

Further reading

Binary numbers	Search for the Binary System on the Grinnell College Mathematics and Statistics website
Binary addition	Search for Binary Calculator on calculator.net
UNICODE	Go to unicode.org

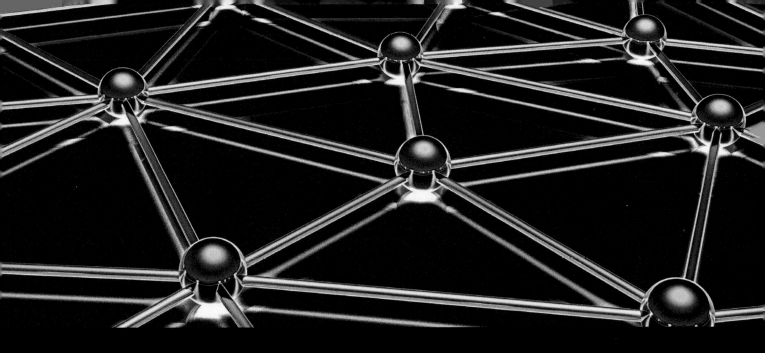

Chapter 13
Organisation and structure of data

Learning objectives

- Explain the purpose of files in data processing.
- Define a file in terms of records and fields.
- Describe how files may be created, organised, updated and processed by programs.
- Explain fixed and variable length fields and records, and give examples of the appropriate use of each type.
- Design files and records appropriate for a particular application.
- Distinguish between master and transaction files.
- Describe sequential, indexed sequential and direct (random) file access.
- Distinguish between the use of serial and sequential file access methods in computer applications.
- Describe and design algorithms and programs for sequential file access and update.
- Explain the purpose of, and be able to use, a hashing algorithm.
- Compare different hashing algorithms.
- Explain the use of multi-level indexes.
- Explain the techniques used to manage overflow and the need for file re-organisation.
- Explain the need for file security, including file backup, generations of files and transaction logs.
- Describe the need for archiving files.

Introduction

In Chapter 1 you have looked at the importance of structuring data with respect to databases and data structures. Most software projects will make use of data structures, such as trees or linked lists, and many larger scale projects will also make use of databases. Databases provide a persistent store of data and a way of providing security and structure. However, databases are not always the best way of storing data. This could be due to the fact that some projects do not need the power of a relational database, the amount of data to be stored is small, or the data to be stored could be represented as a flat file database. Whatever the reason, how data is stored in files is an important part of computer science. In this chapter you will be introduced to how flat file databases can be constructed, the different types of file and how to improve the efficiency of files.

File design

Fixed length records

In order to store data in a file you first must find a way of organising multiple fields. Although there may be scenarios where a list of single field values needs to be stored, it is more likely that multiple fields need to be stored. Consider a simple survey to collect personal data on a group of students, where the data is to be stored in a file. Table 13.1 lists the fields for a simple survey. Each field represents a single set of data and a single record will represent a single student. Each field will have a data type, such as integer or string, and a size measured in bytes.

Field name	Data type	Size
First name	String	20
Last name	String	30
Date of birth	Date	6
Height (cm)	Integer	1
Weight (kg)	Float	4
Eats school lunch	Boolean	1

Table 13.1: Sample data structure from a simple student survey.

Records, as demonstrated above, are a collection of fields that can store a single set of values. Fixed length records have the additional requirement that every record is exactly the same size. In order to implement this requirement, the size of each field, based on the data type, must be stated up front. When you define the sizes it is important to think about what is going to be stored in them, as the number of bytes required will be based on this. Integers will have a size of 1, 2, 4 or 8 bytes depending on the biggest number they will be representing. For example, the height of a student is not going to be over 255 cm, so 1 byte is more than enough to store that value. Strings will be more variable in length so you must consider the maximum number of letters that will be stored. You must use the maximum and not an average, otherwise larger text will be truncated (have the extra characters discarded). Table 13.2 shows the size in bytes for data types, their names and value range. It is important to remember that integers come in two types, signed and unsigned.

Data type	Example	Size in bytes	Alternative names	Value range
Unsigned integer Note – long is rounded	65	1	Byte	0 to 255
		2	Short	0 to 65 536
		4	Int	0 to 4 294 967 296
		8	Long	0 to 18×10^{18}
Signed integer Note – long is rounded	−87	1	Byte	−128 to 127
		2	Short	−32 768 to 32 767
		4	Int	−2 147 483 648 to 2 147 483 647
		8	Long	-9×10^{18} to 9×10^{18}
Floating point	3.14	4	Real	-1.2×10^{-38} to 3.4×10^{38}
		8	Double	Double: -2.2×10^{-308} to 1.7×10^{308}
String	Hello	1 byte per character for ASCII 2 bytes per character for Unicode	Text varchar char (for single characters)	
Boolean	True	1		
Date	5/1/2014	6/8	Time stamp Date/time	

Table 13.2: Relative sizes for primitive data types.

> **Tip**
>
> Table 13.2 is meant for informational purposes only. With regard to the exam, you can make a number of assumptions. Firstly, you will not be expected to know the value ranges or distinguish between signed and unsigned. Secondly, questions which ask you to define sizes will always have a range unless genuinely fixed length is involved (for example, National Insurance numbers are nine characters long, so 9 bytes would be the only correct answer). Finally, you should assume that all text will be stored as ASCII.

Estimating file size

The size of a single record from Table 13.1 can be easily calculated by summing the size of the individual fields within the record. Once you have the size of a single record it then becomes trivial to estimate the size of 20 records by multiplying by the size of one record by the number of records required.

Size of one record = 20 + 30 + 6 + 1 + 4 + 1 = 62 bytes

Size of 20 records = 62 × 20 = 248 bytes

However, the final file size may be slightly bigger due to additional information that needs to be saved. This will include the order, size and type of each field. Also, any indices that are used within the file also need to be saved. This additional information is known as metadata and is required in order to read the file effectively. When estimating the file size it is common practice to add on 10% to accommodate the metadata, as shown here:

Size of one record = 20 + 30 + 6 + 1 + 4 + 1 = 62 bytes

Size of 20 records = 62 × 20 = 248 bytes

Final size with metadata = 248 × 1.1 = 273 bytes

(Note – you always round up. The actual answer was 272.8)

Pseudocode for file access

File access in most programming languages is provided either by the core language or by libraries. It tends to come in the form of classes (if the language is predominantly object orientated like Java) or functions (if the language is more procedural like Python). When defining algorithms that rely on file access, it is important to use Pseudocode rather than language-specific code. Most languages are similar in the way they access files, mainly because they use the same functions from the operating system. To fully appreciate why files are handled the way they are, you should read Chapter 15.

Table 13.3 is a list of Pseudocode that will be used for the rest of this chapter. All of the Pseudocode operations make use of something known as a file handle. When a file is opened, a file handle is returned which can be saved into a variable. File handles are special objects which provide access to open files. To create a file handle, you must open the file first.

Pseudocode	Description	Example
`fh = open (filename, mode)`	All operations on files make use of a file handle (here the variable 'myfile'). Files can be opened in append mode, read mode or write mode. When a file is opened in write mode the original data will be deleted. Here, the mode "r" means "read only".	`myfile = open ("file.txt", "r")`
`fh.close()`	Any open file must always be closed before the end of the program. Files that are not closed could be locked out by the OS from further editing.	`myFile.close()` `close(myFile)`

`fh.read(numBytes)`	This will read a specific number of bytes. Normally used when dealing with fixed length records. Sometimes the argument is omitted to make the assumption that the next field will be read in. When reading data in, you should always save it into a variable or output it.	`myFile.read(10)`
		 `read(myFile, 10)`
		 `read phoneNumber FROM myFile`

`fh.write(data)`	This function will write a series of bytes out to a file. The file must be in append or write modes. If the file is in append mode then new data will be placed at the end of the file.	`myFile. write("hello")`
		 `write(myFile, "hello")`
		 `write phoneNumber TO myfile`

Table 13.3: File access Pseudocode.

Creating, reading and processing files

Later on in this chapter you will have a look at more specific algorithms for file access. In this section, you will look at the basics of creating a simple file and iterating over the records within a file. To create a new file you must put the file into "write" mode or "w".

Write mode will create a new file or delete any existing file. Below is some code that will store a single record as specified by Table 13.1. Assumptions being made are (i) that each write will output the correct number of bytes and (ii) that the variables used contain the correct data.

```
fh = open("singleStudent.txt","w")
fh.write(firstName)
fh.write(lastName)
fh.write(dateOfBirth)
fh.write(weight)
fh.write(height)
fh.write(lunch)
fh.close()
```

In order to process a file it is common practice to read it in line by line. File handlers contain a pointer that will tell the handler where in the file the last read or write operation ended. If a read operation occurs when there is no more data to be read, then it will return an end of file (EOF) designator. If the program attempts to read further, this will, in most modern languages, trigger a run time error. EOF can also be used as a way of ending a loop reading in data from a file. The Pseudocode example below shows how all records within a file could be displayed. The end condition of the while loop makes use of the EOF designator.

```
fh.open("multipleStudnets.txt", "r")
while NOT EOF(fh)
      output fh.read(firstName)
      output fh.read(lastName)
      output fh.read(dateOfBirth)
      output fh.read(weight)
      output fh.read(height)
      output fh.read(lunch)
fh.close()
```

File organisation

The remainder of this chapter will focus on how records are structured in files, and algorithms for manipulating them.

Serial files

The most straightforward method of storing records involves new records being appended to the back of a file. All records are therefore stored in chronological order. When creating a serial file it is important to always ensure that the file is opened in append mode. This forces any subsequent file writes to appear at the end of the file.

Serial files tend to be used for situations (i) that do not require any order, or (ii) where the number of records is small, or (iii) where the data must be stored in the order in which it arrived. For example, recording the times of runners as they cross the finish line would be ideally suited to a serial file.

Sequential and indexed sequential files

Sequential files will order records based on a primary key field. One field in the fixed length record will be used to arrange the records in either ascending or descending order. A sequential file offers a number of advantages over serial files when it comes to searching, and is a prerequisite for implementing an index.

Inserting into sequential files is more complex than simply appending to a serial file. In order to add a new record the position in the file where the record is to be added must be found. It is not possible to move records about easily within a file, as files of whatever type are still physically serial. This means that any inserting or deleting from sequential files must happen in a temporary file.

When inserting, records are copied from the original file into a temporary file. This continues until the point is found where the new record is to be inserted. At this point the new record is added to the temporary file and the remainder of the old file is copied over to follow it. The temporary file then replaces the original file. The same process happens when deleting, only instead of adding a new record, the record to be deleted is skipped.

Below is the Pseudocode to insert into a sequential file.

```
oldFile = open("oldFile.txt", "r")
newFile = open("newFile.txt", "w")
WHILE NOT EOF(oldFile)
    d1 = oldFile.read(field1)
    d2 = oldFile.read(field2)
    IF newRecordField1 > d1 THEN
        newFile.write(newRecordField1)
        newFile.write(newRecordField2)
    END IF
    newFile.write(d1)
    newFile.write(d2)
END WHILE
oldFile.close()
newFile.close()
```

Indexed sequential files will contain an index that makes accessing groups of records much faster for search purposes. The index will group the data into logical chunks, for example, records that start with the same letter, and store the file location where that group of records begin. This means that when searching through an indexed file you only have to search the group of the search item. This will speed up finding records within files greatly, especially if the file contains thousands of records.

Although having an index will speed up searching, it does make insertion and deleting much more challenging. Every time a record is added or removed then the start position of the subsequent groups will be different. This means that all index entries from that point must be updated. This will involve adding or removing the size of a single record depending on whether it is inserting or deleting a record. Figure 13.1 shows an example index where the record size is 64 bytes.

Having an index can speed up searching by limiting the search to a group of records. But what if the index is so large that it takes too much time to first search the index and then find the group of records pointed to by the index? In this scenario, the answer will be to add another level of indexing known as multi-level indexing. The idea of a multi-level index is similar to a normal index, however this time the index is split into a number of levels in a tree structure.

Consider the example in Figure 13.2, where the primary index is split into groups of four. This initial index then points to a secondary index that is split down further. Without the multi-level index, the primary index would contain 16 entries. This means you may have to search through 16 items before you even touch the main data. By using two indexes you

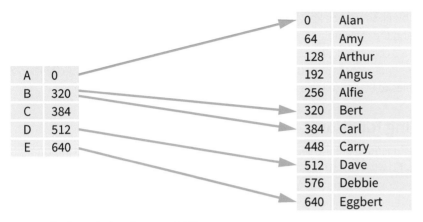

Figure 13.1: Index for an indexed sequential file.

Figure 13.2: A multi-level index showing how groups of records could be organised.

can limit the maximum number of file accesses to eight. The design goal of using multi-level indexes is to limit the number of times the file is accessed, as each access can make demands on the speed of the storage device.

Random files and hashing

Random access in files involves jumping to a record directly without the need to search through numerous records or use an index. Considering the problem in more detail, you need to be able to find a record's start position in a file without having to probe the file in any way. This means the only information you will need is the data you are searching by, which is most likely to be the primary key. You need an algorithm which, when given a key, will produce a position in a file. It must produce the same key every time and must do this regardless of what is already in the file. This form of algorithm is known as a hashing algorithm.

Direct access files are split into blocks where each block contains a fixed number of records. The hashing algorithm will generate the start position of the block and then a serial search can occur on the block to find the file. The file has a maximum capacity, for which space is reserved on the storage device. Each block starts off as blank data but will take up space. If each record has a size S and each block contains R number of records, then each block will be $S \times R$ bytes in size. The number of blocks in the file is decided before any data is added to the file. If there are too few blocks then the chance of having to do a linear search increases. If there are too many blocks then there will be a lot of wasted space due to all blocks being created initially.

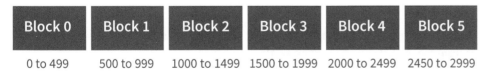

Block 0	Block 1	Block 2	Block 3	Block 4	Block 5
0 to 499	500 to 999	1000 to 1499	1500 to 1999	2000 to 2499	2450 to 2999

Figure 13.3: Block structure of a random file.

The file represented in Figure 13.3 contains six blocks, each made up of ten records. Each record is 50 bytes in size. The total file size is 3000 bytes. The maximum number of records this file could store is 60, however random access files tend not to be filled to capacity. The more full a random access file gets, the worse it performs as more and more searches will result in a linear search. For the files to work optimally, the number of records stored in each block should be kept to a minimum. The ratio between the number of records stored and the maximum number possible is called the load factor. If the structure in Figure 13.3 contained 20 records then the load factor would be 0.33 (calculated by dividing the number of records stored, 20, by the maximum capacity). It is common for random access files to be limited to a load factor of 0.5, or half capacity.

Hashing function

Hashing functions are the secret to how random access files work so it is important to understand what they do and how they are defined. There is not one single hash function to use but rather a collection of functions, each of which spreads information out in different ways. What they all have in common are the following properties:

Deterministic: When given a key, it should always produce the same result.

Uniformity: Keys should be spread evenly over the available block range so as to have the same probability of reducing the number of records in the same block.

Data normalisation: Keys should be normalised before being hashed. For example, all characters should be converted to lower case.

Continuity: Keys that differ by a small amount should result in hash values that also only differ by a small amount.

Non-invertible: It does not hold true that the hash value can be reversed to get the original key.

One simple hashing function for strings is demonstrated by the code below. key.lowercase() normalises the text by turning it all lowercase. The ascii() function will take a single character and return its ASCII value. This hash function is taking each letter in the key and summing up their ASCII values. This number, which could potentially be fairly large, is divided by the block count and the remainder returned. MOD is required here as the hash function's job is to return the block number and not the physical location of the record.

```
function stringHash(key, blockCount)
    key = key.lowercase()
    sum = 0
    for letter in key
        sum += ascii(letter)
    next letter
    return sum MOD blockCount
end function
```

Implementing the above hash function in Python, including some debug lines of code, results in the output shown in Figure 13.4.

```
def stringHash(key, blockCount):
    print "hashing", key
    key = key.lower()
    sum = 0
    for letter in key:
        sum += ord(letter)
    print "total for hashing", key, "is", sum
    return sum % blockCount
```

```
print "final hash is " + str(stringHash("Bert",6))
print "final hash is " + str(stringHash("sally",6))
print "final hash is " + str(stringHash("Betty",6))
```

```
hashing Bert
total for hashing bert is 429
final hash is 3

hashing sally
total for hashing sally is 549
final hash is 3

hashing Betty
total for hashing betty is 552
final hash is 0
```

Figure 13.4: Output of simple string hashing function.

Placing the above records into the file would result in Figure 13.5, but not to scale. Notice that although Sally and Bert are completely different names, they have resulted in the same hash. When two different keys produce the same hash value this is known as a collision. The more collisions you have, the more records get placed in the same block, leading to longer linear searches.

Figure 13.5: Block structure of a random file.

To improve the distribution you can ensure that adjacent letters are not treated exactly the same, by applying a multiplier to them. To prevent the numbers from getting excessively large the multiplier is reset every 4 bytes. The code below generates similar hashes, as the input keys are still relatively small and the number of blocks is small. However, if both of these were increased then the improved hash will produce a better distribution.

Pseudocode:

```
function stringHashImproved(key, blockCount)
    key = key.lowercase()
    sum = 0
    mult = 1
    for letter in subkey
        sum += ascii(letter) * mult
        mult *= 64
        if mult > 64*64*64 then mult = 1
    next letter

    return sum MOD blockCount
end function
```

Python:

```
def stringHashImproved(key, blockCount):
    print "hashing", key
```

```
    key = key.lower()
    sum = 0
    mult = 1
    for letter in key:
        sum += ord(letter) * mult
        mult *= 64
        if mult > 64**3:
            mult = 1
    print "total for hashing", key, "is", sum
    return sum % blockCount

print "final hash is " + str(stringHash("Bert",6))
print "final hash is " + str(stringHash("sally",6))
print "final hash is " + str(stringHash("Betty",6))
```

Comparing hash functions

Comparing hashing functions is different to comparing standard algorithms. Although time and space complexity may be of interest, the key mechanism to compare is the number of collisions that occur. The overall efficiency of any random access file will be based on how many records get placed in the same block. In order to compare hashing functions, you have to run through real data, as the number of collisions will be directly related to the size of the data set and the spread of the data.

Block overflow

As previously discussed, collisions created by the hashing function can lead to more records being stored in a single block. As each block has a maximum record count, what happens if a record block fills up? There are two options, both of which have impacts in terms of cost.

1 Create an overflow area and place the record in there.
2 Create a new file that contains more blocks and re-hash every record to that new file.

Creating an overflow area has the lowest cost in terms of inserting new records, but may cause searches to slow down. When, during a search, you get to the end of the block, the overflow must also be checked. The overflow section will be stored after the standard blocks and would work in the same way a serial file would. If too many records get placed in the overflow part of the file then the overall efficiency of the file will be impacted.

Recreating the file with a larger number of blocks would make inserting potentially very expensive. If this option were to be implemented then the load factor would be the trigger. When the load gets above a certain amount then the probability of collisions will increase, thus increasing the need for overflow. Methods could be put in place to reduce the impact of recreating the file, such as doing it in off-peak periods. Alternatively, selecting a larger initial block size will reduce the chance of it needing to be recreated in the first place. The choice of hash function can also play a part. For example, if, even with a low load factor, the hash function does not spread the records evenly enough, overflow can still occur.

One last thing to consider is that the size of the file grows as each block gets larger and the number of blocks increases.

Master and transaction files

Some files contain vast amounts of data, for example a log of all phone calls made through a mobile phone operator. This data is required for audit purposes, creating bills and data mining. Updating such a file is a slow process. To help speed things up two files are used: one to store the day-to-day interactions and one to store all data. These are known as transaction and master files.

Transaction files will store data collected over a short amount of time, for example, the current month. Although the amount of data this will produce is still large, it is nowhere near the same scale as the data for all months. Transaction files act as a temporary file to help keep the system running quickly, but still storing all of the required data. At the end of a short time scale, which is dependent on the scenario, the data from the transaction file is copied to the master file.

Master files will store all of the data required to perform batch processing operations such as generating bills, or to perform data mining such as deciding which months use more data and less voice. Master files will not be used on a day-to-day basis as they are too large and unwieldy.

Backup and archiving

Backup is the process of copying files from the main area where it is used to a separate area. That way, if a file is deleted the backup can be accessed in order to retrieve the lost file. Every network has a backup policy, as it is very common for files to get deleted or lost.

When creating a backup policy you need to decide:

* where will the backup be stored?
* what will it be stored on?
* how often will the backup be taken?
* how long will a backup be kept?

When you back up your files at home you may use a memory stick or an external hard drive. You may even use a CD or DVD to back up your files. A network will tend to use magnetic tapes or hard drives. The amount of data that needs to be backed up could amount to terabytes (1000 GB), which means that no DVD or external hard drive could fit it all on.

It is common to have a server that is completely dedicated to backing up files!

It can take many hours to back up all of the files on the network, and the procedure can tie up the network for a long time. This means that the backup will occur at night or during off-peak hours. The more often a backup is done, the more secure the data will be; unfortunately this requires very large storage capacity. There is a trade-off between how often you do a backup, how long you can keep the backup and how much storage is required. Eventually, no matter how much storage is used, old backups will need to be deleted in order to make way for new backups. In order to keep the size of a backup small only the files that have changed are backed up. The first backup will copy all files and then each subsequent backup will only copy over the files that have changed. This dramatically reduces the overhead of a backup and means that it can be done more often.

It is common to have backups on the opposite side of the building in a fireproof box. This limits the chance of both the backup and the main server being destroyed by a fire or other accidents. However, to keep data really safe it should be stored off-site, possibly even using a cloud-based service.

Some files are really important and must never be deleted. However, over time, these files build up and take up space in the master files. The more space used up by these records and files, the slower the system becomes overall. If these files are not in day-to-day use then they could be archived. Archiving is the process of moving a file or record from the main system to a separate archived system. Archiving old files will speed up the overall running of the main system but still give access to the files should the need arise.

Chapter summary

- Fixed length records are made up of a number of fields, each one having a specific data type and size.
- Common data types include integer, float, string, date and Boolean.
- Estimating file size requires the size of single records to be calculated, multiplied by the number of records and 10% added on for metadata.
- Files are opened in one of three modes: append, read and write.
- Files are read by iterating over records using end of file (EOF) to end the loop.
- Serial files store records in chronological order.
- Sequential files order records by a primary key field.
- Indexed sequential files will have an index which will point to groups of related records.
- Inserting and deleting from sequential and index sequential files require a new file to be created and the file to be re-organised.
- Multi-level indexes can speed up access to groups of records in larger files.
- Random access files are broken into blocks of records.
- Records are added to blocks by using a hash function.
- Hash functions take a key and calculate a block number. Their key design goal is to ensure a wide spread of blocks for any given set of inputs.
- By looking at the number of collisions, you can compare hash functions.
- Master files store all data while transaction files store data currently being worked on.
- Transaction files are used to speed up access for day-to-day processing of data.
- Backing up files will be based on a policy set up by a company. It will consider how often the back-up will occur, when it should be taken, how long it will be kept and where it will be stored.
- Archiving is the process of moving old files to a separate system in order to speed up the main one.

End-of-chapter questions

1   A school needs to store information about subjects for timetabling purposes.
    They decide to use a fixed length record as shown below. Complete the table.   [6]

Field name	Data type	Size (in bytes)
Subject name		
Number of lessons per week		
Requires ICT?		

2   Using your answer to question 1, estimate the file size for 30 subjects.   [3]

3   A company has decided to store information about their products using a
    sequential file. Each record will store the name of the product, the number in
    stock and the name of the supplier. They want to be able to update the stock
    level when a purchase occurs. In Pseudocode write a function which will
    update stock given the product name and the amount to reduce the
    stock by.   [6]

4   State the advantages and disadvantages of using indexed sequential files
    over sequential files.   [4]

5   Describe how hash functions are used in random access files.   [3]

Chapter 14
Databases and distributed systems

Learning objectives

(A) • Explain what is meant by data consistency, data redundancy and data independence.

• Describe and discuss the benefits and drawbacks of relational database systems and other contemporary database systems.

(A) • Explain what is meant by relational database organisation and data normalisation (first, second and third normal forms).

• Restructure data into third normal form.

• Explain and apply entity relationship modelling and use it to analyse simple problems.

• Describe the use of primary keys, foreign keys and indexes.

• Describe the advantages of different users having different views of the data in a database.

(A) • Explain how the data can be manipulated to provide the user with useful information.

• Explain and apply appropriate techniques for data validation and verification of data in databases.

• Explain the purpose of query languages.

• Construct and run queries using Structured Query Language (SQL*).

• Explain the purpose of a database management system (DBMS) and data dictionaries.

• Explain what is meant by Big Data, predictive analytics, data warehousing and data mining.

- Explain that distribution can apply to both data and processing.
- Describe distributed databases and the advantages of such distribution.

* Candidates should be familiar with the following commands and operators:

```
CREATE TABLE...
PRIMARY KEY
NOT NULL
Int
Char(n)
Numeric(m,n)
DateTime
INSERT INTO ... VALUES
SELECT ... FROM ... WHERE ...
SELECT*FROM ...WHERE ...
IN
AND
OR
ORDER BY
GROUP BY
UPDATE ... SET ...
=
>
>=
<
<=
<>
```

- Candidates should also be familiar with the use of sub queries and parentheses.

Introduction

What is a database?

The ability to hold vast amounts of information is one of the reasons why computer systems have become so widely used. Imagine how many products, customer details and financial transactions Amazon or eBay must hold. Think about how many individual posts, comments, images and links Facebook has to store.

Before the advent of computers, this data would need to be held on paper records in filing cabinets. Entire buildings were dedicated to storing important records for companies or governments. Teams of secretaries were paid to find information and distribute it to those who needed it. Accessing the records held in another town or country was very time consuming.

Computers can store the equivalent of thousands of text documents on a single USB key smaller than a fingernail. But just being able to store this data is only part of the solution. Data is only useful if you can access it quickly and know that the information you are receiving is correct. This is where databases come in. Databases are just data structures that hold vast amounts of data in a way that makes it easy to modify and search. Databases are used to hold product details, customer information, financial records or anything that a user might need to know. Many websites are simply user interfaces for databases, allowing users to search for products and store their personal details for later use. However, storing all this data in one place has led to a number of concerns about privacy and data theft.

Database key terms

Flat file database

In a flat file database information is held in a single table. Each column in the table is called an attribute and each row is a record.

Student ID	Student name	Gender	DOB	Course ID	Course name	Teacher ID	Teacher name	Teacher specialism
67678	Jim Donaldson	M	30/01/2000	GY51	Maths	4445	Mr Surrall	Maths
67677	Jane Jones	F	02/01/2000	FU451	Physics	4445	Mr Surrall	Maths
67678	Jim Donaldson	M	30/01/2000	F4I052	Computer Science	4443	Mr Smith	Physics
67222	Lucy Kid	F	08/03/2000	GY51	Maths	4445	Mr Surrall	Maths

Table 14.1: A flat file database.

Flat file databases are generally used for very small amounts of data. But as they get larger they develop a big problem called *data redundancy*. Data redundancy simply means that lots of data is replicated. Look at Table 14.1, you will see that the same information about Mr Surrall, his ID, name and specialism, occurs three times. Jim Donaldson has his ID, name, gender and DOB occur twice. This repetition has occurred in a really small database. You can imagine how much repetition would occur in a database with thousands or millions of records.

Repetition is a problem for many reasons. Imagine that Mr Surrall changes his specialism to Physics. At the moment that information would need to be changed in three separate places. In a large database it would be easy to miss a record and the data being stored would be inaccurate, which could give you legal problems with the Data Protection Act. Also, imagine that you decide you want to store some extra information, such as students' email addresses. Using a flat file will require you to enter the same information over and over again.

In order to solve the problems with flat file databases, you need to create a relational database.

Relational databases

Relational databases were created to remove the problems with flat file databases. They are made up of lots of smaller tables linked together. This helps to remove the repetition that is such a big problem in flat file databases, but it does mean that the databases are more complex to create and maintain.

The example in Figure 14.1 shows how, by placing the teachers' details in a separate table, you can remove the repetition.

Of course, now the data is in separate tables you need some way to associate the students' records with their teachers' records. For this you need to use primary and foreign keys.

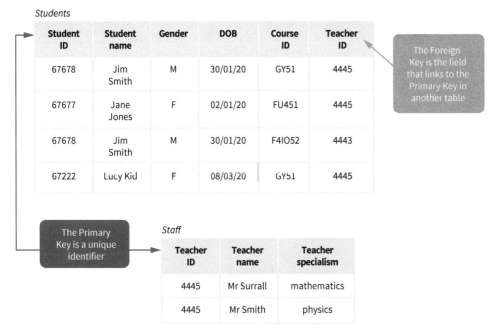

Students

Student ID	Student name	Gender	DOB	Course ID	Teacher ID
67678	Jim Smith	M	30/01/20	GY51	4445
67677	Jane Jones	F	02/01/20	FU451	4445
67678	Jim Smith	M	30/01/20	F4IO52	4443
67222	Lucy Kid	F	08/03/20	GY51	4445

The Foreign Key is the field that links to the Primary Key in another table

The Primary Key is a unique identifier

Staff

Teacher ID	Teacher name	Teacher specialism
4445	Mr Surrall	mathematics
4445	Mr Smith	physics

Figure 14.1: Relational databases contain multiple tables linked together by primary and foreign keys.

Primary key

In a database a primary key is a piece of information in each record that is unique to that record. It is often called a 'unique identifier'. Primary keys are often ID numbers generated especially for that purpose. This is because finding unique information about records is not very easy; there are lots of people with the same first name, postcode and date of birth. Any time you are given an account or user number, you can be sure that it is the primary key in a database somewhere.

Primary keys are vital in creating relational databases. By using the primary key of a record you can link two records together. In the example above, the primary key of the Staff table is 'Teacher ID', so by including 'Teacher ID' in the Students table you can indicate which teacher is responsible for which student.

Foreign key

In a database a foreign key is any field in a table which is the primary key in another table. In our example the 'Teacher ID' field in the Students table is a foreign key because it links to the primary key in the Staff table.

Data consistency, integrity and redundancy

Data consistency ensures that any constraints placed on the database, such as primary and foreign keys, are adhered to. Any database transactions which are about to happen should see all previous changes implemented, otherwise this might lead to unexpected results.

Data integrity refers to the correctness of the data over the lifetime of that data. This means that the data is correct when it enters the database, as it is queried and updated up until the point it is removed from the system. Data must be complete, accurate and consistent. There are three main types of integrity:

1   Entity integrity – every table must have a primary key which is unique and not empty.
2   Referential integrity – foreign keys must point to the primary key of another table but can be empty (meaning that there is no relationship).
3   Domain integrity – all attributes in the database are related to the overall domain that the database is working on.

Data redundancy refers to wasted data or duplication of data. If the data is held in more than one place in the database then this is known as redundancy. Having data in multiple places can impact the accuracy of the data: if one item changes, then two sets of data could differ, even though they should be the same. Data redundancy can lead to a reduction in data integrity.

Normalising the database can enact these three principles.

Normalisation

Normalisation is the process of converting a flat file database (with a single table) to a relational database (with many tables). There are various levels of normalisation that remove repetition to a greater or lesser extent. You will look more at normalisation in a future section.

Indexing

An index is a data structure used to shorten the length of time it takes to search a database. For example, the index might contain the 'surname' column of a database. This would mean that when you are searching for a student, if you know their surname you will find the information you wanted much faster.

Normalisation to 3NF

As you have already seen, normalisation is the process of converting a flat file database to a relational database, that is, going from a database with a single table to one with many tables. The different levels of normalisation are called 'forms' and you need to know the first three of them.

First normal form

A table is in first normal form if each field contains only one piece of data and all the attributes in a table are dependent on the primary key.

Look at the flat file database in Table 14.2:

Student ID	Course ID	Teacher ID	DOB	Gender	Postcode
ST6, James	67TY, 67UI, 67PM	TYM1, TYM3, TYM8	30/01/2000	M	OX68TY
ST7, Charlotte	67TY, 67UI, 67PM	TYM1, TYM3, TYM8	12/05/2000	F	CA80GH
ST8, Julie	67TY, 67UI, 67PM	TYM1, TYM3, TYM8	03/10/2000	F	WR168UY

Table 14.2:

Student ID, Course ID and Teacher ID all have multiple values in each cell. To fix this you need to expand the table, as shown in Table 14.3:

Enrolment ID	Student ID	Student name	Course ID	Teacher ID	DOB	Gender	Postcode
E1	ST6	James	67TY	TYM1	30/01/2000	M	OX68TY
E2	ST6	James	67UI	TYM3	30/01/2000	M	OX68TY
E3	ST6	James	67PM	TYM8	30/01/2000	M	OX68TY
E4	ST7	Charlotte	67TY	TYM1	12/05/2000	F	CA80GH
E5	ST7	Charlotte	67UI	TYM3	12/05/2000	F	CA80GH
E6	ST7	Charlotte	67PM	TYM8	12/05/2000	F	CA80GH
E7	ST8	Julie	67TY	TYM1	03/10/2000	F	WR168UY
E8	ST8	Julie	67UI	TYM3	03/10/2000	F	WR168UY
E9	ST8	Julie	67PM	TYM8	03/10/2000	F	WR168UY

Table 14.3: A flat-file database.

Now that each attribute contains just one piece of data, it is much closer to being in first normal form.

The second requirement for being in first normal form is that all the attributes in a table are dependent on the primary key. This is not true for our current table, as the teachers, courses and students are not uniquely associated with the Enrolment ID; for example, the same Teacher ID appears in many enrolments.

Look at Tables 14.4 to 14.6 below:

Enrolment ID	Course ID	Student ID	Teacher ID
E1	67TY	ST6	TYM1
E2	67UI	ST6	TYM3
E3	67PM	ST6	TYM8
E4	67TY	ST7	TYM1
E5	67UI	ST7	TYM3
E6	67PM	ST7	TYM8
E7	67TY	ST8	TYM1
E8	67UI	ST8	TYM3
E9	67PM	ST8	TYM8

Table 14.4: A flat-file database with grouped items expanded.

Student ID	Student name	DOB	Gender	Postcode
ST6	James	30/01/2000	M	OX68TY
ST7	Charlotte	12/05/2000	F	CA80GH
ST8	Julie	03/10/2000	F	WR168UY

Table 14.5: Students.

Course ID	Course name	Teacher ID	Teacher name	Postcode
67TY	Maths	TYM1	Mr Smith	CA80GH
67UI	Computer Science	TYM3	Mrs Jones	WR168UZ
67PM	Physics	TYM8	Ms Pratt	WR168UB

Table 14.6: Course.

This new layout has removed nearly all the repetition from the tables. Notice that primary and foreign keys are essential for linking the tables together, so they don't count as repeated attributes.

Second normal form

Look at tables 14.7 to 14.9. A table is in second normal form if it is in first normal form and it contains no partial dependencies. For example, in our enrolment table our Teacher ID is only partially dependent on the Course ID, so can be removed.

Enrolment ID	Course ID	Student ID
E1	67TY	ST6
E2	67UI	ST6
E3	67PM	ST6
E4	67TY	ST7
E5	67UI	ST7
E6	67PM	ST7
E7	67TY	ST8
E8	67UI	ST8
E9	67PM	ST8

Table 14.7: Enrolment.

Student ID	Student name	DOB	Gender	Postcode
ST6	James	30/01/2000	M	OX68TY
ST7	Charlotte	12/05/2000	F	CA80GH
ST8	Julie	03/10/2000	F	WR168UY

Table 14.8: Students.

Course ID	Course name	Teacher ID	Teacher name	Postcode
67TY	Maths	TYM1	Mr Smith	CA80GH
67UI	Computer Science	TYM3	Mrs Jones	WR168UZ
67PM	Physics	TYM8	Ms Pratt	WR168UB

Table 14.9: Course.

Now our tables are in second normal form.

Third normal form

A table is said to be in third normal form if it is in second normal form and contains no transitive dependencies. Transitive dependency is tricky to understand; basically, if A is dependent on B and B is dependent on C then A is transitively dependent on C. In our example the course is dependent on the Course ID and the teacher is dependent on the course. So the teacher is transitively dependent on the Course ID and must be placed in a separate table.

Enrolment ID	Course ID	Student ID
E1	67TY	ST6
E2	67UI	ST6
E3	67PM	ST6
E4	67TY	ST7
E5	67UI	ST7
E6	67PM	ST7
E7	67TY	ST8
E8	67UI	ST8
E9	67PM	ST8

Table 14.10: Enrolment.

Student ID	Student name	DOB	Gender	Postcode
ST6	James	30/01/2000	M	OX68TY
ST7	Charlotte	12/05/2000	F	CA80GH
ST8	Julie	03/10/2000	F	WR168UY

Table 14.11: Students.

Teacher ID	Teacher name	Postcode
TYM1	Mr Smith	CA80GH
TYM3	Mrs Jones	WR168UZ
TYM8	Ms Pratt	WR168UB

Table 14.12: Teachers.

Course ID	Course name	Teacher ID
67TY	Maths	TYM1
67UI	Computer Science	TYM3
67PM	Physics	TYM8

Table 14.13: Course.

Our database is now in third normal form.

Tip

Long answer questions often require you to describe how a given flat file database could be normalised.

Database views

A database view allows a number of tables and records to be restricted so that only certain users can see certain sets of data. For example, users who are involved in sales should not be able to see salary information, but someone from management could. It is possible to set a query as a view as shown in the example below. This would create a new table called young_people, which would only show records which have an age less than or equal to 25. This view of the database hides records of people who are older than 25. By combining access rights and creating views, the database developer can restrict data to different groups of users in any way they wish.

```
CREATE VIEW young_people AS
SELECT * FROM personal
WHERE age <= 25;
```

Each table can be restricted so that some users have no access or only partial access to the data. These restrictions are known as database privileges.

The main access rights that can be assigned to a table are:

- Search (run queries)
- Alter (alter the structure)
- Update (edit records)
- Delete (delete records)
- Drop (drop the table).

These can be used in conjunction with views to secure parts of the database. A user, or group of users, will have specific access rights to specific tables.

The key advantages of using database views are:

- Data protection – key data can be protected from different groups of users using a combination of access rights and views.
- Encapsulate complicated SQL queries – if certain queries are complicated enough and are used often enough then it could be worth creating a view for them.
- Simplify access – if data is spread over multiple tables then views can help simplify access for less experienced users.
- Performance – views can be set up with performance in mind and then re-used by other developers. This can be another advantage of encapsulating key queries.

Data validation and verification

In Chapter 3 of Component 1 you were introduced to the concepts of validation and verification.

Databases can implement some validation techniques directly; the rest need to be implemented through the application using them. When specifying a new column in a table you can define the data type so if the type were set to integer then it would reject any attempts to add string data. Columns can be set up to reject null values so they cannot be left empty. This means that if a new record is inserted then this column must contain data, otherwise the whole row would be rejected. Length checks can be set up on text fields by specifying the maximum number of characters. However, it will not reject the data if you do this, rather it will simply truncate the data.

Referential integrity is one validation method that is unique to databases. When linking two tables together, referential integrity stipulates that a record must exist in both tables. More specifically, if the foreign key points to a primary key that does not exist then the record will be rejected. This prevents records being added that form part of a relationship, where the linked table no longer contains the record being linked to.

Format checks are not done by the database but rather must be done by the developer using the database. It is very common for databases to be hidden behind an application, meaning that any additional validation, such as format checks, can be done.

SQL: interpret and modify (list of keywords)

When you have a database, one of the most important things you will need to do is query it. Stored data is useless without being able to access it at a later date. When searching through data from a database, you will have to execute a query. A query is a search on the database. It provides results, which are returned in the form of a new table.

In the early days of computing there were many different types of database. Each required a different way to query the data. This meant that it was very difficult for specialists to transfer skills from one database to another. There was no standardisation, which meant that they were locked into specific database implementations.

Databases often form the cornerstone of computerised systems in business; therefore the demand for skilled database operatives was high. It became clear that there needed to be a standard way of interacting with databases. A committee called the ANSI-SQL group produced the standard for querying a database known as SQL. SQL stands for Structured Query Language and is often pronounced 'sequel'. A query is written in SQL and sent to the database query engine as plain text. The database then executes the query and returns the results in the form of a table. The following examples show some basic SQL commands and their results.

SELECT query

The SELECT instruction returns a specified piece of data from a database. It can return whole rows and columns or the data from a single field.

Student ID	Student Name	DOB	Gender	Postcode
ST6	James	30/01/2000	M	OX68TY
ST7	Charlotte	12/05/2000	F	CA80GH
ST8	Julie	03/10/2000	F	WR168UY

Table 14.14: Students.

SQL Example	Result
`SELECT * FROM Students`	Returns the entire table with everything in it.
`SELECT StudentID FROM Students`	Returns the StudentID column from the Students table.
`SELECT * FROM Students WHERE StudentID = "ST6"`	Returns the whole of the record where the StudentID is ST6.
`SELECT StudentName, DOB FROM Students WHERE Gender = "F"`	Returns the name and date of birth of all the students who have their gender recorded as F.
`SELECT StudentName, DOB FROM Students WHERE Gender = "F" ORDER BY StudentName DESC`	Returns the name and date of birth of all the students who have their gender recorded as F. The list returned will be sorted in descending order by student name.

You can use all the common logical operators you are familiar with in SQL statements, including Boolean operations such as AND, OR, NOT.

INSERT

As well as retrieving data from an existing database, SQL also lets you add records using the INSERT command.

SQL Example	Result
`INSERT INTO Students (StudentID, StudentName, DOB, Gender, Postcode) VALUES ("ST9","Adam","29/01/2001","M","OX69TG")`	Inserts a new record in the Students table.

Be aware that when inserting a record you must include a value for the primary key (in this case StudentID). If you try to insert a new record with the same primary key as an existing record, the database will reject the query.

UPDATE

The UPDATE command is used to edit or modify existing data in the database.

SQL Example	Result
`UPDATE Students SET StudentName = "Joseph"`	Sets every student's name in the database to Joseph.
`UPDATE Students SET StudentName = "Joseph" WHERE StudentID = "ST6"`	Will find the record where the StudentID is ST6 and set the student's name to Joseph.

DELETE

As well as adding and editing data, SQL also enables you to delete data from a database using the DELETE command.

SQL Example	Result
DELETE FROM Students WHERE StudentName = "Joseph"	Will delete every record where the student's name is Joseph from the database.

Creating and removing tables

SQL commands are not just focused on manipulating records. You can also use SQL to create new tables, delete tables you don't want and edit the properties of existing tables.

SQL Example	Result
DROP Students	Will delete the entire Students table and everything in it.
CREATE TABLE Parents (ParentID VARCHAR(4) NOT NULL, ParentName VARCHAR(20) NOT NULL, DOB DATE PRIMARY KEY (ParentID))	Creates a new table with three columns called ParentID, ParentName and DOB. ParentID is the primary key and can be up to four characters long, ParentName can be up to 20 characters long and DOB must be a date. NOT NULL indicates that a field must be set when inserting a record.

Referential integrity

In a relational database every foreign key must correspond to the primary key in another table. For example, there is no point including the Teacher ID TYM9 in our Courses table if there is no record in the Teachers table with TYM9 as a primary key (Tables 14.15, 14.16).

Teacher ID	Teacher name	Postcode
TYM1	Mr Smith	CA80GH
TYM3	Mrs Jones	WR168UZ
TYM8	Ms Pratt	WR168UB

Table 14.15: Teachers.

Course ID	Course name	Teacher ID
67TY	Maths	TYM1
67UI	Computer Science	TYM3
67PM	Physics	TYM9

Table 14.16: Course.

Making sure that each foreign key refers to an existing record is called maintaining referential integrity. Records with a foreign key that goes nowhere are sometimes called 'orphan records'.

There are some specific commands included in SQL to help ensure that a database maintains its referential integrity.

SQL Example	Result
```CREATE TABLE Parents (ParentID VARCHAR(4) NOT NULL, ParentName VARCHAR(20) NOT NULL, DOB DATE, StudentID REFERENCES Students(StudentID) ON UPDATE CASCADE, PRIMARY KEY (ParentID))```	This creates a new Parents table with a foreign key linking it to the Students table. The ON UPDATE CASCADE instruction means that if you update the StudentID in the Students table, the foreign key in the Parents table will be automatically updated to match.

Tip

You should be prepared to have to write or annotate SQL code in the exam.

Just as referential integrity is used to ensure that the links between tables remain correct, record locking is used to ensure that the data itself is correct. Record locking means ensuring that two people can't try and update the same piece of information at the same time and thus override each other's changes.

Database management systems

Databases are stores of data and have no user interface. Their job is to accept database requests and return results. Databases accept requests in the form of SQL commands and return tables via result sets. As a programmer you can use library software to connect to the database and manipulate result sets. In order to connect to a database you must have the following information:

- The network address of the server (IP address)
- The schema name (a database can have more than one schema)
- Username
- Password.

Using a database through a programming language is not normally how the database will be initially created or managed. To maintain the database you will use a database management system or DBMS. This could be GUI or command line based. Command line interfaces allow quick access to SQL queries to be executed while GUIs allow simpler access to rights management and other management tools.

Case study - MySQL

MySQL Community Edition is a free database that is used extensively on the web and in open source projects. The MySQL server will come with a command line DBMS.

You must specify the host, username and password in order to connect. If the database is on the computer you are connecting from then the host name will be localhost or 127.0.0.1.

When MySQL is installed you will be asked for a password for the root account. It is critical you remember that password otherwise you will not be able to connect to the database.

Figure 14.2: MySQL command line interface DBMS.

It is always recommended to add new users to the database (you should never connect as root using a programming language). To do this in MySQL command line you would run the SQL commands:

```
GRANT INSERT,UPDATE,DELETE,SELECT ON mydb.*
TO newuser@localhost;
SET password FOR newuser = password("mypass");
FLUSH PRIVILEGES;
```

This is not a very user friendly way of maintaining a database. However, new users can be created using a script, which may be advantageous for an advanced user. A more user friendly way of maintaining the database is to use the GUI tool for MySQL which is called MySQL Workbench.

Figure 14.3: MySQL Workbench.

MySQL Workbench must be downloaded separately for MySQL and it is possible to maintain multiple databases over a network using it. Server administration allows you to

Activity 14.1

Visit http://www.cambridge.org/
links/kwse6047 and use the 'Try it
yourself' exercises to practise using
MySQL.

set up users and assign privileges. SQL development allows you to create tables and run
general purpose SQL. Data modelling offers a GUI for creating tables and managing the
overall design of the database.

Data definition language

Data definition language or DDL is a language that is used to create and destroy tables
(also known as dropping tables). Using this language you can define the structure, the
fields, primary keys and even indices. This includes:

- CREATE TABLE
- ALTER TABLE
- DROP TABLE

Data manipulation language

Data manipulation language or DML is used to edit or retrieve data from a database. This
means you can insert, update and query using this language.

Common DML statements are:

- `SELECT`
- `UPDATE`
- `INSERT`
- `DELETE`

Data dictionary

There is a lot of data required to define how a database is structured, the users and
their access rights. All of this data, known as the database metadata, is stored in a data
dictionary. It stores the names of all tables, their columns and indexes. For each column it
will store the name of the field, the data type, the size and constraints. The key constraints
include whether it is a key (primary, secondary, composite or foreign) and if that field can
be null (or empty). How tables are linked together is also stored in the data dictionary.
This will be based on each table's keys and whether or not referential integrity has been
enabled.

Big data

The information age is creating an exponential amount of information. It took humankind
24 000 years (approximately) to generate 5 exabytes of data (10^{18} bytes). At the moment
we are generating 5 exabytes of data every two days. This level of growth is given the
overarching title of big data. By using the term big data you are really referring to the
sheer volume of data, both structured (like a database) and unstructured (social media,
random blogs etc). Three main features can be attributed to big data: the volume of data,
the velocity of growth and the variety of formats the data takes. Data can take the form of
video, email, news tickers, audio, animations and many other types of data. As a member
of the information age, one of the key skills you must master is how to wade through big
data. As a computer scientist, you have opportunities to analyse this data to use it for
applications that have never been possible before.

Data warehousing

Data mining and predictive analytics

Computers have enabled corporations and governments to collect vast amounts of data. However, out of context or without a proper understanding of their relationship with other pieces of data, these data are often meaningless. Data mining is the process of finding new patterns in large data sets. Simply put, it is the process of identifying the relationships between different sets of data and setting it in the correct context. It is commonly used in conjunction with modelling to make predictions about the impact of new initiatives based on historical data.

For example, if a supermarket wants to increase the amount of profit it makes from selling milk, it could use the vast amount of data it has on different milk brands, prices, amounts and sales to look for patterns in consumer spending. If it finds that milk sales increase significantly when the price is 5p below that of its competitors it is likely that setting the price at that level for the next month will increase its profits. It is exactly this kind of data mining that has led to supermarket price wars over commodities like milk, bread and beans in the last few years.

Another common use of data mining is fraud detection. Credit card companies have to reimburse their customers if their card details are used fraudulently; this costs the banks a lot of money (an estimated $190 billion per year in the US alone). As a result, the banks have turned to data mining to try to solve the problem by spotting suspicious transactions and stopping them at source. The algorithms used are complex, but, essentially, if all your previous transactions have taken place in London and 98% of them are for items costing less than £100, a sudden one-off payment of £2000 for a new TV in New York is likely to be flagged as a fraudulent payment (someone using your credit card details without your permission). By mining your purchase history, your bank has been able to spot new transactions that don't match the trend and stop them. Of course, this method isn't perfect and many people use their credit cards legitimately on holiday, only to find that their bank has cancelled the card!

Data mining requires fairly advanced technology. A large amount of storage is required to hold all the data, as well as a number of high-specification processors to search all the data as quickly as possible. Finally, complex algorithms are required to ensure that the patterns identified are reliable and represent useful information.

Predictive analytics also can be referred to as data mining, but there are some key differences. Predictive analytics tries to predict the likelihood of an action or event happening. For example, if someone steals your credit card and starts buying things you would never normally buy then predictive analytics could be used to determine if this spending pattern is unusual and trigger an investigation. Data mining, on the other hand, looks at relationships between data and is looking for unknown patterns. When trying to predict future outcomes, predictive analytics will use current and historical data as well as a variety of statistical methods.

In order to enable data mining to take place, data needs to be brought together from many different systems. A data warehouse can be used to bring together and store all of this disparate data. Data is uploaded from active systems, such as current sales, and copied into the warehouse. Reports can then be generated once the analysis has taken place. Data is copied into the warehouse, as current data will change rapidly and that can impact the analysis. As relationships are being determined, it is not essential to have data that is live. However having data that is too stale could lead to links that no longer hold true. One other advantage of data warehousing is that it can act as an archiving system.

Distributed systems

Network services, such as printing or file servers, take the form of servers. Each service that is provided on a network will be carried out by one or more of these servers. In smaller companies this may only be a single server, but in large companies it could be done by many. Distributed systems separate these services over multiple servers or computers.

Databases require a server to run and in most production environments it will be stored on a separate server to the main applications. The application server will communicate with the database server whenever it requires data for processing. It could be the case that multiple application servers work off the same database server, as shown in Figure 14.4.

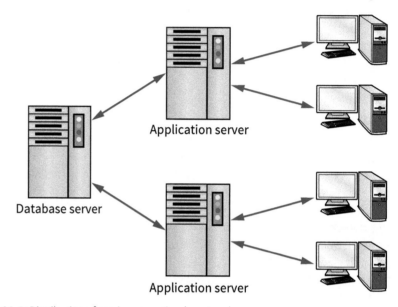

Figure 14.4: Distribution of services on a simple network.

Separation of processing and data is very common and has a number of advantages. Application servers tend to have smaller storage requirements while database requires large, fast file storage. Therefore it makes sense to custom build servers that are more suited to these requirements. Server redundancy and disaster recovery are also key factors to separating data from processing. If the database goes down it can be replaced by a backup server without having to change anything from the application server. Transfer to the backup server can be set up to work automatically to minimise the impact on users. Also, separating the database behind an extra layer of protection limits the chance that an outside hacker can gain access to the database server, even if they have managed to gain access to the application server.

Distributed databases

A database could be split over multiple servers, with each database providing part of the overall system. The diagram in Figure 14.5 shows three different areas of an organisation split over three different databases. Each department would routinely use their own database, but sometimes they may require access to another. For example, when a sale occurs, the sale needs to be recorded and the stock updated. This would mean the transaction would need to update two separate databases. This form of database is known as partition distributed database. The other key type, replicated, is where each database contains exactly the same data for redundancy and optimisation purposes.

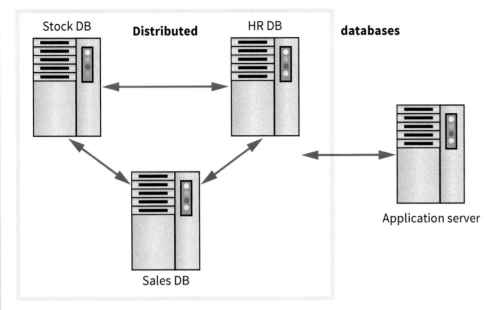

Distributed database

Figure 14.5: Distributed database.

When updating more than one database at a time, transactions become more complicated. If you were to update two databases in a single transaction, what would happen if one of them failed to complete the update? This would lead to data corruption and would impact the integrity of the data. Distributed transactions take an all-or-nothing approach. Either all databases do the update, or none of them do. In order to do this a two-phase commit algorithm is used. In the first phase each of the databases are asked if they are ready to update the data. All of the databases perform the update up until the point where they commit, or finalise the update. The original requesting database will wait until all of the other databases have responded that they are ready. If any respond negatively or not at all then a roll back message is sent out and all databases will undo the change. In the second phase, known as the commit, a message is sent to all databases to commit and asks for acknowledgement. Again if any of them send a negative response, or fail to respond, a roll back is issued.

The advantages of distributed networks are:

- Resilience – if one database goes down, other areas of the organisation can keep working.
- Security – access to entire databases can be limited.
- Scaling – new databases can be added easily allowing for growth.
- Performance – the load on a single database will be reduced, as it is only there to provide part of the overall system.

Chapter summary

- Flat file databases store information in a single large table.
- Relational databases store data in many smaller tables, linked together using keys.
- Primary keys are unique attributes that can be used to identify a record in a table.
- Foreign keys are the primary keys from another table and are used to link tables together.

- Entity relationship models visually describe the relationships between the different entities in a database.
- Normalisation is the process of converting a flat file database into a relational one.
- An index is a data structure used to shorten the length of time it takes to search a database.
- There are different stages of normalisation. The most common is third normal form (3NF). A table is in third normal form if it contains no transitive dependencies.
- Structured query language (SQL) is used to create, edit and delete data in databases.
- Referential integrity is needed to ensure that the foreign keys in one table refer to a primary key in another.
- Data mining and predictive analytics allow analysis of big data to uncover patterns and predict future outcomes.
- Database views allow a restricted view of the entire database for performance and security reasons.
- Database management systems allow users and databases to be managed. They also implement the data dictionary which stores all of the metadata of the database.
- Distributed databases split an organisation's data need between multiple database servers.

Activity 14.2

Imagine you have been responsible for creating a database to hold everything in your school's timetable. Draw a diagram showing the tables and fields you would need, along with any links between primary and secondary keys.

End-of-chapter questions

1 a What is meant by a 'flat file' database? [1]

   b What is a primary key? [1]

2 a What is a relational database? [2]

   b What is the result of running this SQL query: SELECT * FROM Students [1]

   c What is the purpose of referential integrity? [2]

Further reading

Flat file database	Search for Flat File Database on databasedev.co.uk
Relational database	Search for a Relational Database Overview on Oracle's Java Documentation website
Normalisation	Search for Normalisation Example on sqa.org's e-learning website

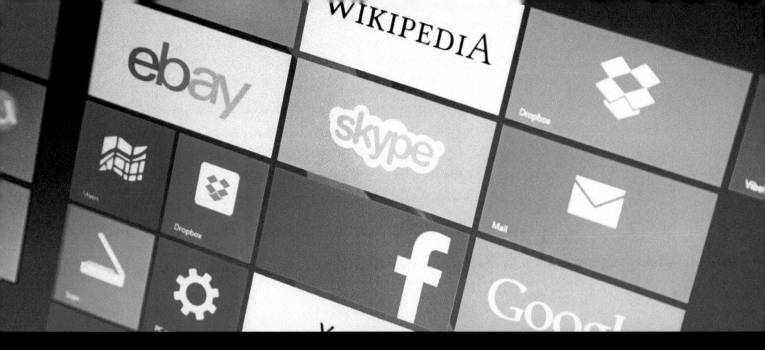

Chapter 15
The operating system

Learning objectives

- Describe the need for and the role of the operating system kernel in managing resources, including peripherals, processes, memory protection and backing store.

- Describe the need for and the role of the operating system in providing an interface between the user and the hardware.

- Explain the hierarchical structure of a directory and describe file attributes.

- Explain the need for and use of a range of utility software.

- Describe the main features of batch processing, real time control and real time transaction systems.

- Identify and describe applications that would be suitable to these modes of operation.

- Explain the following types of system: batch, single-user (standalone), multi-user (multi-access), multi-tasking and multi-programming.

- Explain the need to design systems that are appropriate to the variety of different users at all levels and in different environments.

- Describe a range of conditions or events which could generate interrupts.

- Describe interrupt handling and the use of priorities.

- Describe the factors involved in allocating differing priorities.

- Explain the reasons for, and possible consequences of, partitioning of main memory.

- Describe methods of data transfer, including the use of buffers to allow for differences in speed of devices.

- Describe buffering and explain why double buffering is used.
- Describe the principles of high level scheduling: processor allocation, allocation of devices and the significance of job priorities.
- Explain the three basic states of a process: running, ready and blocked.
- Explain the role of time-slicing, polling and threading.

Introduction

Software can be categorised, with each category responsible for different functionality. System software runs behind the scenes, supported by utility software, and applications run on top of it to allow the user to perform tasks. This division of labour means that application developers don't need to worry about how data is saved to the hard drive; they merely have to invoke the OS to perform that task for them. In this chapter, you will look at the role of system software, with a focus on the operating system.

Systems and application software

System software allows control over the hardware and software of the computer. It is essential for performing even the most basic tasks, such as initialising hardware and handling key presses. The two most common types are the operating system and system start-up software. When considering whether software is system software or application software, it is important to consider whether that software directly manages the hardware and other software. Some software, such as a camera app on a phone, may seem as if it is controlling hardware directly. However, it is simply interacting with the operating system and hardware drivers in order to make use of the hardware indirectly.

Application software is software that allows a user to carry out a specific task. For example, Microsoft Outlook allows a user to send an email.

It is essential to make the distinction between commonly used software and the extra software installed with the operating system. Some software bundled with the operating system may be application (or utility) software. For example, Microsoft Word, although essential for many people, is not system software; it is an example of application software. File Explorer is a utility and does count as system software. Other software types will be explored in more detail in the next chapter.

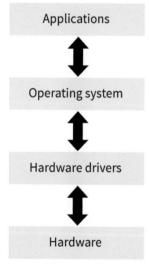

Figure 15.1: The role of an operating system.

Overview of the operating system (OS)

All software, such as word processor or spreadsheet packages, makes use of the OS to perform basic tasks such as saving files or accessing the hardware. Even the simple process of opening a new window is handled by the OS. If an application requires a file to be saved, it asks the OS to save it. In order to save the file, the OS needs to make use of a hardware driver, which performs the final save. The hardware driver is utility software that knows how to talk directly to the hard drive. This separation of responsibilities can be seen in Figure 15.1.

The OS is responsible for managing the computer's resources. These include storage devices, input and output devices, main memory and all the software that is running on the computer. When the computer boots up, it will load the main part of the OS into RAM. This part of the OS is responsible for process management, hardware management and other key low-level tasks. It is known as the kernel. Once this has been loaded, the user interface part of the OS is loaded alongside key utility software.

Overview of operating system tasks

The OS manages input and output devices by:

- communicating with and receiving data input from a keyboard, mouse, etc.
- communicating with and sending data output to a printer, monitor, etc.

The OS manages spooling by:

- storing data on hard disc, in memory, in a queue or in a buffer.

The OS manages the backing store by:

- ensuring that data is stored and can be retrieved correctly from any disc drive
- maintaining a filing system such as FAT or NTFS
- organising files in a hierarchical directory structure.

The OS manages memory (RAM) by:

- ensuring all programs and data, including itself, are stored in correct memory locations
- ensuring all programs and data have enough memory allocated
- utilising virtual memory when there is not enough memory available to run a program.

The OS manages processes by:

- ensuring that different processes can utilise the CPU and do not interfere with each other or crash
- ensuring that all tasks appear to run simultaneously on a multi-tasking OS.

Interface between user and the hardware

Devices come in many different forms and the OS has the job of allowing us to interface with them. In order to do this the OS must first be able to communicate with them using hardware drivers (also called device drivers). When an application asks the OS to save a file or access any connected device, the OS needs to make use of a hardware driver. Hardware drivers are simply software that understands how to talk directly to a given piece of hardware. Drivers of external devices are normally produced by the manufacturer of the hardware, but can also be produced by OS manufacturers and even the open-source community. As all devices are different, the OS needs to have a generic way of talking to devices of the same type. This generic communication is not directly understood by the hardware itself and requires translation into the correct binary control signals. Hardware drivers perform this translation from the generic instructions sent by the OS to the specific instructions understood by the hardware. Drivers are only loaded by the OS if specific hardware has been connected to the PC. Drivers of external devices must be installed before the device is used for the first time. They are modular in nature and can be loaded on demand. Most OS installations will detect what hardware the user has and try to install the required drivers when the OS is installed. This functionality works by each device having two codes, a vendor ID (VID) and a product ID (PID). When a device is connected, the OS queries the device for these two codes. It then checks its database of known vendors and products to see if a suitable device driver can be found. If not, the user will have to install one before that device can be used.

Sometimes the OS will install generic drivers that will not be able to use the full range of features of the device. When setting up a new OS, you will have to install drivers for every piece of hardware on your PC. To see what drivers your system is currently using, you will need to load Device Manager for Windows or System Profiler (sometimes called System Information) on a Mac. On Linux the easiest way to see what devices are installed is to run 'lspci' or 'lsusb' from the command line.

Hardware and software can trigger interrupts (see below) and these are then dealt with by calling an interrupt service routine (ISR), also known as an interrupt handler or a callback. When a device driver loads, it will register interest in a specific interrupt so that, when the interrupt occurs, the code within the device driver will be executed. The ISR does not continuously check the status of the device. As ISRs are part of the device driver, the OS is effectively using the driver to process the interrupt.

Programs written in an event driven language can take advantage of events generated by the OS. Once an ISR is called, the OS will trigger events to any application that is interested. That application will then act upon it as defined by the developer. Consider a simple example of a keyboard press. An interrupt will be sent to the CPU and the ISR for the keyboard will be loaded. This will then trigger an OS event that is sent to an application, which then displays the character typed, or performs an appropriate action (such as 'copy') if it was a keyboard shortcut.

Managing backing stores

Storage devices (sometimes called backing store) all have the same goal, which is the saving and loading of data. How they store that data, however, differs from device to device and even from system to system. There are many different ways, known as file systems, to store files. All storage devices will flatten out the data and remove directory information as the OS manages this information. Therefore it is the job of the OS to provide mechanisms for creating a hierarchical directory structure.

Information about files is stored in an index known as the file allocation table (FAT). How this table is managed, what error detection is used and redundancy in the case of failure are all determined by the file system. Windows has two main file systems: FAT32 and NTFS. NTFS is the most popular as FAT32 has a 32 GB restriction on the volume size. (This was imposed by older versions of Windows installers: the true limit is actually 2 TB).

Macs can read NTFS but they cannot write to it without special software. HFS Plus, used by Macs, can be read by Windows but not written to. Linux can handle both NTFS and HFS Plus but has problems with HFS Plus over 1 TB (possible corruption of data). The Linux community is currently fixing this. The choice of file system is normally the domain of the OS developer, however the end user can sometimes have a say in the choice. Different file systems have different benefits and drawbacks. The exact nature of these is outside the scope of this discussion.

Journaling is used by HFS Plus, NTFS and Linux's EXT3/4 systems. This is a fault tolerance system that is designed to prevent inconsistent states in the case of failure. Journaling is done in two ways. The first is known as meta-journaling where all operations are recorded in a journal (or log) before being committed to the hard drive. For example, if you are going to delete a folder, the journal will make a note of this. If the system crashes half way through the delete then the journal can be consulted to see what state the hard drive should be in. The changes can then be made later. The biggest restriction on meta-journaling is that it doesn't store the data that needs to be saved. Thus, if a save fails, there is still a chance of data corruption.

Block journaling will store the data to be saved in the journal before committing it to the hard drive. This means that data must be saved twice, which has a clear performance penalty. However, block journaling offers the most fault tolerance as, if a write fails, the data can simply be copied from the journal back onto the hard drive, which means that the file will not be corrupted. If a file write fails to add data to the journal then the data is lost but there will be no file corruption.

File allocation table

The file allocation table (FAT) will store the locations of all files on the hard drive. It will also store meta-data about the file, which includes:

- file name
- creation date/modified date
- start sector of the file (address of the first sector)
- file access rights (who can view/edit)
- size of the file.

In order to fully understand the FAT it is important to understand how the hard drive is structured. The hard disc is circular and split into tracks. Tracks start from the middle of the disc and grow outwards in circles. A sector is the smallest unit of storage on the hard drive and tends to be determined by the physical size of the drive. Due to the sheer number of sectors on a hard drive, the file system will group sectors into a cluster. Figure 15.2 shows how the tracks of a hard drive are laid out.

The FAT will store the location of the first sector of each file. As a file could be bigger than a single sector, the file will need to be split over multiple sectors. These sectors will be stored as a linked list, with each sector pointing to the next. The final sector will point to NULL to show that it is the end of the file. This way files can take up many sectors, but the FAT does not have to record every single sector for every file. This has the massive advantage of making the FAT much smaller, but it does mean that files will have to be read in a linear fashion. This is why you have a file pointer when writing file access code that deals with files. Random access of files is only possible once all sectors of a file are known and the software has cached them. Figure 15.3 shows how sectors can be linked together to form a single file.

Files that are stored in a continuous cluster (all sectors on the same track) can be read without moving the read head of the drive. The speed of reading files is determined by how fast the disc spins (measured in revolutions per minute, RPM) and how fast the read head can swap tracks. These speeds determine the time taken for the required sector to come under the read head again (known as the seek time). If the head has to move then the disc may have to make another full turn before the data comes under the read head. If this has to happen more than once then the overall read time will be increased.

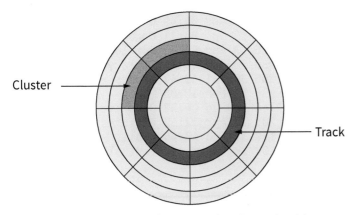

Figure 15.2: Representation of clusters and tracks on a hard drive platter.

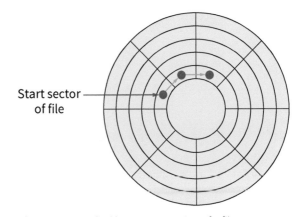

Figure 15.3: Linked list representation of a file.

Files that have their sectors in non-continuous clusters are referred to as being fragmented (Figure 15.4).

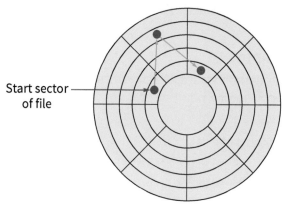

Start sector
of file

Figure 15.4: Example of a fragmented file.

Over time, files will become fragmented and stored in non-continuous clusters. This is especially prevalent if the hard drive is almost full, as it will be harder for the OS to pick continuous clusters of free space in which to save files. Holes will appear where data has been removed or modified. This means the more data the hard drive stores, the more chance that files will become fragmented. This is why you may notice a performance drop on a computer with a hard drive nearing capacity.

The hard drive will have no built-in concept of a directory structure: directories are managed solely by the OS. This is because directory structures can differ greatly between different operating systems. For example, Windows has "drives" while Linux and Mac only have a single folder structure. Devices are treated as folders and mounted in the /media/ folder while Windows will allocate a new drive letter to each device. This may be a simplistic overview of some of the differences, but it is enough to highlight that there is not one standard way of dealing with directories.

The OS, therefore, must manage directories itself. It does this by creating a special file that represents a folder. A folder file will store the following pieces of data:

- links to other folder files (to create the directory structure)
- a list of files stored in that folder
- permissions and other meta-data.

```
adams-iMac:~ mrh$ ls -l
total 0
drwx-------+  16 mrh   staff    544  3 Aug 06:49 Desktop
drwx-------+  10 mrh   staff    340 13 Jul 03:11 Documents
drwx-------+ 114 mrh   staff   3876  3 Aug 07:29 Downloads
drwx-------@  57 mrh   staff   1938 20 Jul 08:21 Library
drwx-------+   9 mrh   staff    306 30 Jul 12:42 Movies
drwx-------+   4 mrh   staff    136 20 Feb 18:05 Music
drwx-------@  66 mrh   staff   2244  3 Aug 06:52 OneDrive
drwx-------+   6 mrh   staff    204 17 Apr 12:52 Pictures
drwxr-xr-x+   5 mrh   staff    170 17 Feb 10:46 Public
drwxr-xr-x    3 mrh   staff    102 20 Feb 05:22 VirtualBox VMs
adams-iMac:~ mrh$ ▮
```

Figure 15.5: Directory listing showing special directory files

The root folder, which is the first folder you encounter when you browse to your hard drive, has a special link stored in the FAT. That way the OS can always find it. Directories are given a special flag so the OS is aware that it must handle that file as a directory.

The screenshot in Figure 15.5 demonstrates this flag. Notice that each item has a "d" at the far left, where the "d" stands for directory.

Utility software

A utility program is designed to perform a commonplace task, for example transferring data from one storage device to another, managing the computer's tasks or combatting viruses. Utility software normally comes bundled with your OS, but can also be installed separately.

File manager utility

File management software enables the user to do simple file manipulation; on its own, it accomplishes very little. The tasks file management software can perform are:

- move files from one directory to another
- copy files
- rename files
- list directory contents.

File management software cannot open files, as this is the responsibility of the application associated with the file. For example the .docx file type is associated with Microsoft Word, which will usually be invoked when a file of this type is double clicked (though the user may designate a different application for this).

Compression software

Compression software is used to compress files to reduce their overall size. When a file has been compressed, it is very close to the minimum size it can be before losing data. Compressing an already compressed file does not result in any further reduction in file size. This is because of the way compression algorithms work and the mathematical theory that underpins them.

When a file is compressed, it becomes unreadable by other software until it is decompressed by the utility originally used to compress it. For example, WinRAR can produce an archive of type RAR. This can only be decompressed by WinRAR or other compatible utilities. So if you 'RARed' a Word document, it would no longer be readable in Word until it was 'unRARed'. This is true for any compression utility.

This kind of file compression is lossless: it retains all the file details, names and folder structures. When the file is decompressed, the exact original file, byte for byte, will be reproduced. A number of files and folders can be compressed together.

Task managers

Task managers allow the user to view the processes currently running on a system and see what resources each one is using. This is useful information when trying to find bottlenecks in a system or when killing unresponsive processes. On OS X (Mac) the utility is called Activity Monitor. It is shown Figure 15.6.

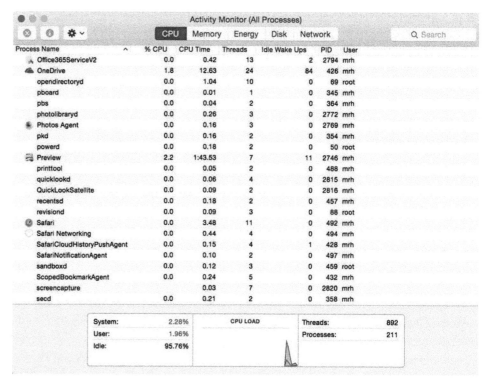

Figure 15.6: Activity monitor.

Anti-virus software

A virus is malicious code that can infect and spread itself though a user's email, secondary storage drives and social networks. Once a virus has infected a system, it can install software to open up a back door for a hacker, monitor a user's keystrokes or simply just wipe (delete) files. Viruses are commonly used by criminal gangs to create armies of infected PCs known as botnets. A criminal can employ botnets to launch denial-of-service attacks and send spam emails. Botnets may be rented out to the highest bidder.

Anti-virus utility software can help to protect the user against these threats. It scans every file and all the memory on the user's system, looking for evidence of viruses and and similar malware. It has a large database of virus signatures, which it can compare to your files. It also monitors suspicious activity and informs the user if it detects anything untoward. When a virus is found, it can try to remove it, delete it or quarantine the file.

There are many different examples of utility software, but those listed in this chapter are the ones most commonly referred to in the exam.

Batch processing

Batch processing performs many similar tasks or jobs serially without the need for user intervention. Each job will only differ in the data it uses.

Computers are very good at number crunching and doing lots of repetitive tasks quickly. For example, computers can easily print off an entire set of electricity bills with little user intervention. Batch processing is the mode used for doing these simple tasks.

Batch processing has the following properties:

- It performs a large number of similar tasks or jobs.
- It can run without user intervention (other than possibly to start it).
- It can run during out-of-office hours (or when there is light load on the computers).

Tip

Types of software utilities.

A batch process will have a list of jobs to do and will work its way through the jobs sequentially. Each job will differ only by the data that it will be working on. Calculating all employees' pay slips, for example, can be done in a batch process, as the process is always the same even though the data it acts upon differs. Batch processes tend to be run at night when there is little load on the servers. They often require large amounts of CPU time and need a long time to complete. The more jobs within the batch process, the more time it will require.

Once a batch process has been started it should not require any user involvement until the job has completed. If an error occurs then that error will be reported to a log file and the batch processing continues. Only if there is a serious error will the batch process stop and require user input. An example of a batch process is generating phone bills.

Figure 15.7: Order of a batch process.

In order for a batch process to work it requires a batch or master file. Data is gathered over a period of time and stored into a batch file for later processing. Under normal conditions this data file will be very large, which means that adding data to it could be slow. In order to solve this problem a temporary, or transaction, file is introduced which collects data over a shorter period of time. This temporary file is merged with the master file at a later date. Figure 15.7 is a diagrammatic summary of these key steps.

Consider a simple example of employees clocking in and out of work. Their hours worked are stored over the week in a temporary file. The times they clock in and out will be recorded into that file. At the end of the week the temporary data file will be merged into the master file. When the end of the month comes, wages can be calculated by using the master data file and a batch process.

Different OS types

There are many different types of OS available, each with different uses and attributes. Windows, for example, works very differently from Android and is used for very different purposes. Devices such as DVD players have a very different OS from a standard desktop PC.

Single-user OS

Single-user OSs are very common, with Windows being a classic example. Although Windows can allow multiple users on a PC, only one of those users can be active at once. Under normal circumstances a user can log into a PC and have sole access to system resources. To help manage different users, a single-user OS creates home directories for each user. Inside these home directories are the user's documents, application settings and browser history, for example. These files are protected by the OS so that only the user and administrator can have access to them. So if another user logs in after you, they will be unable to access these files.

In Microsoft Windows, there is a folder called 'Users' where all user data is stored. Within this folder, each user has their own named folder. In Linux, UNIX and Mac OS, users have their files stored under the home directory.

Multi-user OS

OSs that run on more powerful computers or servers can allow timesharing of system resources by multiple people simultaneously. Instead of having the standard scenario

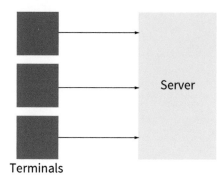

Terminals

Figure 15.8: Terminals connecting to a server.

where someone will physically go up to the PC and log in, a multi-user OS allows users to log in remotely. Each user then has their own display, mouse and keyboard, but is using the internal hardware of the server to which their computer is connected.

Terminals, as the hardware connecting to the server is known, can take the form of any networked device. It could be a specialised thin client terminal, a smartphone, another PC or even an iPad. Even though some of these devices are perfectly capable of using their own resources to run applications, they will connect remotely to the server (Figure 15.8) and run applications there. To enable this communication, a number of different technologies can be employed, for example 'secure shell' and 'virtual desktop'.

Multi-tasking

Multi-tasking is the process of swapping applications in and out of the CPU, giving the illusion that they are running in parallel. All modern OSs have the ability to run more than one program at once. The user is led to believe that the computer is doing many things at once, such as playing music, displaying a document and performing a virus scan. Computers are (with exotic exceptions) serial machines and by definition can do only one thing at a time. In order to implement multi-tasking, the OS ensures that each process is swapped in and out so that the user is under the impression that all processes are running at the same time. This illusion can easily be shattered if a process takes a lot of processing time or crashes, as the user may then see the other processes also hang or become unresponsive.

Multi-programming

A multi-programming computer system stores more than one job in the computer's main memory at the same time. These jobs appear to be processed by the computer's CPU simultaneously.

Multi-programming optimises use of the CPU by preventing it from being idle while waiting for a slower peripheral. The OS may move jobs in and out of memory and allow each job a pre-determined time-slice to access the CPU: this process is called scheduling and is controlled by a scheduler program.

Real-time OS

Real-time OSs must respond within a short amount of time, sometimes considered to be immediate, to input provided to the system. Owing to the speed of computing systems, it is feasible to develop software that can respond to user requests so quickly that it seems immediate. In truth, a few milliseconds would have elapsed. When developing a real-time OS, consideration must be taken away from general computing needs and focused on very specific applications. You would not expect to run a real-time OS on a desktop PC, owing to the unpredictability of the software applications the user may install. In addition, a web page could not load in real time because of the broadband connection bottleneck, no matter how good the OS is. Real-time OSs run only on very specific, usually mission-critical, systems.

Systems that require a real-time OS include nuclear power stations and aircraft systems. If a decision or action is delayed because of software running slowly in a nuclear reactor, it might explode, which would be a disaster. A real-time OS must always respond quickly, so it is crucial that it focuses only on the job of managing the power plant. Some transaction-based systems are also considered to be real time, for example travel agents with multiple stores across the country. If one store books the last seat of a cut-price holiday, it should no longer allow any other store to book. The transaction needs to happen fast enough to stop multiple bookings from occurring and thus is considered to be real time.

Computing in context: Database transactions

Databases form the backbone of almost every computing system and are essential for any form of website that sells services. Most ticket-based systems run over the internet and have a web interface with a database running in the background. Owing to the nature of the internet, it is impossible to time-bound requests for tickets. To prevent duplicate attempts to buy the same ticket, the database uses transactions.

Transactions are a crucial part of databases, but are also very technical. On their most basic level, a series of database transactions are collected together into an all-or-nothing approach. For example, say a customer buys an item that requires two actions: reducing stock and taking money. If only one of the actions is successful, the database will be in an inconsistent state and you can potentially have either a very happy or a very angry customer, depending on which action was successful. If one action fails, both actions must be undone, which is known as a rollback. Both of these actions can be combined into a transaction. This gets even more complicated when more than one database is involved; for example, the bank and the shop will have separate databases.

To prevent other clients changing data that is currently being worked on in a transaction, locks can be used. Locks can be placed on any record in the database, preventing anyone else from writing to that record until the lock has been removed. This is a simplification of what happens 'under the bonnet', but it does give an idea of how tickets can be sold successfully outside of a real-time system.

Interrupts

Process scheduling is handled by the OS and decides when a process will run and for how long. However, it also needs to respond to input devices and other system-wide events, for example, when the hard drive is ready to serve another request or the user has pressed a key on the keyboard. The OS needs to be made aware of these events in order to decide which course of action to take. These signals, sent from hardware to the CPU, are known as interrupts. Software can also generate interrupts during normal execution.

When an interrupt occurs, the CPU will, on the next instruction cycle, automatically run some special OS code that responds to the interrupt. The currently running process will be interrupted so that this event can be handled. It is important for the OS rather than any other software to handle the event, as the OS will have the best idea of the overall context of what the user is doing. When an interrupt occurs, the CPU has the role of informing the OS rather than dealing with the interrupt itself. The OS, if it chooses, can ignore interrupts.

Here is a list of common interrupts:

- Hard drive ready for more data to save or it has retrieved requested data.
- Timer interrupt has occurred.
- Key has been pressed.

- Peripheral requires more data (for example a printer or a scanner).
- The on/off button has been pressed.
- Hardware failure or problem encountered.
- An interrupt may also be triggered by software if it needs to send an urgent message to the OS, for example during an I/O operation.

In order to understand the role of an interrupt, it may help to consider an example. A user wishes to save a 30 MB file onto the hard drive. In order to do this, the file will need to be stored in small chunks of 1 MB. Using the buffer and interrupt system, the first chunk is sent to the hard drive, which, in turn, writes it to the disc. While this is occurring, the CPU will continue doing other tasks, such as dealing with keyboard interrupts or playing music.

Once the hard drive has finished saving the file, it sends an interrupt to the CPU requesting more data, which is duly sent by the CPU. This cycle will continue until the file has been saved. It is important to remember that the CPU is much faster than any other part of the computer, including the user. If the CPU waited for the hard drive to finish saving before it did anything else (i.e. was synchronous), a lot of CPU cycles would be wasted. Interrupts allow the CPU to make much better use of time.

Buffers and interrupts

A buffer is a small block of memory inside hardware devices such as printers, keyboards and hard drives where work currently being handled by that device is stored. When a keyboard key is pressed, for example, an interrupt is sent to the CPU and the key stroke stored in the keyboard's buffer. However, sometimes the OS may not be ready to deal with the keyboard stroke and more keys may have been pressed. Instead of losing the key strokes, the buffer stores the values until the OS is ready. If that buffer overflows, the motherboard warns the user by sounding a beep. Hard drives also contain a buffer; by utilising a buffer the CPU can send a block of data to be saved without having to wait for the data to be physically stored onto the disc. This 'handing off' of tasks is called spooling. It improves system performance by allowing the CPU to work on other tasks.

When data is stored on or loaded from any device, buffers will be used. There is a very specific algorithm used to deal with buffers and interrupts when saving data to a slower device:

- A chunk of data is sent by the CPU to the device and stored in a buffer.
- The device will slowly save the data while the CPU is free to do other tasks.
- When the buffer is empty, an interrupt is sent to the CPU.
- At the start of the next clock cycle the CPU processes the interrupt by informing the OS.
- More data is sent to the device and the cycle repeats. This will continue until all data has been saved.

Sometimes more than one buffer is used at once. This is known as double buffering. Here one buffer accepts data while the other is used for processing. The OS writes data to the first buffer and the device uses the second for processing. Once the data is processed, the OS copies the first buffer into the second and an interrupt is sent. That way there is no delay while the interrupt is being processed, meaning that the device will have a much higher active time.

In another version of double buffering, there is no copying between buffers: their roles are simply swapped after every write. Logically enough, this is known as ping-pong buffering.

Memory management

A standard computer contains memory (RAM) that is shared between processes and managed by the OS. The instructions (machine code) of a process must be stored in RAM as well as any data that is being worked upon. The OS must also have the kernel, the essential part of the OS, in memory, together with any modules required to allow management of the system at a given moment. With all of this data located in RAM, it can get overloaded very quickly, which is one of the key reasons why a memory manager is essential. Before looking at how the memory manager works, you must understand some of the key design goals for memory management:

- Allocate enough memory so that each process can run.
- Split memory up so that it can be allocated to processes (paging/segmentation).
- Ensure security so that other processes cannot access each other's data.
- Allow efficient sharing of memory.
- Extend memory by using virtual memory.

The memory manager must split RAM into workable chunks of storage and allocate those chunks to processes in a fair manner. As processes start and stop at different times and have different memory demands, keeping track of what memory is free becomes a challenge. Allocation of RAM can be done through two managing techniques that will be explored in this chapter, both employing a table to monitor which process has been allocated which chunk of memory. This allows RAM to be shared without worrying about any processes accidentally overwriting each other or gaining unauthorised access, as their access will be strictly monitored by the OS.

Security is a core concern for memory management. If processes could inspect or change each other's memory, this could bypass many security protocols put in place to protect user data. For example, if a process could inspect the data from your web browser, it could very easily manipulate what you see on screen. When a process decrypts something, the decrypted text inside that process's memory would be visible to other processes, making it easy pickings for spyware.

The final consideration is the use of virtual memory to extend memory beyond what is physically available.

RAM will hold:

- the OS
- currently running programs
- current files and data you are working on.

Memory addressing

In order to understand memory management, you need to understand the basics of memory addressing, which is how an individual byte of data can be found in RAM. Instructions and data are all stored in the same memory space. Each byte in memory is numbered, starting from 0, and this number is referred to as an address. In the table below, the text 'hello' is stored, with each letter having its own individual memory address. Memory addresses are essentially the position of a specific byte of data in RAM.

0	1	2	3	4	5	6	7	8	Address
H	E	L	L	O					Data

Figure 15.9: Two processes using virtual memory.

In Figure 15.9, the text starts at address 0 and ends at address 4, using 5 bytes to store the whole word. If a computer has 128 MB of memory, it has a memory address range of 0 to 134 217 728. This address range is calculated by converting the megabytes to bytes, or $128 \times 1024 \times 1024 = 134\,217\,728$ bytes. Most modern computing devices have 2 GB, 4 GB or even more. The memory range for 2 GB is 0 to 2 147 483 648, and 4 GB is 0 to 4 294 967 296.

When talking about addresses, you are normally talking about where to find data in RAM. It is not possible on a modern computer to hard-code memory addresses, as you have no way of knowing beforehand where data will be stored by the OS. The memory manager has the job of allocating memory addresses when a process wants to load or save data, so programs make use of virtual address spaces, which will be explored later.

Paging

When the memory manager uses paging, it allocates fixed sized blocks of memory to processes. These blocks of memory are known as pages and are a physical method of memory allocation. Each process has its own private view of pages and each memory access is made up of two parts: the page number and the offset within that page. All processes use a virtual memory space and are not aware of where in physical memory the pages actually reside, nor are they aware of other processes and where their pages are stored. They will use their own memory address space, known also as logical address space, and it is the job of the memory management unit to translate addresses. In Figure 15.10 there are two processes, each with its own virtual memory space. A paging table will translate the virtual page number to the physical page held in memory. For example, page 1 of process 1 stores the text 'utin' and the paging table shows that this data is actually stored in page 5 in physical memory.

Individual processes view memory as a continuous block, even though this may not be the case. A block of physical memory is called a frame. Page to frame translation is done transparently to the process; if a process attempts to access addresses outside its paging table, an error occurs. When a page is accessed, the page number requested acts as the index to the paging table to get the real page frame.

In order to calculate the physical memory address of a single byte, you must make use of the physical page number and the size of an individual byte. The simple formula below can be used to find out the address of a byte:

$$address = page\ number * page\ size + offset$$

For example, the ':' from page 3 in process 2 would be:

address = page number * page size + offset

address = 7 * 4 + 2 (count from Ø)

address = 30

Virtual address space		Page Table	
Page	Data	Virtual page	Page Frame
0	Comp	0	0
1	utin	1	5
2	g is	2	6
3	Fun.	3	3

Process 1

Physical memory	
Page Frame	Data
0	Comp
1	I li
2	ke c
3	Fun.
4	hees
5	utin
6	g is
7	E :)

Virtual address space		Page Table	
Page	Data	Virtual page	Page Frame
0	I li	0	1
1	ke c	1	2
2	hees	2	4
3	E :)	3	7

Process 2

Figure 15.10: Two processes using virtual memory.

Segmentation

Segmentation is an alternative method of allocating memory to processes, where segments are variably sized rather than fixed. Thus they can logically split RAM into segments of the exact size requested rather than forcing data into fixed sized chunks. This is ideal when storing blocks of code, such as a library, or files where the size is known in advance. In order to allow variably sized segments, the memory manager must store the length of each segment in the segmentation table.

In order to translate memory accesses to physical memory addresses, the segment number and offset are needed. The memory management unit looks for the base address of that segment in a segmentation table, as shown in Figure 15.11. If the memory request is outside the segment, a segmentation fault is raised.

$$\text{address} = \text{segment base address} + \text{offset}$$

One major advantage of segmentation is that memory can be shared between processes, especially when combined with library software. If a block of code used by two processes is needed, it can be loaded into a segment. When a process needs to access code within the segment, all it needs is the segment ID and the offset.

Segmet ID	Start address	Length
1	300	64
2	500	48

Figure 15.11: Example of a segmentation table.

Virtual memory

Virtual memory is commonly used to extend memory. This allows programs to run even when there is not enough memory physically available. When the memory manager sees that some pages have not been used recently, it can decide to move these blocks into virtual memory. Quite simply, the pages identified will be placed into a special file on the hard drive, called the page file (Figure 15.12). The memory manager then makes a note of which pages are in virtual memory.

Image manipulation programs, for example, can use massive amounts of memory. Consider a high-definition image of size 4000 × 3000 in 32-bit colour. Each pixel will need 4 bytes (32 bits) of storage, so:

$$4 \times 4000 \times 3000 = 48\,000\,000 \text{ bytes or } 45.7 \text{ MB}$$

The memory used (for processing purposes and undo) by image manipulation programs is usually double or triple the size of the original image. So you could need over 150 MB just for one image. It is not hard to see how programs will very quickly use up available memory. As the hard drive is much slower than main memory, the choice of which pages should be swapped (moved in or out of virtual memory) is very important. If poor choices are made, there will be a significant reduction in system performance. Until the page is loaded back into main memory, that process is effectively blocked. A process which

Process 1

Virtual address space

Page	Data
0	Comp
1	utin
2	g is
3	Fun.

Page Table

Virtual page	Page Frame	In RAM
0	0	N
1	5	Y
2	6	Y
3	3	Y

Physical memory

Page Frame	Data
0	*7hs
1	Po9a
2	Df54
3	Fun.
4	hees
5	utin
6	g is
7	E :)

RAM

Process 2

Virtual address space

Page	Data
0	I li
1	ke c
2	hees
3	E :)

Page Table

Virtual page	Page Frame	In RAM
0	1	N
1	2	N
2	4	Y
3	7	Y

Page file

Page Frame	Data
0	Comp
1	I li
2	ke c
3	
4	
5	
6	
7	

HDD

Figure 15.12: Page file.

has been swapped into virtual memory is known as suspended. When poor choices are made, lots of pages are continually swapped in and out of main memory, leading to unresponsive processes; this is known as thrashing. This situation can be improved by either updating your OS or getting more RAM, which will result in a lower reliance on virtual memory.

In order to implement virtual memory, page entries in the page table hold a flag that specifies whether that page is located in RAM or saved into the page table. When a page located in the page file is accessed, the memory unit will raise a page fault to the OS. Owing to the speed mismatch between the hard drive and memory, the OS must load the page back into RAM and update the page tables. There is no guarantee that the OS will place the page in its original location, so it must update not only the flag but the frame number (physical location) into which the page has been loaded.

If process 1 requires page 0, which is currently stored in the page file on the HDD, it must swap out another page and update the page tables. Figure 15.13 shows the changes (marked in pink). As process 2 had a page swapped out, its page table needed to be updated along with the page table for process 1. Should process 2 need that page immediately, it would have to be loaded back into RAM and the page tables updated, which would cause a delay. If repeated, this could lead to thrashing.

Process 1

Virtual address space

Page	Data
0	Comp
1	utin
2	g is
3	Fun.

Page Table

Virtual page	Page Frame	In RAM
0	4	Y
1	5	Y
2	6	Y
3	3	Y

Physical memory

Page Frame	Data
0	*7hs
1	Po9a
2	Df54
3	Fun.
4	Comp
5	utin
6	g is
7	E :)

RAM

Process 2

Virtual address space

Page	Data
0	I li
1	ke c
2	hees
3	E :)

Page Table

Virtual page	Page Frame	In RAM
0	1	N
1	2	N
2	0	N
3	7	Y

Page file

Page Frame	Data
0	hees
1	I li
2	ke c
3	
4	
5	
6	
7	

HDD

Figure 15.13: Changes to the page table.

Scheduling

Scheduling is the term the OS uses to define how and when a process is swapped in and out of the CPU, thus enabling multi-tasking. Each OS has a different way of performing scheduling. Many of the specifics on how scheduling occurs in an OS is kept secret from the public, which is especially true of Mac and Windows. A process is a piece of software that is currently being managed by the scheduler inside the OS; the software being managed may or may not be running at any given instant.

Scheduling must not be confused with interrupts. Interrupts are initially handled by the CPU before being passed over to the OS. This differs from scheduling, where the OS makes decisions in its own time on which process should be run next or which ones should be interrupted, known as pre-empting.

Process states

Only one process can be run at once on a single CPU core. This process will be in the 'running state' or just 'running'. Other processes will be either in a 'ready to run queue', waiting for their turn with the CPU, or in a **blocked** state:

- *Running*: when the process has control of the CPU.
- *Ready to run*: a process is in a queue waiting for the CPU.
- *Blocked*: a process is waiting on an input/output (I/O) operation such as reading from the hard drive.

When a process is waiting for a device or external operation to complete, we say that this process is blocked. A process should never be held in the ready to run queue while waiting for an I/O operation to complete, but should relinquish control to another process by placing itself into a blocked state. Consider the state diagram shown in Figure 15.14.

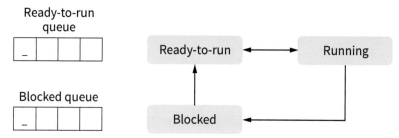

Figure 15.14: Process states.

The OS will have different queues to monitor these three states. Imagine an internet browser which has requested data from the net on a 56 kbs connection. That process could potentially be blocked for a few seconds, which, in processor terms, is a lifetime. If that process was in the ready to run queue, a situation could occur where the process is brought into the running state while still waiting for a device. This would waste CPU cycles, as all the process could do is place itself back into the ready to run queue. A process will only become unblocked when an interrupt occurs, and will always go back into a ready to run state. For example, if a process is waiting for the hard drive it will remain in the blocked state until the hard drive sends an interrupt to the CPU. The process manager will then change the state from blocked to ready to run and the process will join the ready to run queue.

Ready to run queue

A new process is created when the user, or another process, loads an application from the hard drive. Once loaded into memory, the process becomes live and is added to the ready to run queue rather than being placed into the running state. It is the job of the scheduler to decide on which process to run next using a *scheduling* algorithm, and not that of the recently loaded process. However, the scheduler will also decide in what position in the queue the new process should be added. If the new process has a high priority, it may be added higher up in the queue or the scheduling algorithm may decide that the new process should be placed ahead of others.

Running process

In a standard single-core CPU, there will be only one process running at any given time. This process will be given a certain amount of time to run, based on the scheduling algorithm. A running process has a number of options while running:

*   *Complete the task (and close)*: this removes the process from *scheduling* completely and is the equivalent of the user clicking on quit. A process can elect to stop itself or it may have completed the processing. It is important to remember that not all processes are GUI-based applications and could be batch processes.
*   *Be interrupted by the scheduler*: not to be confused with interrupts, which will stop a process so that the OS can deal with an event. This is where the scheduler has decided that the process has had enough CPU time and will swap it for another process. The currently running process is then placed in the ready to run queue based on the scheduling algorithm. When a process is stopped it is said to be pre-empted, which tends to cause schedulers to reduce the priority of the process to ensure system stability.
*   *Become blocked*: in this situation, the process is moved to the *blocked* queue immediately. This is to prevent wasting CPU time.
*   *Give up CPU time*: a process could voluntarily give up CPU access with the intention of getting it back in the near future. A process which does this is known as a well-behaved process and tends to be given higher priority in most modern scheduling algorithms (see the section on multi-level feedback queues).

Process swapping

When a process is running, it will have full access to the CPU. The state of the running process is represented by the data stored in the registers. When the process is swapped out, it is important that the registers are saved. A data structure known as the process control block (PCB) is created, and is used to store the contents of the registers.

The PCB will contain the following pieces of data:

*   *The PC (program counter) register*: this stores the point the process reached, so that it can continue from that exact point when restored.
*   *General purpose registers*: these are temporary values used by the process. Another process could overwrite them, which could throw off calculations. Therefore it is imperative that they are saved.
*   *ACC*: the accumulator stores the value of the last calculation and will be needed by the next calculation that process performs.

- *Variables and state of the process*: any variables linked to the process in memory must be recorded.
- *Priority and process ID*: used by the scheduler for administration.

Once a process has had a PCB created and saved into memory, the registers of the next process are loaded. These will overwrite the current register values. The next fetch–decode–execute–reset (FDER) cycle will then run the new process instead of the old. One key role of the scheduler is to ensure that registers are copied from the CPU first and then overwritten with the values of the new process.

Activity 15.1

This task requires you to use Linux. This can be done by installing a Linux distribution of your choice, using a Raspberry Pi or a virtual machine. The commands listed below will not work in Windows or Mac OS X.

1 Open a command prompt and run the command "**ps**". This command will list out processes running in the current terminal.

2 Enter the command "**ps c -u <your username>**". This will list out all of the processes currently running by that user. The STAT column shows the current status of that process.

3 Look at the main state codes (shown as capital letters). Which of these states can you see in the results of the ps command? You may wish to save the results to a file so you can look in more detail: **ps c -u <your username> > result.txt**

4 Which of the main Linux states matches the blocked state described in this chapter?

5 What does it mean when a process is sleeping? Why is this important for multi-level feedback queues?

```
D Uninterruptible sleep (usually IO)
R Running or runnable (on run queue)
S Interruptible sleep (waiting for an event to
complete)
T Stopped, either by a job control signal or because
it is being traced.
X dead (should never be seen)
Z Defunct ("zombie") process, terminated but not
reaped by its parent.
< high-priority (not nice to other users)
N low-priority (nice to other users)
L has pages locked into memory (for realtime and
custom IO)
s is a session leader
l is multi-threaded (using CLONE_THREAD, like NPTL
pthreads do)
+ is in the foreground process group
```

Process codes to show the state of a process while using the ps command.

Recording interrupts

When an interrupt occurs, a signal is sent to the CPU via a control bus or, in the case of a software interrupt, a flag is set. A special register, known as the interrupt register, is then updated by flipping a bit to 1. Each bit in the interrupt register represents a different interrupt and is referred to as a flag. When a flag is set to 1, it represents an interrupt that needs to be processed. Initially the interrupt register will have all flags set to 0, shown in Table 15.1.

The binary value of 0 shows that the interrupt has not occurred, while if a value of 1 is detected, the processor will need to perform an action. When the interrupt is sent to the CPU, the corresponding flag is set. This does not mean that the interrupt will be dealt with immediately, but rather that the interrupt has been recorded. If the same interrupt happens twice before it is dealt with, only the first one is recorded. Table 15.2 shows that a timer interrupt has occurred:

Sometimes more than one interrupt can be sent to the CPU at the same time, or before the CPU has had a chance to deal with the previous interrupt. This is handled by simply setting multiple flags, but only if they are for two different interrupts. If more than one of the same interrupt is generated before the CPU has had chance to deal with it, the second and subsequent interrupts are ignored. This is a fairly common occurrence for low-priority interrupts such as IO tasks or timers.

Each interrupt will be assigned a priority depending on how critical it is to the system. For example, keyboard interrupts can be safely postponed (have you ever typed on a computer only to wait a few seconds before text appeared?), while interrupts such as hardware switches must be dealt with immediately.

Dealing with interrupts

At the end of a fetch–decode–execute (FDE) cycle, the CPU will check if an interrupt has occurred by looking at the interrupt register to see if any flags have been set. If an interrupt has occurred, the priorities of the currently running process and the interrupt are compared. If the interrupt has a higher priority than the currently executing process, the process must be swapped out by the processor and the interrupt handling code loaded instead. Priorities are checked to ensure that a high-priority process is not being interrupted by low-priority interrupts. If more than one interrupt must be processed, the one with the highest priority will always be selected first, as only one interrupt can be processed at a time. Swapping out an interrupted process requires all of the registers and the state of the process to be copied and saved onto a stack data structure. This includes the PC, accumulator (ACC) and all general purpose registers. A stack data structure is used so that the OS can jump back to the last interrupted process, which could be another interrupt. When restoring a process, the PC, ACC and general purpose registers must be copied back to the CPU so that it can resume from the exact point it was interrupted.

When an interrupt is to be processed, the OS has specific code which is run for each type. For example, if a timer interrupt occurs, every process that depends on timing (anything with animation or a clock) must be informed. In most OSs there will be a number of running processes, all of which make use of a timer event. In order to ensure that all running processes get to respond to the interrupt, the OS must send an event to each of these processes. The processes do not get a chance to do anything about it at this stage they are merely informed so that when they next get a chance to run they will have the option of dealing with that event. Event-driven programming is based around the OS

IRQ flag	Device	Flag
0	Timer	0
1	Keyboard	0
2	Programmable	0
3	COM 1	0
4	COM 2	0
5	Term 2	0
6	Floppy	0
7	Term 2	0
8	RTC timer	0
9	Programmable	0
10	Programmable	0
11	Programmable	0
12	Mouse	0
13	Co-processor	0
14	ATA/IDE 1	0
15	ATA/IDE 2	0

Table 15.1: Example IRQ flags used by an interrupt register.

IRQ flag	Device	Flag
0	Timer	1
1	Keyboard	0
2	Programmable	0
3	COM 1	0
4	COM 2	0
5	Term 2	0
6	Floppy	0
7	Term 2	0
8	RTC timer	0
9	Programmable	0
10	Programmable	0
11	Programmable	0
12	Mouse	0
13	Co-processor	0
14	ATA/IDE 1	0
15	ATA/IDE 2	0

Table 15.2: An interrupt register with a single flag set.

sending events to processes, and interrupts are abstracted by the OS as system events. To stop every process having to deal with every interrupt, a focus system is used, meaning that only the active window will get the interrupts unless the window is still running in the background.

In order that the correct OS code is executed when an interrupt is processed, there is a vector (array) of memory addresses set up, each pointing to the OS code designed to deal with that interrupt. Figure 15.15 represents this vector.

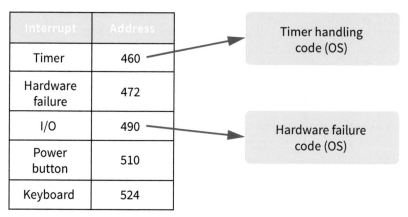

Interrupt	Address
Timer	460
Hardware failure	472
I/O	490
Power button	510
Keyboard	524

Figure 15.15: Vector.

To find the correct interrupt handler the CPU will use indexed addressing mode (see the chapter on assembly code):

$$Interrupt\ handling\ code = Base\ address + (index * 4)$$

(assuming 32-bit addresses)

The base address is where, in memory, the vector exists; the offset is defined by the interrupt that has fired. For example, if the timer interrupt occurs, the offset will be 0, while if the keyboard interrupt occurs, the offset will be 16 (assuming 32-bit addresses).

Stacks and processing interrupts

A stack data structure is key to how interrupt handling occurs. It comes into use when an interrupt is being dealt with by the OS and a higher-priority interrupt is received in mid-process. In this case the interrupt handler must itself be interrupted. By using a stack data structure, the OS will know where it needs to jump back to. Figure 15.16 demonstrates how interrupts can be restored.

Time slicing

Time slicing is commonly used in multi-user operating systems and is where each user is given a set amount of time, or a time slice, for processing. The system then works in a round robin fashion to service all of the active users.

Polling

Asking a device for its status is called polling. Polling is a synchronous activity: the process will block until the device has answered. This is the opposite of an asynchronous activity such as an interrupt, which does not block and uses a callback to register its occurrence

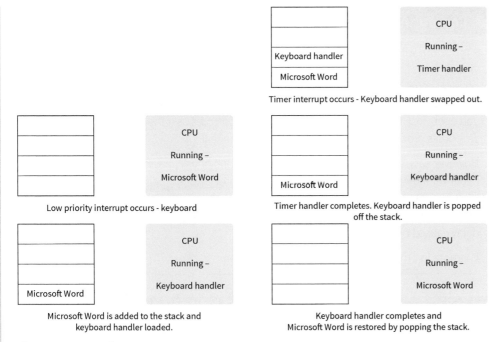

Timer interrupt occurs - Keyboard handler swapped out.

Low priority interrupt occurs - keyboard

Timer handler completes. Keyboard handler is popped off the stack.

Microsoft Word is added to the stack and keyboard handler loaded.

Keyboard handler completes and Microsoft Word is restored by popping the stack.

Figure 15.16: Handling interrupts.

The process may wait until the device responds with a certain status. For example, if the process is waiting for a key press it may simply stop doing anything until it detects one. This is known as busy-wait polling.

Alternatively the process may find other useful things to do and poll the device at regular intervals. This is usually more efficient than busy-wait polling, though not as efficient as relying on interrupts.

Threading

Scheduling is where the OS manages multiple processes. However, a process can split itself up into mini-processes known as threads. Each thread is managed by the scheduler separately, meaning that they can run in no fixed order. As a thread is under the control of the scheduler, it can take advantage of multiple cores and technologies such as hyper threading (see *computing in context below*). A lot of modern applications will use threads to perform background tasks such as spell checking in a word processor, updating the GUI and sending emails in a mail client. Under normal circumstances a task like this would block the program, making it unresponsive, but placing it in a thread can allow it to run in the background, freeing the main application to perform other tasks.

One of the key downsides to threading is synchronisation. You have no control over the order in which threads are executed, which can lead to difficulties if one thread is relying on another having completed. Programming a multi-threaded environment is very challenging, as there are no guarantees on the sequence. Also, because each thread can access the same data, there could be a situation where one thread fails due to changes made by another. It could even be the case that two threads, running on separate cores, access the same data at the same time. Data which is to be shared between threads must be made mutually exclusive, meaning that when one thread is using it, the other must wait. This is sometimes known as a mutex lock.

Computing in context: Hyper-threading

A processor with hyper-threading, an Intel technology, will provide two logical (or virtual) cores for every physical core. This means that a dual core processor, with two physical cores, would appear to have four logical cores. If you have a hyper-threading quad core processor at home then you might be amazed to see eight processors when you open Task Manager. Windows registers logical cores as if they were real cores and schedules processes as if those logical cores were real.

However each pair of logical cores still only has one physical core to run on. What hyper-threading does is make better use of the processor's pipeline and increase the amount that can be done each clock cycle. Although only one instruction will be run at once, hyper-threading can prepare more instructions at the same time, reducing the delay caused by data fetch from RAM.

For more information read about hyper-threading.

Chapter summary

- System software manages the hardware and software of the computer.
- The operating system is responsible for memory management, process management and managing devices.
- A range of utility software is available to help maintain the system. These include file management, compression, task manager and anti-virus software.
- Memory management is done through two mechanisms: paging and segmentation.
- Pages are blocks of memory of fixed sized that are referenced through a paging table. The paging table contains the page number and offset to physical memory.
- Each process has a virtual address space which is translated by the memory unit to physical addresses by the formula

$$\text{address} = \text{page number} * \text{page size} + \text{offset}$$

- Segmentation allows blocks of memory to be used, which are variable in size.
- Each segment is stored in a segmentation table and will record the ID, start address and length for each segment.
- Segments are commonly used to store library software or other blocks of data that are shared across multiple processes.
- Virtual memory is where the hard drive is used as additional memory in order to increase the number of processes that can be active at once.
- When a process is saved into virtual memory it is suspended. When loaded back into RAM for processing it is restored.
- Page tables will record which processes are located in RAM or in virtual memory.
- An interrupt is an electronic signal (hardware interrupt) or a process-generated signal (software interrupt) that is sent to the CPU to inform it that a device or process requires attention.
- Common interrupts are triggered by storage devices, timers, peripherals and failure of power, software or hardware.
- Buffers are used on devices to allow the CPU to perform other tasks while data is being processed.

- Interrupt service routines (ISR) are bits of code that are automatically run when an interrupt occurs; these are normally within a device driver.
- A process can be in one of the following states:
    - running – currently has CPU time
    - blocked – waiting for an operation to complete
    - ready to run – waiting for the CPU.
- Processes are swapped by storing both special and general registers into a process control block. This can then be used to restore the process.
- The main design goal of scheduling is to maximise the throughput of processes. To do this it must minimise starvation and eliminate deadlock.
- Threading is the technique of splitting a process into multiple smaller processes to take advantage of multiple cores.
- There are a number of different types of operating system:
    - single-user
    - multi-user
    - real time.

End-of-chapter questions

1   In order to function, all computing devices require an operating system.

    a   Describe the purpose of memory management in the operating system.   [3]

    b   Describe the purpose behind process scheduling in the operating system.   [3]

2   Describe how page tables are used by processes to manage their memory address space.   [6]

3   Describe, using an example, how and why a process may become suspended.   [6]

4   Describe how buffers and interrupts are used when saving a large file to the hard drive.   [6]

5   Describe the following utility software.

    a   Compression   [3]

    b   Anti-virus.   [3]

Further reading

What are virtual machines?	Search for What Is a Virtual Machine on makeuseof.com
Successor to bios – Unified extensible firmware interface	Search for UEFI BIOS explained on alphr.com
Distributed OS	Look up Distributed operating system on a website such as Wikipedia
Comparison of OS scheduling algorithms	Search for A Comparitive Study of CPU Scheduling Algorithms by Neetu Goel and Dr R.B. Garg on arxiv.org

Chapter 16
The need for different types of software systems and their attributes

Learning objectives

- Explain the use of a range of types of software, including open source software, bespoke and off-the-shelf.

Ⓐ • Explain that some computer applications are safety related and require a high level of dependability, and hence that the development of safety critical systems is a highly specialised field.

- Explain the purpose, use and significance of expert systems.

Ⓐ • Describe common contemporary applications.

- State the nature and scope of computer control and automation.

- Describe the role of the computer in weather forecasting, computer-aided design, robotics and computer-generated graphics and animation.Describe the benefits of automation

Ⓐ • Describe the implications of automation.

- Discuss the possible effects of expert systems on professional groups and the wider community.

- Describe the use of search engines on the internet.

- Discuss the possible effects of the internet upon professional groups and the wider community.

Introduction: Types of software
Open and closed source software

Source code is the raw code produced by developers and defines what they want their software to do. Once software has been produced, tested and packaged, developers have a choice to make. Do they release the source code or not?

Proprietary software does not include the source code and is also known as closed source. When you download or buy software, you normally get proprietary software. This means that you will not be able to get access to the source code, nor will you be allowed to make any changes to the software. Companies commonly do not release source code, because the code may contain trade secrets and other intellectual property (IP), which they do not want others to get hold of; similarly, car companies don't want you to know how their cars are built. Companies invest a lot of money in building their software and they want to ensure that people cannot exploit that investment without paying for it. Closed source software enables developers to protect their knowledge and investments, but it does mean that only they can make changes to the code base. So, if a bug occurs in the code, they will be the ones responsible for fixing it. Developers working on bespoke software will usually be contractually obliged to maintain it for a given period after release, otherwise bugs will not be fixed and remain forever in the software. This is not the case with software provided to the public by companies who have no obligation to maintain it over the years. A recent example is Windows XP, which is no longer supported. Even though there are millions of people still using XP, Microsoft will not fix any bugs that emerge. This means that people either have to upgrade, not always a financial option, or live with software that may have potential security issues.

Closed source software can be free; it is up to the developers and the business model they are using. Apps are mostly closed source and a lot of them are free to the user. Developers may, however, make money in other ways, for example through advertising or in-app purchases. Sometimes closed source software is released for free as a trial for a larger, paid, 'big-brother' version of the software. Examples of this are Microsoft Visual Studio Express and Visual Studio. Express is great for basic programs, but large-scale applications, built by teams of people, will benefit from the paid version of the software.

Open source software is the direct opposite of closed source. For software to be open source, you must be able to download the source code and make changes to it as you wish. There is a big difference between free software and open source. Free software does not usually make the source code available. Open source code tends to have a lot of developers working on it for free, or being sponsored by a larger company. Anyone can join the community of developers to make changes to the code and upload their changes for the rest of the world to see. If the changes are good, they will be merged into the main source code and all users can benefit. Some famous examples of open source software are Mozilla Firefox and the Linux kernel.

In order to understand why open source software is usually governed by a licence, you must take a short look at the history of open source software. In 1983 Richard Stallman, pictured here, started the free software movement by launching the GNU project. He was despondent at the growing trend of companies refusing to distribute source code and felt it was morally incorrect for software developers to impose their view of how software should be used on the people using it. The goal of the GNU project, as well as the free software movement in general, is based around the definition of what free means. Stallman proposed that the ideology behind the word free should be the same as that of free speech rather than free as in 'free beer'. He defines the term 'free software' as:

Computing in context: Software licensing and open software

Most software that users can install on their computing devices is covered by some form of software licence. A software licence defines the exact circumstances in which the software can be used, how many times it can be run, the end user's responsibilities and the developer's liabilities. It makes sense that closed source proprietary software is governed by licences, but the majority of open source projects are also protected by licences. One of the most common licences is the GNU General Public License (GNU GPL or GPL – GNU is a recursive acronym that stands for 'GNU's not UNIX').

A program is free software, for you, a particular user, if:

- You have the freedom to run the program as you wish, for any purpose
- You have the freedom to modify the program to suit your needs. (To make this freedom effective in practice, you must have access to the source code, since making changes in a program without having the source code is exceedingly difficult.) Take a look at http://www.cambridge.org/links/kwse6057.

One issue with open source software is that someone could take the ideas from the software, legitimately; add it to their code, which is allowed; and then release their version as closed source. This would go against the founding principles of the free software movement and thus steps had to be taken to be counter this danger.

In order to ensure that software released as 'free' is kept free, the GPL licence was born. Those who originally produce the software can release it as open source, and can enforce the freedoms using the GPL licence. Anyone breaking the licence can be held accountable in the same way as if someone breaks the licence of proprietary software. This prevents unscrupulous people taking advantage of the movement and trying to make a quick buck from other people's ideas and code.

There are a large number of open source licences, each having their own specific niche. Some insist that any derivations or future versions of the code must be protected by the same licence, while others are more permissive. It is up to software developers to decide what licence they wish to use.

Bespoke and off-the-shelf software

Closed source programs, as introduced in the last section, tend to come in one of two forms; bespoke and off-the-shelf. Bespoke software, also known as custom built, will be created for a single or small group of customers. They will have identified a need within their business which no existing system will fully solve (at least within their budget). Any software which is built will be specific to this business need and therefore will not be portable to other companies or problems. Moreover, it may be in the customer's best interest that bespoke software is not transferable, as it may give them a competitive edge over their rivals.

Any business contracting developers to build a bespoke system will have to bear the full cost of development themselves. The biggest cost of any software system is paying the software engineers for their time, which means that even a small system can prove to be very costly. It is not unusual for larger systems' costs to run into the millions. Due to the large financial commitment that goes with bespoke software it tends to be only larger organisations that can afford it. Although you will get software which meets the needs of your business directly, there are a number of issues to consider. First of all, development time can run into years for more complicated projects. This means that you will have to wait for the solution to be finished before using it. This can be mitigated by using different methodologies and implementation methods, such as an incremental phased approach, but there will always be a delay. Additionally, due to the smaller number of people testing the software, there may be more bugs or other problems with bespoke. Support will only be offered by the developer, or partners of the developer, which means that maintenance and support contracts are essential and potentially expensive.

Off-the-shelf software is software which you can buy ready made. This type of software is not cheaper to make than bespoke as the development costs will still be as high. The end user only pays less due to the cost being shared amongst everyone who will buy it. The more people who buy the software, the cheaper the developers can make it per unit item. Off-the-shelf software may not fully solve the problems that the business has and more often than not the business may have to change some of its practices in order to get the best use out of the software. This could mean changing procedures and policies, which will offset some or all of the cost-saving. However, the software will be available immediately and will be well supported. The more popular the software is, the more people will have tested the software and reported issues leading to an overall more stable solution. The company can also source support and knowledge from third parties and internet sites rather than just relying on the development company.

Safety critical systems

Systems which are classed as safety critical cannot be allowed to fail. For a system to be considered safety critical then one of the following is likely to arise from a failure by the system:

- death or serious injury
- loss or severe damage to company assets
- damage to the environment or wildlife.

One classic example of a safety critical system is the on-board computers for an aeroplane. Should this fail, the plane could crash. This type of software is tested using combinations of simulations, automated testing techniques, test flights and real flights. Whenever a fault is detected all planes which carry that software must be grounded. It is not acceptable for software like this to fail. Any software which is designated as safety critical must be dependable.

In the case that failure does occur, safety critical systems will provide methods to get the system back under control.

Fail-safe systems are ones where manual overrides are in place should failure occur. For example, if life support should begin to fail, it would alert the medical staff and keep working long enough for them to intervene manually.

Fault-tolerant systems will have redundant systems in place and be split out into sections. Should one section fail then it can be bypassed or a redundant system be brought online. In this way the system will keep working and give the maintenance team the chance to diagnose and fix the problem.

An auto-pilot, on the other hand, is an example of a fail-passive system. It may indeed fail, but if it does so the pilot is able to regain manual control.

Developing software which is fault tolerant, well tested and will keep operating once problems occur is a difficult task. Automated testing using logical deduction, for example, is a current area of research and not something the average developer would be able to do. Safety critical systems are a highly specialised field as, if mistakes are made, the result can be very serious.

Knowledge-based (expert) systems

Using a knowledge-based system, a user can interrogate a vast knowledge base to find a solution. The user enters the information he or she already has, and the knowledge-based system infers an answer. If the system cannot reach a conclusion, it requests more information. This process is continued until either the system has a high degree of confidence that it knows what the solution is, or it is sure that, having exhausted every line of inquiry, it does not know the solution.

Consider a car mechanic who has very specific and detailed knowledge on how to repair cars. The mechanic knows that if a car is exhibiting certain symptoms, it is likely that X or Y is the problem. The process is not always exact and sometimes the mechanic has to look deeper in order to diagnose the issue. The mechanic follows a simple algorithm:

While problem has not been solved:

mechanic asks the client questions

client responds to the questions

mechanic infers what the problem may be based on the information given so far.

A knowledge-based system works in the same way and consists of different parts:

- *Knowledge base*: is a database containing expert knowledge.
- *Inference engine*: attempts to work out the answer to the user's query by using the rule base.
- *Rule base*: links knowledge together through facts.
- *User interface (HCI)*: allows the user to communicate with the system. HCI stands for human–computer interface.

The rule base works by using logic and probabilities. For example, consider a patient who has a headache and a runny nose. The patient could have a cold or flu. It is much more likely to be a cold, but there is a chance that it could be flu. The rule base sets these links and probabilities for the inference engine to use. Based on the two symptoms, a probability is placed on the two possible outcomes. The more likely scenario, a cold, has a higher weighting (however, the relative seriousness of the two conditions must also be taken into statistical account in real life implementations). At this stage the inference engine may not have enough information to make a diagnosis, so it could ask for more information, such as 'Do you have a fever?' or 'Are you fatigued?'

The inference engine is interactive and will not just work serially by taking the input, doing some processing and then providing an answer. At any point it may require more information to help it arrive at the correct conclusion.

The inference engine is responsible for making one of three decisions:

- It has enough information to arrive at an answer.
- It requires more information.
- It cannot reliably come up with an answer.

Probabilities of which answer is correct are built up over time. Every question eliminates some answers and makes others much more likely to be correct, enabling the expert system to make an educated guess.

Tip

Questions on knowledge-based systems are normally based around a scenario that requires some form of diagnosis using expert knowledge. You must be able to relate the main parts of a knowledge-based system to the context. Make sure you revise the four main parts.

Contemporary application software

Some application software allows a user to carry out a specific task, such as sending an email. Other applications can each be used for many different tasks, and these applications constitute a subset of application software known as generic application software. Examples are word processors and spreadsheets.

Tip

Recall, from Chapter 2, the distinction between commonly used software and the extra software installed with the operating system.

Presentation software

Presentation software, such as Microsoft PowerPoint or Apple's Keynote, allows the user to create presentations to convey information. It is designed to be shown on a screen while a speaker is talking to the audience. Features of presentation software include animations, multimedia, interactive links and speaker notes. Text tends to be large (defaults to size 24 to 26 point) so that it can be viewed easily at a distance. Simple animations may increase the visual appeal of the presentation. By using animations as a form of output, the user can present information in a different way or draw attention to key aspects.

Presentation software is generally used in meetings or in educational environments such as schools or training courses. Each slide contains only a small amount of information, as the bulk of it is delivered by the speaker. Sometimes speakers use notes, which can be displayed to them but not to the rest of the audience, as shown in Figure 16.1.

 Tip

For each major type of application software, you need to know common uses for it and be able to identify the type of scenario for which it would be most suitable. In order to be able to justify your answer, you must remember the key features of each type of software.

Figure 16.1: Presentation software with user notes, which are hidden from the audience.

Desktop publishing

Desktop publishing, or DTP, allows the creation of many different types of publication, for example manuals, posters and banners. There is a common misconception that DTP software, such as Microsoft Publisher, is used for the same tasks as a word processor. DTP software allows the user much finer control over the layout of a publication and is not designed to handle (or at least to input or edit) large amounts of text; conversely, word processing focuses on producing essays, letters and reports rather than graphical publications. When selecting between DTP and word processing, the final result has to be considered. If it is text heavy, a word processor is more suitable.

Two of the key features of DTP software are templates and the layout of text and images. You can use templates to set up the page size, orientation and basic layout, along with various text styles, for a variety of commonly used types of publication. It is also common to set up templates for general use within a company. This dramatically improves productivity, by allowing you to focus on content instead of setting up and imposing the styles and layout yourself.

Spreadsheet packages

Spreadsheet packages are primarily focused on dealing with numbers and financial information. They can be used for storing simple databases, but this is not what they are good at. A single spreadsheet is known as a workbook and contains one or more worksheets. A worksheet is split into a grid system, with letters representing columns and numbers representing rows. A single box in the grid is known as a cell. Cells can contain calculations that refer to the numbers in other cells. The results of these calculations are automatically updated when the numbers in the other cells are changed; this is one of the most important features of a spreadsheet. An example calculation is = A1 + A2, which adds the contents of cells A1 and A2 and displays the result. Any change to the value held in cell A1 or in cell A2 automatically triggers recalculation of the answer.

Drawing packages

Drawing packages come in two main types, bitmap and vector. They both allow the user to draw images, but they do so in different ways. Vector images are made up of lines and shapes. Because they are mathematically defined, they can be dynamically resized without loss of quality. Vector images tend to be used in diagrams for use in publications, including computer science diagrams. Data flow diagrams (Figure 16.2), flowcharts and UML (Unified Modelling Language) diagrams are all examples of vector images. Typefaces are also defined as vector images.

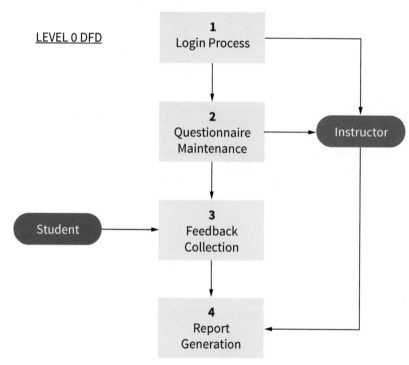

Figure 16.2: Data Flow Diagram.

Bitmap images are made up of thousands of coloured dots known as pixels. Bitmap image software tends to be used for photos and more complex artwork than line-drawings. Software such as Adobe Photoshop, the *GNU Image Manipulation Program* (GIMP) or Adobe Fireworks offers many advanced tools to manipulate bitmaps. To cope with the loss of fidelity as an image is manipulated or transformed, it is important to start off with a high-quality image. Figure 16.3 shows that the closer you zoom in to a bitmap image, the more you notice the individual pixels. This pixellation occurs because the software has no mathematical definition (such as that used for vector images) to rely on when enlarging the image.

Bitmap images are produced by digital cameras and scanners. If you need to edit these, bitmap drawing tools are your only option, unless you use OCR (optical character recognition) to gather the text from the images.

Figure 16.3: Example bitmap icons for apps.

Bitmap images tend to be high-quality images produced by high-end cameras, and the file sizes are massive. Consequently, compression is required to allow them to fit onto secondary storage or to be downloaded quickly over the internet. A popular image compression format is JPEG (Joint Photographic Experts Group), which uses a lossy compression method to achieve enormous savings in file size. Lossy compression, although very efficient at saving file space, loses some of the overall quality of the image. This is why professional photographers will not take photos in JPEG format, preferring to use the uncompressed RAW format.

Database packages

A database is a structure in which data is organised into tables, fields and records. Databases are used to store vast amounts of data required for specific purposes. Databases form the backbone of most ICT systems, including large-scale websites. For example, your bank records, health details and even the time you arrive at school are all stored on a database, and the BBC website is run entirely from a database, with news stories and images recorded in tables. This is commonly referred to as content management. Databases are much better equipped to deal with large amounts of data, while spreadsheets are better equipped to deal with numeric data.

One of the key features of a database is the ability to search and sort data quickly. This is done by querying the data within the database. Microsoft Access, which is used in schools and small businesses, has a graphical way of generating queries, as shown in Figure 16.4. In larger-scale databases, queries are written in a special language called SQL (Structured Query Language). Large organisations, such as banks and the owners of substantial websites, will use database software such as MySQL, Microsoft SQL Server or Oracle. Microsoft Access can also make use of SQL; the details of SQL are covered in Chapter 5.

Mobile phone apps

The small but powerful applications (apps) that run on smartphones have revolutionised the way mobiles are used and given small application developers access to massive

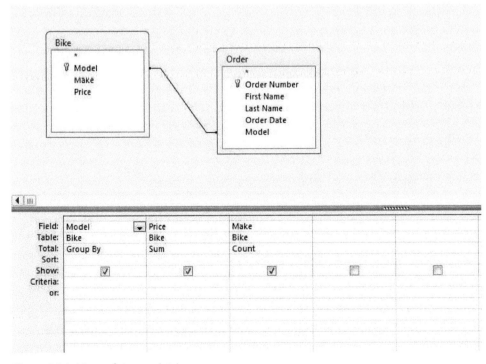

Figure 16.4: Microsoft Access database.

marketplaces, such as Apple's App Store and Google's Play Store. Apps, which are of low cost to the end user, or supported by advertising, have allowed mobiles to become true mobile computing platforms rather than simply something on which to play Angry Birds.

Unlike desktop applications, mobile apps tend to be small and focused on a number of very specific tasks. Users can download and install apps to enable them to perform the tasks they are interested in doing. Owing to smartphones' menu-based interface, small-screen 'real estate' and comparatively low processing power (when compared to desktops), apps are, by their very nature, simple. It is their basic and simple nature that has led to their popularity, and people who do not normally make use of desktop programs happily make use of mobile apps.

Mobile apps are developed in a number of programming languages and environments, depending on the destination platform. Apps for iPhones are written in Objective-C, apps for Android are written in Java, and apps for Windows are written in .NET. This poses a problem to software developers, who have to port their programs from one platform to another if they want to reach the widest possible market. In reality, this does not always happen and many apps are available only on the iPhone and on Android. There are some programming environments, such as Unity, that enable developers to produce their programs and publish them to all of the different platforms.

Animation and computer-generated graphics

Drawing packages allow 2D images, both bitmap and vector, to be produced. 3D images and animation can be generated by specialist 3D modelling software using techniques such as ray tracing. This type of software will allow the user to sculpt or model objects, apply textures, set up a scene and then provide light sources. The computer will then generate an image, known as rendering.

Wireframe models are made up of thousands of surfaces, each made up of a number of points known as vertices. Each surface will have specific properties which will dictate how light will bounce off it. The artist can specify properties such as colour, how reflective the

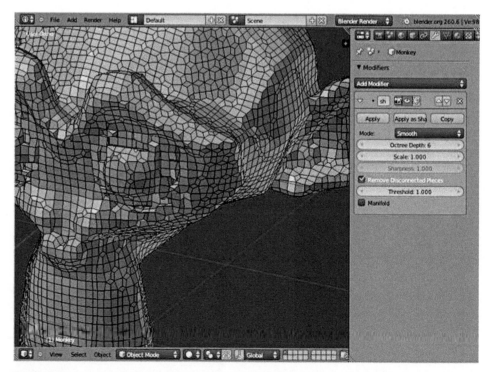

Figure 16.5: From wireframe representation to 3D model.

surface is or even if it is slightly transparent or not. Virtual light sources will illuminate the objects in the form of rays which are directed from the source to the scene. These virtual rays will bounce off objects using the properties of the object and arrive at the virtual camera, which will then record the final value of each pixel, very much as it works in real life.

Figure 16.6: Example ray traced image.

3D modelling software also allows animation. Objects are moved in a scene by stating a start and end state. Objects can move, rotate and resize between the start and end state. The software will interpolate more states between the user-defined start and end to give the appearance of a smooth animation. This process is known as an animation tween (short for in-between). Additionally to moving objects, the animator can move the camera and light sources to produce things such as car with headlights moving realistically or flying around a city. These effects are commonly used in films and computer games.

There are also other advanced features most 3D modelling software provides. Setting up 'bones', or pivot points, within a model allows it to move more naturally. Figure 16.7 shows how a simple human model could have bones to allow it to walk, wave and perform other actions. Any bone can be rotated at the intersection points and all of the vertices around that bone will move accordingly.

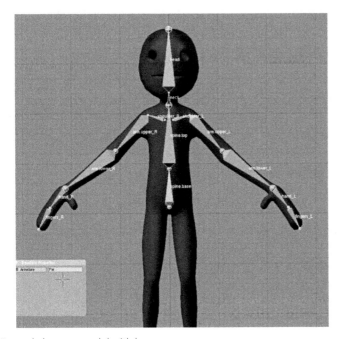

Figure 16.7: Example human model with bones.

Other advanced features include particle effects like explosions or hair and fluid dynamics to represent fabric and water.

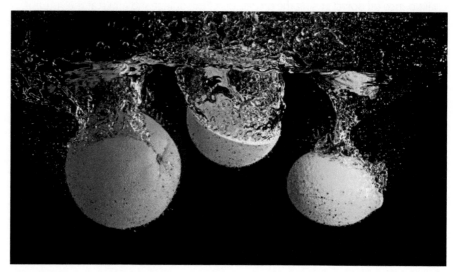

Figure 16.8: Example rendered image showing fluid dynamics representing water.

Weather forecasting

Weather forecasting is based on science and mathematics rather than folklore and guesswork. A lot of industry such as sea transport, aircraft and tourism relies on accurate weather forecasting. Predicting natural disasters such as tropical storms or hurricanes is crucial for preserving life. Forecasting accurately, and as far into the future as possible, is crucial. In order to do this, data must be collected such as rainfall, temperature, humidity, pressure and wind speed. The amount of data recorded across the country and out at sea can only be processed by computers, as the sheer volume would make it impossible for a team of humans to process quickly enough.

Weather forecasting software assimilates all of the data recorded to create a numerical model of the atmosphere. Any change in the atmosphere will result in changes to the weather. These models involve billions of calculations, for which the MET (meteorological) office uses a supercomputer.

Computer automation and robotics

Computer automation refers to the control of something in the physical environment by some form of computing system. The object controlled may be a door, a factory production line or a robot. The range of scenarios where computer automation can play a role is vast but what they all have in common is that they gather input using sensors and produce output using actuators. Some systems may also use more traditional input and output devices in addition to sensors and actuators. For example, a robot which fits chips onto a circuit board may have a visual display unit to show current progress.

Sensors can be found in a wide range of devices such as mobile phones, cars, cookers and even games consoles. A sensor will record data from the physical environment. Common sensors include:

- pressure sensor
- mercury tilt switch/accelerometers
- luminance (light) sensor
- humidity sensor
- infrared sensor.

When a sensor is used to record data it will be processed by a computer. Based on the results of this processing, some form of output will occur. If this is a physical motion, then an actuator must be used – an output device which can cause physical movement. An example would be a conveyor belt controlled by an infrared sensor.

There may be a feedback loop between sensors and actuators. When a sensor detects a change it will order an actuator to perform an action. This can, in turn, cause a change in what the sensors are detecting which in turn can cause further activation of the actuator. This feedback loop is very common with such systems. The cycle is shown in Figure 16.9.

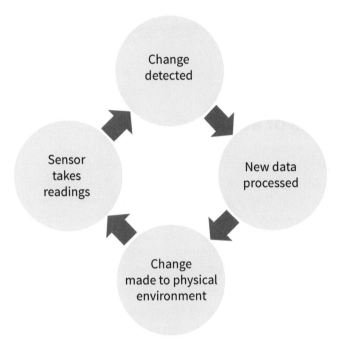

Figure 16.9: Feedback cycle for sensors and actuators.

Computer-aided design and computer-aided manufacturing (CAD/CAM)

Computer-aided design and computer-aided manufacturing (CAD/CAM) is the process of designing a product on a computer, testing it using simulations, and then manufacturing many thousands of copies based on a single design.

Almost all of the things we use in modern life have come from a factory assembly line. From toothpaste to iPods, most products are manufactured using a CAD/CAM process.

Computer-aided design (CAD) software enables designers to try out different designs for a product. CAD allows the designer to place parts together (some of which may have been pre-designed), scale and rotate in three dimensions, change colour and even run simulations to test how the design might react in the real world. Designers can try out different ideas and styles without having to make physical prototypes until they are sure that the design is sound. It isn't possible to test every aspect of a design using CAD because of the vast number of variables; a prototype will usually have to be built at some point. By using CAD, the number of prototypes can be kept to a minimum, potentially saving millions of pounds during research and development.

For example, when designing a car it is important, from a safety standpoint, that the design is tested to see what would happen at different speeds and in different weather conditions. It is not worth creating a prototype that would fall apart at the first sign of bad weather. Running simulations of the car in use through the CAD software generally allows most problems to be spotted and solved before any prototype is built.

As consumers, we expect everything we buy to be perfect. By enlisting machines to produce our products, we can guarantee, within a small error margin, a stable quality level. In computer-aided manufacturing (CAM), machines rather than people make products. Specifications are fed into a CAM system, which drives an assembly line. The specifications say exactly what the product looks like, its materials and the steps required to assemble it. CAM systems rely heavily on sensors and actuators and commonly make use of feedback loops. CAM machines offer the following advantages over hand assembly:

- They will always produce products that are exactly the same.
- They do not get tired.
- They do not make mistakes (unless they break down!)
- They can work 24/7.

Implications of automation

As shown in the last section, automation in the form of CAM has a number of key benefits. However, there are wider social issues at stake resulting from automation. As robots do the job of repetitive actions faster, more precisely and with fewer breaks than a human ever could, this has meant a shift in the job market. There are fewer lower skilled manual labour jobs available, meaning that certain groups in society struggle to find employment. Although manual labour jobs have reduced, jobs maintaining and monitoring robotic automation have increased. This shift in jobs forms part of the digital divide and areas which traditionally employed people in manufacturing have had to deal with higher unemployment. This tends to be in areas which were already poorer.

People fear automation and worry that robots, specifically those equipped with artificial intelligence, will supersede humans. Films such as The Terminator play on our fears that sentient computers will overthrow and exterminate humankind. Although these types of film are clearly just sci-fi fantasy, the fear of change is real. In some cases, robots have taken over key roles, such as manufacturing, which further feeds people's fears.

Search engines and impact on the wider community

In 2015 there were calls for exam boards to allow Google to be used in exams. In fact, the term "Google something" has become such a commonly used phrase that it has been added as a verb to the Oxford dictionary. Most students will direct questions to Google – the very same questions they would have directed to their teachers only years before. There is a shift in the way we deal with knowledge: we are now learning to manage the flow of information rather than to remember that information. This is one of the key arguments being put forward in allowing Google within exam rooms.

Information now takes many forms which gives people a choice in how they consume that information. In education, for example, students can learn about programming from a textbook, online tutorials or through interactive websites (http://www.cambridge.org/links/kwse6058). As more and more information is being digitised, using Google to quickly search and focus in on material has led to a society able to access information to which, years ago, they would have had limited access.

As Google lays a lot of answers at our fingertips, some say that our ability for critical thinking has diminished. We are less likely to think for ourselves and much more likely to look to Google for the answer. Also, due to the immediacy of gathering information, we are more likely to accept it at face value rather than questioning its validity or bias. A lot of younger people, including people in their twenties and thirties, have a much lower tolerance for boredom after growing up with a vast array of information and entertainment. A study of 2000 people, conducted by eDigitalResearch in 2012, showed that 80% used a device while watching TV. The way we consume media and information has changed and part of the reason for this is the easy access we get to information via search engines.

Almost every business will have a web presence, which can range from small sites which advertise goods to massive online shops. Most consumers will, before buying an item, search for it on the web. Increasingly people are also looking at online reviews before making purchases, especially of services or larger items such as electronics. The implication of this for businesses is that they need to manage the flow of information very carefully. It is common for companies to have their own Twitter feeds, Facebook pages and teams of people searching and managing the company's profile online. It is not uncommon for companies to try and shut down blogs or online reviews which are scathing of their business.

One key concern for every businesses is what comes up when they are 'searched' in any of the big search engines: Google, Bing and Yahoo for example. If I did a search for "best TV" would my company's web store appear in the results or will a competitor's? If your website is not in the first page of popular search terms linked to your business then your business will suffer from lost sales. Also, if negative reviews are the first things that appear when your company's name is searched for, then again this could have a negative impact. Companies spend a lot of money ensuring that their websites, which they can control, are some of the first that appear in search engines. This requires a combination of spending money with the search engines to have sponsored results and manipulating the page rank algorithms used by them.

Companies can improve their page rank by a number of approaches. Page rank reflects (i) the number of hits on links to you in the search engine's results and (ii) the number of websites that link to your own. There are a number of ways of improving these and other measures. Having a single web portal, rather than lots of sub-domains, will stop hits on your site being diluted. It is common for companies to have links to partners and testimonials on why they are partnered. People who come to websites will have done so by entering a series of keywords linked to your business. It is possible to analyse the search terms people use and ensure they are emphasised more on your site than other terms. It is better to focus on a small number of keywords which are more commonly used than taking a blunderbuss approach (which the search engines may detect anyway). For example, TV manufactures will probably use terms like "smart tv", "3D" or "Netflix".

Searching the Web

The World Wide Web consists of billions of webpages spread across tens of millions of servers. This can make finding the exact piece of information you want very, very difficult. Before search engines appeared on the scene, you had to know the domain name of every website that you wanted to visit; this dramatically cut down the number of websites that you could access.

Search engines provide a number of ways for you to find information quickly and efficiently from anywhere on the web. The concept of a search engine is really simple: you type some keywords and it returns a list of websites that contain those words. The reality, however, is much more complicated. Which website should go at the top of the list? The first one found, or the one that contains your keyword the highest number of times? Early search engines struggled to return relevant, useful results. They could find millions of related sites but you had to trawl through and find the one most relevant to you. Modern search engines use complex indexing and ranking algorithms to ensure that you get instant access to the most relevant websites – or at least to the websites the search engine algorithms most want you to visit.

Search engine indexing

Search engines collect information about webpages using automated bots called web spiders. These bots scour the internet, following links and recording keywords and the addresses where the keywords were found. This information is then transmitted back to the search engine provider, for example Google or Yahoo. The information sent back is then ordered and stored according to an index, for example keywords. When we use search engines we are not searching the World Wide Web – we're simply searching the search engine's index of the Web. This approach means that results can be returned very quickly.

PageRank algorithm

Search engine companies analyse their indexes using algorithms. The PageRank algorithm is Google's way of generating a rank order for the websites found in response to users' searches. It was named after its inventor, Larry Page. The PageRank algorithm works by counting the number of links to a page from other websites. This gives Google a rough estimate of how important a website is; more important websites are returned higher up the search results. The information about webpages (like the number of links) is gathered by an automated web spider called Googlebot.

The algorithm represents all the webpages as vertices on a directed graph data structure and the hyperlinks between pages are stored as edges within the same structure. Vertices are assigned a numerical value representing their importance (based on the number of links to them). PageRank is no longer the only algorithm used by Google but it was the first and is still the best known.

Chapter summary

- Open source software tends to be free and will always give access to the source code for people to read, edit and share.
- Closed source software will not give access to the source code, but may be free to use.
- Proprietary software is also referred to as closed source.
- Off-the-shelf software can be bought immediately but may not be able to offer the same level of functionality that custom built software can.
- Safety critical systems are classified as any system which could lead to death, injury or loss to company assets.
- Safety critical systems must have fail-safes and fault tolerance and are much harder to produce than regular software.
- Knowledge based systems, also known as expert systems, are broken into four parts; knowledge base, rule base, inference engine and GUI.
- Utilities are software which help the user accomplish tasks and tend to come shipped as part of the operating system.
- The modern trend in software is moving towards a higher number of smaller specialised apps rather than larger monolithic applications.

- Applications such as 3D ray tracers can produce detailed computer-generated images and animation.
- Weather forecasting is based on mathematical models and is backed by vast amounts of data.
- Computer automation makes use of sensors to record the physical environmental and actuators to control it.
- Computer-aided design allows designers to try ideas out on the computer, including modelling how the product will react in different scenarios and simulations, without having to build expensive prototypes.
- Computer-aided manufacture will take designs and produce exactly the same product using an assembly line.
- Search engines give greater access to a wider range of information.
- The PageRank algorithm will determine where a website appears in search results.
- A company's online reputation must be carefully managed as negative information can have an impact on sales.

End-of-chapter questions

1   Describe three parts of a knowledge-based system.   [6]

2   Describe the difference between bespoke and off-the-shelf software.   [4]

3   Discuss the difference between open source software and free software.   [8]

4   Explain how the PageRank algorithm determines the order of search results.   [2]

Chapter 17
Data security and integrity processes

Learning objectives

(A) • Explain the special security and integrity problems which can arise during online updating of files.

• Describe the dangers that can arise from the use of computers to manage files of personal data.

• Describe contemporary processes that protect the security and integrity of data including standard clerical procedures, levels of permitted access, passwords for access and write-protect mechanisms.

(A) • Describe the need for and the purpose of cryptography.

• Describe techniques of cryptography and their role in protecting data.

• Follow algorithms and programs used in cryptography.

• Compare cryptographic methods and their relative strength.

• Describe the purpose and use of contemporary biometric technologies.

• Describe the benefits and drawbacks of biometric technologies.

• Describe the complexities of capturing, storing and processing biometric data.

• Describe the various potential threats to computer systems.

• Describe contingency planning to recover from disasters.

• Describe malicious and accidental damage to data and identify situations where either could occur.

(A) • Describe types and mechanisms of malicious software and their vectors.

• Describe black hat hacking, white hat hacking and penetration testing.

Security risks in modern computing

Most companies have an online presence which, although necessary in the modern world, does open the company up to hacking and security threats. Protecting files, from database files to webpages, is a top priority to all firms. There are a number of key risks to files which include:

- outside access and manipulation of files
- unauthorised reading or copying of files
- corruption of files
- loss or deliberate deleting of files.

Threats can be broken into two main categories, internal and external. Internal threats include disgruntled employees, employee mistakes or incompetence and social engineering. Social engineering is a key issue for any company where their employees can be contacted by the public. It is much easier to trick a human into giving you access to files than it is to break 2048-bit encryption. External threats are posed by *black hat hackers*, described later on in this chapter.

Another key issue for file integrity is down to how files are managed when multiple users have access to them. The integrity of data is important as, if data is incorrect in any part of the system, mistakes can be made which ultimately could lead to loss of profits or other problems. Consider two users who both make a copy of the same file and update it separately. There are now three versions of the file; which one should be used? If one person overwrites the changes of another then data could be lost. Also, if they both try and save the data at the same time, the file can become corrupted.

Protecting files and data

There are a number of methods which can be used to protect files and data within an organisation. Some of these will be technical and others based on a company's policy. Software is not always the weakest link when protecting data; employees tend to be the biggest risk.

In order to ensure that data is secured correctly a company must put policies in place. These tend to define how data is to be used by those who do have access rights. There is no software on the planet which could prevent a system administrator writing their password down in their diary and leaving it on the bus. Policies should state the complexity of passwords, which can then be enforced by software; how data is accessed; and steps that should be taken to secure access. For example, hard copies of files should be disposed of by using confidential waste management (i.e. shredding and then disposal using a special service) and should never be left out in the open. Workstations should be locked when not in use, even if you have just popped out for a coffee.

Passwords are the next level of security and it is important that clerical procedures are clear for employees when setting them. It is common for companies to enforce passwords which must contain a mixture of upper and lower case letters, numbers and symbols. The more access a person has, the more important this becomes.

Access levels can help secure files. Some groups may be able to read but not to write to or delete certain files, while others may not be able to see them at all. Reducing the number of people who have access to certain files minimises the risk of employee mistakes and the number of targets for social engineering.

Files defined as read-only tend to be ones which contain data needed by all staff, for example the policy of acceptable internet usage. Although everyone must be able to read it, only a few people should be able to change it. By combining read/write permissions with access levels, sensitive files and data can be protected.

Cryptography

Cryptography, also known as encryption, is simply the act of scrambling a piece of plain text into cipher text so that it can't be immediately understood. Cryptography is an area of computer science focused on how best to enact encryption. Decryption is the process of unscrambling the encrypted message to reveal the original piece of text. The piece of information needed to decrypt the message is commonly called the key.

Encryption has been carried out for thousands of years. Julius Caesar is thought to have been one of the first people to use encryption when sending messages to his supporters and generals. As his messages were encrypted, it didn't matter if they were intercepted, as whoever stole them couldn't read them anyway!

The Caesar cipher (or shift cipher) that Caesar used is a very simple one to understand, so it makes a useful example, as shown in Tables 17.1 to 3.

A	B	C	D	E	F	G	H	I	J	K	L	M	N	O	P	Q	R	S	T	U	V	W	X	Y	Z
A	B	C	D	E	F	G	H	I	J	K	L	M	N	O	P	Q	R	S	T	U	V	W	X	Y	Z

Table 17.1

First you write out the alphabet in the top and bottom rows of a table:

Then shift the bottom alphabet along a set number of places. You can choose any number you want, and that number becomes your key.

This example shifts the bottom alphabet along two places, so the key to this message is two. Notice that letters from the end of the alphabet are 'wrapped around' so that they don't get lost:

A	B	C	D	E	F	G	H	I	J	K	L	M	N	O	P	Q	R	S	T	U	V	W	X	Y	Z
Y	Z	A	B	C	D	E	F	G	H	I	J	K	L	M	N	O	P	Q	R	S	T	U	V	W	X

Table 17.2

The next step is to write out your message using normal English. Finally you encrypt this message by replacing each letter with its shifted equivalent, so all the As become Ys, Bs become Zs and so on:

C	O	M	P	U	T	I	N	G		I	S		B	R	I	L	L	I	A	N	T
A	M	K	N	S	R	G	L	E		G	Q		Z	P	G	J	J	G	Y	L	R

Table 17.3

You can now send your message 'AMKNSRGLE GQ ZPGJJGYLR'. Only someone with the key knows how to decrypt it.

Of course, in modern terms, the Caesar cipher is very weak (weak encryption). A computer could break this code in milliseconds simply by trying all possible combinations (brute-force hacking), but in 30 BC this was thought to be a very effective method of encryption.

Encryption in the modern world

For hundreds of years, encryption was only really used by the military. However, with the explosion in electronic communication (many people send tens of electronic communications every day), encryption is becoming more and more important in everyday life. At the same time, powerful computers can crack most traditional forms of encryption (like the Caesar cipher) in seconds.

Computing in context: Alan Turing and Bletchley Park

Alan Turing is often referred to as the grandfather of computing. He is responsible for many of the ideas and concepts that still underlie the computers we use today.

As well as writing a number of ground-breaking academic papers on computing, he was largely responsible for the creation of the world's first electronic computer.

During the Second World War, Turing worked as a code breaker at Bletchley Park in Buckinghamshire. For the duration of the war the country house and its grounds were requisitioned by the military and used to house a top-secret code-breaking unit. The code breakers were successful in breaking a number of Nazi ciphers and their work is thought to have shortened the war by a number of years.

Breaking the Nazi encryption required a great deal of complex and repetitious mathematics, which Turing thought could be more accurately carried out by a machine. Together with the other code breakers and engineers at Bletchley Park, he designed and built Colossus, an electronic computer capable of rapidly and accurately breaking the incredibly complex Nazi codes.

As all digital communications over the internet can potentially be intercepted, the need for data to be encrypted becomes clear. When sending sensitive data, such as credit card information, you would not want people snooping on that data. Such an attack, which will read packet data as it passes through a node, is known as a man-in-the-middle attack. Most modern day applications rely on cryptography to protect data, from storing your passwords in an encrypted file to using secure socket layers (SSL) to transmit data over the internet securely. Without encryption online banking and commerce could not be trusted.

Symmetric and asymmetric encryption

Symmetric encryption means that the process of decryption is simply the opposite of the process used to encrypt. For example, in the Caesar cipher the message is encrypted by replacing each letter with another one a set number of places down in the alphabet. Decrypting the message is simply a case of swapping each letter in the encoded message with another that is a set number of places up the alphabet. As the process of decryption is just the opposite of the process used to encrypt the message, the Caesar cipher is a symmetric encryption algorithm.

Symmetric encryption algorithms have the advantage that they are quick to set up and easy to execute. Every encryption technique created before 1975 was essentially a symmetric technique. The problem with symmetric techniques is that they are very easy for modern computers to crack. A computer can crack an encrypted message simply by trying thousands of different alternatives and in a short amount of time.

In asymmetric encryption algorithms the encryption and decryption keys are different. If someone knows the encryption key, they can encrypt information but not decrypt it. Likewise, if someone possesses the decryption key, they can read the information they receive but can't encrypt their response using the same algorithm. Asymmetric algorithms were almost impossible for computers to crack, and until the 20th century nobody had thought of the concept, much less implemented it. So when the American computer scientist Whitfield Diffie invented the asymmetric key in 1975, it was a discovery that revolutionised the fields of cryptography and electronic warfare.

Asymmetric encryption is also called public key encryption and is best explained using an example.

Suppose Adam wants to send Charlotte a message. Charlotte keeps her decryption key secret (this is referred to as a private key), but publishes her encryption key on the internet (this is referred to as a public key). When Adam wants to send Charlotte a secret message, he simply uses the public key (which anyone can find out) to encrypt the message and then sends it to Charlotte.

It doesn't matter if anyone intercepts the message because only Charlotte has the private decryption key, so only she can read the message.

The system sounds simple but in reality it is incredibly complex. It requires the creation of a one-way mathematical function, a function that can only be reversed under a single circumstance. In fact, when Diffie first came up with the idea of asymmetric encryption it seemed likely that no such mathematical functions even existed!

Fortunately, within two years of Diffie's discovery, three American mathematicians, Ron Rivest, Adi Shamir and Leonard Adelman, developed such a function. Called the RSA cipher (based on the inventors' initials), it went on to become the foundation of all modern encryption techniques.

In the 'Computing in context' box, overleaf, is a short overview of how the RSA cipher works, adapted from Simon Singh's The Code Book: the Secret History of Codes and Code Breaking (Fourth Estate, 2002).

Computing in context: Mathematics of the RSA cipher

1. Charlotte picks two large prime numbers, w and q. These should be massive but for simplicity's sake we'll say $w = 17$ and $q = 11$.
2. Charlotte multiplies these numbers together to get N. In our example $N = 187$. She then picks another number, e; let's say $e = 7$.
3. Charlotte now publishes e and N on the internet. These become her public key.
4. To encrypt a message it must first be converted into a number M, for example by joining together the ASCII (American Standard Code for Information Interchange) codes that make up the message. M will turn out to be very large for any text more than a few characters long.
5. M is then encrypted to create cipher-text C using the formula $C = Me(MOD\ N)$

For example:

If Adam wants to send Charlotte a single kiss (X), he converts this to its ASCII value 1011000, which is the equivalent to the denary number 88. So $M = 88$.

He then calculates the value of C using the formula $C = 887(MOD\ 187)$. So $C = 11$. He then sends this to Charlotte.

Exponents in modular arithmetic are one-way functions, so it is incredibly difficult to work backwards to the original message unless you know the private key.

6. The private key d is calculated by Charlotte using the formula $e \times d = 1(MOD(w{-}1) \times (q{-}1))$. In our example this eventually gives us $7 \times d = 1(MOD\ 160)$ or $d = 23$.
7. To decrypt the message Adam has sent her, Charlotte simply uses the following formula: $M = Cd(MOD\ 187)$. This resolves as $M = 1123(MOD\ 187)$ or $M = 88$, which is X in ASCII.

The brilliant part is that the function can be personalised by choosing w and q. Therefore only the person who knows these values can decrypt the message.

Diffie released his asymmetric encryption algorithm for free on the internet, which meant that everyone in the world suddenly had access to incredibly strong, military-grade encryption. Many governments (not least Diffie's own American government) were deeply upset by Diffie's actions.

Comparing cryptographic methods

Fundamentally, when comparing ciphers, the question to ask is, "How easy is this to break?" Claude Shannon, an American mathematician, is known as the father of information theory. Part of his work was to define what is meant by a good cipher and is listed below:

*   The amount of secrecy should determine the amount of work needed to encrypt and decrypt.
*   The cipher must work on all types of data.
*   The algorithm should be simple to minimise implementation errors.
*   If an error is introduced it should not impact the rest of the message.
*   The size of the cipher text should be no larger than the original plain text.

Most encryption algorithms are well known, but their strength relies on their key rather than the process used by the cipher. Therefore the goal of any attack on encrypted data involves trying to work out what the key is. This can be done through brute-force, by trying to guess the key by trying every possible one until a match is found. Alternatively statistical analysis can be used: if certain groups of characters appear more often than others in the cipher text then the frequencies can be compared with the frequencies of certain groups of characters in plain English.

Consider the example of using Caesar's cipher with an unknown offset. The cipher text is shown below along with a frequency analysis of the letters (Figure 17.1) which appear in the cipher text.

AJYNULPEKJ DWO XAAJ YWNNEAZ KQP BKN PDKQOWJZO KB UAWNO. FQHEQO YWAOWN EO PDKQCDP PK DWRA XAAJ KJA KB PDA BENOP LAKLHA PK QOA AJYNULPEKJ SDAJ OAJZEJC IAOOWCAO PK DEO OQLLKNPANO WJZ CAJANWHO. WO DEO IAOOWCAO SANA AJYNULPAZ, EP ZEZJVP IWPPAN EB PDAU SANA EJPANYALPAZ, WO SDKARAN OPKHA PDAI YKQHZJVP NAWZ PDAI WJUSWU!

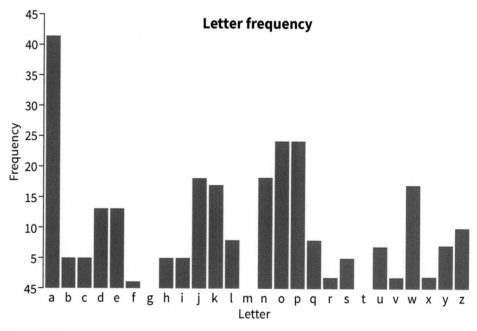

Figure 17.1:

The most common letter in the alphabet is "e" which occurs 12.702% of the time, followed by "a" which occurs 8.167% of the time. It stands to reason that the letter with the highest frequency in our cipher text must be an "a" or an "e". In the cipher text "a" appears the most often suggesting an offset of 0 if "a" is really an "a", or 4 if "a" is really an "e". Trying an offset of 4 gives the following text. Our first educated guess was correct, which goes to show how weak the Caesar cipher is.

Encryption has been carried out for thousands of years. Julius Caesar is thought to have been one of the first people to use encryption when sending messages to his supporters and generals. as his messages were encrypted, it didn't matter if they were intercepted, as whoever stole them couldn't read them anyway!

When looking at the strength of an encryption algorithm it is important that it adds diffusion. Diffusion will ensure that each letter of plain text will impact more than one letter in the cipher text. By combining different letters together in different ways you limit the predictability of the resultant cipher.

The resultant cipher can also be combined with random (strictly speaking, pseudorandom) data to further guard against frequency or dictionary attacks. By using Exclusive Or (XOR) and a random seed, a stream of random data can be created. This operation can be undone by the destination if it knows the random seed, as the values produced by any random number generator will be the same if the seed is the same. This process is known as salting.

Finally the strength of the key will depend on how vulnerable the cipher text is to a brute-force attack. Small keys, which are under 56 bits, can be broken by modern computers in a few days. However larger keys, 128-bit or above, would take millions of years to break by brute-force.

Biometric data

Humans are unique in many ways. Although we have some common characteristics which we may share with others, no one else has the exact same combination. Using the human body as a method of gaining access to computing systems uses human measurements and metrics, known as biometrics. In order to use biometric data it first must be recorded and stored into a database. With the idea of each metric, or combination of metrics, being unique, each person effectively becomes the primary key.

Some physiological metrics which can be measured include:

- face
- finger prints
- iris/retina scans
- DNA
- palm print.

There are a number of active biometric systems today. Some smartphones have fingerprint scanners. The scanner will use capacitance, in a similar way to the touch screen, to detect ridges along the skin. The patterns of your fingerprint actually make up a number of ridges and valleys, so when you press your finger on the scanner not every part of the finger will touch it. This is picked up as variations in capacitance and converted into a pattern. This form of fingerprint scanner cannot be fooled by a print out of someone's finger as it does not work by taking a picture.

Biometric passports use a combination of facial recognition, iris recognition and finger prints. UK passports contain an RFID chip which contains your passport number, your name and your date of birth. This is linked to a database which contains your photo and your biometric data. The data comes from your photo directly. The system uses facial recognition and iris recognition software to analyse it.

Facial recognition works by measuring how far apart, relative to one another, your eyes, jaw, nose and cheekbones are. Figure 17.2 shows what some of these measurements would look like. One of the key issues with facial recognition is that, when the image is captured for comparison, it must be done under good conditions with the person's face clearly visible. Although some systems can work by building a 3D model of the face, it is much more accurate when facing straight on, face passive and good uniform lighting over the subject. This is why you are asked to look straight ahead on a passport photo and when you go through security at the airport.

Figure 17.2: Female face with facial recognition overlay.

Facial recognition is currently being used by other major technology firms and is a key area of research. Facebook has a feature where it can automatically detect faces in images, compare it to other members, and suggest tags. This feature has to be deliberately enabled by the user following a privacy ruling by the European court, but it is a remarkably accurate tool. It can also be used in conjunction with existing CCTV systems to help spot wanted criminals.

Biometric technology has a number of key advantages. It has the potential to be much more secure than conventional passwords as it is very difficult to replicate the data. Your biometrics cannot be lost, stolen or forgotten, unlike conventional passwords. No one can social engineer your biometric information out of you, short of tricking you into logging in on their behalf. It can help speed up conventional queueing systems, such as school canteens or airport queues, by linking your biometrics to your data.

Disadvantages of biometrics include a lack of reliability under some circumstances. Biometrics are not always 100% accurate, especially when the conditions where the metrics are read cannot be controlled. People change over time due to ageing, illness and injury. Finally a lot of people have privacy concerns with regards to biometric data. They have a concern about how the data will be used and how it can be linked back to other aspects of their lives. For example, using facial recognition can detect which shops we go into in order to target advertising.

Malicious software and hacking

There are three purposes to hacking which are named black, grey and white hat hacking. Black hat hackers will break into systems for their own purposes. This could be for financial gain, political motivation, to test their skills or just for fun. White hat hackers will use their skills to break into a system to expose flaws and then advise on how they can be fixed. They will work directly for the company, or be hired by that company, to perform penetration testing. Grey hat hackers are white hat hackers who are not directly hired by a company but perform penetration testing anyway to expose flaws. The hope is that they will be hired by the company, but they run the risk of being prosecuted under the Computer Misuse act.

Penetration testing is done by all three types and involves trying to break into a system by exploring vulnerabilities in the OS, application flaws, poorly configured systems and user behaviour. The goal of this testing is to find flaws in the security in order to exploit them or fix them, depending on who is doing the testing. Penetration testing is broken down into a number of phases:

1   Reconnaissance
2   Scanning
3   Gaining access
4   Maintaining access
5   Clearing tracks.

Reconnaissance is all about collecting as much public data as possible. This could include software in use, names of employees, IP addresses and other such data. The key here is not to set off any alarm bells by trying to access protected information too early. Once this is done, phase two will start, which will probe the system defences in more detail. Here the plan is to scan available ports, find software versions, find out the addresses of all public computers and create a blueprint of the target. Once this information is gathered then it is time to look for software or personal vulnerabilities. If software has not been updated then it could have security flaws which the hacker could exploit. The final phases will result in changing passwords, creating back doors and clearing logs. Getting caught during the hack can lead to a black or grey hat hacker receiving a lengthy jail term.

Once a hacker has broken into a system, it will be up to them what they want to do next. Commonly they will install malicious software to help maintain their access or perform the mischief they had originally intended. Some of the key malicious software types are described below.

Virus – A virus is software which will attempt to spread over the network by infecting emails, removable storage devices or known software vulnerabilities. Once a virus is in play it will deliver one or more other pieces of software known as the payload. The attack vector for a virus tends to be through emails or infected websites.

Trojans – These work in a similar way to a virus only they are hidden in files or programs. When these files are opened, the Trojan is activated, delivering its payload. Tricking users into downloading files or using illegal peer-to-peer networks is the common attack vector for Trojans.

Spyware – This will track key presses and software use, details of which are then sent back to the hacker. This is commonly used to commit identity fraud. The spyware attack vector tends to be from other malicious software such as a virus.

Scare-ware/ransom-ware – Scare-ware will try to scare the user into buying fake or further malicious software. It will pop up messages suggesting that your system is compromised and only their software can fix the problem, at a price. Ransom-ware uses similar tactics but will delete, collect or encrypt files which they will ransom back or threaten to publish. Ransom-ware can also take control of webcams. Scare-ware tends to be used on comprised websites while ransom-ware tends to have an attack vector as the payload of a virus.

Botnets – These will create a back door to your computer allowing a hacker to use it without your permission. The hacker will then use your computer as part of a larger group of compromised computers to launch further attacks, normally denial of service. Again, this tends to be the payload of a virus.

Contingency planning

With all of the potential risks associated with computers it is sensible for companies to create a contingency plan. This plan will be enacted should a disaster happen such as an 'act of God' (earthquake, tsunami etc.), server failure or hacking attack. When creating a contingency plan it is important to understand what data is stored, how each area of the business interconnects, how each area of the business would be impacted in the event of a disaster and identifying the key risks. Disaster recovery, which will be enacted by the contingency plan, will include the following key elements:

- Backup of systems – See Chapter 4 for more detail on backup.
- Redundant servers – These can activate should the original servers fail. They may be kept off-site and even offline to ensure that they are not compromised by any virus.
- Relocating key personnel – If the system is to be housed on an external site in the event of a disaster then key personal will be need to go to the new site and maintain it.

Contingency plans need to be created, tested and maintained. As a business will change over time, so should the contingency plan. If the plan is not updated every time the IT system is, then it can become too outdated to get the business going again, which could cost millions.

Malicious and accidental damage

So far in this chapter we have considered the threats that companies face relating to computers and methods to mitigate these risks. The next step, which is related to contingency planning, is to determine what the impact of security breaches would be. Once a system has been compromised, either through malicious intent or accident, it will need to recover. Understanding what the impact of a security breach would be means that you can better understand what contingencies need to be put into place.

Malicious damage includes the deliberate targeting of critical parts of the system. The motivation of the hacker determines the targets. For example, if the hacker is politically or ideologically motivated, they may wish to disrupt the business by deleting key files or using denial of service to bring down public websites. The hacker group Anonymous tend to be more ideologically motivated, so they tend to launch denial of service attacks. This type of hacker may also wish to publically shame people or groups of people by breaking into email accounts and other repositories of information. By leaking this information, the public image of that company or individual can be permanently tarnished. Recent examples include the hack on Sony's email by "guardians of peace" who leaked emails between Sony executives and celebrities. This caused substantial embarrassment for Sony and their stock price fell by 6.6 percent. Although it is difficult to attribute the hack to the drop in share price directly, it would most certainly be a factor.

Financially motivated hackers target either credit card details from customers or sensitive files which can be ransomed back. In this scenario the hackers in question are keen to stay under the radar as much as possible and it is much less likely that anyone would admit to being the perpetrator. The damage to the company could be huge. Although credit cards are insured and ransoms can be tracked, what cannot be easily repaired is the lost reputation for that company. Lost business, over time, can be much more costly than the actual initial monetary loss. For example, eBay suffered a hack in 2014 where 145 million accounts were compromised. They tried to keep the hack secret, stating that they thought customer data was safe. Then, when the hack was made public, they got everyone to change their password. Shares for eBay dropped by 1.43% as a result of the hack.

The final group of malicious hackers forms part of an internal threat to all companies: the disgruntled employee. One of the biggest issues with disgruntled employees is that they tend to be behind security features. They will already have access to the site and a password to get onto the system and would not need to do any hacking at all. It is common for disgruntled employees to leak information, delete files and disrupt internal procedures. However, as they are internal, it is much easier to track and identify culprits.

Accidental damage is when employees move, delete or update files when they were not supposed to. Although accidental, the impact of this disruption is exactly the same as if it were done maliciously. The biggest difference is that accidents tend to be one-off issues rather than a sustained approach with clear goals or outcomes. Because accidents are not predictable they are harder to protect against. It is easy to formulate plans when considering what the high profile targets in a company might be, but not so easy to consider every possibility relating to accidental damage. Accidents tend to happen due to lack of training, insufficient security on key files and fatigue. The latter cause, which can be also linked to stress, is important for every employer to consider. Humans suffering from sleep deprivation lose focus and, in extreme cases, can perform worse than someone under the influence of alcohol. This is why drivers are informed that they must not drive when tired.

Chapter summary

- Security risks to modern systems include outside access of files, corruption of data, unauthorised reading or duplication and loss or deliberate deleting.
- Policies ensure that staff use data responsibly and minimise risk of data loss.
- Passwords need to be strong in order to protect data and files.
- Access levels restrict which users can access sensitive files and data.
- In symmetric encryption the process of decryption is the opposite of the process used to encrypt. The Caesar cipher is an example of symmetric encryption.
- In asymmetric encryption algorithms the encryption and decryption keys are different.
- Cryptographic methods can be compared by looking at how well they diffuse information and how hard they are to break by brute force.
- Biometric data uses human metrics to identify individuals.
- Common biometric methods include facial recognition, finger prints, iris scans, DNA and palm prints.
- Biometric data is unique to individuals, which makes it very difficult to impersonate.
- Biometric data can be inaccurate if recorded in sub-optimal conditions.
- Privacy concerns arise as a result of using biometric data.
- Black hat hackers will break into systems for their own ends while white hat hackers use their skills to identify and fix security flaws.
- Malicious software comes in many forms including viruses, Trojans, spyware, ransom-ware and botnets.
- Contingency planning allows companies to develop disaster recovery procedures. The plans must be tested and constantly updated to ensure the business has limited exposure to down time.

End-of-chapter questions

1 Describe 2 methods of protecting files and data. [4]

2 Explain why a shift cipher could not be used for online banking. [4]

3 Heathrow airport is using facial recognition and retina scans to help fast-track UK citizens when arriving home. What issues would they face when developing this system? [6]

4 Explain two methods a company could employ when contingency planning. [4]

5 Describe how a school could mitigate the issue of accidental data loss. [3]

Further reading

Dubin, J. (2012) The Little Black Book of Computer Security 2E, Create Independent Publishing Platform. ISBN 978-14375286243.	
How do biometrics work?	Search for How Biometrics Works on howstuffworks.com

Glossary

Artificial intelligence: Intelligence that has been built into a computer, enabling it to perform tasks normally undertaken by humans.

Assembler: A form of translator used when converting assembly code to machine code.

Association: The order in which logical connectives of the same type are used does not change the overall truth.

Attribute: A characteristic of an object.

Automata: Finite state machines created for each expression during lexical analysis.

Bandwidth: A measure of how much data can be fitted onto a cable at any point in time.

Biconditional equivalence: Both sides of the equivalence must be true.

Binary: A base-two number system that is used to represent information in computer systems.

BIOS: Basic input and output system – initialises and runs basic tests on connected hardware before running the boot loader to trigger loading of the operating system.

Bit rate: The rate at which data is sent over a network (bits per second). It is not a measure of speed, rather the amount of data that can be sent at a given time.

Blocked: A process that is waiting for a resource to become available. Blocked processes will not be moved into the running state until they unblock.

Buffer: Temporary memory used to store data to be saved onto slower storage or output devices. Use of a buffer enables the processor to work on other processes.

Cache: Memory that runs much faster than standard memory and sits in between RAM and the processor.

Centralised computing: Server model of computing where services are provided at a single point of contact.

Checksum: An error checking method used by TCP. It will perform a calculation on data, producing a short value that can be added to the packet for verification purposes.

Cipher text: The scrambled code produced by encrypting the plain text message.

Circuit switching: A route across the network is set up in advance and all packets are then sent down the same route.

CISC: Complex instruction set computer.

Client–server: Services, such as file storage, are made available on servers to which clients connect in order to access the services.

Client-side processing: Programs are executed by the client; a common example is a JavaScript file.

Clock cycle: One increment of the CPU clock.

Cloud computing: A system allowing companies and individuals to store all their data online rather than on their own computers.

Command line: A means of interacting with a program where the user (or client) issues commands to the program (command lines). Commands can take one or more arguments.

Commutation: The order of propositions combined using a logical connective does not matter and does not change the overall truth.

Compiler: Produces an executable file from source code. Commonly used when releasing closed source software.

Compression: A reduction in the number of bits in a file. Usually achieved by removing duplicated bits.

Conjunction: Used to combine propositions where both have to be true in order for the whole statement to be true.

Constructor: A special method called when a class is instantiated. Co-processor

Co-processor: An additional processor used for a specific task.

CPU: Another term for a processor. It stands for central processing unit.

CSS: Cascading Style Sheets contain the formatting information for HTML documents.

Cybercrime: Criminal activity carried out over the internet.

Data dictionary: A database that stores every item of data, the size of that data, the type of the data and a comment to explain what that data means.

Data link layer: Focuses on the transmission medium and ensures that a packet is packaged correctly for either wired or wireless transmission.

DHCP (dynamic host configuration protocol) server: Used by ISPs to assign an IP address to a device when that device connects to the internet.

Disjunction: Used to combine propositions where either can be true in order for the whole statement to be true.

Distributed computing: Services are spread across many computers, each of which plays a part in providing a single service.

Distributed processing: In peer-to-peer networking, peers share the processing load for complicated calculations.

Distribution: Propositions, which are combined with statements in brackets using a different logical connective, can be expanded.

Double negation: A double negative always results in the original truth value.

Duplex: A method of transmitting data over a physical cable. Data can be sent in simplex, half duplex or (full) duplex.

Edge: A link between two items in a graph.

EEPROM: Electronically erasable programmable read-only memory

Element: The name given to a variable within an array. Usually accessed using its position in the array.

Encapsulation: The hiding of the implementation of a class and controlling access to its methods and attributes.

Fetch, decode and execute (FDE) cycle: Uses the cache to improve the processor's efficiency.

Flat file database: A single large table is used to hold all information.

Foreign key: The primary key of one table is included in a record in another table to link the two entities.

GPU: Graphics processing unit. A co-processor usually used to handle graphics but also suitable for a number of other tasks.

Handshaking: A process in which two communicating devices agree on a set of protocols to use.

Hash: A unique string of data.

Hash function: Used to produce the location in a hash table where a piece of data should be stored.

Heap: A large pool of memory.

Hertz (Hz): The number of clock cycles per second.

HTML: Hyper Text Markup Language, the language in which all webpages are written.

Identifier: A text name, not starting with a number, used to identify variables, constants or functions.

Implication: Given a logical statement we can infer further truth.

Increment: Adding to something; e.g. adding new functionality to a product.

Inheritance: The idea is that something is being passed down through some form of relationship.

Instantiation: The process of creating an object.

Intermediate code: Generic machine code for a general purpose computer. Used for languages that are both compiled and interpreted.

Interpreter: Reads source code in line by line, translating each line into machine code as it goes.

Interrupts: A signal sent to the CPU to inform it that an event has happened. Interrupts are recorded in the interrupt register, which is evaluated at the end of each Fetch–Decode–Execute cycle.

IP masquerading: Private LAN networks sharing a smaller number of external IP addresses to connect to the internet by using network address translation.

Iterative: Repeating an action; e.g. repeatedly improving the functionality of a product.

JavaScript: A scripting language commonly used with webpages.

Least significant bit (LSB): The rightmost bit in a byte, so called because it represents the lowest value.

Leeching: A term used in peer-to-peer networking, describing the initial stages of a file download process.

Literal: A hard-coded number or string found within source code.

MAC: Media access control layer. Hardware addresses used by the data link layer.

Machine code: Instructions in binary notation that can be executed by the CPU. Machine code instructions will only work on a specific machine architecture.

Method: A piece of code that implements one of the behaviours of a class.

Mission creep: A situation where objectives shift gradually during the course of software development, resulting in new, unplanned features and escalating costs.

Mnemonic: A symbolic name.

Mnemonics: A human readable representation of the machine code instruction set. A single mnemonic, such as ADD, would represent a single machine code instruction.

Model, methodology: A particular way of implementing the systems lifecycle.

Most significant bit (MSB): The leftmost bit in a byte, so called because it represents the highest value.

Motherboard: The main circuit board of a computer, which contains connectors for attaching additional boards.

Negation: Reverses the truth of any given statement. True becomes false and vice versa.

Network layer: Handles routing and is used to navigate the internet to get a packet to the correct destination.

NIC: Network interface card. Hardware responsible for placing packets onto network cables in the form of electronic signals, or bursts of light if the cable is optical.

Node: The part of a data structure that holds the data.

Normalisation: The process of converting a flat file database into a relational one.

Object: A combination of data and the actions that can operate on that data.

Opcode: A specific binary value that represents a single instruction from the processor's instruction set.

Overclocking: Increasing the speed of a processor beyond the manufacturer's specifications; it will probably void the warranty.

Packet: Data to be sent over a network containing additional data needed to correctly transmit the data.

Packet switching: Packets take independent routes through the network.

Page: A fixed sized memory block used when assigning memory to processes.

PageRank algorithm: Used to prioritise some webpages over others in the results provided by search engines.

Paging table: A table that maps virtual memory spaces used by processes to physical locations in RAM.

Parallel processor: An additional processor that works on the same task as the primary processor.

Parser: Reads text or tokens and provides context to that text. For example, parsers are used during syntax analysis.

Peer-to-peer network: Each computer, or peer, in a network has the same status as the others. No computer acts as a server, meaning that peers must work together to fulfil the required task.

Pipelining: The process of fetching one instruction while executing another, which enables higher throughput of instructions in the CPU.

Plain text: The original message prior to its encryption.

Pointer: A variable that holds a memory address, denoted with a * in many programming languages.

Polymorphism: The ability for an object of one class type to appear to be used as another.

Port: A point of contact for networking. Software ports have packets redirected to a specific application while hardware ports can be used to route packets.

POST: Power-on self-test - started when the computer boots and runs basic tests on connected devices. A report is generated and shown to the user as long as quiet boot has not been enabled.

Primary key: A unique piece of information used to refer to an individual record.

Process: A running program.

Processor: Runs instructions from memory and controls the rest of the computer.

Proposition: An atomic logical statement that can be either true or false.

Protocol: A set of rules that govern communication.

Protocol stack: A number of protocols chained together.

Prototype: A functioning but limited version of an application system, usually created to give the customer a rough idea of what to expect.

Recursion: A function that calls itself.

Relational database: A number of tables are used to hold information; these are linked together using primary and foreign keys.

Requirement: A key feature of a system that must be present in the final implementation.

Requirements specification: A document that contains the exact requirements of the new system.

RISC: Reduced instruction set computer.

ROM: Read-only memory – non-volatile memory that is used to store essential systems software.

Scheduling: Part of the operating system that is responsible for managing the order of processes and how they will be managed to achieve multitasking.

Scope: The lifetime of a variable. A variable can have either local or global scope.

Search engine indexing: A technique for speeding up the response time and relevance of search engine results.

Secondary key: A piece of information that can be used to sort a database or search for a group of items.

Segmentation: A variable sized block of memory that can be shared between processes. A common example would be the use of dynamic libraries.

Segmentation table: A table that stores the location of segments to map between virtual and physical memory addresses.

Server-side processing: Programs are executed by a server. Such programs are commonly written in server-side languages such as PHP.

Sign and magnitude: A method of indicating whether or not a binary number is negative using the MSB.

Source code: Human-readable code written to perform tasks. Must be translated into machine code before it can be run on any CPU.

SQL: Structured Query Language. A language created to help modify and query databases.

Strong encryption: Encryption that is very difficult to break.

Suspended: A process that has been moved to virtual memory.

Systems software: Software that manages the hardware and other software such as the operating system or system start-up software.

Tautology: Regardless of the truth values of the individual propositions, the overall value must always be true.

Translator: Software that takes source code and converts it into machine code. Examples of translators include assemblers, compilers and interpreters.

Transport layer: Has the choice of a reliable stream of data (TCP), or an unreliable 'fire and forget' datagram (UDP).

Two's complement: A way of displaying negative numbers using binary.

Unary operator: An operator with only one operand.

Unit tests: Tests created by programmers to ensure that the code they have written is working as expected.

USB: Universal serial bus – a common type of connection for external devices such as memory sticks, mice and keyboards.

Vertices: The set of all the values in a graph.

Von Neumann architecture: A software development model in which the different stages are arranged in order, with each stage cascading down to the next.

Weak encryption: Encryption that is easy to break.

WIC: Wireless interface card. Needed if the connection to the network is wireless.

Wireless access point (WAP): A device that allows wireless devices to connect to a wired network using Wi-Fi or another similar standard.

Index

Acknowledgements

Cover © 2013 Fabian Oefner **www.FabianOefner.com**

All images used in the chapter openings are courtesy of Shutterstock, except for Chapter 6 Sasha Suzi/Getty Images..

3.6 Shutterstock; 3.25-3.27 Fotofolia, Chapter 9, Computing in Context image Corbis; 9.2, 9.3 Aljazeera; 0.3 Shutterstock; 1.1 SPL; 1.5 Alamy; van Neumann, Corbis; 2.4, 2.5, 2.6, Shutterstock; 2.10 SPL; 4.3 Alamy; Richard Stallman, Corbis; Alan Turing, SPL; 9.6 Corbis; 9.8, 9.11 Shutterstock; Department of Justice, Corbis; 14.2, 14.3 Aljazeera.